主 编 徐建义

Editor–in–Chief: Xu Jianyi

人间仙境菩提岛

Puti Island: A Fairyland on Earth

中国旅游出版社

China Travel & Tourism Press

编纂委员会

主　　　编：徐建义

执行主编：何宗禹

副　主　编：田书和

执行副主编：孟庆忠　　刘庆文

编　　　委：徐建义　　何宗禹　　孟庆忠　　刘庆文　　呼景山　　刘文秩

　　　　　　田书和　　邓树民　　张海军　　习洪业　　董宗仁

摄　　　影：刘江涛　　张志刚　　徐亚平

插　　　图：陈亚杰

英文翻译：列　文　　张济英　　于　曼　　王露西　　刘海乐

装帧设计：吕泽雯　　王　源

Contents

Preface ··················· Xu Jianyi   8

Foreword ···18

Chapter I ···18

Chapter II: The Origin of Puti Island ··············24

Chapter III: Cultural Heritage of Puti Island ······26

I. Historical Figures ··································26

1. The First Qin Emperor in Search of Immoralty ··············26

2. Cao Cao and His Poem *Gazing at the Immense Ocan* ······28

3. Shi Hu Stationing Troops and Storing Grain ·················28

4. Yang Guang Watching the Sea at Mortarlsle ·············30

5. Li Shimin and Nineteen Isle ·····························34

6. Wanyan Dan Hunting on the Island ···················36

7. Yu Chenglong Burnt Down the ChaoyangNunnery ·········36

8. Martial Champion Li Guoliang ·······················40

9. Monk Faben, Abbot of the Chaoyin Temple ···········48

10. Shi Lü jin Wrote Antithetical Couplets ···············52

11. Ge Yuzhi and Monk Faben ·····························52

12. Li Dazhao, Co-founder of the CPC ···················56

13. Han Zuozhou Wrote Antithetical Couplets for the Chaoyin Temple ······································66

15. General Luo Ruiqing Inspected Mortar Isle ·············76

14. Liu Zhensheng, the First Disciple of Huo Yuanjia ·········68

II. Poetry and Prose ··································78

1. Poetry ···78

(1) *Tour to Xiamen*, by Cao Cao of the Han Dynasty ···········78

(2) *Watching the Sea*, by Yang Guang of the Sui Dynasty ····78

(3) *Watching the Sea with Your Majesty*, by Yu Mao of the Sui Dynasty ···82

(4) *Watching the Sea on a Spring Day*, by Li Shimin of the Tang Dynasty ···84

(5) A Response to Your Highness's Poem Watching the Sea on a Spring Day, by Yang Shidao of the Tang Dynasty ·······86

(6) *Observing the Sea (Climbing onto Mortar Isle)* By Dugu Ji of the Tang Dynasty ···························88

(7) *In Memory of Boyi and Shuqi,* by Wang Shipeng of the Song Dynasty ···90

(8) *Staying the Night by the Luanhe River,* by Nanlan Xingde of the Qing Dynastyr ·································92

(9) *Mortar Isle,* by Shi Menglan of the Qing Dynasty ·········92

(10) *Mortar Isle,* by Yang Zaiwen of the Qing Dynasty ········96

(11) *Mortar Isle,* by Song Luo of the Qing Dynasty ···········98

(12) *A Travel to Mortar Isle,* by You Zhikai of the Qing Dynasty ···100

2. Odes and Prologues ································104

(1) *Ode to Mortar Isle,* by Huang Yi of theQing Dynasty ···104

(2) *Prologue to Tour of Nineteen Isle,* by Yin Zhenyou of the Qing Dynasty ·······································108

(3) *A Brief Record of Mortar Isle,* by Han Xiangting of the Republic of China period ·····························112

Appendix: A Brief Biography of ·····················114

Chapter IV: Stele Inscriptions ·····················116

1. *Stele Inscriptions of the Chaoyang Nunnery,* by Li Zhongshu of the Qing Dynasty ·······················116

2. *A Brief Record of Chaoyang Nunnery,* by Yin Zhenyou of the Qing Dynasty ·································120

3. *Stele Inscriptions of Chaoyang Nunnery,* by An Rulin, etc. of the Qing Dynasty ·································124

4. *Stele Inscriptions for the Buddhist Hall of Guanyin Temple* ·····································128

5. Stone Stele in Commemoration of the Establishment of Chaoyin Temple, written by Zhao Zuming of the Qing Dynasty ·······································130

6. Gravestone for Monks Jing'an and Puji of the Linji Sect ···136

Chapter V: Religious Sites ························138

I. The History of Chaoyang Nunnery ·················138

II. Monk Faben and Chaoyin Temple ················142

III. Couplets in the Chaoyin Temple ·················150

IV. The Origin and Filiations of the Zen Sect

目 录

序……………………………………………徐建义 9

第一章 前言………………………………………19

第二章 菩提岛的形成………………………………25

第三章 菩提岛文化溯源…………………………27

第一节 相关历史人物…………………………………27

一 秦始皇派人上岛求仙………………………………27

二 曹操观沧海………………………………………29

三 赵武帝石虎屯兵储粮………………………………29

四 隋炀帝石臼坨望海…………………………………31

五 唐太宗驻跸十九坨…………………………………35

六 金熙宗岛上狩猎……………………………………37

七 于成龙火烧朝阳庵…………………………………37

八 武状元李国梁………………………………………41

九 潮音寺住持法本……………………………………49

十 史履晋撰写楹联……………………………………53

十一 葛翰林与法本结善缘……………………………53

十二 中国共产党创始人之一李大钊…………………57

十三 韩湘亭与潮音寺楹联……………………………67

十四 霍元甲大弟子刘振声……………………………69

十五 罗瑞卿大将巡视石臼坨…………………………77

第二节 诗词赋序…………………………………………79

一 诗词………………………………………………79

（一）步出夏门行……………………汉 曹操 79

（二）望海……………………………隋 杨广 81

（三）奉和望海………………………隋 虞茂 83

（四）春日望海………………………唐 李世民 85

（五）奉和圣制春日望海……………唐 杨师道 87

（六）观海（登石臼坨）……………唐 独孤及 89

（七）咏史怀夷齐……………………宋 王十朋 91

（八）菩萨蛮·宿滦河………………清 纳兰性德 93

（九）石臼坨…………………………清 史梦兰 95

（十）石臼坨…………………………清 杨在汶 97

（十一）石臼坨………………………清 宋荦 99

（十二）游石臼坨……………………清 游智开 101

二 赋序………………………………………………105

（一）石臼坨赋………………………清 黄倄 105

（二）游十九坨序……………………清 阴振猷 109

（三）石臼坨纪略……………………韩湘亭 113

第四章 碑刻与碑记………………………………117

一 朝阳庵碑记………………………清 李中淑 117

二 朝阳庵记略………………………清 阴振猷 121

三 朝阳庵碑记………………………清 安汝林等 125

四 观音庙佛堂碑记…………………………………129

五 创建潮音寺碑……………………清 赵祖铭 131

六 临济宗派寺僧静安普济墓碑……………………137

第五章 宗教名胜…………………………………139

第一节 朝阳庵的兴衰与变迁…………………………139

第二节 法本与潮音寺…………………………………143

第三节 潮音寺楹联诠释………………………………151

第四节 菩提岛禅宗门派源系…………………………157

第五节 潮音寺供奉佛像………………………………159

一 前殿………………………………………………159

（一）东方持国天王……………………………………159

（二）南方增长天王……………………………………159

on Puti Island ································156

V. Buddhist Statues in the Chaoyin Temple ···············158

1. Front Hall ·····························158

(1) Chiguo Heavenly King of the East ···············158

(2) Zengzhang Heavenly King of the South ···············158

(3) Guangmu Heavenly King of the West ···············158

(4) Duowen Heavenly King of the North ···············158

2. Great Hall (or Tathagata Hall) ···············160

(1) Sakyamuni Buddha ···············160

(2) Manjusri Bodhisattva ···············162

(3) Samantabhadra Bodhisattva ···············162

3. Rear Hall ························162

(1) Amita Buddha ···············162

(2) Avalokitesvara Bodhisattva ···············164

(3) Mahasthamaprapta Bodhisattva ···············164

4. The Eighteen Arhats ···············166

5. Five Hundred Arhats ···············170

Chapter VI: Ten Sights on Puti Island ··········**182**

I. Zhubi Pavilion ···················182

II. Bodhi Trees ·····················184

III. Fuhe Spring ·····················186

IV. Preaching Terrace ·················186

V. The Front Gate of Puti Island ···············186

VI. Zhengjue Lake and Kwan-yin Terrace ···········188

VII. Emperor-Greeting Mulberry Tree ···········188

VIII. Mandarin Duck Trees ···············188

IX. Wish Tree ·····················190

X. Three Suns Shine Together ···············190

Chapter VII: Plants on Puti Island ··············**192**

I. Ligneous Plants ·················192

II. Herbaceous Plants ···············202

III. Medical Herbs ·················206

ChapterVIII: Animals on Puti Island··············**216**

I. Birds ·····························216

1. Swimming Birds ···············216

2. Wading Birds ···············222

3. Terrestrial Birds ···············226

4. Singing Birds ···············228

5. Scansorial Birds ···············232

6. Predatory Birds ···············234

II. Marine Animals ···············238

III. Other Animals ···············240

Chapter IX: Hot Springs on Puti Island··········**242**

1. Slightly Alkaline Natrium
Bicarbonate Springs ···············242

2. Chlorinous Natrium Bicarbonate Springs ···········244

3. Sustainable Development ···············244

4. Ecological Hot Springs ···············244

Chapter X: Historical Celebrities of

Laoting County ····························**246**

I. Politicians and Officials ···············246

II. Jinshi of Past Dynasties ···············268

III. Local Celebrities ···············272

IV. Famous Businessmen ···············276

V. Provincial and Ministerial Officials after the Founding of
the People's Republic of China ···············278

VI. Generals after the Founding of the People's
Republic of China ···············282

VII. CAS and CAE Members ···············284

Postscript ····························**286**

（三）西方广目天王 ·········· 159
（四）北方多闻天王 ·········· 159
二 大雄宝殿（如来殿）·········· 161
（一）释迦牟尼 ·········· 161
（二）文殊菩萨 ·········· 163
（三）普贤菩萨 ·········· 163
三 后殿 ·········· 163
（一）阿弥陀佛 ·········· 163
（二）观音菩萨 ·········· 165
（三）大势至菩萨 ·········· 165
四 十八罗汉 ·········· 167
五 五百罗汉 ·········· 171

第六章 菩提岛十景 ·········· 183
一 驻跸亭 ·········· 183
二 菩提树 ·········· 185
三 和尚井 ·········· 187
四 讲经台 ·········· 187
五 菩提山门 ·········· 187
六 正觉湖与观音台 ·········· 189
七 盼王桑 ·········· 189
八 鸳鸯树 ·········· 189
九 许愿树 ·········· 191
十 三日同辉 ·········· 191

第七章 菩提岛上的植物 ·········· 193
一 木本植物 ·········· 193
二 草本植物 ·········· 203
三 药用植物 ·········· 207

第八章 菩提岛上的动物 ·········· 217
第一节 鸟类 ·········· 217
一 游禽 ·········· 217
二 涉禽 ·········· 223
三 陆禽 ·········· 227
四 鸣禽 ·········· 229
五 攀禽 ·········· 233
六 猛禽 ·········· 235
第二节 鱼虾类 ·········· 239
第三节 其他动物 ·········· 241

第九章 菩提岛上的温泉 ·········· 243
一 微碱性碳酸氢钠泉 ·········· 243
二 含氯碳酸氢钠泉 ·········· 245
三 确保可持续发展 ·········· 245
四 建设生态温泉 ·········· 245

第十章 乐亭历代名人录 ·········· 247
第一节 历代政要 ·········· 247
第二节 历代进士 ·········· 269
第三节 历代名人 ·········· 273
第四节 商界名人 ·········· 277
第五节 新中国成立后省部级干部 ·········· 279
第六节 新中国成立后将军 ·········· 283
第七节 中国科学院、中国工程院院士 ·········· 285

后记 ·········· 287

Preface

Over the three years from September 25, 2006, to December 23, 2009, I was lucky to participate in the takeover, development and construction of Puti Island, which became sweet and unforgettable memories in my life.

It was by chance that I got to know the island and finally decided to take over it.

One of my old friends in army, Tan Shuqiang, returned to his hometown and became director of the Defense Department of Laoting County, Tangshan City. He called several times to invite me to his home. Tan ever won first-grade medal for his heroic performance at the counterattack against Vietnam, and his company was granted the title of "Heroic Company in Laoshan Battle" upon the ratification of Deng Xiaoping, then chairman of the Central Military Commission. As the company commander, he was invited to give speech around the nation after the war. Moved by his warmth, I set out to Laoting to meet him in the early summer of 2006, where I unexpectedly received a grand welcome from the business promotion delegation of local government there.

The memory remains fresh as if it happened yesterday: Li Dongsheng, then member of the county's Party committee and secretary of Political and Legal Commission, Meng Xianfu, then executive vice county magistrate, and other members of the delegation introduced me to all kinds of local investment projects. It was already at noon that they elaborated the 37th project. I interrupted them and joked, "Don't starve yourselves for my reason. Why not continue your introduction at dinner table?" Mr. Meng replied, "We can continue after lunch. If none of the projects we mentioned this morning doesn't interest you, perhaps the Puti Island development project could be your destiny…" The high praise that Mr. Meng gave to Puti Island evoked my curiosity, and I then consulted him about more details about the island. However, Mr. Meng seemed not hurry to answer my questions, but said, "Let's have lunch first. You will know everything about the island when you personally visit it." His words aroused thunderous laughter.

The next day, I went to the island with the accompaniment of Mr. Li and Mr. Meng.

Our ship cruised on the sea. Viewed from the distance, Puti Island appeared like an oasis floating on the Bohai Sea, comprising a fantastic sight like a mirage.

As we disembarked onto the island, the first thing that entered our sight was a vast expanse of knee-high reeds and wormwoods, which swayed gracefully in the breeze and

序

公元2006年9月25日至2009年12月23日，我经历了接收管理与开发建设菩提岛三年时间的全过程，在人生旅途中留下了一段美好而难忘的记忆。

说起接管菩提岛的起因，其实很简单，而且生动有趣。

老部队的老战友谭树强，从野战部队平调回到距离家乡不远的唐山乐亭任县武装部部长，几次来电话邀请我去他那里走一走看一看。谭树强曾经是老山前线防御作战一等功荣立者，还是曾经得到军委主席邓小平签署命令授予的"老山作战神炮连"荣誉称号的连长，参加过英模报告团在全国各地巡回演讲。此次调任地方武装，于情于理都应该前去表示慰问。未曾想，2006年初夏时节前去见面时，却受到了乐亭县委县政府招商团的隆重接待，这是我始料未及的。

当时的情形历历在目。时任乐亭县委常委、政法委书记李东升，常务副县长孟宪福以及招商团成员逐一介绍各种招商引资项目。当时针指向中午12点时，介绍到了第37个项目，我插话说："不要因为我来，让大家陪着一起饿肚子。咱们边吃边谈怎么样？"孟副县长见状，接过我的话题："可以先吃饭，下午再作介绍。如果对以上项目不感兴趣呢，我们乐亭县还有一个海岛，名叫菩提岛，准备招商引资进行旅游开发……"听孟副县长夸菩提岛如何如何好，我便接连追问了几个有关该海岛的问题。这时，孟副县长却站起身来，调侃着卖了一个关子："先吃饭。要想知道详细情

emitted slight but soul-refreshing fragrance. Then, we took an electric cart toward a virgin forest that was only hundreds of meters from the shore. The rarest arboreal species in the forest is the Armur Linden, which is endemic to northern China. Perhaps due to their unique appearances, those ancient trees looked like gigantic bonsais in the sea breeze. Then, we visited the Chaoyang Nunnery that is said to be constructed during the reign of Emperor Wanli of the Ming Dynasty (1368-1644) and the Chaoyin Temple built in the reign of Emperor Guangxu of the Qing Dynasty (1644-1911).

No wonder the island is praised as "a fairyland on earth" and "a dreamlike paradise."

Impressed by its picturesque landscapes, I turned to Wang Fengting, then director of the county's Tourism Bureau, who stood aside, and remarked, "The never-before-touched ecosystem of Puti Island deserves our special protection. Such an idea must be followed in the process of its development. It's hard to forest an island, but easy to destroy it."

"The city of Jinzhou is a famous producer of apples," I added. "In the autumn of 1948, when the Liaoxi Campaign was fought there, local apple trees were overgrown with fruits, but none of PLA soldiers snatched apples from local farmers. During the Korean War, Chairman Mao Zedong required all officers and soldiers of the Chinese People's Volunteer Army to protect every mountain, river, and tree in North Korea as much as they could, and take no single belongings of Korean people."

Later, I reached an agreement with leaders of Laoting government, including Fan Shaohui, then secretary of the Party committee of Laoting, and Yuan Zhigang, then magistrate of the county, on the cooperative development of Puti Island. According to relevant procedures, the agreement we signed would not come into effect until it was ratified by the municipal government of Tangshan. Before I left the county, I entrusted some local friends to find some historical records and other documents about the county.

The island further impressed me as I acquired an insight of its history.

Astonishingly, the small island was associated with so many celebrated historic figures, including the First Qin Emperor and his prime minister Li Si, as well as such emperors as Liu Che, Cao Cao, Yang Guang, Li Shimin, Wanyan Dan, and Kangxi. Surprised at its profound cultural accumulation, I began to ponder why so many monarchs and historic celebrities were in favor of the island.

Historical records reveal that Laoting was established as a county in the Jin Dynasty (1115-1234). In ancient times, "locals paid great attention to education, and sent their children to school only if their families had enough to eat and clothe." Throughout the Ming Dynasty, many passed imperial examinations. From the time of Emperor Qianlong, martial arts began to prevail in the area. By the end of the Qing Dynasty, the county had become home to 55 *jinshi* (successful candidates in the highest imperial examinations) and 167 *juren* (those who

况，且等看了菩提岛以后再说！"引得哄堂大笑。

翌日，李东升和孟宪福两位领导专程陪同我前往菩提岛进行参观考察。

乘船渡海途中顺着手指的方向，伴随着海浪的起伏，远远望见菩提岛好似漂浮在渤海之上的一片绿洲，蜿蜒起伏，犹如海市蜃楼。

登上菩提岛后，首先映入眼帘的是齐腰深的芦苇和蒿草，放眼望去，婀娜多姿，婆娑荡漾，不时地飘过一缕缕草香，叫人心旷神怡。乘坐电瓶车过几百米，便驶进古树丛林里，其中尤以北方所独有的小叶菩提树最为罕贵。或许是树种的原因，或许是海风吹拂摇曳的作用，棵棵古树造型都好似硕大的盆景一般。在菩提树林的掩映下，我们先后游览了据说始建于明朝万历年间的朝阳庵遗址和建于清朝光绪年间的潮音寺。

真是人间的仙境，梦想中的乐园。

面对如此美景，我一时兴起，当着时任县旅游局局长王凤亭的面，随口吟诵出了："锦州那个地方出苹果，辽西战役的时候，正是秋天，老百姓家里有很多苹果，我们的战士一个都不去拿"，以及抗美援朝时毛泽东主席给中国人民志愿军的指示："中国同志必须将朝鲜的事情看做自己的事情一样，教育指挥员战斗员爱护朝鲜的一山一水一草一木，不拿朝鲜人民的一针一线。"[1] 菩提岛可是原汁原味的原始生态，一草一木轻易都不能动。一定要坚持保护与开发并举。在这海岛上，长出一片生态难，毁掉一片绿色易啊！

在与时任县委书记范绍慧和县长袁志刚等乐亭县委县政府的领导洽谈好合作意向后，县里还需要向市里报批，临返回之前我委托有关同志寻找带回了当地不同年代的几本县志和有关的一些文史资料。

不看不知道，一看吓一跳。

一个区区弹丸之小海岛，竟然与秦始皇和丞相李斯、汉

注释：①参见《毛泽东选集》第五卷。

passed the imperial examinations at provincial level), including one literary *zhuangyuan* (No.1 scholar at the highest imperial examinations), one military *zhuangyuan*, one *bangyan* (No.2 scholar at the highest imperial examinations), and one *tanhua* (No.3 scholar at the highest imperial examinations).

This just evidences the county's abundance in resources and talents.

Throughout history, countless literati wrote poems and essays to chant the praises of Puti Island. The First Qin Emperor once came here to look for a meeting with immortals, and Emperor Wudi of the Han Dynasty (202BC-220) followed the suit. Over centuries, many men of letter traveled the island and left behind numerous beautiful poems that are still shining like bright pearls in every corner of the island. A systemic discovery, research and compilation of those cultural relics can made them priceless treasures of the island. This is also the reason why I compiled this book.

After taking over the trusteeship of the island, we organized a series of campaigns to rescue and restore some ruined stone steles with historic and cultural value in the Chaoyang Nunnery and the Chaoyin Temple, redeemed some ancient bricks, stones, and utensils that originally belonged to the island, and reconstructed the gates of those temples. In addition to protecting their architectural buildings, we also endeavored to resume their fame as a center of religious activities as alike as in the Ming and Qing dynasties. Within the 1,000 days and nights I spent together with the island, I personally witnessed

its misty scenery as marvelous as a fairyland, its scenic views that embodied the loyal love, and its fantastic sights that feature three suns and three moons shining together. I also experienced the island's tranquility and singularity. Every time I heard the roaring of violent wind and rain on the island, an inexpressibly sweet feeling would hit my heart.

Later, due to the need of united development of Puti Island and the other two islands, the municipal government of Tangshan decided to withdraw our trusteeship of the island. Life seems like a relay race. It is good to pursue the dream, but it needs more courage to give up. Thanks to the leadership of Xue Shubin, director of the Tanshan Bay International Travel Island Development and Construction Headquarters, our original concepts concerning the development of Puti Development have been retained and even further improved.

It has been more than a year since I said goodbye to Puti Island. Today, *Puti Island: A Fairyland on Earth* has finally been unveiled to readers. Perhaps this is what we could do for the development of the island.

I sincerely hope that Puti Island will develop into an "unprecedented resort" as our ancestors wished, and serve as a tranquil hideaway for our offspring.

Xu Jianyi
May 10, 2011

武大帝刘彻、魏武帝曹操、隋炀帝杨广、唐太宗李世民、金熙宗完颜亶、清康熙帝玄烨等都有着历史的渊源或关联。如此厚重的文化底蕴，更加令我惊羡不已。为何历史上这么多帝王将相结缘菩提岛呢？

细读历朝历代县志，乐亭自金置县，"雅重读书，村氓衣食稍足，亦必令子弟就塾。明自洪武至隆万，科第不绝"。"逮乾隆初，武风鼎盛，会元鼎甲，接迹连镳，时俗艳之。"迨至清末，该县出过进士55人，举人167人，其中文状元、武状元各1人，探花、榜眼各1人。

诚如斯言：物华天宝，人杰地灵。

在浩瀚历史长河中，有许多文人墨客为菩提岛写就诗词、歌赋、碑记，如"秦帝曾经此，登临翼飞翻"、"汉武雄心兮，寄遗踪于飘缈。羡门高蹈兮，传佳话于空濛"、"老骥伏枥，志在千里。烈士暮年，壮心不已"、"仙源真世外，何必觅蓬莱"、"风帆沙鸟结人世之奇缘，云影波光开天然之画本"，等等。秦皇汉武来此求仙，骚人墨客探奇览胜，优美的诗赋篇章就像一颗颗珍珠，散落在历史的各个角落里，如果系统加以发现、考证和整理，用历史文化这条主线把它们串起来，便可以成为菩提岛所独有的弥足珍贵的传世之宝。这是主持编写本书的初衷。

接管菩提岛以后，我们对具有历史文物价值的朝阳庵和潮音寺的残碑组织进行了抢救性保护和修复，费重金赎回了一些原本属于菩提岛的旧砖石器物，复建了山门。在保护好朝阳庵和潮音寺遗址基础上，着力恢复明清时期"佛事鼎盛，闻名遐迩"的历史风貌。在心系菩提岛的1000多个日日夜夜里，我目睹了菩提岛罕见的宛若仙境的岛霭蜃气、见证爱情忠贞的"海枯石烂"和三日同辉、三月同耀的神奇美景，亲身体验了菩提岛的"古、幽、奇、静"，无数次倾听了菩提岛狂野的风声和雨声，内心铭刻了几多美妙、遐想与情思。

出于"三岛"旅游统一开发的需要，唐山市委市政府决定收回菩提岛。其实，人生的每一个阶段都好似接力赛，追逐梦想是美好的，舍得放弃也是一种超脱和美德。令人欣慰的是，在唐山湾国际旅游岛开发建设指挥部薛树滨主任主持下，菩提岛原来的一些开发理念得以继续，并且更加恢弘博大。

离开菩提岛已经一年有余了，《人间仙境菩提岛》一书终于付梓出版以飨读者，算是同人们善始善终为菩提岛的开发建设添砖加瓦吧！

衷心希望菩提岛能够实现先人"终古之胜"之夙愿，亦能够为后人留下一方清幽与宁静。

是为序。

徐建义

2011年5月10日

（一）明　乐亭县地图

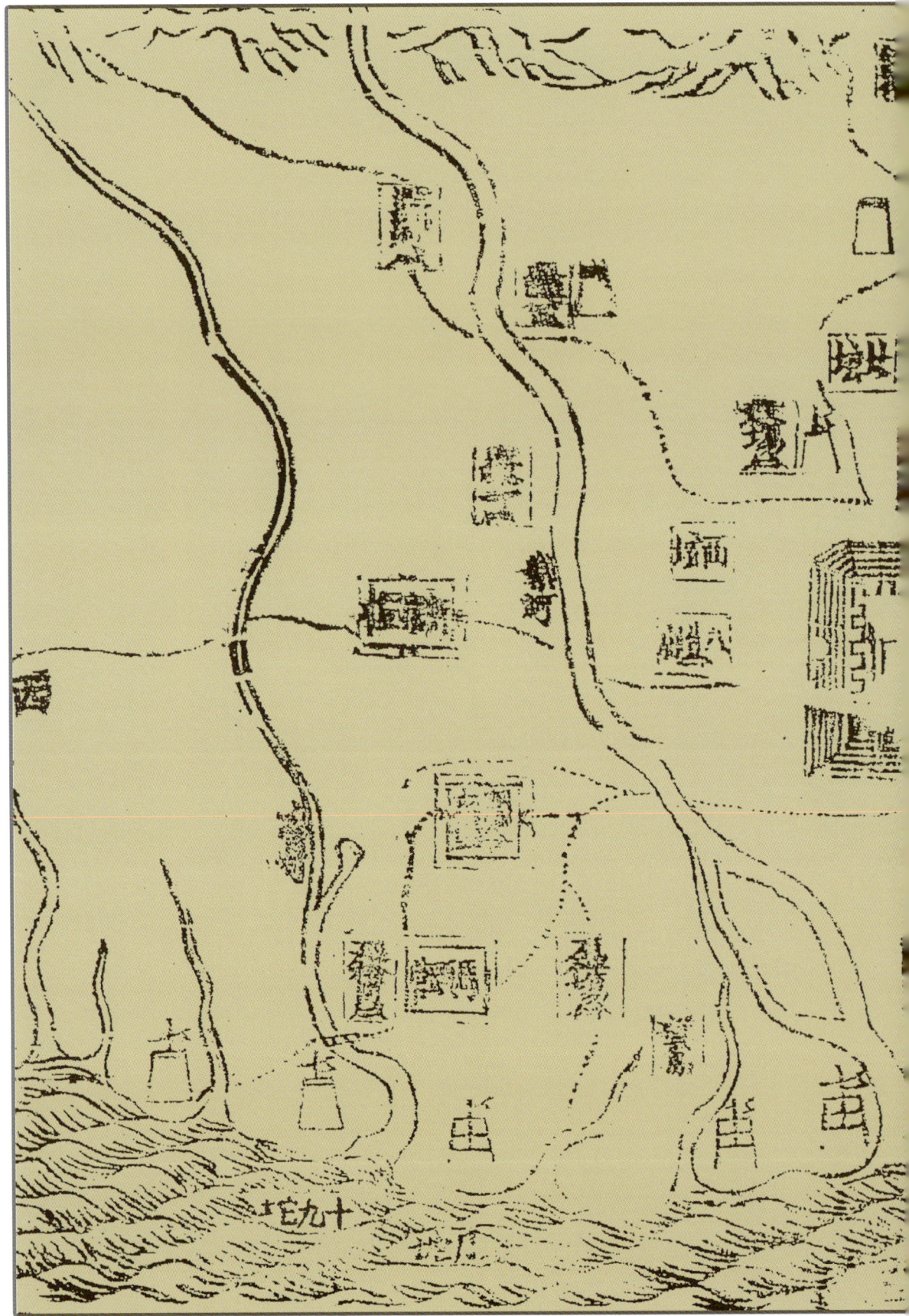

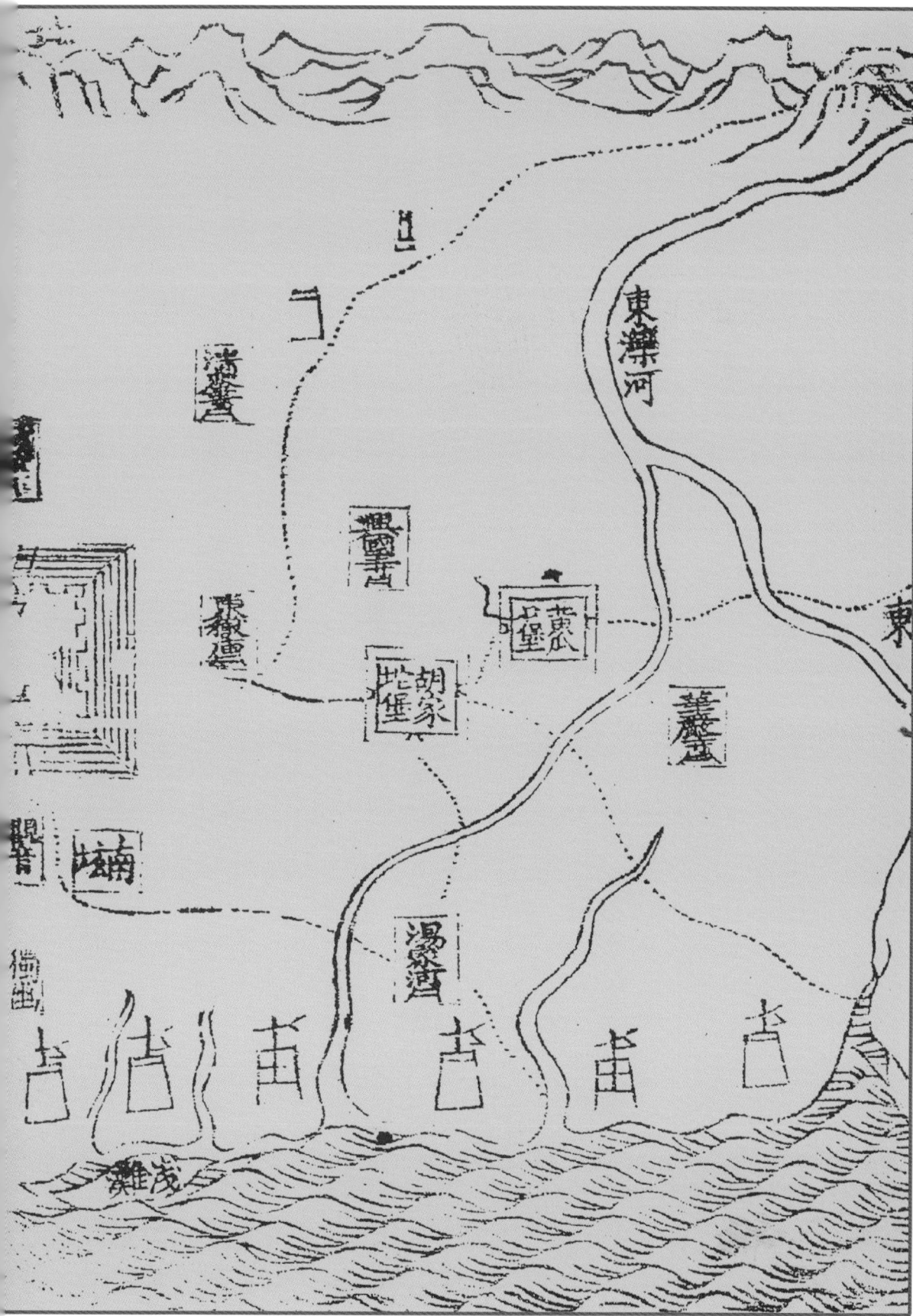

（二）清　乐亭县地图

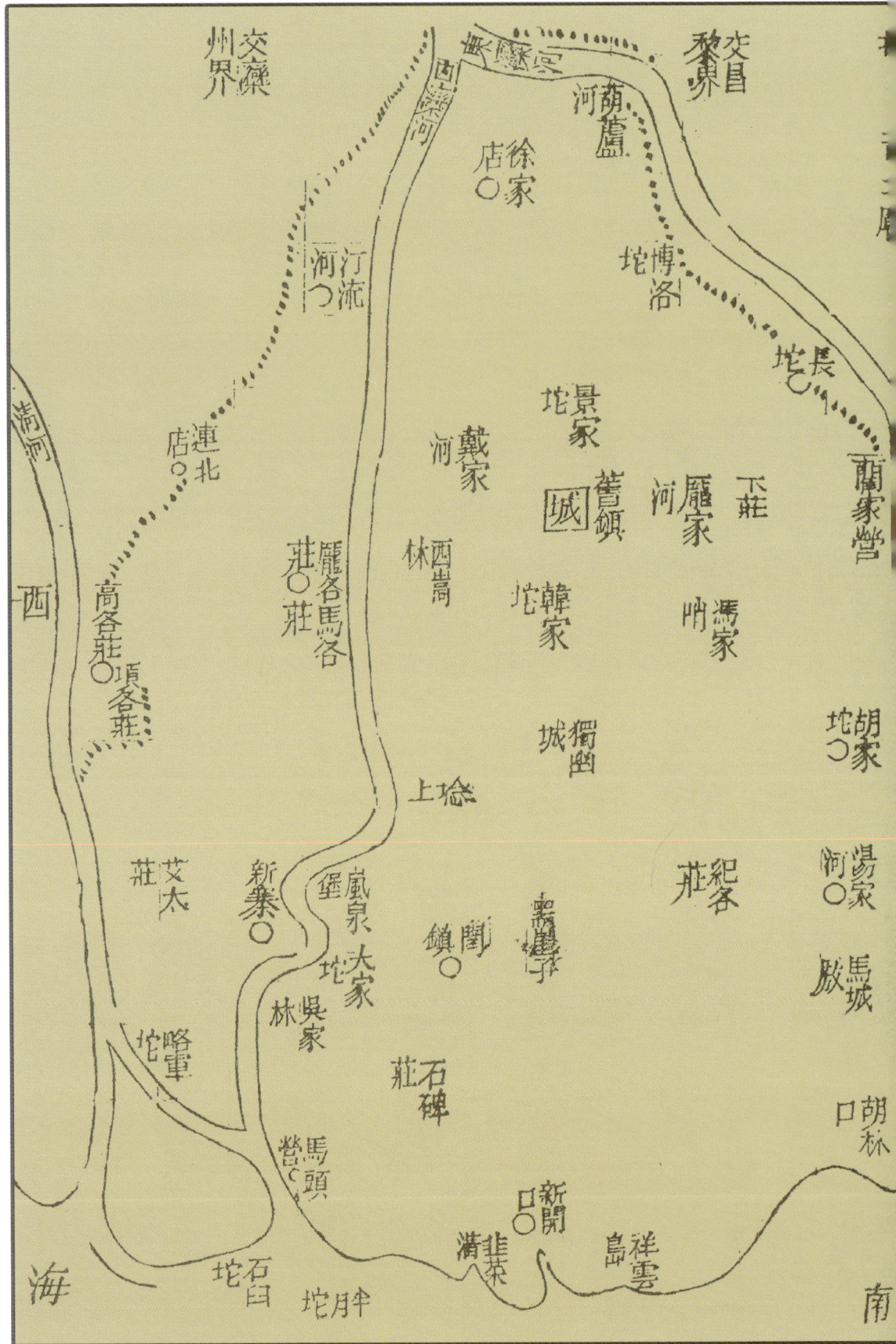

合境全圖

東

海

百壑營

左家營

黃佃莊

灘質

周家營

木瓜

黃瓜口

羊闌溝

坨

老米

野猪口

泉水

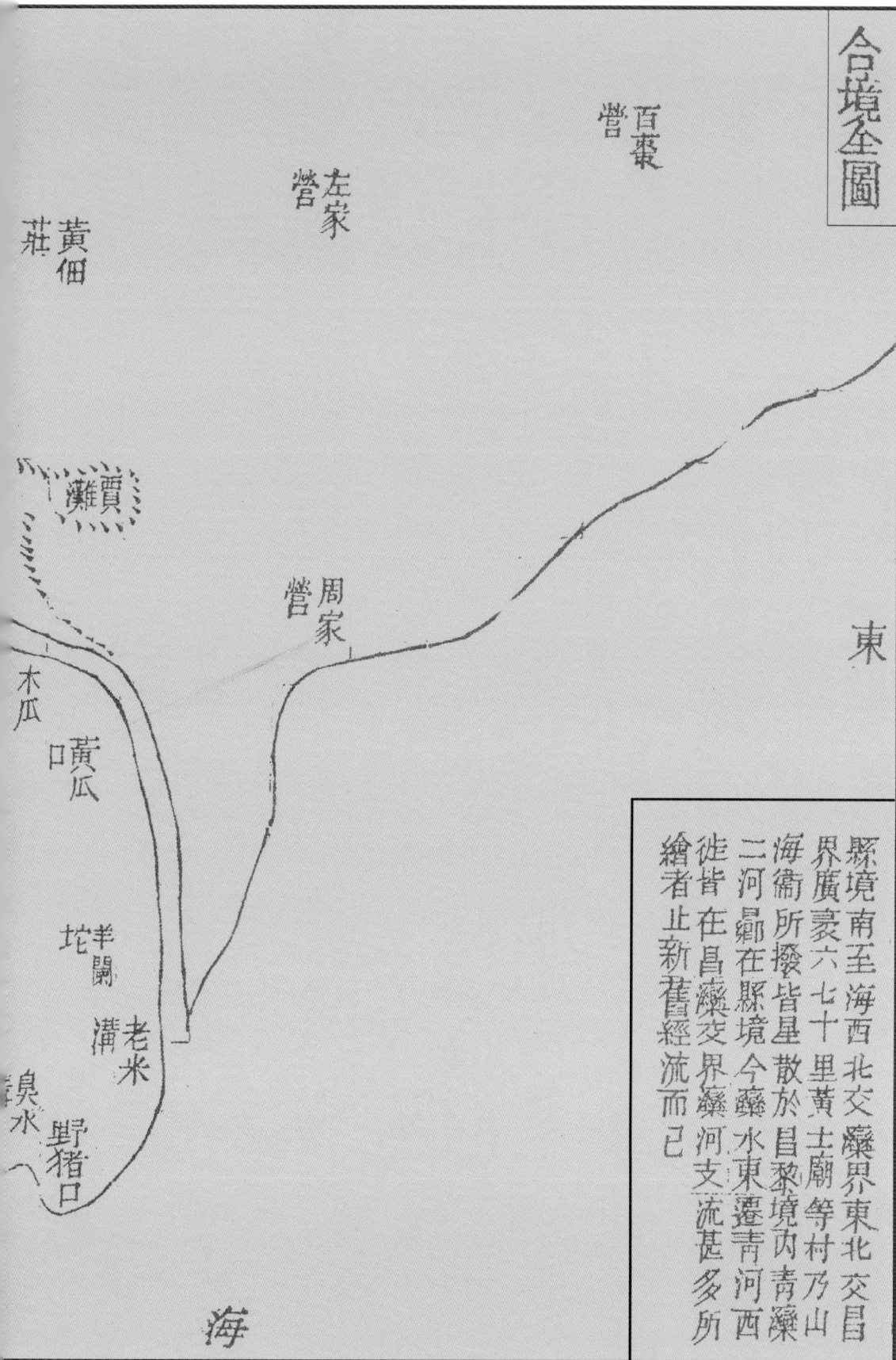

縣境南至海西北交灤界東北交昌
界廣袤六七十里黃土廟等村乃山
海衞所撥皆星散於昌黎境內青灤
二河皆在縣境今灤水東遷青河西
徙皆在昌灤交界灤河支流甚多所
繪者止新舊經流而已

Chapter I Foreword

Stretching in the Bohai Sea, 30 kilometers southwest of the county seat of Laoting, Hebei Province's Tangshan City, is a small island that measures three kilometers from north to south and two kilometers from east to west. It is Puti Island.

The island features lush plants, hovering birds, and diverse wildlife, and appears like a shining gem inlaid on the Bohai Bay. There, lucky tourists can observe the fantastic view of three suns or three moons shining together, as well as spectacular mirages.

A favored child of Mother Nature, Puti Island was formed due to joint efforts of the ancient Luanhe River and the Bohai Sea. The Luanhe River originates at the Dagudao Valley in Xiaoliang Mountain in the northwest of Fengning County, Chengde City, and flows to Laoting County via the Inner Mongolia Plateau and the Yanshan Mountains of Hebei Province. Its lower reaches, which is popularly called Daqing River, jumps into the sea in Laoting. The river carries tremendous amounts of sand from its upper reaches to the sea, where its torrent slows down due to the obstruction of tides. With the passage of time, more and more sand aggregated there. Washed by tides over millions of years, the sand finally formed a mortar-shaped island, with its edges protruding upwards and its center sunken. Such a terrain is easy to withhold rainwater. Meanwhile, the island can turn seawater into freshwater due to the filtration of its sandy soil. Although surrounded by seawater, therefore, the island abounds in underground freshwater. Since remote antiquity, the island has been seldom touched by human footprints, so it preserves a primitive ecosystem. Living on the island are more than 200 species of plants, 400 species of birds, and over 40 kinds of wild land animals.

Puti Island is a botanical kingdom. The particularly astonishing fact is that such species as linden and kapok, which are endemic to humid, hot southern regions and rarely seen in the areas north of the Yellow River, grow vibrantly on the island. Some deem it as the blessing from Sakyamuni Buddha, and others attribute the strange phenomenon to migratory birds carrying seeds from the south, which didn't digest and then took roots on the island together with the birds' excrements. However, migratory birds are also found in nearby areas. So, it remains a mystery why those trees only thrive on Puti Island.

Puti Island is also a paradise for birds. Its dense forests and vast beaches provide plentiful food for wild birds. Meanwhile, its untouched environment is a favorable habitat for birds to breed. There have been discovered 379 species of migratory birds and 29 resident species, including seagulls, mallards, and eastern imperial eagles. Even such endangered species as Saunder's gull, Asiatic dowitcher, and short-tailed albatross are often found on the island. So far, the island has become a world-renowned destination for bird watching. In spring and autumn, numerous bird lovers travel afar from around the world to watch birds on the island.

In addition, Puti Island is a utopia for wild animals. There are more than 40 species, including fox, badger, mallard, pheasant, hare, mole, hedgehog, and lizard. Records about those wildlife species are found in many local historic books. For instance, According to *Record of Laoting County's Local Products* that was revised in 1755, pheasants and lizards were already found in the county during the Qing Dynasty. Historical records reveal that "local adult lizards measured five inches in length, and featured golden-and-green bodies."

More importantly, Puti Island abounds in historic and cultural relics.

After he united China, the First Qin Emperor conducted five inspection tours around the country between 220BC to 210BC. Except for his first tour westwards to Longxi, the destination of all tours was the East China Sea. On one hand, the emperor tried to demonstrate his "unparalleled dignity and power" in this way, and on the other hand, he aimed to look for elixir of life. During his inspection tours, the emperor left stone steles at seven sacred mountains, including Yi, Tai, Zhifu, Langya, Dongguan, Jieshi, and Huiji.

Some local elders declared that a stone stele with inscriptions of Li Si, prime minister of the Qin Dynasty, was

第一章　前言

在河北省唐山市乐亭县城西南30多公里的渤海之中，有一个南北长约3公里、东西宽约2公里的狭长状岛屿，这就是菩提岛。

岛上植被茂盛，飞鸟群集，物种丰富，像一颗孤悬

菩提岛方位图

在渤海湾中的闪亮明珠，让人心驰神往。登临菩提岛，可以欣赏到三日同辉的壮丽，三月同耀的美景，海市蜃楼的奇观。

菩提岛是大自然的造化。古滦河与渤海共同造就了菩提岛。滦河发源于承德丰宁满族自治县西北小梁山大古道沟，流经内蒙古高原及河北燕山山区，进入乐亭县境。滦河的下游大清河，是滦河最初在乐亭县的一条入海口。滦河从上游裹挟着大量的泥沙奔腾入海，由于海潮侵蚀阻挡，河水的流速减缓下来，这样在入海口前的水流和大海潮流相抵的地方泥沙逐渐沉积，且越积越多。涨潮时海浪将裹挟的泥沙推到高处，退潮时泥沙就在高处滞留。千万年的日积月累，终于形成了四周隆起、中间低凹，状似石臼的海岛。这种独特地形，使雨水难以外流，而主要由泥沙构成的岛屿既能滤水又能涵水，过滤下去的是原来沙土中的盐碱，涵养下来的则是淡水。因此，岛的四周虽被海水包围，而岛上掘地盈尺，

则甘泉清冽。再加上自古人迹罕至，所以保持着原始的生存状态，岛上植物达200种，鸟类400余种，陆生野生动物超过40种。

菩提岛是植物的王国。最让人百思不解的是，菩提、木丝棉等树种主要生长在南方温湿地带，整个黄河以北地区几乎是绝无仅有，在这里却枝繁叶茂，生机勃勃。有人说这是释迦牟尼的法力显圣，未免唯心与神话；还有人把这种奇迹归因于迁徙的飞鸟，它们粪便中排泄出自南方带来的树种，经高温消化使树种变异，但飞鸟迁徙落在附近陆地的也很多，难以解释为何唯独菩提岛才能使它们生根发芽并茁壮成长。

菩提岛是鸟的世界。这里植物茂密，滩涂广阔，食料丰富，人为影响较小，对鸟类栖息繁殖十分有利。岛上共发现候鸟379种、留鸟29种，海鸥、野鸭、白肩雕时隐时现，世界上存量极少的黑嘴鸥、半蹼鹬、短尾信天翁等珍稀鸟类也经常到这座岛上栖息觅食。每年春秋两季，世界各地的许多观鸟爱好者不远万里聚集到这个国际知名的观鸟基地参观考察。

菩提岛是野生动物的天堂。狐、獾、野鸭、山鸡、野兔、鼹鼠、刺猬、四脚蛇等有40多个物种，其中在历代史志中均有记载。譬如，在清朝乾隆二十年（1755年）修订的《乐亭县志·物产》记载："凡羽之属……雉……"并引用《尔雅》注释："雉绝有力奋，北方曰鹨。""雉"就是指"山鸡"，也称"野鸡"。四脚蛇也称"蜥蜴"，或"石龙子"。据同年的《乐亭县志·物产》记载："凡虫羽之属……石龙子……"并引用《滦志》注释："大者长四五寸，身有金碧色，或谓即蜥蜴。"

菩提岛还有丰富的历史和文化底蕴。

秦始皇嬴政统一全国后，从公元前220年至公元前210

discovered in the county during the 1960s. According to *Record of Laoting County's Mountains and Rivers* that was compiled in 1877, previous historical records showed that "it was said the county preserved Li Si's stone stele." However, it is still unknown whether the stone stele was that of Mount Jieshi. The *Biography of the First Qin Emperor in the Records of the Grand Historian*, written by Sima Qian, reveals that the emperor once "left a stone stele on Jieshi Mountain."

So far, historians haven't reached consensus on the location of Jieshi Mountain. Some claim that the ancient Jieshi Mountain was already submerged in the estuary of the Luanhe River that is near to Puti Island in the southwest of Laoting County, while others assert that the mountain mentioned in the historical book is actually Mount Jieshi in the north of today's Changli County. However, Mount Jieshi in Changli County is encircled by other mountains and doesn't face the sea, which offers an important evidence that the original Jieshi Mountain is in today's Laoting County.

Liu Che, or Emperor Wu of the Han Dynasty, also ever visited Jieshi Mountain to seek immorality. According to the *Biography of Emperor Wu in the Records of the Grand Historian*, in 110BC, Emperor Wu of the Han Dynasty held a grand ceremony to worship Mount Tai, and he then "traveled eastwards to the sea in search of the legendary island of Penglai, and northwards to Jieshi Mountain." Li Daoyuan, a noted geographer in ancient China, recorded in his *Commentary on the Waterways Classic* that "the Ru River flows southeastwards to Lei County's Jieshi Mountain… Emperor Wu of the Han once climbed onto the mountain to observe the immense ocean." Ban Gu, a prestigious historian of the Eastern Han Dynasty, also mentioned the coastal mountain in his *Ode to West Capital*. Later, Huang Yi, a scholar from Fujian Province in the Qing Dynasty, mourned the hopeless journey of Emperor Wu of the Han to seek immorality in his *Ode to Mortar Isle*. Unfortunately, nothing has been left to evidence the emperor's visit to Puti Island.

In 207, Cao Cao, a powerful warlord in the Three Kingdoms Period (220-265), passed Jieshi Mountain after he defeated Yuan Shao and Wuhuan, where he wrote a famous poem to express his feeling. Titled *Gazing at the Immense Ocean*, the poem reads:

> Come east of Jieshi Cliff
> I gaze out across the ocean,
> Its rolling waves
> Studded with rocks and islets;
> Dense the trees and bushes here,
> Rank the undergrowth;
> The autumn wind is soughing,
> Huge billows are breaking.
> Sun and moon take their course
> As if risen from the sea;
> The bright galaxy of stars
> Seems sprung from the deep.
> And so, with joy in my heart,
> I hum this song.

According to the landscapes depicted in the poem, the mountain that Cao Cao visited was probably Jieshi Mountain in Laoting County, and the islands he saw in the sea were perhaps Puti Island and nearby Xiangyun and Yuetuo Islands.

Yang Guang, the second emperor of the Sui Dynasty (581-618), passed Jieshi Mountain when he led an expedition against Korea. He left behind a poem titled *Watching the Sea*.

> Although delighted to watch the blue ocean,
>
> I remain a little disappointed for not seeing the legendary Golden Terrace.
>
> Rolling waves smash on banks,
> While distant islands look blurry in clouds.
> Against roaring billows,
> Docile seagulls play with humans,
> On the shore carpeted with lush trees and bushes.
> The scenery is so beautiful,
> That I need never travel afar

年五次巡游天下，除第一次是在公元前220 年西巡陇西外，第二次至第五次都是到海边巡游，一方面为了颂扬他"横扫六合，威震四海"的丰功伟绩；另一方面也为了求仙问药，长生不老。在巡游过程中，曾在七处刻碑立碣，分别是《峄山》、《泰山》、《之罘》、《琅琊》、《东观》、《碣石》、《会稽》。

据乐亭县三岛附近的许多老人回忆，在20世纪60年代"破四旧"之前，有人曾见到过李斯书写的碑刻。清光绪三年（1877年）编纂的《乐亭县志·山川》记载：旧志云，祥云岛上"人传中有李斯碑"。李斯是秦始皇当朝丞相，其是否就是《碣石》碑刻，至今不得而知。查阅《史记·秦始皇本纪》，有如下记载：

三十二年，始皇之碣石，使燕人卢生求羡门、高誓。刻碣石门。坏城郭，决通提防。其辞曰：

遂兴师旅，诛戮无道，为逆灭息。武殄暴逆，文复无罪，庶心咸服。惠论功劳，赏及牛马，恩肥土域。皇帝奋威，德并诸侯，初一泰平。堕坏城郭，决通川防，夷去险阻。地势既定，黎庶无繇，天下咸抚。男乐其畴，女修其业，事各有序。惠被诸产，久并来田，莫不安所。群臣诵烈，请刻此石，垂著仪矩。

对于"刻碣石门"，学术界有多种说法，争议最大的有两个：一说在六朝以后，古碣石山沉入乐亭县西南旧滦河入海口处，即临近菩提岛的位置；另一说是指昌黎县城北的碣石山。而昌黎城北的碣石山是在群山环抱中，并不能面临大海，很难理解"决通堤防"，这是有利于石碣山原在乐亭县境内的重要佐证。

汉朝武帝刘彻，也曾到过碣石山巡幸求仙。据《史记·孝武本纪》记载，元封元年（前110年），汉武帝到泰山

行封禅大礼，"蓬莱诸神山若将可得"，"乃复东至海"，"望冀遇蓬莱"，"北至碣石"。郦道元《水经注·濡水》对此记述："濡水又东南至絫县碣石山……汉武帝亦尝登之，以望巨海。"东汉史学家班固在《西都赋》也提到"扬波涛于碣石，激神岳之嶈嶈"。清朝乾隆年间福建侯官举人黄佾在《石臼坨赋》中曾写道："汉武雄心兮，寄遗踪于缥缈；羡门高蹈兮，传佳话于空濛。"可惜，汉武帝在菩提岛是何等佳话已经随着时光流逝而湮灭。

魏武帝曹操在建安十二年（207年）击败袁绍、征讨乌桓之后，绕道碣石山，留下抒怀名篇———《观沧海》：

东临碣石，以观沧海。

水何澹澹，山岛竦峙。

树木丛生，百草丰茂。

秋风萧瑟，洪波涌起。

日月之行，若出其中。

星汉灿烂，若出其里。

幸甚至哉，歌以咏志。

根据"水何澹澹，山岛竦峙"诗句判断，曹操登临的很可能就是乐亭境内的碣石山，而能看到的海岛也有可能就是菩提岛以及临近的祥云岛和月坨岛。

隋炀帝杨广于大业八年（612年）东征高句，"出碣石道"，并留下诗作《望海》：

碧海虽欣瞩，金台空有闻。

远水翻如岸，遥山倒似云。

断涛还共合，连浪或时分。

驯鸥旧可狎，卉木足为群。

方知小姑射，谁复语临汾。

To admire the famous Gushe Mountain in Linfen.

In 644, Emperor Li Shimin of the Tang Dynasty led military forces to suppress Korea. According to *Record of Laoting County's Mountains and Rivers* compiled in the time of Emperor Guangxu, the emperor stayed for 19 days on Puti Island, which was thus named Nineteen Isle. During his stay, the emperor composed the poem *Watching the Sea on a Spring Day*, which reads as follows:

Putting on a robe,

I look afar at the immense ocean.

Lying against the handle of my chariot,

I feel intoxicated in the beautiful spring views.

The running river disappear at the horizon,

As though it flowed to heaven.

Hidden in haze are three legendary islands on the sea,

While spring breeze gently blows.

Piercing through waves,

The sun shines with dazzling light.

Colored clouds confuse wild geese,

Which then fly disorderly.

Despite my humble ambition,

I dare to shoot with bow.

Although with boundaries,

The ocean cannot be measured with a gourd ladle.

Although without a source,

The ocean cannot be emptied with a gourd ladle.

From time to time,

The ocean can turn into mulberry fields.

As Mount Zhifu reminds me of Emperor Wu of the Han,

Mount Jieshi reminds me of the First Qin Emperor.

Not as ambitious as them,

I merely wish a peaceful, harmonious society.

About five nautical miles southwest of Puti Island stands a stone stele carved with *Record of the Caofeidian Lighthouse*, which reads like that: "Facing the Bohai Sea and backing Luanzhou Harbor in eastern Hebei Province, the watercourse serves as an offshore corridor linking to Tianjin. Historically, the Tang emperor stayed here for several days. Unfortunately, his favored concubine, Cao, died here. The emperor then built the Caofei Palace in memory of the dead concubine on an isolate island. This was how the place got its name. Legend goes that numerous fishermen died on the violent sea. During the Qing Dynasty, Monk Faben traveled here and constructed a lighthouse to guide fishing boats. A local official had a crystal lamp at his home. Hearing the news, the monk came to ask for it. He didn't succeed until he burnt one of his fingers. The lighthouse remains in use till today."

The Chaoyin Temple on Puti Island began to be built by Monk Faben in 1889. The temple formed a certain scale over 27 years of expansions. After Faben died in 1917, his disciple, Zhenkong, spent 17 years further constructing the temple, which was eventually completed in 1933.

Besides the Chaoyin Temple, the Chaoyang Nunnery is another historic building on the island. Historical records reveal that the nunnery was first constructed in the reign of Emperor Wanli of the Ming Dynasty. However, the stone stele in memory of Monks Jing'an and Puji there indicates that the nunnery can "be traced back to the Tang Dynasty."

Nowadays, those ruined pillars and steles scattered amidst linden trees still remind visitors of the island's profound history and splendid culture.

唐太宗李世民于贞观十八年（644年）讨伐高句丽，传说在这里驻跸停留19天，菩提岛因此留下十九坨的旧称。光绪三年《乐亭县志·山川》对此记载道："相传唐太宗征高句丽，住此十九日，故坨名十九。"唐太宗还赋诗《春日望海》：

披襟眺沧海，凭轼玩春芳。

积流横地纪，疏派引天潢。

仙气凝三岭，和风扇八荒。

拂潮云布色，穿浪日舒光。

照岸花分彩，迷云雁断行。

怀卑运深广，持满守灵长。

有形非易测，无源讵可量。

洪涛经变野，翠岛屡成桑。

之罘思汉帝，碣石想秦皇。

霓裳非本意，端拱且图王。

距菩提岛西南5海里的曹妃甸刻有一块石碑《曹妃甸灯塔记》，其中说道："滦州故地，冀东新港，渤海滨沙岛，天津外水廊。背陆地而有浅滩，面大洋而有深槽。唐王于兹歇马，曹妃就此驻魂，唐王伤怀爱妾，兴曹妃殿于孤岛。此为该地得名之始。汪洋千里，碧波无尽。船工不幸每遇海难而夭亡。龙王饕餮，常借黎民以果腹。以至满清，法本僧游方于此，感念苍生之不幸，欲竖灯塔以指海道。闻道台有水晶灯盏，竟自燃其指乞化，方得以赠。是由，灯塔遂起，遗泽于今。"

菩提岛现存的佛教寺院潮音寺，是在清光绪十五年（1889年）由法本和尚始建，历经27个寒暑，寺院粗具规模，法本大师于1917年圆寂。他的弟子真空又经过17年艰辛努力，最终于1933年将潮音寺建成。

菩提岛除了潮音寺，更具悠久历史的是朝阳庵。据《乐亭县志》记载，朝阳庵始建于明朝万历年间。但是现存的纪念临济宗僧人静安、普济所立石碑却刻有"朝阳庵由唐至今……"

菩提林掩映着散落的柱础基石，残缺的碑文诗赋，述说着菩提岛的历史变迁，还有那说不完的人文情趣。

Chapter II: The Origin of Puti Island

Geologists reveal that the ancient Luanhe River flowed along the Yanshan Mountains and formed the land of Laoting County, and such local offshore islands as Puti, Yuetuo and Xiangyun were results of tide movements of Bohai Bay.

Nestling in the vast Bohai Sea, Puti Island is four kilometers from the coast. A geological survey shows that the Luanhe River, which originates at the Dagudao Valley in Xiaoliang Mountain in the northwest of Fengning County, Chengde City, and flows to Laoting County via the Inner Mongolia Plateau and the Yanshan Mountains of Hebei Province, carries tremendous amounts of sand from its upper reaches to the sea. When it reached Laoting, the torrent slows down due to the county's flat terrain. With the passage of time, more and more sand aggregated there, causing the rise of riverbed and the obstruction of watercourse. Historical records show that prior to the Ming Dynasty, the mainstream of the Luanhe River was split into the East Luanhe (today's Erluan River) and the West Luanhe (today's Old Luanhe). In ancient times, the upper reaches of the West Luanhe, popularly known as the Daqing River, flew into the ocean in Laoting. Year after year, the river carried sand from its upper reaches into the sea, where it was blocked by tides. So, more and more sand aggregated at the river estuary, which finally caused the West Luanhe River plugged. Then, waves transported sand that was already dumped into the sea and formed a sandy barrier islet almost parallel to the coastline. Because it looked like a stone mortar, locals named it Mortar Isle. Later, Emperor Li Shimin of the Tang Dynasty ever stayed here for 19 days during his expedition against Korea, so the island was renamed Nineteen Isle. In recent years, locals began to call it Puti (meaning "Bodhi" in Sanskrit) Island due to bunge hackberries growing there, which appear like Bodhi trees.

第二章　菩提岛的形成

据地质学家介绍，沿燕山山脉顺流而下的滦河，造就了乐亭这方土地，渤海湾潮汐的作用，造就了乐亭陆地前沿渤海中的菩提岛、月坨岛与祥云岛等沿海离岸岛屿。

孤悬于浩瀚的渤海之中的菩提岛，距海岸线4公里。地质部门勘察考证发现，发源于承德丰宁满族自治县西北小梁山大古道沟的滦河，流经内蒙古高原及河北省燕山山区，由于上下游河道落差大，在承德境内汇集了沿途各支流带来的大量泥沙。浊流冲出燕山山脉后直奔乐亭广袤平原，水势相对变缓，河水中的泥沙开始沉积，河床抬高，造成河道淤积，经常泛滥改道。史料记载，在明朝前，滦河在乐亭境内其干流分为东滦河（今二滦河）和西滦河（今老滦河底），西滦河的下游就是大清河，是滦河最初在乐亭县的入海口。

由于上游泥沙逐年流淌下泄，下游大海潮汐周而复始，阻止泥沙入海，在两者相互作用下，使沉积在这里的泥沙越来越多，当西滦河渐渐淤塞，上游断了泥沙来路，大海波浪对已入海的滦河泥沙重新进行横向搬运和分选沉积，从而形成了以中细沙粒级为主体的与岸线近于平行的滨岸沙坝，逐渐形成了一座沙质的蚀余岛。因此岛形似石臼，故人们叫它石臼坨；后因唐王李世民东征在此驻跸十九日，所以又叫十九坨；近年来，有人见岛上遍生小叶朴（又名棒棒木），此树酷似菩提树，遂取其梵意命名为菩提岛。

Chapter III:Cultural Heritage of Puti Island

I. Historical Figures

1. The First Qin Emperor in Search of Immorality

After he united China, the First Qin Emperor began to construct roads and canals in order to reinforce his sovereign. Accompanied by Prime Minister Li Si and other chancellors, the emperor conducted inspection tours around the country. One day, when the emperor arrived in Qi Prefecture, a local official reported to him, "On the sea are three legendary islands respectively named Penglai, Fangzhang, and Yingzhou. Occasionally, those islands appeared in sight, on which one could see blurry towers and pavilions hidden in lush bushes. The immortals who lived there could fly in clouds and fed themselves on morning dew or mountain spring water, and ate elixir of life. Your majesty! Why not send some to the islands to seek methods to immortality?" The emperor believed what the man said, and then sent him to search elixir on the mythical islands. However, the man returned without finding anything, and explained to the emperor this was because he hadn't enough fortune to meet immortals. Though depressed, the emperor forgave him.

However, the emperor never gave up looking for elixir of life. One time, he visited the area around today's Qinhuangdao on the shore of the Bohai Sea. He ordered to build a palace on the cliff of Jinshanzui at Beidaihe, where he stayed for months in hopes of witnessing the legendary islands.

One day, the sun came out after rain, and the ocean rippled with green waves. Suddenly, three islands showed on the sea in the southwest direction, which looked like a mirage in mist. The three islands didn't disappear until several hours later. Observing the fantastic sight, the emperor made sure that what the Qi man said was true. He then promulgated a decree to recruit alchemists who could find immortals on the mythical Penglai Island.

Lu Sheng, an alchemist from Yan, came to the emperor and declared that he could fulfill the mission. The emperor doubted, "Previously, a Qi man devoted painstaking efforts to seek elixir but failed. Why are you so sure you can do it?" Lu replied, "I knew two immortal alchemists, Xian Men and Gao Shi, who are practicing Taoism on Mortar Isle. The island is home to many immortals and rare medical herbs. It will be easy to find elixir if I ask help from them. I'd like to take the task." Deeply pleased, the emperor promised Lu a great reward if he could fulfill the mission. The next day, escorted by Prime Minister Li Si and other officials, the emperor went to the coast that faced today's Puti Island. However, it wasn't safe to reach the island by boat due to the surging tide. The emperor and his companions thus stayed onshore.

Lu and his disciples took a boat to the island. However, they didn't find Xian Men and Gao Shi across the island, let alone elixir of life. Feeling ashamed, Lu didn't return to meet the emperor. But, the story has been handed down from generation to generation.

The First Qin Emperor's daydream of immortality made himself a joke for later generations. Records about his inspection tour to Yan can be found in the *Record of the Grand Historian*, which translates as follows:

In 215BC, the First Qin Emperor visited Jieshi Mountain and sent Lu Sheng to look for immortal alchemists Xian Men and Gao Shi. Also, he erected a stone stele on Jieshi Mountain, and destroyed the city wall to build river dikes. The inscriptions on the stone stele read:

The emperor sent army to overthrow evil rulers, put down rebellions, annihilate mobs, and liberate common people, thus winning respect from all people. Then, the emperor rewarded outstanding officials according to their merits, and united the country with morality. He demolished the old Guandong City and built river dikes. The fields are leveled, and people are exempted from forced labor and lead a peaceful life. Men devote themselves to farming, while women focus on weaving. Everything goes well. Thanks to our wise and brilliant emperor, all people can live and work in peace and contentment. Thus, the stone stele is erected to commemorate our emperor's marvelous achievements.

第三章　菩提岛文化溯源

第一节　相关历史人物

一　秦始皇派人上岛求仙

秦始皇统一中国后，为巩固大秦江山，加紧修驰道、浚水路，在丞相李斯和臣僚的陪同下巡视各郡县。一日，驾临齐地，忽有齐人御前奏道："此地滨海有'蓬莱'、'方丈'、'瀛洲'三座仙山，隐现无常，显现时楼台殿阁，丛林树木，依稀可见。仙人们驾云长天，纵情遨游，饮的是山泉甘露，吃的是长生不老之药。陛下若想长命百岁，何不派人去寻仙问药呢？"始皇听罢，信以为真，当即降旨，令齐人究其虚实。秦始皇派齐人到滨海仙山寻药未果，齐人回来言称自己命薄福浅难以见到仙人。始皇帝闻听龙心不悦，转念想，此等凡夫俗子，焉能容易见到神仙！此事只好暂时作罢。

始皇巡幸至燕，寻仙求药之事时时萦绕于怀。一日来到渤海湾沿岸的今秦皇岛地域，让人在北戴河金山嘴山岩上筑造行宫小住，意在待仙山再现。

天逢艳阳，沛雨过燕，万里海疆，碧波荡漾。倏然间，西南方海面上升起三座仙山，似海市蜃楼，隐约显现。三座灵峰，异彩纷呈，变幻万千，约一炷香时辰方冉冉隐去。始皇见后大悦，信齐人所奏是真，便四处张贴榜文，广招天下去蓬莱求仙之士。

燕地一方士卢生见到榜文后，速到行宫见驾，言能寻仙问药。始皇问："前有齐人为孤求药，费尽千辛，一无所获，尔等有何能耐？"卢生答道："小辈无能，燕地有两个仙家奇士，名曰羡门、高誓，他们住在石臼坨海岛上修行。那里群仙云集，药材遍岛，如能找到他们，仙药唾手而得。小人无才，愿意领旨前往。"秦始皇闻奏龙心大悦，说："上士如能引得寡人得见二仙玉成此好事，孤必有重赏。"翌日，在丞相李斯等陪同下始皇帝嬴政率众浩浩荡荡直奔菩提岛而来，不料，正遇大潮，舟楫难渡，遂驻跸在菩提岛对岸的陆地上。

卢生和弟子们驾船来到石臼坨，踏遍仙岛，千呼万唤也未找到羡门、高誓，更没能寻到仙药。卢生此举，无颜面对始皇帝，岂敢回归交旨，因而给后世留下了这段奇异的传说。

始皇帝梦想长生求药，为后世留下讥笑之谈。秦始皇东巡燕地，《史记》有载，含义如下：

三十二年（前215年），始皇前往碣石，派燕国人卢生访求方士羡门、高誓。在碣石山门刻石立碑。毁坏了城墙，挖通了堤防。所以碑文说：

皇帝兴师用兵，诛灭无道之君，要把反叛平息。武力消灭暴徒，依法平反良民，民心全都归服。论功行赏众臣，惠泽施及牛马，皇恩遍布全国。皇帝振奋神威，以德兼并诸侯，天下统一太平。拆除关东旧城，挖通河川堤防，夷平各处险阻。地势既已平坦，众民不服徭役，天下都得安抚。男子欣喜耕作，女子修治女红，事事井然有序。皇恩覆盖百业，合力勤勉耕田，无不乐业安居。群臣敬颂伟业，敬请镌刻此石，永留典范规矩。

2. Cao Cao and His Poem *Gazing at the Immense Ocean*

Gazing at the Immense Ocean, written by Cao Cao, is a poem known far and near. The poem, in fact, is closely associated with Mortar Isle (today's Puti Island) in Laoting County. In 200, Yuan Shao, then governor of Bohai, launched a war against Cao Cao. Their armies fought at Guandu, and Cao Cao finally won the battle. After the death of Yuan Shao, his sons, Yuan Tan, Yuan Xi, and Yuan Shang, went to the Wuhuan tribe for shelter. In 207, Cao Cao mobilized an army to drive the Wuhuan tribe out of the Great Wall.

The following year, in order to restore social order of North China, Cao Cao led an army to defeat pirates led by Guan Cheng. Later, he recruited soldiers and accumulated provisions and fodder mainly through having garrison troops open up wastelands and grow grain. His chancellor, Dong Zhao, dug up Pinghu and Quanzhou Canals for river transport. One of them started from the Jiyun River and stretched eastwards to the Luanhe River, which linked the two rivers together. Meanwhile, a new manmade river was opened at the lower reaches of the Luanhe River. Then, a cargo wharf was constructed nearby Mortar Isle at the estuary of the new river. The canals formed a water transport network that linked rivers and the sea, thus facilitating the transportation of military troops and provisions. On the other hand, outlanders migrated to Laoting County, where they reclaimed wastelands and prospered agricultural production. To strengthen the control of immigrants, Cao Cao set up an official post to administrate farming affairs. He also awarded farmers with animal power allowances, so as to encourage their enthusiasm in agricultural production. Moreover, he ordered to "exempt farmers from agricultural taxes in case of drought and flood" without "increasing taxes in case of harvest." Therefore, many immigrants flooded into Laoting and reclaimed an enormous amount of wastelands.

After two years of agricultural development, Cao Cao earned tremendous returns, which provided strong backings for his military expeditions. He not only stored sufficient provisions for his military operation against the Wuhuan tribe, but also laid a solid foundation for his future conquering of the Wu and Shu kingdoms.

Due to its favorable geographic location and convenient land and water transportation, Cao Cao made Laoting his base camp. He ordered to build grain storehouses on the coastal areas, especially at the estuary of the Daqing River nearby today's Puti Island, so that grain could be transported conveniently via the sea. In the autumn of 207, Cao Cao got ready for the war against the Wuhuan tribe. He hired Tian Chou, a native of Yutian, as the guide, and personally led troops to conquer the Wuhuan, thus restoring peace in North China. When returning from victory, he passed Laoting and climbed onto Jieshi Mountain, where he left behind the famous poem, *Gazing at the Immense Ocean*.

> *Come east of Jieshi Cliff*
> *I gaze out across the ocean,*
> *Its rolling waves*
> *Studded with rocks and islets;*
> *Dense the trees and bushes here,*
> *Rank the undergrowth;*
> *The autumn wind is soughing,*
> *Huge billows are breaking.*
> *Sun and moon take their course*
> *As if risen from the sea;*
> *The bright galaxy of stars*
> *Seems sprung from the deep.*
> *And so, with joy in my heart,*
> *I hum this song.*

3. Shi Hu Stationing Troops and Storing Grain

After the collapse of the Western Jin Dynasty (265-316),

二 曹操观沧海

曹操的《观沧海》诗，享誉古今中外。然而，这首诗却与乐亭沿海的石臼坨有着不解之缘。东汉建安五年（200年），渤海太守袁绍聚大兵伐曹，曹操与之进行了举世闻名的"官渡之战"，大败袁绍。袁绍死后，其子袁谭、袁熙、袁尚分别投奔了乌桓部落。建安十二年（207年），为绝袁绍之后患，曹操集重兵征讨，逐乌桓于塞外。

曹操为稳定北方的社会环境，第二年秋，率兵东讨海贼管承，获得了胜利。此后，他着手养兵蓄锐，广积粮草，其主要措施是"屯田"，准备北征乌桓。首先，由大臣董昭负责开通"平虏渠"和"泉州渠"两条漕运。其中一支西由蓟运河始，横向开挖东延至滦河，沟通了蓟、滦两河间的水上通路，向滦河下游开挖出一条"新河"，并在新河口处地理位置优越的石臼坨附近建立了转运码头。两漕运开挖成功后，在冀东形成了一条河海相通、利于兵员运输和军需物资供应的水运网络，在北方水陆交通环境下具一定规模。另外，充分利用乐亭平原荒地优势，从外地移民垦牧，发展生产。为加强管理，特设立了负责屯田的官称"屯田都尉"；为鼓励农民耕种菽粟，给以牛人之费。同时制定"大收不增谷，有水旱灾除"等一系列奖励措施。因此，大量外地移民移居乐亭，大面积荒地得到开垦。"屯田"调动了农民垦殖的积极性，使农业获得了大丰收。

经两年"屯田"，给曹操带来了巨大的经济效益，很快使曹操的军需充盈起来。不仅为征乌桓蹋顿提供充足的粮草，更为后来南征吴蜀奠定了物质基础。

曹操出于战略需要，将地理位置优越、水陆交通便捷的乐亭作为基地，在沿海一带建立仓廒，储备粮草，特别是在地处菩提岛附近水陆交通枢纽的大清河口储备了大部粮草辎重，时刻准备向外发运。建安十二年（207年）秋，曹操粮草充足，兵强马壮，他见时机成熟，由熟悉地域情况的玉田人田畴做向导，亲率大军从孤竹出塞北进，一举征服了乌桓，平定了夷狄祸患，稳定了北方局势，巩固了大后方。他班师时，一路风光，途经乐亭沿海，特意登临碣石山，放声吟诵出大气磅礴的传世名篇《观沧海》：

东临碣石，以观沧海。
水何澹澹，山岛竦峙。
树木丛生，百草丰茂。
秋风萧瑟，洪波涌起。
日月之行，若出其中。
星汉灿烂，若出其里。
幸甚至哉，歌以咏志。

三 赵武帝石虎屯兵储粮

西晋（265—317年）灭亡后，北方进入十六国时期，匈奴、羯、鲜卑、氐、羌等五个部族入主中原，北方地区连年混战。《乐亭县志》记载：晋武帝太康五年（284年），鲜卑族首领慕容廆（wěi）进犯辽西，杀掠甚众。献帝遣幽州诸军迎击，大战肥如，廆兵大败。

晋成帝司马衍咸康四年（338年）、后赵建武四年（338年），后赵武帝石虎谋伐昌黎（今辽宁义县）郡，遣派渡辽将军曹伏率青州兵众渡海驻蹋顿城（《晋书》指今

North China was divided into 16 small kingdoms, including such nomadic tribes as the Huns, Jie, Xianbei, Di, and Qiang. At the time, people suffered from years of wars. According to *Records of Laoting County*, in 204, Xianbei chieftain Murong Wei led troops and invaded western Liaoning Province, where they killed numerous civilians and plundered countless households. Emperor Xian sent Youzhou's garrison troops to defeat the Xianbei army in Feiru.

In 338, Shi Hu, who was historically known as Emperor Wu of the Later Zhao Kingdom, planned to conquer Changli Prefecture (today's Yixian County, Liaoning Province). He ordered General Cao Fu to station his troops on an island in Tatun (today's Matouying), and then transported 3 million *hu* (a measurement tool in ancient China) of grain there as provisions. The island was believed to be today's Puti Island. Embraced by the sea, the island abounded in underground freshwater and was thus ideal to station troops and store grain. At the time, the island served not only as a military base of strategic importance, but also as a water hub for grain transportation.

Moreover, Shi Hu ordered to expand the canal built by Cao Cao and connect it to natural river courses around Yaozhou. He also trained a naval army and recruited artisans to build ships. Meanwhile, he expropriated 300 civil boats to transport 300,000 *hu* of grain to Korea. Then, he disposed another 10,000 soldiers at the coatal area of Matouying in Laoting. The result of the war would be certain ultimately after all of these got ready.

In 340, Shi Hu won the war against Changli. Then, he dispatched an army via the sea to fight Murong Huang, the monarch of the Former Yan Kingdom. To back the army, he organized a fleet of 10,000 ships to transport a million *hu* of grain to Le'an (today's Laoting). Such a large scale of military transportation via the water hadn't been seen ever before.

4. Yang Guang Watching the Sea at Mortar Isle

Historical records reveal that Yang Guang, historically known as Emperor Yang of the Sui Dynasty, once traveled in the coastal county of Laoting, where he composed poems together with his chancellor Yu Mao.

After succeeding the throne, Yang Guang tried his utmost to suppress the threat from ancient Korea. In 611, under the pretext that ancient Korea didn't abide by its conduct as a dependency, he ordered a punitive expedition against Korea. All garrison troops across the country assembled in Zhuo Prefecture. The next year, a total of 1.13 million soldiers gathered in the prefecture to form an army that the Sui declared to comprise two million people. Under the command of the emperor, the grand Sui army formed a procession that extended hundreds of kilometers, with military banners floating together and thunderous drumbeats reverberating in the air. In ancient historical records, the military expedition was declared as "a mission with greater grandeur than ever before."

As he led the army via Laoting County, Yang Guang disembarked on Mortar Isle (today's Puti Island). Impressed by its lush plants and picturesque landscapes, he wrote a poem titled *Watching the Sea*.

Although delighted to watch the blue ocean,

I remain a little disappointed for not seeing the legendary Golden Terrace.

Rolling waves smash on banks,

While distant islands look blurry in clouds.

Against roaring billows,

Docile seagulls play with humans,

On the shore carpeted with lush trees and bushes.

The scenery is so beautiful,

That I need never travel afar

To admire the famous Gushe Mountain in Linfen.

Yu Mao, a chancellor who accompanied the emperor during the

马头营），屯兵海岛，并运粮300万斛（十斗为斛）作为给养。菩提岛因其地处滦河入海口，四面环海，掘地成泉，淡水资源丰富，便于屯兵储粮。由此可见菩提岛在当时的重要地理位置，不仅是重要的军事和运输基地，亦是石虎大军转运补充粮草的水上运输枢纽。

石虎为谋取战争主动权，疏浚了当年曹操开辟的新河，加深加宽，使之与幽州诸郡河道连成一体。石虎在军队增设水军，加强训练，充分利用河海水运优势，一面组织工匠，建造运输船只；一面征用民船，先后共集船300余艘，运粮30万斛至高句丽，使典农中郎将率兵万余，屯兵乐亭沿海马头营一带，形成了恢弘的战略举措，取得了战争的主动权。

咸康六年后赵建武六年（340年），石虎在取得伐昌黎之役的胜利后，又继续利用河海水运，派将讨伐前燕慕容皝（huàng）具船万艘组成强大的水运船队，自河通海运粮豆一百万斛于乐安城（今乐亭）以供军需，如此强大的军事水运规模，是历史上前所未有的。

四 隋炀帝石臼坨望海

史载，隋炀帝杨广曾来乐亭沿海游览、吟诗，大臣虞茂并做诗奉和。

隋炀帝杨广继位后，念念不忘高句丽之患，一直在寻找借口讨伐高句丽。公元611年，隋炀帝以高句丽不遵臣礼为由，下诏征讨。他命自己管辖范围内的兵卒，不论远近，都到涿郡集中。次年正月，全国应征的军士全部到达涿郡。共计113.38万人，号称200万，统由炀帝亲自指挥。各军首尾相接，鼓角相闻，旌旗相连长达千里，声势浩大，史称"近古出师之盛，未之有也"。

隋炀帝率大军东征，途经乐亭沿海，见海中的石臼坨（今菩提岛），花繁树茂，风景宜人，亲自登岛游览，不禁诗兴大发，遂写了一首《望海》。

碧海虽欣瞩，金台空有闻。
远水翻如岸，遥山倒似云。
断涛还共合，连浪或时分。
驯鸥旧可狎，卉木足为群。
方知小姑射，谁复语临汾。

随隋炀帝一起出征的大臣虞世基（字茂世，亦称茂），也奉和了一首咏海诗，题名《奉和望海》。

清眸临溟涨，巨海望滔滔。
十洲云霭远，三山波浪高。
长澜疑浩日，连岛类奔涛。
神游藐姑射，睿藻冠风骚。
徒然随观海，何以效涓毫。

附：隋炀帝杨广小传

隋炀帝，名杨广（569—618年），隋文帝次子，公元581年封为晋王，因他在灭陈和抵御北方突厥的过程中，立有大功，从而笼络人才，要取代兄长杨勇的太子地位。杨

military expedition, responded with another poem titled *Watching the Sea with Your Majesty*.

> *Tide surges up on the ocean.*
> *Afar in clouds and billows,*
> *Emerge ten mythical continents and three legendary islands.*
> *Your Majesty,*
> *Your brilliant poem even dwarfs all poetic classics.*
> *Though lucky to accompany you in watching the sea,*
> *I feel ashamed of my humble contribution to the country.*

Appendix: A Brief Biography of Yang Guang

Yang Guang (569-618), historically known as Emperor Yang of the Sui Dynasty, is the second son of Emperor Wen. In 581, he was conferred on the title of Prince Jin. Due to his remarkable contribution in the battles overthrowing the Chen Dynasty and defending the Turks, a nomadic tribe in North China, he won support from many generals. He then conspired to replace Crown Prince Yang Yong, who was already disfavored by their father for his luxurious life. To win favor from Emperor Wen, Yang Guang pretended to lead a simple life. He colluded with Yang Su, a powerful chancellor, to frame a case against Yang Yong, who was then dethroned into a plebeian. Then, Yang Guang was declared to be the crown prince.

In July 604, Yang Guang cooperated with Yang Su to murder Emperor Wen in illness. They counterfeited the emperor's last will to sentence Yang Yong to death and enthrone Yang Guang. Soon after he ascended the throne, Yang Guang unveiled his camouflage and began to live an incontinent and sumptuous life, making himself one of the most notorious emperors in Chinese history. The first year after his enthronement, he decided to relocate the capital to Luoyang, where he built magnificent and luxurious palaces.

To construct the new capital, he forced farmers to transport building materials from around the country, and many died for overwork en route. The magnificent West Garden he built in Luoyang boasted numerous pavilions and towers, as well as flowery plants blossoming all year round. The same year, Yang Guang forced a million laborers to build the Grand Canal that stretched over 2,000 kilometers from Zhuo Prefecture (today's Zhuozhou City, Hebei Province) to Suzhou and Hangzhou in southeastern China. The project cost six years to complete. In addition, more than 40 palaces were erected along the canal for the emperor to temporarily stay during his tours to the south. Many laborers died in the construction project. One time, Yang Guang ordered to bury more than 50,000 overseers and workers alive because the section of canal they dug was a little shallower than required. Starting in August 605, Yang Guang went onto three tours to Jiangdu along the Grand Canal. The dragon boat he took measured nearly 70 meters long and 15 meters high and had four stories, which was escorted by thousands of gorgeously-decorated boats used to carry accompanying concubines, chancellors, monks, and nuns. All of those boats comprised a fleet that extended over 100 kilometers. More than 80,000 trackers were hired to drag the boats. When night fell, those boats lit up as bright as daytime, on which Yang Guang entertained himself with drinking and music while observing scenery on the banks. Excessive food was buried before the fleet set sail to next destination. Although its construction cost tremendous money and manpower, the Grand Canal played an important role in transportation within the following millennium. Pi Rixiu, a poet in the Tang Dynasty, asserted that the Grand Canal "remains in use although its construction resulted in the collapse of the Sui Dynasty; To some extent, Yang Guang could parallel Dayu in terms of water conservancy if he didn't build the canal for personal pleasure." During his reign, Yang Guang launched three wars against ancient Korea, but all failed. Ultimately, his brutal governance resulted in an outbreak of farmer rebellions in 611. Soon, rebels took over most parts of the country, and

勇由于生活奢侈，渐渐失去了隋文帝的欢心。杨广善于伪装，不露声色，文帝为他的生活俭朴、心怀仁慈等假象所迷惑。他勾结杨素，诬陷太子杨勇。杨勇于公元600年被文帝废为庶人，改立杨广为太子。

公元604年七月，杨广乘文帝病危与大臣杨素谋杀了文帝。又派人假传文帝遗嘱，将杨勇杀死，就这样，杨广以弑父杀兄的手段夺取了皇位，史称炀帝。杨广一夺到帝位，就显露出荒淫奢侈、残虐人民的本性，成为中国历史上著名的荒淫无道的暴君。即位的第一年，就决定迁都洛阳，建东京宫室，起造显仁宫。

在营建洛阳过程中，征集各地的奇材异石，运送洛阳。强迫农民运输，致使许多人活活累死在路上。他在洛阳建筑的西苑，亭台楼阁，十分壮观。整个西苑被点缀得四季如春。同一年起，杨广为了游玩和加强对南方的统治，征调民工百万，历时六年，修建了一条东北起自涿郡（今河北省涿州市），东南到苏杭，全长4000多里的大运河。沿河设置了40多座行宫。开挖运河的过程中，许多民工累死在河中。有一段河道挖得浅了些，杨广竟下令将挖掘这一段的官吏和民工5万多人全部捆住手脚，活埋在岸边。在客观上，从大业元年（605年）八月起，杨广三次通过大运河到江都巡游，他乘着长200尺、高45尺，上下四层的大龙舟。随行的妃嫔、王公大臣、僧尼道士分别乘几千艘华丽的大船，首尾相望，绵延200多里，拉船的纤夫就有8万多人。一到晚上，灯火通明，鼓乐喧天。杨广在船上纵情饮酒作乐，观赏两岸风景。珍馐美味吃不完，开船时就挖一个坑埋掉。虽然杨广开凿大运河劳民伤财，但大运河在此后的近千年都发挥着重要作用，唐代诗人皮日休曾说："尽道隋亡为此河，至今千里赖通波。若无水殿龙舟事，与禹论功不较多。"杨广在位先后三次发动了对高句

丽的战争，耗尽民脂，众生涂炭，皆无功而返。杨广暴虐的统治，终于在公元611年激起了农民大起义。隋朝的大部分土地已为起义军所控制，隋军只是困守着洛阳、江都等几座孤城，他怕江都不安全，准备迁都到长江南面的丹阳（今江苏省南京市），命令民众给他修建宫室。大业十四年（618年）三月三日，将作少监宇文智与中郎将司马德戡，直阁裴虔通等人发动兵变，乘机推右屯卫将军宇文化

only a few cities such as Luoyang and Jiangdu were under the control of the Sui rulers. For the sake of his safety, Yang Guang ordered to relocate the capital to Danyang (today's Nanjing City, Jiangsu Province) south of the Yangtze River, and forced local residents to build his royal palace there. On March 3, 618, several officials and generals organized a coup to overthrow Yang Guang. As rebel soldiers attacked the royal palace, Yang Guang changed his clothes and fled to the West Pavilion, where he was strangled by rebels.

5. Li Shimin and Nineteen Isle

Li Shimin, historically known as Emperor Taizong of the Tang Dynasty, was one of the most prominent strategists in Chinese history. During his reign, the Tang Dynasty boasted strong military strength, and all neighboring states except for Korea submitted to its rule.

In 642, Yeon Gaesomun, a powerful general of Goguryeo, launched a coup to kill King Yeongnyu and some chancellors, and appointed himself the Prime Minister. He declared that Goguryeo no longer "acknowledged allegiance to the Tang" and would recapture the land that the Sui Dynasty seized from Goguryeo before. He dispatched an envoy to ally with Syr Tardush, a nomadic tribe in the north; On the one hand, he reinforced the border fortifications constructed during the time of King Yeongnyu; On the other hand, he disposed troops and constructed forts around the Yalu River and the Qianshan Mountains in eastern Liaoning Province. Moreover, many fortresses were further reinforced to form a secondary line of defense used to block the Tang army. Moreover, he ordered to clear the fields so that the Tang army wouldn't get replenishments in wartime. The military confrontation irritated the Tang rulers, and Li Shimin then hatched a military expedition against Goguryeo.

In 644, Yeon Gaesomun sent army to invade Silla, another kingdom in ancient Korea. Silla asked help from the Tang

Dynasty. In order to reoccupy eastern Liaoning, Li Shimin personally headed the military expedition against Goguryeo. The Tang troops reached Laoting's Mortar Isle in March. Impressed by the beautiful spring views on the coast and the boundless ocean, the emperor expressed his feeling with a poem titled *Watching the Sea on a Spring Day*:

> *Putting on a robe,*
> *I look afar at the immense ocean.*
> *Lying against the handle of my chariot,*
> *I feel intoxicated in the beautiful spring views.*
> *The running river disappear at the horizon,*
> *As though it flowed to heaven.*
> *Hidden in haze are three legendary islands on the sea,*
> *While spring breeze gently blows.*
> *Piercing through waves,*
> *The sun shines with dazzling light.*
> *Colored clouds confuse wild geese,*
> *Which then fly disorderly.*
> *Despite my humble ambition,*
> *I dare to shoot with bow.*
> *Although with boundaries,*
> *The ocean cannot be measured with a gourd ladle.*
> *Although without a source,*
> *The ocean cannot be emptied with a gourd ladle.*
> *From time to time,*
> *The ocean can turn into mulberry fields.*
> *As Mount Zhifu reminds me of Emperor Wu of the Han,*
> *Mount Jieshi reminds me of the First Qin Emperor.*
> *Not as ambitious as them,*
> *I merely wish a peaceful, harmonious society.*

Yang Shidao, an official who accompanied the emperor, responded with another poem that reads:

> *On a spring morning,*

及为主，煽动士兵，于傍晚时杀入宫中，杨广闻变，仓皇改换服装逃入西阁后，被叛变的士兵勒死。

五 唐太宗驻跸十九坨

唐太宗李世民是中国历史上最为卓越的军事家之一。贞观年间，大唐朝名臣集聚良将如云，兵强马壮，边患基本扫平，此时唯有属国高句丽桀骜不驯。

贞观十六年（642年），高句丽西部盖苏文发动政变，杀国王高建武及大臣，自号莫离支，专擅国政，对唐"不奉正朔"，声称要讨还隋末侵占高句丽的500里之疆土。他首先遣使前往漠北，用"厚利"挑唆薛延陀汗国与唐的关系，在北面对唐朝进行牵制。在战备上，一面加固高建武时代建造的"长城"，一面在辽东和鸭绿水（今鸭绿江）以及千山山脉之间广大地区集结兵力，构筑军事据点。企图封锁唐军的水陆进攻线路和登陆港口，并在这些地方实行坚壁清野，伺机在唐军粮饷匮乏之时乘机反攻。盖苏文以东方盟主自居，走上了一条与唐朝进行全面对抗之路。他这样明显的敌对行动，当然是大唐王朝所不能容忍的。因此，唐太宗李世民就召集大臣们谋划东征高句丽。

贞观十八年（644年）正月，大莫离支（最高摄政）盖苏文率军南侵新罗，新罗求救于唐。唐太宗为平番贼，收复辽东，亲自带领兵将东征高句丽。东征大军逢山开路，遇水搭桥，一路浩浩荡荡，所向披靡。当年三月，他率兵来到乐亭沿海的石臼坨海岸，此时正是春和景明，茫茫海岸，望不尽绿草红花，大海碧波万顷，水天相连，他不禁高声吟诵出《春日望海》诗：

披襟眺沧海，凭轼玩春芳。
积流横地纪，疏派引天潢。
仙气凝三岭，和风扇八荒。
拂潮云布色，穿浪日舒光。
照岸花分彩，迷云雁断行。
怀卑运深广，持满守灵长。
有形非易测，无源讵可量。
洪涛经变野，翠岛屡成桑。
之罘思汉帝，碣石想秦皇。
霓裳非本意，端拱且图王。

唐太宗吟罢，紧跟在他后面的中书令杨师道也步其韵随之奉和了一首：

春山临渤海，征旅辍晨装。
回瞰卢龙塞，斜瞻肃慎乡。
洪波回地轴，孤屿映云光。
落日惊涛上，浮天骇浪长。
仙台隐螭驾，水府泛鼋梁。
碣石朝烟灭，之罘归雁翔。
北巡非汉后，东幸异秦皇。
搴旗羽林客，跋距少年场。
龙击驱辽水，鹏飞出带方。
将举青丘缴，安访白霓裳。

I stood by the Bohai Sea,

With my campaign grown off.

What I see quite differs from Lulong and Shushen that I passed,

Which have been separated by the sea.

Against the setting sun,

The ocean merges the sky in distance.

On the immortal islands,

Hornless dragons drag chariots,

And huge tortoises form a bridge to the Dragon Palace.

As the mist thins out on Jieshi Mountain,

One can see wild geese hovering over Zhifu Mountain.

Unlike the Qin and Han emperors

Who came here in search of elixir,

Our king comes for a unification mission.

Our heroic warriors cross the Liao River.

What we desire from immortal abodes

Aren't white feather gowns,

But divine arrows that can help us defend the nation.

As the emperor looked afar at the ocean, Mortar Isle shrouded in auspicious clouds appeared like an emerald inlaid on the water. After days of trekking from the capital, the emperor and his officers were already exhausted, but the picturesque scenery cheered their spirit up. Yang Shidao then advised the emperor to pay a visit to the island. The emperor agreed. Then, escorted by General Xue Rengui, the emperor mounted onto the island by boat. With lush trees and singing birds, the beautiful landscapes on the island impressed them. They traveled every corner of the island, but were still reluctant to leave. Thus, Emperor Taizong stayed on the island for 19 days, hence its later name "Nineteen Isle."

6. Wanyan Dan Hunting on the Island

Wanyan Dan, historically known as Emperor Xizong of the Jin Dynasty, once hunted on today's Puti Island. According to

the *Annals of Laoting County*, in 1140, Emperor Xizong hunted on the island during his inspection tour to the coastal area of Laoting.

Wanyan Dan was the oldest son of Wanyan Zongjun, and his grandfather was Wanyan Hao, the first emperor of the Jin Dynasty. In 1132, Jin aristocrats elected Wanyan Dan as the heir of the dynasty. In 1135, Wanyan Dan succeeded the throne, and his reign lasted 14 years.

Before he ascended the throne, Wanyan Dan learned Confucian culture from Han Fang, a scholar from the Han Nationality. He didn't cease learning Han classics even after he became the emperor, which helped him enhance the political, cultural, and military strength of the Jin Dynasty. This also played an important role in accelerating the dynasty's social development.

7. Yu Chenglong Burnt Down the Chaoyang Nunnery

Of all ancient relics on Puti Island, the Chaoyang Nunnery was the earliest to be found in historical records. However, its origin remains controversial: Some believe its history can be traced back to the Tang Dynasty, and others assert that it was constructed by Master Xianguang during the Ming Dynasty. Due to the prevalence of Buddhism in China, Buddhist temples are considered sacred places. However, the Chaoyang Nunnery was once burnt to the ground by Yu Chenglong, then magistrate of Laoting County. Some may wonder why he did so, but the mystery could be explained by social situation of that time.

During the reign of Emperor Kangxi of the Qing Dynasty, there were two high-ranking officials named Yu Chenglong, and both were noted for their incorruptness and administrative capacity.

The older Yu Chenglong was a native of Yongning (today's Lüliang City, Shanxi Province). He was born in 1617 and died

唐太宗极目远眺，苍苍茫茫中的石臼坨恰似大海浮翠，彩练环珠，祥云缭绕，风光旖旎，好醉人的风景啊！连日来，大军由长安出发，长途跋涉，甚是疲劳，君臣见石臼坨如此美景，都想亲临坨上看看。杨师道见唐太宗此时兴致正浓，就建议陛下上坨游览一番，太宗点头默许。杨师道马上招来船只，并叫来大将薛仁贵，护送陛下到石臼坨上游览。他们君臣乘船上坨，但只见，坨上绿草茸茸，群芳竞秀，绿树参天，菩提蔽日，渔歌阵阵，百鸟争鸣，着实让唐朝君臣赞叹不已。他们君臣从南到北，由东至西仔仔细细地游览了一遍，但仍是余兴不减。太宗皇帝决定在此驻跸，谁知一住就是十九日，因之后人叫作十九坨。

六 金熙宗岛上狩猎

金代皇帝熙宗完颜亶（dǎn）以其民族特有的方式，表达了对菩提岛的推崇。据清光绪三年（1877年）《乐亭县志·卷三》记载：熙宗四年冬十一月，完颜亶巡幸乐亭沿海，上岛狩猎。

完颜亶是金太祖完颜旻嫡长子完颜宗峻之长子。天会十年（1132年），在完颜宗干、完颜宗翰、完颜宗辅、完颜希尹等诸宗亲勋贵的支持下，受任为谙版勃极烈，确定为皇位继承人。天会十三年（1135年），金太宗死，继帝位，是为金熙宗，在位14年。

金熙宗继位前曾受教于汉人文士韩昉，他喜雅歌儒服，善用汉文赋诗作字。继位以后，尤勤于汉文典籍的学习，提高了金朝的政治、文化、军事水平，对当时刚建立不久的大金王朝的社会发展起到了重要的促进作用。

七 于成龙火烧朝阳庵

查阅菩提岛历史，朝阳庵最早见诸史籍。这座寺院究竟

为唐朝所建，还是明朝万历年间临济宗住持显光上人始建，仍有待于继续考证。自释教东传，佛门净土世人多恭而敬之。但是到了清朝康熙年间，乐亭知县于成龙却一度在盛怒之下将朝阳庵付之一炬。后人对此多有困惑，要想解开这一疑团，需要从于成龙职宰乐亭时所处的社会环境说起。

清朝康熙年间，曾出现过两位叫于成龙的官员，他们都身居高位，且都以清廉务实、政绩卓著而名垂青史。

年长的于成龙，人称大于成龙，字北溟，号于山，山西永宁州（今山西省吕梁市离石区）人。生于明万历四十五年（1617年），逝于清康熙二十三年（1684年）。自清顺治十八年（1661年）起，历任广西罗城知县、四川合州知州、湖北黄州同知、武昌知府、湖广下江陆道道员、福建按察使、福建布政使、直隶巡抚、两江总督。

另一位于成龙，字振甲，别号如山，奉天盖州（今辽宁省盖州市）人，年龄比大于成龙小21岁。生于明崇祯十一年（1638年），逝于康熙三十九年（1700年）。历任乐亭知县、滦州知州、通州（今北京通州区）知州、直隶巡抚、兵部尚书兼都察院御史、镶红旗汉军都统、河道总督等职，谥号"襄勤"。小于成龙曾经先后两次任乐亭知县。第一次是在清康熙七年（1668年），第二次是在康熙十年（1671年）。

清朝初年，由于朝代更替，社会秩序混乱，地处渤海之隅的乐亭同样处于动荡之中，官员乡绅肆行妄为，盗贼横行称霸，再加上滦河经常泛滥，致使民不聊生，饿殍遍野。于成龙首任乐亭后，查询时弊，了解民情，对于破坏社会治安、扰乱百姓的海匪、流寇进行抓捕、训教、处置，严厉地

in 1684. From 1661, he consecutively acted as magistrate of Luocheng, governor of Hezhou, governor of Wuchang, administrator of Huguang, supervisor of Fujian, administrator of Fujian, imperial inspector of Zhili, and governor-general of Jiangsu and Jiangxi.

A native of Gaizhou (today's Gaiping County, Liaoning Province), the other Yu Chenglong was 21 years younger. He was born in 1638 and died in 1700. Consecutively, he acted as magistrate of Laoting, governor of Luanzhou, governor of Tongzhou (today's Tongzhou District, Beijing), imperial inspector of Zhili, minister of national defense, and governor-general of waterways. Historically, he was appointed as magistrate of Laoting twice in 1668 and 1671, respectively.

Early in the Qing Dynasty, Laoting suffered a social disorder like many other areas. Ordinary people were exposed not only to the oppression of local officials and aristocrats, but also to the threat of bandits and pirates. Moreover, floods often occurred along the Luanhe River, so many starved to death. After he became Laoting magistrate, Yu Chenglong took measures to restore deteriorated social order and arrest pirates. Gradually, locals lived stable, safe lives. One time, several Laoting prisoners successfully escaped through jailbreak. The Qing emperor dismissed Yu Chenglong for breach of duty. Many locals knelt before the official who came to announce the decree, begging for leniency. However, their request was refused.

As Yu Chenglong left, locals lined up on roadsides to say goodbye with tears in their eyes. Later, his superior found that Yu Chenglong "was honest and duteous in the administration" through investigation. Many officials at different levels pleaded Yu Chenglong in their reports to the throne. Thus, Emperor Kangxi reappointed him as magistrate of Laoting. Delighted at the news, locals lined up to welcome him. During the period when Yu was dismissed, bandits reassembled to plunder local

people. After he resumed his post, Yu took stronger measures to crack down bandits, which incurred hatred from those bandits.

In November 1681, when Yu Chenglong went onto business trip, bandits disguised themselves as merchants. After entering the county, they began to attack the government seat. Chen Zhuguo, head of the guards, mobilized soldiers to fight against intruders while sending someone to report the news to Yu Chenglong. In the battle, bandits captured Chen and then brutally killed him. Bandits also captured Yu Yongzhen, the oldest son of Yu Chenglong. Although being only 16 years old, Yu Yongzhen showed no fear, but reviled the bandits. He was also killed by irritated bandits. Then, bandits began to loot households across the county.

Receiving the news, Yu Chenglong led troops back to the county seat, but the bandits fled before his arrival. After conciliating victims, Yu mobilized soldiers to chase those bandits. Soon, the bandit ringleader was arrested and beheaded. The rest bandits fled to Puti Island, where they took the Chaoyang Nunnery as their lair. Sometimes they crossed the sea to plunder coastal residents. To eliminate the threat of those bandits, Yu Chenglong ordered to burn down the nunnery.

Local scholars, including An Rulin, An Yude, and Chen Yongqing, recorded the history on a stone stele in the rebuilt nunnery: "To eliminate pirates, County magistrate Yu had to burn the nunnery they occupied. Later, he donated money to rebuild six halls of the nunnery." Today, the stone stele can be still found on Puti Island.

欢舞如狂，迎接于成龙再次到任。于成龙第一次来乐亭，给予土匪、流寇狠狠打击，因此他们恨之入骨。当于成龙因故被撤职后，他们又开始危害百姓。于成龙第二次上任后，加大了整治匪寇稳定社会的力度。那些匪盗流氓受到打击后，伺机报复。

康熙十年（1671年）十一月，土寇探得于成龙有事外出离开县城，他们见时机已到，纠集百余人伪装成客商混进城中，进攻县衙。守城把总陈柱国一面派人向于成龙报告，一面组织护衙兵丁与群寇搏斗。在混战中陈柱国负伤被抓，后被匪徒残忍杀害。匪徒们在县衙内搜捕于成龙家人，于成龙年仅16岁的长子于永祯不幸落入匪徒之手。面对匪徒的嚣张气焰，于永祯昂首不屈，大骂贼人不止，气急败坏的匪徒将其杀害。众匪徒走出县衙后，又到处烧杀抢掠，霎时乐亭城内哭喊一片。

于成龙在外得到报告，急速带人赶回县城，匪徒们闻讯仓皇逃窜。看到县城被匪徒们蹂躏的惨状，于成龙悲愤不已。他一面抚慰受害的百姓，一面组织官兵在全县清剿匪徒，不久匪首梁氏被缉拿归案，斩首示众。少部分匪徒则逃匿到菩提岛上，霸据朝阳庵为匪巢，仍不时过海侵害百姓。在追剿匪徒过程中，盛怒之下于成龙下令焚烧朝阳庵，捣毁了海寇的藏身之地。

关于于成龙焚毁朝阳庵的这段历史，邑庠生安如林、通议大夫安于德、儒学教谕陈永清等人撰写的《朝阳庵碑记》中有"于翁职宰乐亭，以海寇故，不得已遂焚其庵，后复捐资首倡而修大殿六间"的记述，现石碑仍存留在菩提岛上。

打击了他们的嚣张气焰，使百姓生活日趋安定，社会治安大有好转。于成龙首次任乐亭知县期间，有在押犯逃跑，他因此受到连累被撤职。乐亭百姓闻知后，聚拥县衙给宣旨官员下跪极力挽留，无奈官命难违。

于成龙离开时，县城内外百姓含泪依依送别。由于于成龙在乐亭的突出业绩，百姓感念，各级官属上奏保举，经上司调查核实，于成龙确是"操守清廉、治理有方"。因此，康熙皇帝重又下旨，于成龙第二次复任乐亭知县。乐亭百姓

8. Martial Champion Li Guoliang

During the Qing Dynasty, martial arts prevailed across Laoting County. The period witnessed emergence of many martial arts masters, including Li Guoliang, Xu Shouchun, and An Tingzhao, of which the most famous was Li Guoliang who ever the title of Martial Champion in imperial examinations.

Li Guoliang was born in 1729. During the time of Emperor Kangxi, his ancestors moved from Fengrun County to Laoting County's Xugezhuang Village. When he was young, his family led a poor life. At the age of six, he began to work for the An Family together with his mother.

A local rich clan over generations, the An Family spent considerable money inviting famous tutors to teach their children literature and martial arts.

As a child, Li Guoliang showed remarkable capacity in learning and boasted prominent physical strength. It was said that he could raise considerable weight.

After he entered the An Family as a servant, Li Guoliang was assigned to serve the family's children in reading and practicing martial arts.

In 1751, An Tingzhao, the oldest son of the An Family, won third place in imperial martial examinations and appointed as an imperial guard. Li Guoliang attended An Tingzan and other An youngsters when they learned literature and martial arts.

A lover of martial arts, Li Guoliang enjoyed his job very much. Every time his masters read or practiced martial arts, Li stood aside to learn together. He remembered what the teachers taught, and went over them time and time again at night. His diligence was rewarded. Years later, Li was accomplished at both literary and martial arts.

In 1757, Li Guoliang accompanied An Tingzan to attend an imperial martial examination held in the capital. Qi Dayong, a native of Changli and supervisor of the imperial examination, learned that Li Guoliang was expert at both literary and martial

arts, and particularly approved him to participate in the examination. Li Guoliang passed the examination, and was nominated as the Martial Champion by the emperor. Moreover, he was appointed as a First-Grade Imperial Guard.

In the autumn of 1761, Li Guoliang was appointed as assistant general of Fujian and Zhejiang. He was noted for his duteousness and incorruptness. He kept fairness in allotting army provisions, and prevented the troops under his command from oppressing local people. As he acted as associate general of Xiangshan, Emperor Qianlong inspected Daqing. Li took the mission to escort the emperor during his stay. The emperor awarded him two pieces of martens and four bundles of satin for his outstanding performance.

In the spring of 1769, Li was promoted associate general of Taizhou; In 1772, he once again acted as commander of Xiangshan; In the autumn of 1773, he was appointed as garrison commander of Dinghai; In 1774, he became army governor of Zhangzhou, Fujian Province. During the period, he and Huang Yi, a scholar who taught in Fujian's Donghai Academy, swore to be blood brothers. After Li's mother died, Huang Yi accompanied him to return his hometown for his mother's funeral. The emperor promoted Li to be Huguang Governor to reward his filial piety. Four years later, the emperor appointed Li as governor of Zhili so that he could take care of his old father. When Li's father died for illness, the emperor particularly issued a decree to condole with him. In 1787, Li died at the age of 58. Before this, when Li was on the sickbed, the emperor dispatched a court physician to treat him. After Li's death, the emperor sent representatives to express sympathy. Meanwhile, the emperor wrote a funeral oration for him and granted him the honorary title of "guardian of crown prince."

Throughout his life, Li Guoliang was noted for his righteousness, generosity and loyalty. He did all he could to help those in need. He restricted his relatives and friends from riding roughshod over the weak. In addition, he led a

八　武状元李国梁

清代，武风一度鼎盛的乐亭县，相继出现过武状元李国梁、武榜眼徐寿春、武探花安廷召、武进士安廷赞等武林人物。纵观乐亭武林史，声名最为显赫者当属武状元李国梁。

李国梁，字简侯，号静斋，生于雍正七年（1729年）。原籍丰润县，康熙年间其先人率族人由丰润迁到乐亭南乡徐各庄。传至其父李瑞掌门，家道贫困，难以聊生。为生活计，李国梁六七岁随其母到乐亭南乡名富安家打工数年。

安家世代为乐邑旺门，不惜花费重金为其子弟聘请文武名师来家塾授业教习。

李国梁自幼聪明好学，博闻强识，且膂力过人。世传力能过顶，在乡有谐音"力过顶"（李国鼎）之名。

李国梁到安家后，安老爷见其生得眉清目秀，相貌不俗，身板结实，且有把子好力气，便让他侍候少爷们念书习武。

安家少爷中习武者，大少爷安廷召已于乾隆十六年（1751年）得武探花，授侍卫。李国梁进入安家，正值三少爷安廷赞等人学文习武之际。

儿时便热心拳、脚、棍、棒的李国梁，遇此天赐良机，可谓大喜过望。每逢少爷们在塾攻读习武，他必伺候在现场听讲观看。教者无心，学者有意，他对家塾先生、武术教师所教课程及所授一招一式，听在耳里，看在眼里，记在心间，事后连夜抓紧时间暗中背诵演练，直到每一篇文章，每一个细微动作都熟悉精练为止。功夫不负苦心人，经过几年勤学苦练，李国梁学得满腹经纶、全身武艺。

乾隆二十二年（1757年），朝廷在京开设武科。李国梁跟随三少爷安廷赞进京参加考试。此次考试中，由人举荐，主考大员齐大勇（昌黎人）得知安的随从李国梁文

武全才，身手出众。在其提携下，以当场严格考试得中进士，后经御前面试，中头名武状元，并授"御前头等侍卫"的官衔。

乾隆二十六年（1761年）秋，李国梁出任福建、浙江等处参游副总，授浙江提标中军参将。李国梁在任忠于职守，清正廉明，以治军严谨、清勤垂范著称军中，或督练兵勇，或分发粮饷，必亲检查对，严防部下贪污腐化，鱼肉乡民。升任象山副将时，正逢乾隆皇帝南巡大庆。李国梁精心帮办筹划，亲自派办差务，因而受到皇上嘉奖，赐貂皮两张、大缎四匹。

乾隆三十四年（1769年）春，升任台州副将；三十七年（1772年）再度被调任象山；三十八年（1773年）秋调任定海总兵；三十九年（1774年）调福建漳州任陆军提督。在此期间，与掌教东海书院的福建侯官举人黄俌结拜为异姓兄弟。在任期间，李国梁母亲病逝，义兄黄俌陪同李国梁从福建归乡奔丧。返任后，圣上念其至忠至孝，奉诏署理湖广提督，并赏顶戴花翎。四年后，皇上体恤国梁家中尚有九旬老父，为使其就近奉承老父，将李国梁调入直隶任提督。其父病故，皇上曾命军机传旨嘱谕："伊父年过九旬，不必过于伤悼！"乾隆五十二年（1787年）李国梁卒于任上，终年58岁。卧病期间，皇上亲问病情，并派太医前来诊治。国梁死后，皇上又亲派官员前来御祭，并赐碑文，谥恪慎，赠太子少保。

李国梁一生，清正廉洁，慷慨义气，亲戚、族属、乡里遇有急难者，必尽其全力予以周济。其在任上，有亲朋来投，多不使外出，以免仗势欺人、行为不轨。平日衣着俭朴，粗淡饮食；暑期骑乘，从不张盖旗伞；酷暑严冬，教场操典练兵，从不惧辛劳，以身示范。

有几则李国梁之趣闻逸事流传于民间。

simple life. He set a good example for his soldiers in course of trainings even in scorching summer and chilly winter.

The following are several stories about Li Guoliang that prevail amidst local people.

Won Fame Overnight

In 1757, Li Guoliang accompanied An Tingzan, the third son of the An Family, to attend an imperial martial examination held in the Qing capital. Qi Dayong, a native of Changli and supervisor of the imperial examination, particularly met examinees from his hometown Yongping. Some examinees, who were acquainted with Li Guoliang, recommended him to Qi, and begged for a chance for Li to attend the examination.

At the contest field, Qi looked Li up and down, and was impressed by the young man's robustness, heroic spirit, and style of conservation. "The court has no restriction on talent recruitment. It would be a great regret if you didn't attend the examination. Are you willing to do so?" Qi asked with smile.

"My master is expert at archery and equestrianism, but he already lost to an opponent from Luoyang. How dare can I..." Before Li finished, other examinees urged him onto the contest field.

The first round of examination was archery. Holding a bow on horseback, Li consecutively shot three arrows to the target with a coin in the center. The first arrow hit the central hole of the coin, the second arrow hit the first one and pushed it through the hole, and the third arrow shot down the coin. His marvelous archery stirred up thunderous applause. Then was the examination of arm strength. Examinees were required to pull back the strings of huge bows, and the one who pulled the most would be the winner. Li totally pulled three of such bows without any difficulty. His performance once again won applause from the audience.

Then, Li passed all of the rest examinations. Impressed by

Li's outstanding performance, Qi was going to announce him as the champion. At the moment, the examinee from Luoyang stood out and asked Qi angrily, "Sir, Li and I scored equally in examinations. Why will you choose him as the champion? It is unfair if the reason is he comes from your hometown."

Although irritated, Qi laughed, "As the examination supervisor appointed by the emperor, I must maintain fairness. If you don't agree with the result, you can challenge Li's arm strength."

"Alright!" The Luoyang examinee replied. "But pulling the bow isn't the best way to test arm strength."

"Do you think which way is better?" Qi asked.

The examinee thought for a while and said, "One of us stands steadily, and the other pulls him, Then vice versa. The one who doesn't move will be the winner."

Qi agreed on his suggestion. At first, Li pulled his opponent. With his sleeves rolled up, Li seemed not consume much effort to hold up his opponent from the ground, which evoked a hail of cheers from the audience. Then, it was his opponent's turn to pull. Although making every effort he could, his opponent didn't move Li, who appeared like taking root on the ground. Ashamed and exhausted; his opponent vomited some blood and fell down to the ground. Escorted by his servant, the opponent fled back to Luoyang.

Then, Li was nominated as the Martial Champion and appointed as the First-Grade Imperial Guard.

Stone Roller in the Tree

After he was granted the title of Martial Champion, Li Guoliang was permitted to offer sacrifices to his ancestors in his hometown. He was escorted by a procession of honor guards all the way home. As the messenger reached Xugezhuang, Li's parents were working in the field at the moment. His neighbors got to know the good news first, and then rushed to the field to

初露锋芒

年逢丁丑，大清朝依制开设武场科考取士。李国梁跟随安家三少爷进京赴试。验试将毕，主考大员昌黎人齐大勇，出于乡情破例接见了永平府前来应试的考生。乡人熟知安廷赞的随从李国梁身手不凡，当面向齐举荐，要求给予了李国梁一个参试的机会。

齐大勇把李国梁从上到下打量了一番。只见李弱冠年华，身材魁伟，气度不凡，浑身透出一股勃勃英气。言谈间更觉此人气质不俗，恢弘大度，很是招人喜欢。齐当场笑着答道："朝廷取士不拘一格，李生能有如此天赋，朝廷幸甚，漏掉人才，实属可惜，当场一试有何不可呢？"

李国梁推辞道："我家少爷弓马娴熟，当场比试尚落于洛阳举子之后。国梁何德何能敢争人先，我看……"众人不容分说，百般怂恿，硬是把李国梁推上了武场。

试外场：李国梁纵马擎弓，坐骑沿马道跑起之后，只见他伸手从背后取出三支雕翎，放开马缰，搭箭开弓，照定箭靶上的金钱眼就是一连三箭。第一箭名为"凤凰单展翅"，箭射钱眼后，雕翎旁垂；第二箭名为"凤凰夺窝"，后箭将前箭由金钱眼抵出；第三箭射掉金钱，谓之"金钱落地"。随着三箭中靶，场内一片欢腾，场外人声鼎沸，比赛的将校无不交口称赞。比试箭法后，需试膂力，按场规应试者要当场拉开三百担大弓。李国梁进场后，同时拉开了三张三百担大弓，且是气不长出，面不改色。众人见后更是喝彩不迭。

外场其他科目，李国梁全部顺利通过。等到内场试过"武经"之后，齐大勇喜出望外，手提朱笔就要当场定选。此时，只听场外有人大喊一声："且慢！"接着便从场外走进一人，来者不是别人，正是眼看胜券在握的洛阳举子。此人满脸愠色，走到主考大人面前，愤愤问道："主考大人，统观内、外两场，我和李生相比，功夫不相上下，那么为啥

要点他为魁呢？难道因他来自永平，就只讲乡谊而不再秉公取士了吗？"

齐大勇一听，几乎气炸了肺，他压压怒气，思忖片刻，随之哈哈大笑起来。齐公案前落座后，手捋长髯，朗声答道："我乃朝廷命官，食君奉禄，事关社稷，奉旨选贤怎可当众徇私？尔要不服，可与李生当场比试膂力如何？"

"好！不过拉弓射箭乃平日练习之力，以此较力，不足为凭。"

齐大勇问道："那么依你之见，怎样比试方可信服呢？"

洛阳举子想了想说："我二人各自拉开骑马蹲裆之势谁个要是不被拉动，即为胜者。"

"好！就依你之见！"

齐大勇命李国梁当场和洛阳举子进行比试。先是洛阳举子站定架势，由李国梁来拉。只见李国梁抹肩挽袖，走至近前双手叉腰只轻轻一托，未费多大力气，便将洛阳举子高高托起。众人又是一阵喝彩。随后，李国梁勒紧腰带，站好架势，由洛阳举子来拉。洛阳举子运足气力刚要动作，李国梁气沉丹田，使出平日练就的"千斤坠力"之功，任凭洛阳举子左拉右拽，使出吃奶的气力，也未能将李国梁动起地面分毫。洛阳举子羞愧万分，连气带累，"哇"地一口鲜血喷在地，当即由随从扶出场外，抱病返回洛阳老家去了。

李国梁被点中新科武状元，封为"御前头等侍卫"的官衔。

上树的碌碡

李国梁金榜题名，蒙圣恩荣归祭祖。一路上前呼后拥，好生气派。报喜人先行一步，手捧喜帖赶到乐亭徐各庄时，李国梁的老父老母在地里干活儿。忽见田头呼啦啦走来一群人，到近前一看，全是村中三老四少，其中还有许多平日并

tell his parents. Many showed more respect than before, and even some rich people who looked down on the old couple began to display unusual courtesy. "Uncle Li," some said with humble smile. "Why are you still working in the field. Your son is a high-ranking official now. You need never labor like before any more." Knowing not what they said, Li's father replied, "How will a farmer feed himself if he doesn't work in the field? There is no such thing as free lunch."

Some gabbled in hopes of bootlicking Li's father.

"Don't worry! My barn is your barn."

"Hurry! Just give Uncle Li a cart of firewood from our warehouse."

......

"Thanks, but I can feed my family by myself," Li's father replied.

As soon as they returned home, the messenger arrived. He knelt down to Li's parents and presented a bulletin with both hands. "Congratulations," he said. "Your son has been titled Martial Champion in the imperial examination."

Li's parents didn't believe what they heard at first. After making sure they didn't daydream, the old couple burst into tears due to excitement. They tried to compensate the messenger, but found nothing valuable at home. Subsequently, their neighbors raised some money as award to the messenger.

After a short while, three bangs of salute guns broke the silence of the village. Escorted by honor guards holding banners, gongs, umbrellas, and fans, Li Guoliang arrived at his home. He first greeted his parents, and then his neighbors. The following day, Li Guoliang worshiped his ancestors at their graveyards. He then decided to stay home for a few days to accompany his parents.

The next early morning, Li Guoliang got up for a walk while most villagers were still in sleep. As he roamed in the village, he was shocked when seeing a gigantic stone roller in a big

scholar tree. The stone roller appeared hundreds of kilograms in weight. "Who could do this?" Li wondered. "He must be extraordinary strong."

As he pondered under the tree, Liu Maolin, a hired laborer of the nearby Gao family, passed by while shouldering two water barrels. "Lord Li," Liu said. "You must be astonished at how the stone roller was put onto the tree."

"Yes," Li asked. "Do you know who did this?"

"I don't know either," Liu replied. "But it happened several times. Every time we took the stone roller off, we found it was put onto the tree again the next morning."

Then, Li took the stone roller off the tree with his hands. "There must be something unusual," he told himself. To find out who did this, he disposed several sentries to watch at night.

One early morning, around 2 o'clock, a watchman saw a porter drawing near from the south, with two buckets on his shoulder. He put down his shoulder pole for a rest under the tree. Seeing that the stone roller was already taken off, the porter spoke to himself, "Let me put you onto the tree again." He went down to hold the holes on both sides of the stone roller with two hands, and put it onto the tree.

At the moment, the watchman jumped out and shouted, "Who're you?" Frightened by the sudden sound, the porter stammered, "I… I'm a fish vendor."

"All right," the watchman said. "My master wants to see you."

"Please forgive me," the fish vendor begged. "I can take the stone roller off. Selling fish is a hard business. I'm hurrying to the market before my fish deteriorates…"

"Shut up! Just come with me," the watchman stopped him.

Hearing the news that they had caught the man who elevated the stone roller to the top of the tree, Li rushed out of his home. "Don't frighten him," Li told his sentries.

Never seeing such a high-ranking official before, the porter got scared. "Please forgive me," he begged. "I did this just for fun. Please let me go. I need to sell fish as quickly as possible,

无来往的望门大户。这些人在老夫妻面前，有的称叔，有的叫婶，有的以手相搀，有的躬身施礼。平日见面多以白眼相对的财主们也是笑脸相迎："哎呀，我的李老太爷，你们怎么还在地里呀？令公子高官得做，从此再不用下地干活啦！"李老汉愣怔怔道："庄户人家，不下地干活，吃什么，天上会掉馅饼？"

"粮食咱家有的是，快！给李老太爷先送过几斗来！"

"去！先从咱家给李老太爷拉车柴火来！"

……

李老汉笑呵呵地说："不劳众位操心，此情我领啦！"

李老汉老两口刚回到家，报喜之人报门而进，见到老两口一个响头磕在地，双手捧上喜帖，连声说道："恭喜二老，贺喜二老，贵公子李国梁金榜题名，得中头名武状元啦！"

老两口一听，好像是在梦境之中，可是掐掐手，手疼，捏捏肉，肉疼。抬头一看金灿灿的日头正悬在头顶，连自己的影子都被照在了残垣之上。老两口顿时百感交集，不觉潸然泪下。原想给报喜人一些赏赐，却又身无分文，最后还是由众位穷乡亲凑了些银两，寒酸地打发走了报喜之人。

工夫不大，只听村头三声炮响，旗、锣、伞、扇涌满长街。武状元李国梁在众人簇拥之下来到了自家门口。他首先拜过了二老，再拜过村里乡亲。翌日又祭拜过祖上坟茔之后，决定在家小住几日以慰藉双亲。

次日清晨，李国梁早早起来趁众人还未起床，来到街上散步。他沿村街信步走到一棵大树下，抬头往上一看，不觉愣在了树前。只见一个五六百斤重的大碌碡被人放置在槐树杈上。李国梁心想，这是何人所为，好大的力气呀！

李国梁正在树前望着碌碡出神，对门高家伙计刘茂林担着水桶笑哈哈地走了过来。他见李状元正在树下发愣，便往树上

一看，情知缘由，笑着说道："李老爷，你这是看稀罕吧？"

"是啊！"李国梁顺口答言，"这是谁举上去的？好大的一把力气呀！"

"谁知是谁干的，好多次了。我们把它整下来，第二天早起一看，又给搁上去啦！"

"唔！"李国梁说着，用手一托，把碌碡托下树来。心想里面一定有勾当，遂命令侍从暗中守候，查明此人是谁。

当天夜里，天近四更时分，只见从正南走来一个挑担之人。走到树下放下担子，把扁担往两个筐上一横，就势坐在了扁担上。他一看碌碡又被人放下树来，嘴里自言自语道："又给放下来了，好！看我再给你搁上去。"说着走到碌碡跟前，蹲下身子，双手抠住碌碡两端的眼儿，只听他口中磨叨"起"，一用力，那碌碡又被他稳稳当当地放回到树杈上。

这一切动作，被躲在一边守夜的差人看了一个清清楚楚。守夜人突然站了出来，大声问道："你是什么人？"挑担人被突然出现的守夜人吓了一跳，回答说："我，我是跑海卖鱼的。"

"好极啦，那就跟我们见老爷去吧！"

"别价！哥们儿，我把碌碡给你们放下来就是了。小本生意不容易，我赶天亮得卖鱼去呀，要不然会臭了的。"

"少说废话，快跟我们走吧！"

"这……"

"不要惊动这位大哥！"李国梁得知逮住了放碌碡的人，忙从家中走了出来和颜悦色地说。

跑海的见是一位大官，胆战心惊地求饶说："老爷开恩，小的是无意开开玩笑，我把碌碡给老爷放下来就是了，你让我走吧。我得赶紧去卖鱼，不然耽搁了时间，把鱼放臭了，我们全家人就得饿肚子啦！"

or my family had to starve today."

"Don't worry," Li smiled. "I can buy all your fish. Will you please stay at my home for three days? I'll compensate you for your loss."

Delighted at the offer, the fish vendor agreed.

"But you must stay with me within the three days," Li added. "And you cannot eat anything in the following three days and three nights. I'll treat you with a banquet on the fourth day."

"Ok," the porter replied after thinking for a while.

In the following three days, the fish vendor accompanied Li wherever he went, and they both ate nothing. On the fourth day, the porter almost starved, but Li seemed as same as usual. Li requested the porter to lift the stone roller up to the tree. No matter how hard he tried, however, the fish vendor failed to do so.

Disappointed at the porter, Li stopped him and said, "Don't injury yourself. Let me try." He seemed not consume much effort to elevate the stone roller onto the tree and then took it off. Li's amazing strength shocked the porter.

Li ordered servants to prepare meals to feast the fish vendor. After the dinner, he gave the fish vendor some money before he left. Later, someone asked why Li did so. "I tried to test his real strength. However, his strength came from food, and thus cannot become a real useful person. So, I finally let him go."

First—Grade Imperial Guard

One time, Emperor Qianlong went out for autumn hunting at the Mulan Hunting Ground. This was a traditional custom for the royal family. Hidden in lush forests of the hunting ground were numerous wild birds and animals, including wolves, bears, tigers, leopards, roes, and deer. As the emperor and his warriors approached, those animals fled deep into the forests. Then, the emperor told the warriors accompanying him, "You

shoot them! Those who captured rare birds and beasts will be rewarded."

Encouraged by his order, those armed warriors escorted the emperor to chase their preys.

As the emperor chased a Mongolian gazelle, his horse stumbled against the cragged path. The emperor lost his balance and almost fell from horseback, and his red-laced whip got rid of his control and flied like an arrow to the sky. Li Guoliang, who escorted the emperor in rear, urged his horse forwards and shouted, "Your majesty, let me help you." Then, Li jumped from horseback, caught the whip in the air, and sat back onto his horse. He returned the whip to Emperor Qianlong, who seemed delighted at Li's brave act and acute skills. After they finished hunting, the emperor particularly met Li and said to him, "I've long heard your arm strength is amazing and you're skilled at all kinds of weapons. But, I never knew you have so marvelous light skill. I hereby appoint you as a First-Grade Imperial Guard. From now on, you're my trustworthy bodyguard."

Testing a Little Monk

Li Guoliang was appointed by the emperor as a First-Grade Imperial Guard. In 1761, he became a general defending Fujian and Zhejiang. One time, he and several attendants entered an ancient temple during a military expedition against bandits. The temple boasted skyscraping trees and prosperous Buddhist activities and was as magnificent as any famous monastery around the country. Numerous pilgrims came to worship Buddha.

Along a zigzagging path, Li Guoliang reached the temple's kitchen, where several little monks were cooking. The spacious kitchen was shrouded in steam and smoke. Perhaps due to their long history, color paintings on the girders already faded except for dragon patterns on four pillars. The stove was

李国梁笑着说:"这位大哥别急,这鱼我全买下啦!不仅如此,你每天跑海能赚多少钱我给你多少钱,请你在我家陪我住上三日怎样?"

跑海的心想,这可是打着灯笼难找的好事,便满口答应下来。

李国梁微微一笑说:"不过我有个条件,在这三天里,你得答应和我住在一起,三天三夜不许吃东西,第四天我请你赴宴如何?"

跑海的想了想说:"中,中中的!"

从当天起,李国梁叫跑海的跟在自己身边寸步不离,他走那里,跑海的跟在那里,三天三夜饮食未进。跑海的饿得饥肠寡肚咕咕直叫,而李国梁却没事似的。就在四天头上,李国梁又把跑海的带到树下,指着碌碡说:"这位大哥,劳驾你,请你再把这碌碡放到树上如何?"

跑海的遵命,双手把碌碡端将起来,可是用尽了吃奶的力气也未能把碌碡举上树去,只好有气无力地将碌碡放在了地上。

李国梁见此光景大失所望,他对跑海的说:"不用瞎费力气,免得伤身,你看我的。"说着,双手一托,稳稳当当地将碌碡安放到了树杈上,接着双手一托,又将碌碡取下轻轻放回原处。跑海的在一旁看呆啦!

碌碡放在地上之后,李国梁吩咐家人备饭待客。饭后,又备些银两给跑海的便叫他走了。

事后,人们问起李国梁为啥这样做。李国梁不无遗憾地说:"我是想试试他是否有真力气,能否成为一个习武之人,可惜此人乃饭力之辈,难成大器,故而放他回去啦。"

众人听罢连连点头称是。

猎场飞身抄鞭　御赐带刀侍卫

有一年,乾隆皇帝遵照祖制,到木兰围场进行秋狝。举目远看,偌大围场,草木葱茏,禽兽繁多。乍见人迹,那狼、熊、虎、豹、獐、狍、麋、鹿四散逃避。眼望众多猎物,乾隆君臣好不喜欢。乾隆皇帝一时兴起马上传旨:"尔等赶快上前射捕,获有珍禽异兽者,朕将重重有赏!"

众军从闻听,人人奋勇,个个争先,挟弓带箭簇拥着乾隆直奔猎物。

正当乾隆皇帝兴冲冲地策马穷追一只黄羊,山地崎岖,草林茂密,不幸坐骑偏崴前蹄,险些栽下马来。由于身体失衡,红缨皮鞭脱手而出,恰似一支箭镞直射天际。乾隆身后的李国梁见状,从马上纵身跃起,开口喊道:"陛下别急!"说时迟,那时快,飞身将马鞭抄在手中,复坐鞍上,驱马紧追只有几步,便将马鞭拱手交与皇上,乾隆皇帝龙颜大悦。围猎事毕,回到山庄传旨将李国梁唤至面前,言道:"朕只知李爱卿膂力过人,对于十八般兵器样样熟稔,未想到你的轻功却如此了得!朕封你为御前头等侍卫,今后尔可带刀随身护驾。"

巧试小和尚

李国梁授职御前头等侍卫,备受皇帝恩宠。乾隆二十六年(1761年),被放外任来到闽、浙等地。一次在剿匪的行军途中,得知附近有一处古刹,遂带着几名侍从来到寺中。这是一座像模像样的功德丛林,其建筑格局不亚于名山大寺。树木参天,气势宏伟,佛事昌盛。山门内外游人如织,善男信女前来拜佛者络绎不绝。

李国梁一行沿着寺内曲径由前到后依次观赏,信步到了寺内庖厨所在。入内,只见几个小沙弥正在烧火做饭。宽敞的大厅内烟气蒸腾,梁上的彩绘模糊不清,但四根画龙明柱依稀可见。灶内火焰熊熊,灶台边放有几捆毛竹。只见一个烧火的小和尚,悠闲地坐在小竹凳上,用手不停地向灶膛内填放着毛竹。为使火势燃旺,伸手拿起数根毛竹,张开拇食

fueled with bamboo sticks. Sitting on a bamboo stool, a little monk easily smashed a piece of bamboo stick into pieces with his thumb and forefinger, and threw it into the stove.

Stuck by what he saw, Li Guoliang stood there for an hour. "What great kung fu!" Li said to himself. "The temple must be a hideaway for talents. A little monk can do so, and his teacher must be much better. I must pay extra attention to suppressing bandits." To test the little monk's strength, Li Guoliang secretly lifted a gigantic column with his hands and pressed it onto the front of the monk's garment. He then turned to the little monk, and said, "Could you stand up, little master?"

The little monk turned around and tried to stand up. However, no matter how hard he tried, he couldn't stand up because his garment was restrained by the column.

"Somebody helps me," the little monk cried. "I don't know what happened to my garment."

A group of monks flooded into the kitchen, but none of them could help the little monk out.

"Don't be silly," someone suggested. "Just take off your garment."

"Let me help you," Li Guoliang said.

He lifted the column again and freed the little monk. Astonished at his marvelous strength, those monks were frozen for a while. "Sorry," Li apologized. "I played with the little master just now. You can smash a bamboo stick with two fingers, but why you cannot move the column?"

"We were trained to smash bamboo with fingers since we were young," one monk explained. "In fact, we have never learned martial arts. For us, it is easy to smash a bamboo stick into pieces, but impossible to move such a column."

"I see," Li Guoliang then said goodbye to those monks.

Watching his back farther and farther, the monks turned up their thumbs and exclaimed, "What an amazing man!"

9. Monk Faben, Abbot of the Chaoyin Temple

In 1839, Monk Faben was born as Guo Chuncheng in Beitang, Ninghe County. As a child, he learned sailing from his father. Later, he was hired to pilot ships shuttling between Tianjin, Hebei, Shandong, and Liaoning. One time, as he sailed on the sea nearby Caobeidian, he saw a sandy island, on which there was a Buddhist temple named Caofei Hall. So, the island was popularly called Caofeidian. The island extended 3.5 kilometers long and two kilometers wide, and the bay in front of it featured torrential currents and huge billows. Therefore, it was easy for boats to wreck there, especially on nights due to blurry vision. At the time, a local saying went that "Caofeidian is the graveyard even for heroic boatmen." When he was young, Guo witnessed many boats wrecked there, and thus swore to

二指，由粗到细熟练地轻轻紧捏，只听根根毛竹"嘎嘎"作响，立时被捏得粉碎，填入炉膛。

李国梁见状好生吃惊，站在一旁不声不响，直呆呆看了足有半个时辰。心中暗想：好厉害的功夫啊！看来佛门净地确实藏龙卧虎，一个小沙弥尚且如此，其祖师的功夫那还了得？难怪此地匪情如此猖獗，靖化地域须当十分注意。为试其膂力，李国梁悄悄绕至小和尚的背后，靠近明柱，单臂缠紧往起一拉拔，竟将那明柱拔起半尺多高，顺势将小和尚的袄襟压在了柱子下面，之后道了一声："这位小师父请了。"

小和尚见有人说话，急忙起身相迎。刚想站立起身，不料自己身后的衣襟被压在了明柱之下，左扯右拽，怎么也动弹不得。

小和尚情急喊道："快来人啊！快来人，阿弥陀佛，奇事，怪事，我的袄襟怎被压在柱子下边了呢？"

听见喊声，呼啦来了一群小和尚。大家一见都被惊得呆若木鸡，你看着我，我看着你，一筹莫展，谁也救不起那袄襟被压在柱子下的小和尚。

有人在一旁喊道："还愣着干什么，快把袈裟脱掉吧！"

李国梁见状言道："小师父们别慌，让我来！"

李国梁说着，俯身弯臂，再次拔起明柱，那小和尚立即站起身来。小和尚们被惊得半晌没人说话。最后还是由李国梁开口问道："小师父们，对不起，方才是在下和小师父开了个小小的玩笑。请问，方才你们烧火之时，用手捏碎毛竹不费吹灰之力，一根小小明柱压住衣襟却为何动它不起呢？"

小和尚们笑着答道："施主有所不知，小僧们双指捏开毛竹乃自幼为之，天长日久练就的指力，身上并无半点功

夫，捏开毛竹易，要想挪动如此偌大的一根殿中明柱，势比登天还难啊！"

"哦！原来如此。"李国梁向众僧告别便走出殿外。

众和尚望着李国梁走远的背影，个个伸出拇指，万分叹服地说："真神人也！"

九　潮音寺住持法本

法本俗姓郭，名醇诚。道光十九年（1839年）生于宁河县北塘，自幼随父亲学习航业，受雇于人，往来于津冀、山东、辽宁等沿海。在航行中，他见到曹北甸海域海面宽阔，迎海一面有一道横贯东西的大沙岗，形成北侧水浅，南侧水深。当地人称此沙岗为曹北甸。在沙岗上建有一座佛殿，名曹妃殿，所以人们又将这半沙岛，称为曹妃甸。此海域横亘一道东西长3.5公里、宽2公里的大沙岗，岗前水深莫测，造成风高浪险，水流湍急，险象环生，凡由此地经过的船只，特别是在夜间，因视线模糊，常常遇险遭难，因有"英雄好汉，难过曹妃甸"之说，凡驾船之人，都谈之色变。年幼的小醇诚，曾亲眼见到过行船在此遭难，因此发誓要在此建立一座灯塔，以利夜间船只航行。然建灯塔需用一笔相当大的资金，况此时年纪尚小，只靠他一个人是难以完成的。咸丰七年（1857年），19岁的郭醇诚因不同意家里给他办婚事，就逃婚到京北红螺山古台寺受戒出家。因其立下过建灯塔的夙愿，遂告别师父及寺中僧众托钵化缘，苦行劝募，历时四年，筹集够资金后，在曹妃甸建成了引航灯塔。自此，他日夜守护，为过往船只夜间航行提供了方便，受到了船工们和当地百姓的赞扬。光绪年间，法本云游途中见到了石臼坨上的朝阳庵，他得知此庵自唐朝以来就是佛门圣地，规模宏大，但日渐衰微，于是决意在此修建新寺院。为筹集建寺资金，他组织一部分僧人铲除岛上杂草，

build a lighthouse for sailors. However, the project would cost a tremendous amount of money, which seemed an impossible mission for the child to fulfill alone. In 1857, at the age of 19, Guo fled home because he dissented from the marriage that his family arranged for him. He converted to Buddhism at the Gutai Temple in northern Beijing. Since then, he called himself Faben. To fulfill his pledge of building the lighthouse, Faben left the temple and spent four years traveling around to raise money for the construction of the lighthouse. After the lighthouse was completed, Faben stayed there day and night to guide boats sailing on the nearby sea. His beneficent act won applause from boatmen and local people. During the reign of Emperor Guangxu, Faben visited the deteriorated Chaoyang Nunnery on Mortar Isle. Knowing that the nunnery had been a sacred land for Buddhists since the Tang Dynasty, Faben made up his mind to restore its past prosperity. He mobilized some monks to reclaim wastelands to grow crops and produce salt on the coast. Moreover, he built ships and piloted them to trade cargos around northeastern China. After a decade of tireless efforts, he finally raised enough funds to rebuild the nunnery. He bought stones from North Hill and timber from western Liaoning. He first shipped the building materials via the Luanhe River to the coast, and then transferred them to Mortar Isle. As all materials got ready, Faben invited experienced artisans from around the country to reconstruct the nunnery. They altogether constructed a gate, a front hall, six major halls, and ten rear halls, as well as dozens of rooms for monks and visitors to dwell. Each stone pillar of the reconstructed temple measured three meters in height and was decorated with exquisite carvings. After its reconstruction, the nunnery was renamed the Chaoyin Temple.

Unlike other Buddhist monks, Faben didn't preach sermons much, but committed himself to charity undertakings. He often helped disaster-stricken people. In the spring of 1913, locals suffered a severe famine. He donated large amounts of grain and money, thus rescuing many from starving. On December 4, 1917, Faben, then abbot of the Chaoyin Temple, summoned all of the temple's monks. He died when he recited Buddhist sutras for them.

His stories are found in the *Philosophy of Chuncheng* written by Han Zuozhou.

开垦出荒地数百亩，种植五谷；一部分在就近沿海晒盐；并建造大船（大木鱼、小木鱼等），亲自带人驾船出航经商，往来于燕齐、东北等地。历时10余年，他带领僧众，不畏寒暑，不畏艰险，克服了重重困难，积累了大量资金，主要用于购置建寺物料。他从北山采石，从辽左伐木，用船从滦河上游运来，然后从海上转运到石臼坨上。物料备齐，待建寺时机成熟，就四处选能工巧匠，精心设计，择吉日动工建设。先后建成山门前殿、正殿六楹（座），后殿十楹，僧房、客房等五六十间。仅建设用的大殿石柱就有一抱多粗，一丈多高，上面精雕细刻着各种纹饰图案，并将朝阳庵改为潮音寺。

法本是个特殊的佛教之徒，不尚说法，注重实践，干事敬业，戒律严谨，并雅性慈善，经常赈济灾民。在1910年春天闹饥荒，他就运米320石，制钱3000缗赈济灾民，救活了很多人。1917年12月4日拂晓，病中的法本召集全寺僧人，说《大悲咒经》毕，跌坐示寂（端坐着故去）。

附：《醇诚传》 韩作舟

醇诚字法本，石臼坨潮音寺住持僧也。俗姓郭氏，原籍宁河，幼习航业，往来于直、鲁、奉天各海岸。因见曹北店海面弯阔，横亘沙冈，经过风帆，动遭覆没。乃发愿誓筑灯塔一座，以利夜航。然事大用宏，只手未易举办。咸丰丁巳，时年十九遂逃婚入京北红螺山古台寺，披剃受戒，托钵远游，苦行劝募。不四年而塔成，中外便之。嗣悉石臼坨朝阳庵自唐称为圣地，惟经营无人，榛芜未辟。乃卓锡认师，督领僧众，昕夕勤苦，诛除草菜，垦地数百亩。躬率僧徒，树艺禾黍，一面亲操航业，冲犯波涛。盛暑祁寒，险艰不避。所积赢余，用以伐石采木，起造丛林，前后数十年往返数千里，费款数万金。计修佛殿、山门、经堂、僧舍以及庖湢、垣墉之属，无不塑绘庄严。规模宏丽，至石佛石柱镌刻尤为精工。遂改朝阳为潮音，宣统二年，春大饥，运米三百二十石、制钱三千缗赈济沿海贫民，全活甚众。一生志操孤洁，梵行清贞，苦力虔修，深入佛海。民国六年丁巳，旧十二月四日拂晓，招集全寺僧人，说大悲咒经毕，跌坐示寂。县贤达葛养田、王麟徵、安蕴璞等，呈请国府特予褒扬。

10. Shi Lü jin Wrote Antithetical Couplets

In 1880, Shi Lüjin passed the imperial examinations and was conferred on the title of *jinshi*. Later, he was consecutively appointed as justice minister and circuit supervisor of Liaoning and Shaanxi. During the Republic of China period (1912-1949), he acted as director of the Central Industrial Department.

Shi Lüjin was the third son of Shi Menglan, the No.1 scholar in eastern Beijing at the time. It is said that before the birth of Shi Lüjin, his father made a strange dream, in which a scholar accidently disturbed a tiger in sleep by trampling its tail, but the tiger didn't bite the scholar but carried him on its back across the mountain forest. As he woke up from his dream, Shi Menglan was informed that his wife gave birth to a boy. Shi Menglan deemed that his dream coincided with the "Jin diagram" as depicted in the *Book of Changes*. Thus, he named his son Lüjin. He hoped the son would become a noble and useful person in future.

Since he was young, Shi Lüjin had been clever and studious. Under the instruction of his father, he finally passed the imperial examinations and was appointed as an imperial supervisor.

At the time, many officials adored Shi Menglan for his outstanding literary achievements. For this reason, they showed a favorable attitude to his son, Shi Lüjin. Of course, Shi Lüjin didn't disappoint them. He worked hard and never corrupted, and the upper class regarded him as a talented person. After the founding of the Republic of China, he was elected director of the Central Industrial Department. Dr. Sun Yat-sen mentioned in his *Strategies of Founding a Nation* that he planned to build "a harbor" at the north beach of Laoting. In fact, Shi Lüjin provided Sun with relevant materials for the book.

Faben, the abbot of the Chaoyin Temple on Mortar Isle, was an intimate friend of Shi Lüjin. When Shi Lüjin died, Faben led a group of monks to his mansion in order to release his soul from purgatory. In 1923, when he acted as manager of Zhili Industrial Corp., Shi Lüjin wrote a pair of antithetical couplets for the Chaoyin Temple, which were then hung on the pillars of the temple's front gate.

Humble in preaching, boundless Buddhist doctrines offer a spiritual utopia to all people in suffering;

Rather than white lotus terrace, immense ocean and sky are abodes for Bodhi living.

11. Ge Yuzhi and Monk Faben

In the late Qing Dynasty, Ge Yuzhi, a Hanlin academician, was a household name in Laoting. His stories, including growing from a smart boy to a member of the Hanlin Academy after passing the imperial examinations, as well as his benevolent deeds of assisting local residents, were known near and far, but few knew he was an intimate friend of Monk Faben, abbot of the Chaoyin Temple on Mortar Isle.

Monk Faben adored Ge for his knowledgeableness and

十 史履晋撰写楹联

史履晋字康侯，光绪庚寅（1890年）科进士。曾任刑部郎中、升经辽沈、陕西道监察御史。民国年间，出任中央实业司司长。

京东第一才子史梦兰有三个儿子，史履晋是其第三子。相传，史履晋出生前，史梦兰做了个梦，梦见一个书生踩了老虎的尾巴，这老虎被踩醒后，不但没咬这个书生，反而让书生骑在背上，驰骋于山林之中。史梦兰梦醒之后，家人报知说夫人生下一子。史梦兰认为此梦与《易经》的"晋卦"相合，便为此子取名曰"履晋"。他希望此子长大后，成为清正纯洁，胸怀坦荡，光明磊落，同时又沉着冷静，机敏细致，有所作为的人。

史履晋自幼聪慧，刻苦攻读，再加上其父专心指导，终于在光绪庚寅科中了进士，并被朝廷命为记名御史。

当时，朝中的一些老官员对史梦兰都很敬重，因之对其子史履晋亦高看一眼，厚爱一层，格外重用，且史履晋也不负众望，为官清廉，工作认真，被上层社会一致认为是一位极有本事的人才。故民国建立后，被推举为实业司司长。孙中山撰写的《建国方略》中关于在乐亭王滩拟建"北方大港"，其原始材料就是史履晋为其提供的。

石臼坨潮音寺的住持法本与史梦兰过从甚密，史履晋对法本的为人了解且敬重，史梦兰逝世，法本曾亲率僧人去大港村史府为其念经超度。潮音寺建成后，时任直隶实业司司长的史履晋，于1923年正月在北京的官邸里，书写了潮音寺山门的楹联：

佛法本无边努目低眉度娑婆众生苦恼皆成极乐界
菩提应不住白莲青石看海天万顷庄严满布祇陀园

十一 葛翰林与法本结善缘

晚清时，在乐亭邑内提起翰林葛毓芝，可谓无人不知，无人不晓。人们只知葛翰林（毓芝）幼年聪慧，得中进士，殿试二甲，授翰林院庶吉士，他做官清正廉洁，在乡行善于民，誉满乡梓，但鲜为人知的是，他与石臼坨上潮音寺住持法本交往甚厚。

法本仰慕葛翰林为官清廉，足不入权贵之门，敬重他敏捷多才，通达经学；而葛翰林则是尊崇法本虔修佛门，为在曹妃甸建灯塔，苦行劝募，立志建潮音寺，志操孤守，梵行

uncorrupted spirit, while Ge respected Faben for his devotion to Buddhism and his charitable acts to build the Caofeidian lighthouse and reconstruct the Chaoyin Temple. Their friendship set a good example for later generations. According to local elders, there is a legendary story about how their friendship began:

As Faben led other monks to prepare for the construction of the Chaoyin Temple, one of his friends, Wang Linhui, told him that Ge Yuzhi returned from capital to his hometown Gezhuang after his retirement. During his tenure, Ge was noted for his righteousness and loyalty. He once wrote a poem as his mottos, which read that "Never too far to seek truth; Never too old to learn knowledge." Thus, Faben wished to meet Ge. One day, one of his disciples went to the county seat, who came back with a good news: To help local people suffering from flood and famine, Ge asked assistance from his former colleague Xiong Xiling, and raised enough money to build a flood drainage channel that stretched southwards from Daocha to Hantuo Village. At the moment, Ge was leading local people to dig the channel. Hearing this, Faben became more eager to get to know Ge.

The following early morning, Faben pulled on his gown and headed for the county seat of Laoting. As he arrived at Daocha and Hantuo Villages, an almost-completed channel presented itself before his eyes. Numerous laborers were still working on the construction site. Faben climbed onto the dike by the channel, and bowed towards Gezhuang while chanting "Amitabha." Then, he sat on the dike to chant Buddhist sutras until sunset.

The monk drew attention from those laborers, who then reported to Ge. Before long, Ge came to the dike and asked respectfully, "Master, what your name?"

"You can call me Faben," the monk replied.

"Master, what're you doing here?" Ge asked in humility.

"I heard Mr. Ge, a native of the village, set a good example

of morality. He is a righteous person and has helped thousands of local households. So, I came to pray for blessing for him," Faben replied, with his eyes closed.

"I don't deserve such praise," Ge said modestly.

Faben opened his eyes, and saw an old man who wore simple clothes and behaved gracefully. He then asked, "Are you Mr. Ge?"

"Yes, it's me."

"Amitabha! I've long heard your name. Finally, I have the luck to meet you today," Faben bowed to Ge.

"I just do what I can do for local people, and don't deserve your praise," Ge bowed back.

"I've long adored you for your well-knownknowledgeableness and benevolence are known near and far. Today must be my lucky day so that I can meet you here." Faben asserted.

Impressed by his sincerity, Ge then invited Faben to stay the night at his home. Faben didn't refuse his kind invitation, but bowed with gratitude.

Ge ordered his servants to escort Faben to his home. In the living room, Ge treated Faben with tea, and the two began conversation. The topics they discussed included Buddhist doctrines, as well as how Faben raised funds for the construction of the Chaoyin Temple. They didn't stop talking until midnight. Within the following three days, they kept talking with each other. Their conversation would continue if Faben didn't leave due to some emergencies occurring in the construction of the Chaoyin Temple.

Since then, they became intimate friends. Once he encountered any difficulty in the construction of the Chaoyin Temple, Faben would come to consult Ge. And Ge concerned about the temple. In his spare time, Ge often visited Mortar Isle to admire island views and compose poems.

On December 4, 1917, Faben summoned all monks in the Chaoyin Temple. He died while reciting Buddhist sutras. Hearing the news, Ge fell into deep sorrow. For the reason of

清贞。他二人因而结缘，其友情流芳后世。但他们的交往究竟是从何时开始的，据老人们说还有一段故事。

那一年，法本正在带领僧众修建潮音寺，他听县内故友、乡贤王麟徵说，城西葛庄葛养田（毓芝）自京城还家，其人在任为官清廉，淡漠荣华，急公好义，不事权贵。自撰联语云：义理无穷，活到老学到老；光阴有限，过一年少一年。葛翰林的为人风范为邑内人称道。法本闻此，对葛翰林顿生仰慕之情。一日，一徒弟去县内办事，又带来一个好消息：葛翰林为解决城西一带多年来沥涝之灾，饥民困苦，去京城找当年同僚熊希龄，并奔波于府、县之间集资，终于求得善款，要修一条北起道岔村南，南至韩坨村东入长河的泄水渠。现在，他正在带领城西百姓挖渠。听了这一消息，更激起了法本和葛翰林交往的急切心情。

第二天拂晓，他披上袈裟，托起云钵，直奔乐亭城西而来。他到了乐亭城西，只见从道岔村到韩坨一带人山人海，车水马龙，一条即将挖成的新渠道展现在眼前，法本无限感慨。他迈步登上渠首大堤，面向葛庄，双手合十，躬身一揖，口念："阿弥陀佛。"而后，就在堤上打坐念起经来，看看红日渐渐西沉，但他仍在那里打坐念经。

法本的行动引起了人们的注意，马上有人报告了葛翰林。葛翰林闻知，立即带人来到现场，果然见一老和尚闭目打坐在大堤上默祷。他趋步上前施了一礼，恭敬地说："请问师父，法号怎么称呼？"

法本答道："小僧法本，施主请了。"

葛翰林说："师父来敝地有何见教？"

"不敢。久闻贵地出了一位葛翰林，善于奖掖后进，敦厚乡风，经常劝人行善去恶。且急公好义，利普万家，我在此祝他善行善果，流芳百世。"法本嘴里说着，身子却一动不动。

葛翰林谦恭施礼，说："师父过誉，敝人实在汗颜。"

法本闻听来人口气，慢睁双眼，见身旁站着一位朴素典雅、文质彬彬的老人，一看就让人产生敬慕之情。连忙开口道："这么说先生就是葛翰林了？"

"不敢，正是老朽。"葛翰林忙说。

"阿弥陀佛，久仰大名，今日得以相见，幸会，幸会！"法本又是一揖。

"老朽只是为乡民办些力所能及之事，师父之言，羞煞老朽了。"说完，连连施礼。

"先生才高八斗，声名远播，所做善事，千古流芳，老衲仰慕已久，今日得见，乃三生有幸！"法本说完感慨不已。

葛翰林见法本如此谦恭，很是感动，忙对法本说："天色已晚，有请师父到寒舍一叙。"

法本听后，并不谦让，只是深深一揖，说："叨扰了。"

葛翰林让家人搀起法本，直奔葛家而来。到家后，葛翰林将法本让进客厅，下人摆上清茶，二人就在大厅内畅叙起来。他们说法论佛，谈经讲道，乃至潮音寺的资金筹集和建设，直到夤夜月照中天。一连三日，二人长聚在客厅里，总是有说不完的话，法本大有相见恨晚之慨。三日后，法本因

his old age, Ge already couldn't visit Mortar Isle to mourn his friend. He wrote a pair of elegiac couplets that read "Ascending to heaven in search of Buddhist truth, leaving on earth a lighthouse to guide people." He then delivered the elegiac couplets to Mortar Isle to express his grief towards his friend.

12. Li Dazhao, Co-founder of the CPC

On October 29, 1889, Li Dazhao was born into a peasant family in Laoting County, Hebei Province. His father died for illness before his birth, so did his mother when he was 16 months old.

At that time, the corrupted Qing government oppressed its people, but submitted to foreign intruders. Thus, numerous ordinary people lived in sufferings. In his childhood, Li Dazhao witnessed so much social darkness that he determined to "rescue the nation from decline through political reform." In 1907, before he graduated from Yongping Prefecture Middle School, Li Dazhao entered Tianjin Northern Law and Political Science School in hopes to find a solution to rescue his motherland from suffering.

In October 1911, Dr. Sun Yat-sen led a revolution to overthrow the Qing Dynasty. Li embraced great expectations for the republic founded by Dr. Sun Yat-sen. However, Yuan Shikai, a powerful warlord at the time, hijacked the 1911 Revolution and became the president. Moreover, he managed to resume emperorship, which deeply depressed Li Dazhao. In December 1911, Li Dazhao and Bai Yayu, a member of the Republic Federation, masterminded and launched the Luanzhou Uprising that aimed to overthrow the reign of Yuan Shikai. After the uprising failed, Li Dazhao began to publish essays to criticize corrupted warlords and bureaucrats.

In the winter of 1913, with the help of Tang Hualong, Li Dazhao went to Japan's Waseda University to study politics. During his stay in Japan, Li Dazhao got to know many revolutionists and intellectuals. Abe Isoo's socialist thoughts cast a deep influence on Li. In addition to studying Marxism and socialist thoughts originating in Europe, Li also participated in patriotic activities against Yuan Shikai organized by the General Association of Overseas Chinese Students.

In May 1914, Yuan Shikai enacted the *New Constitution* as a step to resume emperorship in China. In November, Li Dazhao published *National Situation* to reveal the plot that Yuan Shikai colluded with imperialists to restore emperorship. The same year, Li Dazhao founded Chinese Society in Japan to secretly promote campaigns against Yuan Shikai. After Yuan Shikai signed the infamous Twenty-One Demands with Japan, Li Dazhao published *The Letter to People All Over China*, calling on people throughout the country to fight against Yuan Shikai. On February 2, 1916, Li Dazhao quitted school and returned to China in May. In July, upon the invitation of Tang Hualong, Li Dazhao came from Shanghai to Beijing to found the newspaper *Morning Bell*. Later, he quitted his job due to the intervention of some politicians. Then, he was hired as an editor of Jiayin Daily, a newspaper founded by Zhang Shizhao. During the period, Li Dazhao published *Youth* to encourage youngsters to shake off pessimistic thoughts and dedicate themselves into social revolution.

On November 7, 1917, the October Revolution broke out in Russia. It victory encouraged Li Dazhao tremendously. After that, he gradually converted to Marxism and rethought the fate of his motherland, which marked that he began to transform from a follower of patriotism and democracy to a communist. Consecutively, he published View on Comparison of French Revolution and Russian Revolution, *Victory of Common People* and *Victory of Bolshevism*, singing for the victory of Russian October Revolution, revealing the in-depth nature of the World , and calling on Chinese people to walk onto a revolutionary path like Russia. In his essays, Li Dazhao declared, "Just look at the future of the world; it is bound to be a world of red flags!"

潮音寺建设事急，才不得不依依惜别回到了石臼坨。

从此，二人成了莫逆之交。法本在建设潮音寺过程中，有什么疑难之事，常是登堂向葛翰林请教；而葛翰林也对法本的潮音寺的文化氛围非常关注，并在闲暇之时，亦来到石臼坨上欣赏海岛风景，吟诗作赋。

1917年腊月初四，为佛事操劳一生，卧病在床的法本长老召集潮音寺僧众，同念起《大悲咒经》，诵罢，他面带微笑，跌坐示寂。葛翰林得到了法本圆寂的消息，但他此时年事已高，已不能亲自到石臼坨上去吊唁，只得含着悲痛写下了"天上送佛极乐国，人间留泽指航灯"的挽联，派人送到石臼坨上，以示他悼念故友之情。

十二　中国共产党创始人之一李大钊

李大钊，1889年10月29日生于今河北省乐亭县大黑坨一个农家。在他诞生前父亲病亡，母亲生下他不满16个月病逝。

此时的清朝政府，腐败无能，对内残酷压榨，对外卖国求存，广大人民群众生活在水深火热之中。李大钊从小目睹中国黑暗的社会现实，"感于国势之危迫，急思深研政理"。1907年，李大钊在卢龙永平府中学没有毕业，毅然考入天津北洋法政专门学校，立志为苦难的中国寻求出路。

1911年10月，孙中山领导辛亥革命推翻了清王朝。李大钊对孙中山建立的民国寄予了很大希望。可是不久，辛亥革命的胜利果实被袁世凯窃取。袁世凯倒行逆施，甘冒天下之大不韪，引起了李大钊极大的"隐忧"和"哀痛"。1911年12月，李大钊参与、策划了共和会白雅雨等人领导的"滦州起义"，以期推翻袁世凯领导的北洋军阀政权。起义失败后，他开始发表文章深刻揭露军阀官僚的黑暗统治。

1913年的冬天，李大钊为了寻找救国救民的道路，在汤化龙等人的资助下，来到日本就读于东京早稻田大学政治本科。留学期间，李大钊结识了一批革命者和有识之士。安部矶雄教授以"人类爱"为中心的社会主义思想，对李大钊产生了深刻的影响。在校他一面研究马克思和欧洲的社会主义思想，一面参加中国留学生总会，进行反对袁世凯复辟帝制的斗争。

1914年5月袁世凯颁布了《新约法》，妄图实现他的封建统治。11月李大钊发表了《国情》一文，揭露帝国主义与袁世凯暗相勾结妄图称帝的阴谋。同年在日本发起组织了"神州学会"，秘密进行反袁活动。当日本公然向袁世凯提出灭亡中国的"二十一条"的侵略阴谋透露后，李大钊奋笔疾书，撰写并向国内寄发《警告全国父老书》，一针见血地揭露了日本帝国主义的侵略实质与袁世凯的卖国阴谋，号召国民奋起自救。因参与反袁斗争，1916年2月2日，被学校除名。为推动反袁斗争，他毅然放弃了学业，起程回国。袁世凯在全国人民的一片唾骂声中死去。5月，李大钊回到祖国。7月，应汤化龙等人的邀请由上海回到北京创办《晨钟报》，由于政客们的干扰而辞职，后受聘担任章士钊主办的《甲寅日刊》编辑。在此期间，李大钊发表了《青春》一文，这篇文章除批判悲观厌世的人生观外，着力宣传了青春宇宙观和人生观。他倡导青年应"本其理性，加以努力，进前而勿顾后，背黑暗而向光明，为世界进文明，为人类造幸福，以青春之我，创建青春之家庭，青春之国家，青春之民族，青春之人类，青春之地球，青春之宇宙"。

1917年11月7日，俄国爆发了十月革命。十月革命的胜利，使李大钊受到极大的鼓舞。从此他开始用无产阶级的世界观来观察中国的问题，重新考虑中国的命运，从一个爱国主义和革命民主主义者开始了向共产主义者的转变。先后发表了《法俄革命之比较观》、《庶民的胜利》和《布尔什维

In February 1918, upon Zhao Shizhao's recommendation, Li Dazhao became head librarian of Peking University. During his tenure in the library, he committed himself to the research of Marxism and published a number of essays. Due to his unparalleled knowledgeableness and morality, Li Dazhao won respect from teachers and students throughout the university and was elected into the university's highest council four times. A survey amongst the university's students revealed that Li Dazhao was ranked among the top ten respectful figures, together with Lenin and Sun Yat-sen.

In November 1918, Mao Zedong and two dozens of Hunan students who planned to study in France came to Peking University. Under the influence of Li Dazhao, Mao Zedong changed his mind and determined to stay for further research of China's social problems. Upon the recommendation of Yang Changji, Li Dazhao appointed Mao as a secretary of the library, who was paid eight yuan each month. Mao was deeply influenced by Li's thoughts, virtues, and publications, so he considered Li Dazhao his "real teacher."

In December 1919, Mao Zedong visited Beijing once again as the head of the Hunan petition delegation. Li Dazhao recommended him to join Youth China Society. Under the influence of Li's doctrines, Mao devoted much energy to the research of Marxism and transformed from a revolutionary democrat to a Marxist. Just as Mao ever said, "I quickly converted to Marxism when I acted as assistant librarian of Peking University Library under the supervision of Li Dazhao." During his stay in Peking University, Li Dazhao guided a number of youngsters, including Mao Zedao and Zhou Enlai, to walk onto the road towards Communism.

Before the May 4th Movement broke out, Li Dazhao did a lot to spread revolutionary thoughts. On December 22, 1918, he and Chen Duxiu co-founded *Weekly Review*. In January 1919, he published *New Era*, calling on Chinese people to "do

something good for mankind" by taking chance of the victory of Russian October Revolution. Moreover, he acted as tutor or advisor for such magazines as *National People* and *New Tide*, and often published essays on those magazines to discuss new thoughts and social problems, which played an active role in urging the outbreak of the May 4th Movement.

After the May 4th Movement, Li Dazhao devoted more effort to the research and spread of Marxism and began painstaking preparation of the founding of the Communist Party of China (CPC). From September to October 1919, he published *My Perspective of Marxism* in *New Youth*, giving a systematic elaboration of the three important components of Marxism: historical materialism, political economy, and scientific socialism. By the time, he had basically been a Marxist.

In addition to spreading Marxism across China, Li Dazhao also endeavored to found revolutionary organizations and magazines. In the winter of 1918, he founded Marxism Research Society in Peking University. In May 1919, he helped *Morning Post* in the founding of the column *Research of Marxism*. In July, he co-founded Youth China Society together with Wang Guangqi in Beijing. In March 1920, he organized Research Society of Marxism Theory in Peking University, and then founded Kangmu Charity Studio as the base for the study and research of Marxism. In July 1920, he was appointed as professor and head librarian of Peking University. He taught courses such as "modern political science," "research of historical materialism," and "socialism and social movements" in the university, and often gave lectures at colleges and universities like Female Teachers' College, Normal University, Chaoyang University, and University of China to publicize Marxism doctrines.

The revolutionary organizations and publications founded by Li Dazhao played an active role in the dissemination of Marxism, thus laying an ideological and organizational foundation for the founding of the CPC.

和列宁、孙中山的名字排在一起，列在前十名，成为当时青年学生心目中的大人物之一。

1918年11月，毛泽东和湖南20多名准备去法国勤工俭学的青年，来到了新文化运动中心的北京大学。在李大钊等人的影响下，毛泽东改变了主意，决意留在国内研究中国问题，在杨昌济的介绍下，李大钊为他在北大图书馆安排了一个"书记"的职务，每月工薪8元。毛泽东受到李大钊的道德、人品和文章的深刻影响。毛泽东说李大钊是他"真正的老师"。

1919年12月，毛泽东率领湖南"驱张代表团"赴京请愿，第二次来北京时，李大钊介绍毛泽东加入"少年中国学会"。在李大钊的思想影响下，年轻的毛泽东对马克思主义的研究日益倾注热情，实现了从一个革命民主主义者向马克思主义者的转变。

李大钊是毛泽东成为马克思主义者的领路人。正如毛泽东后来所说："我在李大钊手下担任国立北京大学图书馆助理员的时候，曾经迅速地朝着马克思主义的方向发展。"李大钊在北大工作期间，"教育团结了包括毛泽东、周恩来等一大批革命青年，引导他们走上了共产主义的道路"。

五四运动之前，李大钊做了大量的思想发动工作。1918年12月22日，与陈独秀共同创办了《每周评论》，1919年1月发表《新纪元》一文，号召人们趁着十月革命开

主义的胜利》等三篇文章，热情歌颂十月革命的伟大胜利，深刻揭露帝国主义发动第一次世界大战的本质，号召中国人民走十月革命的道路，向全世界郑重预言："试看将来的寰球，必是赤旗的世界！"

1918年2月，在章士钊的介绍下，李大钊出任北京大学图书馆主任。这期间李大钊潜心钻研马克思主义，撰写并发表了大量文章。他以自己的学识人品，独特的人格魅力和崇高理想，赢得全校师生的尊重，四次入选北大最高决策机构评议会。在北大的一次学生民意测验中，李大钊

Li Dazhao was among the first who initiated the idea of founding the CPC. Early in 1920, he joined hands with Deng Zhongxia to mastermind the founding of the Party. After he was released from prison, Chen Duxiu went to Shanghai for a shelter from persecution of the Government of Northern Warlords, and Li Dazhao escorted him. On their way to Tianjin, they discussed about the founding of the Party, too. In March 1920, when Voitinsky and other delegates from the Communist International visited China, Li Dazhao introduced Voitinsky to meet Chen Duxiu in Shanghai, while another Communist International representative stayed in Beijing to assist Li Dazhao prepare for the founding of the Party. In May, Chen Duxiu wrote a letter to Li Dazhao, in which he consulted Li about the name of the party to be founded. Li Dazhao replied that it definitely should be Communist Party. In October, Li Dazhao founded the Communist Group, which was renamed CPC Beijing Branch one month later, and Li was elected secretary of the branch. The founding of the Communist Group further accelerated ideological and organizational preparation for the founding of the Party.

In June 1921, Malin visited China on behalf of the Communist International. Li Dazhao met him to talk about issues concerning the official founding of the Party and its first congress. Then, he sent Zhang Guotao to escort Malin to meet Li Hanjun in Shanghai for further discussion. Before long, the preparatory committee of the Party issued a notice to require all Communist organizations across China to send two representatives to participate in the Party's first national congress in Shanghai. Li Dazhao was absent from the meeting because he was busy leading teachers from eight national colleges and universities in the struggle for salaries and education funds in Beijing.

After the founding of the CPC, Li Dazhao was dedicated to leading the Party in the north and organizing worker and peasant movements. From 1925 to 1926, he published Land

and Peasants and *Red Spear Fraternities of Shandong, Henan, and Shaanxi Provinces*, giving an in-depth elaboration on how to solve peasant problems and how to organize peasant armed forces.

In June 1922, the CPC Central Committee advocated to "set up a united democratic front" at the second national congress. At the Special Meeting of the CPC Central Executive Committee held by West Lake in Hangzhou, Malin suggested CPC members join the Kuomintang in name of individuals, which stirred up wide objections at the meeting. Li Dazhao agreed with Malin, and finally persuaded most dissenters to accept the suggestion, thus realizing the first cooperation between the Kuomintang and the CPC and enabling the happening of national revolution and the North Expedition. After the meeting, Li Dazhao met Dr. Sun Yat-sen in Shanghai, and they discussed about how to rejuvenate the Kuomintang and China. Impressed by Li's knowledgeableness and morality, Dr. Sun Yat-sen recommended him to join the Kuomintang.

In June 1923, Li Dazhao participated in the CPC third national congress held in Guangzhou, at which representatives discussed on whether CPC members should join the Kuomintang as individuals. Before the conference, the first cooperation between the two parties was already on the way. However, Fan Ruilin proposed to restrict Kuomintang members from joining any other party at the Kuomintang first national congress. In fact, his real purpose was to urge the Kuomintang to close door to CPC members and further prevent the cooperation between the two parties. Li Dazhao opposed the proposal, saying that "the purpose of CPC members joining the Kuomintang is to make contribution to national revolutionary undertakings, but not promote Communist movements by taking advantage of the Kuomintang." He added, "Dr. Sun Yat-sen once agreed Kuomintang members to join the Communist International's organizations in China. So, it's righteous for CPC members to join the Kuomintang." Li's speech gained

辟的一线光明，"努力前去为人类活动，做出一点有益人类（的）工作"。并在《国民》、《新潮》等杂志社任导师或顾问，经常在这些杂志上发表论述新思潮和社会问题的文章，积极领导五四运动，并和改良主义思潮作斗争。

五四运动以后，李大钊对马克思主义进行了更加深入的研究，在此基础上他在国内积极宣传马克思主义，为创立中国共产党而艰苦奋斗。1919年9月至10月11日，李大钊在《新青年》上连续发表了《我的马克思主义观》，系统地介绍了马克思主义的唯物史观、政治经济学和科学社会主义学说。此时的李大钊已基本成为一个马克思主义者。

李大钊在大力宣传马克思主义的同时，积极组织进步团体，创办进步刊物。1918年冬，他在北大组织了《马克思研究会》。1919年5月，他协助《晨报》开辟"马克思研究"专栏，刊载马克思著作。7月，他参与了北京王光祈等人发起建立的"少年中国学会"。1920年3月，他在北大组织"马克思学说研究会"，之后指导研究会建立了专供学习和研究马克思主义用的"亢慕义斋"。1920年7月他被聘为北京大学经济学教授，兼任图书馆主任。他在北大政治系、史学系、经济系和法学系开设了现代政治、唯物史观研究、社会主义与社会运动等课程，同时还在女子高等师范、师范大学、朝阳大学、中国大学等高校讲学，利用高校这一阵地，在知识分子中大力宣传马克思主义。

李大钊发起组织的这些进步团体及其创办的这些进步刊物，积极传播了马克思主义，为中国共产党的建立在思想上、组织上做了准备工作。

李大钊是最早提出建立中国共产党的领导人之一。1920年年初，他与邓中夏就曾酝酿成立中国共产党。陈独秀出狱后去上海避难，李大钊在送其去天津的路上，就曾讨论过建党的事情。是年3月，共产国际远东局局长威金斯

基和马迈耶夫等人来华后，他介绍威金斯基去上海会见陈独秀，马迈耶夫继续留在北京帮助李大钊筹备建党事宜。5月，陈独秀从上海来信向李大钊询问党的名称，李大钊明确地回答：叫共产党。10月他在北京建立了共产主义小组，11月底正式定名为中国共产党北京支部，李大钊任书记。北京共产主义小组的成立，进一步加强了对工作的宣传教育和组织工作。

1921年6月，共产国际代表马林来中国，李大钊与他商谈有关召开党的代表大会正式建党的问题，并派张国焘陪同马林去上海与李汉俊等人商谈有关事项。不久，党在上海的发起组织发出通知，要求各地党组织派两名代表到上海参加党的第一次全国代表大会。李大钊则因为在北京领导国立八所大专院校的教职员工代表进行索薪和争取教育经费的斗争，没能参加这次会议。

中国共产党成立之后，李大钊代表党中央长期负责领导北方党的工作。他以极大的热情领导了北方的工人运动，大力开展农民运动。1925年至1926年，先后发表了《土地与农民》、《鲁豫陕等省的红枪会》等文章，对农民问题和农民武装问题进行了精辟的论述。

1922年6月，中央提出了"建立一个民主主义的联合战线"的主张，这一主张在党的"二大"就已提出。在杭州西湖召开的中共中央执行委员会特别会议上，马林提出中国共产党员要以个人资格参加国民党。与会多数同志思想不通。李大钊同意马林的提议，经过李大钊在会上做的大量深入细致的思想工作，除个别人以外，多数同意了马林的提议，从而使国共两党的合作得以实现，并在此基础上掀起了轰轰烈烈的国民革命和北伐战争。西湖会议之后，李大钊在上海会见了孙中山。两人讨论了振兴国民党与振兴中国的问题。孙中山对于李大钊的渊博学识、人格魅力十分欣赏，亲自主盟

applause from most representatives at the meeting. Through allying with the left wing of the Kuomintang, Li Dazhao defeated the right wing of the Kuomintang and urged the congress to pass the three policies of "uniting Russia, uniting CPC, and supporting peasants and workers." He played a vital role in realizing the first cooperation between the Kuomintang and the CPC. Later, he was chosen into the Kuomintang Central Executive Committee, and then became director of the Organization Division of the Kuomintang Beijing Executive Department in North China.

In May 1924, Zhang Guotao betrayed the Party and confessed to the Beijing warlord government that Li Dazhao was the major Party leader in the north. Then, the government announced Li as a wanted criminal. Li Dazhao left Beijing and hid a dozen days on Xiangyun and Puti Islands and Wufeng Mountain. In June, he received a notice from the CPC Central Committee to appoint him as the head representative of the CPC delegation to the 5th Congress of the Communist International held in Moscow.

The 5th Congress of the Communist International was held from June 17 to July 8, 1924, in Moscow, which attracted more than 500 representatives of over 60 parties and organizations from 49 countries. At the meeting, Chinese delegation submitted the report drafted by Li Dazhao. During his 5-month stay in Soviet Union, Li Dazhao was impressed by the fact that what he long dreamed had already become realities there: The former summer resort of aristocrats and bourgeois in the suburb of Moscow already transformed into a holiday paradise for ordinary workers and children; Sailors from every corner of the world can enjoy the library and entertainment facilities in the International Sailors' Home in Leningrad; The former Royal Club on the outskirt of Leningrad already turned into an orphanage, where orphans led happy lives. He concluded that ordinary workers and peasants truly became the owners of the socialist Soviet Union. Such an experience enhanced his desire for

socialism and his resolution to overthrow oppressors and realize socialist system in China.

After returning to China, Li Dazhao immediately devoted himself to revolutionary struggles. In November 1924, Dr. Sun Yat-sen planned to hold a preparatory meeting for the National Congress. To crack down the pending National Congress, the warlord government under Duan Qirui held a meeting of warlords and bureaucrats. Following the instruction of the Party, Li Dazhao organized activities to fight back, spreading revolutionary activities across the nation.

In the early winter of 1924, Dr. Sun Yat-sen, then premier of the Republic of China, visited Beijing from Tianjin despite his serious illness. His illness increasingly worsened. Before the death of Dr. Sun, the Kuomintang right wing represented by Zhang Ji conspired to split the Kuomintang through distorting Dr. Sun's last words. However, the plot was disintegrated by left-wing representatives like Li Dazhao, He Xiangning, and Soong Ching-ling.

On March 8, 1925, the Kuomintang right wing founded the Kuomintang Comrades Club and began to publicly drive CPC members from the Kuomintang. They declared to abolish the three policies of "Uniting Russia, Uniting the CPC, and Supporting Workers and Peasants." Li Dazhao held a meeting of the Northern Party Committee to oppose Kuomintang right wing's plot aiming to destroy cooperation between the two parties.

On March 12, 1925, Dr. Sun Yat-sen died for illness. Representatives from all walks of life organized a funeral committee, and Li Dazhao worked with the committee's Secretariat. Zhang Ji and some Kuomintang right wing members proposed that Dr. Sun's coffin should be escorted by them, who declared themselves as Dr. Sun's "close friends." Due to the persistent argument of Li Dazhao, the pallbearers included right, left, and middle-wing representatives of the Kuomintang. On April 2, Dr. Sun's coffin was moved to the

介绍李大钊加入了国民党。

1923年6月，李大钊到广州参加了党的第三次全国代表大会。会议的中心是讨论中国共产党全体党员要以个人身份加入国民党的问题。会议之前，国共两党合作的道路已被打通，可是在国民党"一大"28日的会议上，国民党代表方瑞麟提出，党章中要增加禁止本党党员跨党的建议。其目的在于想禁止共产党员以党员的身份加入国民党，实质上是反对孙中山同意的国共两党实现合作的主张。李大钊当场发言予以驳斥，他说："我等之加入本党，是为有所贡献于本党，以贡献于国民革命的事业而来的，断乎不是取巧讨便宜，借国民党的名义，作共产党的运动而来的。""本党总理孙先生亦曾允许我们仍跨第三国际在中国的组织，所以我们来参加本党而兼跨固有党籍，是光明正大的行为，不是阴谋鬼祟的举动。"李大钊义正词严的谈话，博得了多数与会者的赞赏，方瑞麟的提案终于被否决。李大钊在会上联合国民党左派，击败了国民党右派的进攻，保证了大会的顺利进行，通过了实行"联俄、联共、扶助农工"三大政策的宣言和党章。李大钊在促成国共合作中起到了十分关键的作用，他被选进了国民党中央执行委员会，终于实现了国共两党的第一次合作。不久，被任命为国民党北京执行部组织部长，开始领导国共两党在北方的工作。

1924年5月中旬，由于张国焘的叛变，供出了李大钊北方地下党主要负责人的身份。北京政府以"共产党首领鼓动罢工，宣传赤化"的罪名下令通缉李大钊。为了躲避敌人的追捕，李大钊离开北京，先后到乐亭祥云岛、菩提岛和昌黎五峰山避居十数日。同年6月，接到党中央通知，委派他为中共代表团首席代表率团赴莫斯科出席共产国际第五次代表大会。

共产国际第五次代表大会于1924年6月17日至7月8日在莫斯科举行，参加会议的有来自49个国家的60多个政党、团体共500余名代表。在这次会议上，代表团向大会提交了由李大钊起草的中国代表团的报告。在苏联居住的四五个月里，给李大钊留下了深刻印象，他感到自己多年的梦想已经在苏联得到了实现。他在莫斯科近郊马拉霍英卡看到了原来贵族和资产阶级避暑的场所，现在成了工人和儿童避暑的地方。在列宁格勒，他发现被称作"国际海员之家"的海员俱乐部里，那里的图书馆和种种娱乐设施，不管来自何方的海员都可以尽享。他还看到列宁格勒郊区的"皇家村"已经成为儿童村（孤儿院），那里的孤儿过着幸福的生活。他感到在苏联社会主义国家里，工农大众真正当家做了主人。所有这些美好的感受，增进了他对社会主义的向往，这就更加坚定了他要在中国推翻压迫者，建

Biyun Temple. At the funeral, Li Dazhao acted as a pallbearer, and more than 100,000 citizens flooded onto the streets to mourn for Dr. Sun. Under the leadership of Li Dazhao, the Northern Party Committee turned the funeral into an enormous anti-imperialism and anti-warlord demonstration.

At the Fourth CPC National Congress, Li Dazhao was once again elected member of the Central Executive Committee. Meanwhile, he acted as secretary of the Northern Party Committee to take charge of organizational work in a dozen provinces and municipalities including Beijing, Tianjin, Hebei, Jilin, Shanxi, Rehe, and Suiyuan. Li Dazhao paid great attention to uniting ethnic minorities, and once presided over the founding conference of the Great Alliance of Workers, Peasants and Soldiers in Inner Mongolia.

During his tenure as secretary of the Northern Party Committee, Li Dazhao devoted particular concern about the formulation and implementation of the Party's military strategies and tactics. His tireless endeavor was rewarded by the support from national revolutionary army led by Feng Yuxiang, Hu Jingyi, and Sun Yue. He once persuaded General Feng Yuxiang to swear to join the Northern Expedition in Wuyuan.

In 1925, the May 30th Movement broke out in Shanghai. Li Dazhao and Zhang Shiyan announced their support for the movement in Beijing. They organized Shanghai Massacre Revenge Association amongst students, as well as Revenage Association of Workers, to support the struggle of Shanghai protestors.

On March 12, 1926, a Japanese warship bombarded the Dagu Forts in Tianjin, and Chinese troops fought back. Japan then united eight other countries including Britain and the United States to send an ultimatum to the Beiyang Government under Duan Qirui, demanding the Duan government to dismantle all defense establishments at the Dagu Forts. Li Dazhao called on all walks of life in Beijing to unite together against the invasion of Japanese imperialists.

On March 17 and 18, tens of thousands of people from over 200 public organizations gathered for a demonstration in front of the Tian'anmen Gate. Li Dazhao was a member of the demonstration's leading council. Subsequently, Li Dazhao and more than 2,000 protestors gathered in front of the government headquarters in Tieshizi Lane, where they encountered bloody attack by armed soldiers ambushing there. Totally, 47 protestors were killed, and more than 200 injured. This incident was historically known as the March 18th Massacre.

After the massacre, the Zhili and Liaoning warlords jointly listed Li Dazhao as the wanted. So, Li Dazhao was forced to hide in an abandoned barrack in the Soviet Union Embassy together with his family, and the headquarters of the Kuomintang and CPC northern committee also moved there. Even under such as circumstance, Li Dazhao still devoted himself to work all day and night. On April 6, 1927, although against international laws, Zhang Zuolin dispatched 300 soldiers to siege the embassy and arrested more than 80 Kuomintang and CPC members, including Li Dazhao and his family.

No matter how much enemies tortured or lured him, Li Dazhao was utterly fearless and didn't release any secret about the Party. He also argued strongly for justice, displaying dauntless heroism. Within the 22 days of his imprisonment, he leaked nothing confidential to enemies, but leaving a poem titled "My Last Words in Prison" to express his loyalty and fearlessness.

The arrestment of Li Dazhao stirred up great concern in public. People from all walks of life, including academicians, politicians, workers, journalists, and militaries, did their utmost to rescue him. Some railway workers even organized a squad, trying to break into the jail. However, Li Dazhao stopped them for the purpose to save revolutionary forces, and persuaded them not to take any imprudent actions, demonstrating his high sense of responsibility for the Party and others.

立社会主义制度的坚定信念。

李大钊回国后，立即投入了紧张的革命斗争。1924年11月，孙中山北上，准备在北京召开国民会议预备会。段祺瑞政府为了抵制国民会议，召开了由军阀头目和官僚政客参加的"善后会议"。按照党的指示，李大钊与之进行了坚决的斗争，有力地推动了全国革命运动的发展。

1924年初冬，孙中山自天津抱病来到北京后，病情急剧恶化，就在先生病危之际，以张继为代表的右派势力，蓄意分裂国民党，妄图篡改孙中山的遗嘱。李大钊、何香凝、宋庆龄等国民党左派厉言陈词，不准其恣意诽谤篡改总理遗嘱的一字一句。

国民党右派遂于1925年3月8日成立了"国民党同志俱乐部"，公然扯起了"反共"、"分共"的旗帜，向社会宣称要把共产党员从国民党中排挤出去，取消联俄、联共、扶助农工的三大政策。李大钊闻讯召开北方区党委会议，坚决反对国民党右派破坏国共合作的阴谋。

1925年3月12日，孙中山不幸病逝，社会各界组成了孙中山先生治丧委员会，李大钊参加了治丧处秘书股的工作。在抬灵问题上张继等人相继提出应由他们这些所谓的孙中山先生的"亲密战友"抬灵。在李大钊等人据理力争之下，达成妥协，由左、中、右三派派人共同抬灵。4月2日，孙中山先生的灵柩移奉西山碧云寺。出殡那天，李大钊扶灵执绋，10余万市民为孙中山送行。李大钊领导北方区委把这次移灵演变为一次悲壮的反帝、反军阀的群众大示威。

孙中山逝世后，中国共产党第四次全国代表大会再次选举李大钊为中央执行委员。他还担任了新成立的中共北方区委书记，负责北京、天津、河北、吉林、山西、察哈尔、热河、绥远等10余个省市党的领导工作。李大钊非常注意党在少数民族地区的工作，他亲自到张家口主持了内蒙古"工农兵大同盟"成立大会。

李大钊担任北方区委书记期间做了许多工作。他非常关注党对抓军事工作的政策和策略。当时冯玉祥、胡景翼、孙岳率领的国民军所以倾向革命，都与李大钊对他们做过大量工作有关。冯玉祥在北方五原誓师北伐，就是李大钊做的工作。

1925年5月30日，"五卅"运动在上海爆发以后，李大钊、赵世炎等人在北京立即响应。他们在学生中组织"沪案雪耻会"，在工人中组织"工人雪耻会"，声援上海市人民的斗争。

1926年3月12日，发生了日本军舰入侵天津大沽口事件。日本政府借此蓄意制造的口实，联合英、美等八国向段祺瑞政府提出所谓的"最后通牒"，要求中国拆除大沽口防

On April 28, 1927, despite the strong opposition from the public, the brutal and cowardly enemy hanged to death Li Dazhao and other 19 revolutionists, which was executed at 2 p.m. in the Capital Jail. Li Dazhao was the first to step onto the gallows, without showing any fear. Before he was hanged, Li declared, "The great Communism will never die even if you gibbet me today. Our comrades have taken root around the world. We firmly believe the Communism will definitely see glorious victory in China and even across the world." He died at an age of only 38. Li Dazhao contributed his young, precious life to the liberation of the nation.

13. Han Zuozhou Wrote Antithetical Couplets for the Chaoyin Temple

Han Zuozhou, a native of Yinhao Village, Laoting County, was born into an intellectual's family. As a child, he was famous for his cleverness and studiousness. Before the imperial examination was abolished at the end of the Qing Dynasty, he was admitted as a *gongsheng* (candidate in provincial-level imperial examination, who could directly enter the Imperial Academy). Later, he was admitted into the Yongping Prefecture Middle School.

After his graduation from the school, Han became headmaster of Xiyuan Primary School in Laoting County. During the period, he participated in the compilation of the *History of Laoting County* in the Republic of China Period. At the time, the Chaoyin Temple on Mortar Isle was almost completed. The temple's abbot, Monk Zhenkong, invited Han to write couplets used to hang on columns of the temple's halls. Han, then 54, accepted the invitation and stayed in the temple for three days. After he finished those antithetical couplets, Han also compiled Philosophy of Chuncheng and included into the *History of Laoting County* (Republic of China edition). Later, he was appointed as magistrate of Guangping County in southern Hebei Province. During his tenure, Han realized outstanding achievement in administrative affairs and supervised the compilation of the *History of Guangping County*.

After he left Guangping and returned to his hometown, Han began to act as president of Laoting Detention Center. Because Han ever worked for the puppet government of Japanese invaders, some accused him of betraying his motherland. However, he didn't do anything really evil. In 1951, he underwent a trial and was sentenced as a criminal. However, he was released on the site for his insignificant guilty.

In 1952, the government invited him to revise the *History of Laoting County* in the Republic of China Period. Han and Li Dazhao were schoolmates at the Yongping Prefecture Middle School. So, he added the philosophy of Li Dazhao to the revised edition.

御设施。为了抗议日本帝国主义的侵略，李大钊积极发动北京各界群众起来斗争。17、18两日，北京200多团体，数万人在北京天安门集会，抗议日本军舰制造大沽口事件和日、英、美、法等八国政府为中国政府发出的最后通牒。在这次大会上，李大钊担任主席团成员。会后，李大钊随同2000多群众到执政府所在地铁狮子胡同请愿。不料遭到事先埋伏好的执政府卫队的血腥镇压。当场有47名示威群众被打死，200多人受伤。这就是中国历史上段祺瑞执政府制造的震惊中外的"三一八"惨案。

"三一八"惨案后，直、奉两派军阀联合发出通缉令，到处搜捕李大钊。李大钊被迫率北方国共两党的领导机关与自己的妻子儿女搬进苏联大使馆西院的一个旧兵营，日以继夜地为党工作。1927年4月6日，控制了北京政府的张作霖不顾国际惯例，调动300多名士兵包围并闯入苏联大使馆，李大钊和妻子儿女连同国共两党80多人被逮捕。

李大钊被捕入狱后，敌人对他进行严刑拷打，威逼利诱，但他始终严守党的秘密，大义凛然，拒理力争，表现了一个共产党员威武不屈的高贵品质。在他被关进监狱的22天里，敌人从他身上没能得任何东西，得到的只有一纸他那肝胆可对天地的《狱中自述》。

李大钊被捕，在社会上引起了极大的震动。北京学界、政界、工人、北京报界，驻陕国民军以及他的同乡友好，对他进行了积极的营救。铁路工人组成敢死队，准备劫狱。大钊得知后，为了保护革命力量，表示坚决反对，并理智地劝说大家不要盲目行动，表现了一个共产党人对党的事业高度负责的革命精神及爱护他人胜过自己的高尚人格。

1927年4月28日，反动军阀置社会舆论于不顾，判处李大钊等20人绞刑。下午2时，在西交民巷京师看守所执行绞刑时，李大钊第一个走上绞刑台。他从容自如，大义凛然，慷慨陈词："不能因为今天你们绞死了我，就绞死了伟大的共产主义！我们已经培养了很多同志，如同红花的种子撒遍各地！我们深信，共产主义在世界、在中国，必然要得到光荣的胜利！"为了民族的解放事业，李大钊献出了年轻而又宝贵的生命，时年仅38岁。

十三 韩湘亭与潮音寺楹联

韩作舟，字湘亭，乐亭县新寨乡迎好村人。出身于书香门第，自幼聪慧好学。在清朝末年废除科举前，曾考中副贡（副贡也称陪贡，在乡试入取名额以外列入的备取举人，可直接入国子监读书）。后清政府废科举，兴学堂，韩作舟考入永平府中学读书。

韩作舟从永平府中学毕业后，回乡担任了乐亭县严坨西原高等小学的校长。在这期间，参与了《乐亭县民国志》的编纂工作。此时，石臼坨上的潮音寺建设已基本完工，该寺住持真空大师邀请韩作舟登石臼坨岛，求其为潮音寺内各殿的廊柱书写楹联。时年54岁的韩作舟欣然而往，在潮音寺内住了三天，写完大部楹联之后，还为《乐亭县志》（民国版）写了《醇诚传》。后来，经人介绍，韩作舟去河北省南部的广平县当了一任县长，政声很好，且主持纂修了《广平县志》。

韩作舟由广平解任回乡后，又出任了乐亭"感化院长"，因其在日伪时期担任过县长、"感化院长"，有汉奸之嫌，但他在乱世中保持了自己的民族良知，没有沦为大奸大恶，故在1951年镇反运动中，他只当了个陪绑的角色，被当场释放。

1952年，韩作舟受人民政府聘请，重新审定编纂了民国乐亭县志稿，因他和革命先烈李大钊是永平府中学同学，在县志修订稿中，补写了李大钊出生传记。

14. Liu Zhensheng, the First Disciple of Huo Yuanjia

Huo Yuanjia, a Chinese martial artist, is a household name in China. However, his most famous disciple, Chen Zhen, is only a fictional figure in movies and novels. Historically, Huo had a disciple named Liu Zhensheng, who ever lived in Laoting County and acted as martial arts tutor for General Zhang Xueliang.

Liu Zhensheng (1883-1960), a native of Shandong Province, moved to Laoting's Hexinzhuang Village from Tianjin during the Republic of China period. Despite his short physique, he was skilled at martial arts, particularly *qinggong* (light skill), hence his nickname "Lightning Catcher and Flying Swallow."

Liu Zhensheng was born into a poor family. When he was a child, his father died. As a child, he had to work at a Tianjin factory to support his family. During the period, he got acquainted to Boss Liu, a merchant from Laoting who later became his godfather. Then, Boss Liu recommended him to Huo Yuanjia to learn kung fu. Wandering across the country together with his heroic teacher, Liu won great fame as the "first disciple of Huo Yuanjia."

Once, Huo Yuanjia fell into conflict with some Japanese warriors, who then colluded with the corrupted Qing government to list Huo among the wanted. Then, Liu Zhensheng began to drift together with his teacher in hopes to escape arrestment.

After Huo was murdered, Liu Zhensheng converted into a Buddhist. Today, it is already unknown where he became a monk. Some declared he became a monk at the Faxing Temple in Tianjin's Jixian County, and others believed he converted to Buddhism on Laoting's Puti Island.

His mother tried to find Liu Zhensheng, but failed after searching through such major cities as Shanghai and Tianjin.

In fact, Liu resumed secular life soon and hid in northeastern China, with his real identity concealed. In Shenyang, capital of Liaoning Province, he got to know Du Huilin, a local wealthy man who hired Liu as his bodyguard. However, Liu disliked the extravagant life that the Du family led. Particularly, Du's favorite concubine usually had at least eight courses for breakfast and was rigorous towards her servants. Thus, Liu quitted his job at the Du family.

Because he adored Liu's martial arts and morality, Du Huilin attempted to persuade him to stay by presenting Liu one of his shops for free. However, Liu refused.

After he left the Du family, Liu Zhensheng found the Sanguangmen Martial Arts Club outside the north gate of Shenyang, where he taught students and started an escorting business. Upon the introduction of Du Huilin, General Zhang Zuolin hired Liu as a martial arts tutor. During the period, Zhang Xueliang and Zhang Xuesi, both sons of Zhang Zuolin, ever learned martial arts from Liu Zhensheng. Furthermore, Liu and Zhang Xueliang became intimate friends.

In 1928, Zhang Zuolin died in a blast schemed by Japanese invaders at Huanggutun. This event urged Liu Zhensheng to hate Japanese further. When the 9.18 Incident broke out, Chiang Kai-shek, then generalissimo of China, implemented the policy of "Pacifying the Interior before Resisting Foreign Aggression" and ordered Chinese troops not to fight back. Upon Chiang's order, Zhang Xueliang retreated his troops from northeastern China to Hebei. Liu Zhensheng took the same train with the retreating troops. Discontent with Zhang's nonresistance, Liu jumped off the train at Luanxian County and then went to his godfather in Laoting for shelter. Afterwards, Zhang Xueliang once sent his guards to Laoting to invite Liu back.

At the time, Liu Zhensheng was recommended by his godfather to the Liu Guoliang's family, where he served as a private guard. Later, he brought his mother from Tianjin to live

十四 霍元甲大弟子刘振声

武林中人霍元甲家喻户晓，其弟子陈真历史上并无其人。但是，霍元甲确有一位弟子名叫刘振声，不仅与乐亭菩提岛有缘，而且还曾经当过张学良的武术老师。

刘振声（1883—1960年），原籍山东与河北交界处的景州虎头庄人，民国年间由天津迁居乐亭县何新庄村。因其武艺超群，身材矮小，轻功见长，拳路、手法迅猛快捷，江湖盛称其为"闪电手飞燕子"。

刘振声自幼家贫，早年丧父，为生活计，幼年时家人带领他到天津静海一家工厂当童工。在此期间，结识了乐亭县王道滩人刘姓老板，并认为义父。义父见他身手敏捷，便引领其拜霍元甲为师学武，成为霍元甲的早期弟子，并跟随师傅闯荡江湖多年。从此，江湖上霍元甲大弟子刘振声闻名遐迩。

霍元甲与日本浪人发生矛盾，日本浪人勾结腐败无能的清政府对霍元甲进行迫害。霍元甲受官府追缉后，刘振声随师傅浪迹天涯。

霍元甲遇害后，刘振声悲痛欲绝，曾落发为僧，一说是曾在天津蓟县法兴寺出家，一说是曾在乐亭菩提岛当过和尚，但都无据可考。

家中老母派人到处打听刘振声的下落，但找遍上海、天津等大城市，未见刘振声的踪影。

原来，刘振声出家不久即还世俗，一度隐姓埋名辗转到了东北，在沈阳结识了富豪杜惠林。杜惠林欣赏刘振声人品端正，武艺高强，二人相处极为投缘，遂结为好友。刘振声一度成为杜惠林的私身保镖，兼看家护院。刘振声看不惯杜府花天酒地的奢侈生活，特别是杜惠林小姨太太，一顿早餐得专为她做十样八样饭菜，而且对待下人脾气刁钻泼辣，形同妖妇。刘振声不满杜家家风，执意请辞，离开杜府。

（刘振声女儿刘彩霞提供照片）

杜惠林看重刘振声的精湛武艺和高洁品格，为挽留刘振声，曾让刘振声从他十几处买卖中挑一处商号相赠，以保刘振声的生活来源。尽管杜惠林如此厚爱，用心良苦，却未能动摇刘振声离开杜家的决心。

刘振声离开杜府后，在沈阳北门外开设"三光门武术馆"，教授徒弟，兼设镖局，为人护路保镖。张作霖从杜惠林口中得知刘振声的为人，把刘振声聘进大帅府教授武功多年。在帅府执教期间，张学良、张学思兄弟俩跟随刘振声学习武功。刘振声和少帅张学良相处投契，后来成为要好朋友。

1928年，张作霖在皇姑屯被炸死后，日本人在华更加

together with him.

Since ancient times, martial arts have prevailed in Laoting. After Liu settled in Laoting, locals nominated him and Song San, a chief guard in the Liu family in Shishige Village, as "South Liu and North Song."

Nicknamed "Iron Crotch Song," Song San was a strong, square-faced man with thick whiskers and loud voice. In addition to his extraordinary strength, he was skilled at all sorts of weapons. After he opened a martial arts school in the county seat of Laoting, Song heard Liu Zhensheng was also a famous martial artist. Then, he expected a chance to compete with Liu.

One day, as Liu Zhensheng and his oldest disciple, Yu Jilou, roamed at a local market, they encountered Song San. Before this, Liu had heard that Song wanted to compete with him. However, Liu wasn't willing to fight before the public in fear of uncovering his identity. Deluded by Liu's short physique and ordinary looking, Song insisted on fighting one-to-one. Liu postured to display his modesty, and let Song attack first. Song quickly kicked three times, but Liu neatly stood aside to successfully avoid Song's assault. His acute movements even dazzled Song, who then began to attack with hands. Song's assault with hands didn't work, too. Before Liu counter fought, one of Song's disciples sneaked behind Liu to raid him with a blade. Because it was too late to hide, Liu tightened every muscle of his back to knock away the blade, which was inlaid into a door frame more than ten meters away. "Why did you do so? Didn't we already agree to fight one-to-one?" Liu asked angrily. Ashamed for what his disciple did, Song apologized, "It's my fault, and I lost. See you later." And he walked away. Later, with the help of Xie Enbo, the two became reconciled. Since then, Song had been completed convinced by Liu's accomplishment in martial arts.

The Lu family was a wealthy and influential clan in Laoting's Huangzhuang Village. At the end of the Qing Dynasty, one member of the clan passed the imperial examinations.

Then, the family hired a famous martial artist from Shandong Province, who was nicknamed "Big Feet Zhang," as a private guard. It was said that Zhang was good at fighting, especially kicking techniques, and never lost in combats along the Yellow River in Shandong. Many came to learn kung fu from him after Zhang settled in Huangzhuang.

Just as a Chinese saying goes, "A high tree catches the wind." Soon, the news that Liu Zhensheng won Song San in competition at the county seat was disseminated to Huangzhuang. Then, some of Zhang's disciples went to Hexinzhuang, where they watched Liu's disciples practicing martial arts. "Nothing special," they mocked. "Your master doesn't deserve his reputation."

Liu Zhensheng didn't concern much about their mocking, and admonished his disciples not to retaliate. Ignoring his warning, He Qingrui and his brother, both Liu's students, came to Huangzhuang. Zhang's disciples were practicing kicking techniques as the brothers peeked and mocked their inexperienced skills. Then, Zhang's disciples besieged the brothers, asking for an immediate competition. However, all of them were defeated, and someone then reported to their teacher, Zhang. Irritated by He Qingrui's mock, Zhang fought with him and kicked He away. After he heard the thing, Liu Zhensheng summoned his disciples to the Lu family in Huangzhuang, in hopes of apologized to Zhang.

However, the patriarch of the Lu family misdeemed that Liu Zhensheng came for revenge, and then warned Zhang to deal with the incident carefully. Irritated by the thought that his employer looked down upon him, Zhang swore to beat Liu, or he would disappear forever in Laoting.

At first, Zhang treated Liu with distain. Although Liu explained he came for apology, Zhang persisted in competing with him. Zhang declared he would leave Laoting if he failed, and asked Liu what bet he would take. Liu replied, "I will close my martial arts club and disappear in Laoting if I

猖狂，新仇旧恨，使得刘振声对于日本人的种种无耻行径恨之入骨。"九一八"事变后，蒋介石实行"攘外必先安内"的政策，对日采取不抵抗主义，张学良受其挟制，关东军从东北退守河北，拱手让出东北大好河山。刘振声不满张学良对日本人的妥协态度，随军向关内撤退，走至滦县境内，不辞而别，乘机跳下火车，投奔了乐亭王道滩年迈的义父。之后，张学良曾派手下到过乐亭，邀请刘振声返回少帅身边。

此时，经义父介绍，刘振声已到徐各庄原武状元府李国梁宅第看家护院，并从天津接回了老母和他共同生活。

自古以来，乐亭武风盛行。刘振声来到乐亭县后，一时有"南刘"、"北宋"之盛称。所谓南刘，即刘振声；北宋，即有"京东第一家"称号的乐亭县刘石各庄刘家的护院总管宋三。

宋三，人称铁裆宋，此人生得膀阔腰圆，络腮胡，四方脸，说话大嗓门，力大无穷，谙熟十八般兵器，从小练就金刚童子铁裆。从刘石各庄来城关开设武馆后，声闻人称闪电手飞燕子刘振声进入乐亭，总想找个机会与之过手，一决雌雄。

一日，刘振声带着大徒弟于继楼来到城关赶集，凑巧和宋三撞了个正着。刘振声早有耳闻，宋三正在伺机要与自己交手，隐居乡间的刘振声原本不愿与人过招，以免暴露身份引来事端。宋三见刘振声身材瘦小，相貌平平，依仗自身武艺，大有以强凌弱之势，故意找碴儿要和刘振声交手。刘振声为避免事态扩大，要求事先言明是群打还是单斗。宋三认为战胜刘振声易如反掌，主动提出单个和刘比武。刘振声站立一个门户，叫宋三进招，宋三好不客气，接连就是三腿。刘振声身轻如燕，手如电闪，纵前跃后，如猿猴戏大象，把个铁裆宋三弄得眼花缭乱。宋三见看家本领"追魂取命腿"一招也未能奏效，随即改用八卦连环手，接连出手，却是招

招落空。刘振声找准时机就要进招，宋三的徒弟看师父要吃亏，悄悄转至刘振声背后，手执砍刀，从暗处照准刘振声搂头就是一刀。刘振声觉知背后暗器近身，躲闪不及，遂提起丹田之气，将砍刀磕出，"当"的一声，飞到四五丈远的门框上。刘振声随即跳出圈外，问宋三："君子有言在前，暗处伤人，这是何意？"宋三怒视了一下徒弟，抱歉地说："在下认罪服输，你我后会有期！"说完，羞愧地走出圈外。事后经谢恩博从中说和，二人以礼相见，言归于好。由此宋三对刘振声的武功佩服得五体投地。

乐亭黄庄鲁家为显门大户，清末出过功名人，家称人值，从山东雇来人称飞虎弹腿的武林高手"张大脚"为之看家护院。据说那张大脚，功夫了得，善使飞虎连环腿，在山东打遍黄河两岸无敌手，来到黄庄后，收了不少徒弟，练习武功。

俗言：树大招风。刘振声在城关比武的消息很快传到了黄庄。张大脚得知此消息未动声色，但徒弟们却是跃跃欲试，纷纷来到何新庄偷看练武，看后谮语伤人："什么飞燕子闪电手，一见徒弟便知师父，不过具虚名而已！"

对于黄口小儿狂言伤人，刘振声根本没放在心上，并再三警告徒弟们不许去黄庄观武滋事。

一帮血气方刚的徒弟们那能容得如此侮辱，何庆瑞兄弟二人，一商量偷偷地来到黄庄，见张大脚的徒弟们正在练腿，个个武艺平平，练到高潮处，何庆瑞情不自禁地叫了一声倒好。张大脚的众徒弟立即将何家兄弟围在当中，口出不逊，并要何家兄弟出场过招。双方经过较量，张大脚的徒弟们个个不是何家兄弟的对手。有人将武场发生的事情添油加醋地报告了张大脚。张大脚出门想看个究竟，被不知天高地厚的何庆瑞三言两语激怒，过招后，张连使三腿，把何庆瑞踢出一丈多远。何家兄弟回来后，恐怕师傅责怪，未敢声

lose." Confident about his kicking techniques, Zhang asked whether Liu dared to compete in kicking. "As you wish," Liu answered carelessly. During the competition, three wooden poles that Zhang used to practice martial arts were broken as Zhang kicked them. Then, it was Liu's turn. Five rest wooden poles were leveled as Liu kicked. The following day, Zhang disappeared as he swore.

In fact, Zhang returned his hometown in Shandong, and told his teacher Tan Tianhua what happened to him in Laoting. Upon Zhang's description, Tan concluded the man who defeated his disciple would be his foe when he ran a martial arts club in Shenyang many years ago.

As Liu Zhensheng quitted his job in the Du family and opened the Sanguangmen Martial Arts Club outside the north gate of Shenyang, he became a rival for Tan who then ran security business there. One time, Tan led his disciples to pick a quarrel at Liu's martial arts club, but he was defeated by Liu and fled back to Shandong. In the following three years, Tan dedicated himself to practicing whip skills. Before Tan returned to Shenyang for revenge, Liu had left the city for a long time. Tan didn't figure out his foe's whereabouts until his disciple told him the news. He then sent Zhou Qing, his second disciple, to investigate the truth in Laoting.

A smart person, Zhou Qing was accomplished both literarily and martially. He learned steel whip skills from Tan Tianhua. Though he looked more like a literati, Zhou Qing was noted for his kung fu around Shandong Province. He wormed his way into Liu Zhensheng's club, with a pretext of learning martial arts. Soon, Liu saw through his real intention. Then, Zhou Qing took a chance to assassinate Liu with his steel whip. Before the steel whip fell onto Liu's body, he snatched it. With his bare hands, Liu broke the steel whip into nine pieces and threw them to Zhou Qing, who then fled away with horror.

On the day of Lantern Festival, the wife of Liu Zhensheng dried clothes in their courtyard. At the moment, two strangers who looked similarly black-faced entered. They were Tan Tianhua and Big Feet Zhang.

As soon as they came into his sight, Liu Zhensheng recognized his foe Tan Tianhua. He knew they didn't come for peace. Liu invited them into the living room, where the two guests took seats flanking Liu's. As Liu poured tea for Tan, the latter locked Liu's wrist with his left hand, attempting to break Liu's arm. At the same time, Tan clutched Liu's throat with two fingers of his right hand, while Zhang kicked towards Liu's crotch. At the moment of maximum peril, Liu pushed the two attackers with all strength. As a result, Tan fell down to the ground, and Zhang tumbled and rolled on the ground, with his face seriously injured. Then, Zhang fled out of the living room. Tan stood up and kicked towards Liu. Then, Liu caught Tan's ankle, and threw him into the courtyard.

"Let's go," Tan shouted, and then ran towards the gate together with Zhang. Liu attempted to beat Tan's left arm, but mishit the brick wall beside the gate, leaving a deep hole. Tan and Zhang fled away and never returned to Laoting.

Liu Zhensheng had an intimate relationship with the Chaoyin Temple. Legend goes that he once helped the temple punish villains.

One day, Liu Zhensheng visited the Chaoyin Temple. The abbot led monks to meet Liu at the temple gate, and treated him with tea in the room. As they conversed with each other, a little monk reported Liu Si'er, a local ruffian, was forcing monks in the kitchen to cook pheasants and hares that he hunted on the island. Although the monks explained that Buddhists couldn't kill, but he didn't listen.

The abbot looked depressed and sighed, "What a sin!" Liu Zhensheng then asked, "Master, is there anything I could do for you?" The abbot told Liu how Liu Si'er and other local villains committed all kinds of outrages on the island:

Although an inland resident, Liu Si'er often bullied and oppressed local fishermen. Several days ago, he led some

张。没过几天，这件事就被刘振声知道了。刘振声集合起徒弟们问清事情的经过。为显"三光门"的气度，决定带着徒弟亲自去黄庄鲁府，找张教头赔礼道歉。

刘振声带着何庆瑞兄弟来到了黄庄，鲁家老爷不知刘振声的来意，以为是前来报复，遂找来张大脚当面嘱咐，谨慎处理此事，不可小看飞燕子的不速造访。张大脚以为鲁老爷小瞧自己，当面声称，如果与飞燕子过招不是他的对手，从此不在乐亭见人。

张、刘二人相见，张大脚根本没把刘振声放在眼里，尽管刘振声百般解释来意，张大脚自恃武艺高强，一意孤行，决意要和刘振声过招，并声言自己要是败阵从此离开乐亭，并狂妄地追问刘振声，你如败阵，将作如何处置。刘振声毫不含糊地说，要是输给张大脚，从此摘下"三光门"的牌子，乐亭再没有他刘振声。张大脚自以为他的飞虎连环腿举世无双，主动提出敢不敢和他比试腿功。刘振声毫不在乎地说："悉听尊便。"张大脚运足气力，照定练武的梅花桩"啪、啪、啪"就是三腿，三根碗口粗的梅花桩齐刷刷应声折断。张大脚以挑战的姿态让刘振声进招。刘振声提了提丹田之气，旋身扫地"啪啪"就是几腿，只见练武场上的五根梅花桩全被擦地扫平。比试过后，第二天人们再去找张大脚，早已不知踪影。

张大脚回到山东老家，找到他的老师谭天华，将发生在乐亭的事情诉说一番。他的老师谭天华听后为之一惊，根据张大脚的描述，所说的刘振声不是别人，很可能就是他多年前在沈阳开武馆时的武林仇敌。

那年，刘振声从杜惠林处请辞，到沈阳北门外开设"三光门武术馆"，因抢了谭天华的保镖生意，谭天华领徒弟们来砸刘振声的场子，二人话不投机，当场动武，谭天华被刘振声打得惨败，无颜在沈阳立足，抱愧回到山东老家，决心

精深自身武功。习武三年，练就盖世鞭功，谭天华自觉武艺高强，伺机回到沈阳以雪当年的奇耻大辱。到了沈阳一打听刘振声早已离开沈阳，无奈返回了山东，到处打探刘振声的下落，始终不知刘振声的去向。今日听徒弟张大脚一讲，似觉乐亭的刘振声定是当年沈阳的飞燕子刘。为探听虚实，他派二徒弟周青前往乐亭卧底看个究竟。

谭天华的二徒弟周青，生得白白净净，文武兼备，足智多谋，跟随师父谭天华学成九节钢鞭，看其外貌，活脱脱一介书生，论其鞭法在齐、鲁也算小有名气。他到乐亭后以慕名求师为由住进刘家，时间不长，他的行藏便被刘振声识破。周青卧底败露，利用献艺的机会，舞鞭出毒招想置刘振声于死地。鞭到近身，刘振声闪手将鞭收在手中，用力一搓，鞭环脱落，钢鞭碎成九节，随手掷向周青。周青见状，仓皇逃窜。

春节刚过，转眼到了元宵节。刘振声的夫人正在当院晾晒衣物，忽见从门外进来两个陌生人。前面的那人，身材高大，面貌黝黑；身后那人长相和前边那汉子活似一对双胞胎，来人不是别人，正是周青的师父谭天华和谭的大徒弟张大脚。

谭天华见到刘振声假意寒暄。刘振声见是谭、张不速而至，立即想起在沈阳和谭比武与张大脚在黄庄过招一节。此二公来乐的目的不问自明。刘振声立即提高警惕，刚刚吐出一个"请"字，谭天华和张大脚，径直朝向室内走去。进屋后，三人分宾主坐定，谭天华、张大脚一前一后将刘振声夹在当中。刘振声为客人倒茶，茶杯刚到谭的面前，谭天华左手一把将刘振声的手腕死命钳住不放，妄图将刘振声的胳膊生生掐折，右手钳起二指，照准刘振声的咽喉狠狠就一把。与此同时，张大脚顺势找准部位，狠狠朝刘振声的下裆掏去。刘振声说声"好狠毒"，两臂

villains to the temple on Puti Island. The abbot was forced to treat them with superb accommodation and diets, for which he even purchased rare vegetarian food far from the temple. However, those villains weren't satisfied, but forced monks to cook meat for them.

Guided by a monk, Liu Zhensheng went to the eastern courtyard inhabited by those villains. As soon as he entered the courtyard, Liu heard those villains burst into dirty words. Along with his approach, Liu saw those villains, who were untidily dressed, scolding monks in the kitchen. "The Chaoyin Temple is a sacred Buddhist place. Why are you so angry?" Liu Zhensheng asked politely. "Who're you? It's none of your business!" Liu Si'er shouted.

Although extremely angry at their bad behaviors, Liu Zhensheng didn't want to fight with them at the sacred temple. "Don't you feel shameful for your misconduct?" Liu Zhensheng attempted to persuade. "Bullshit!" A villain shouted and assaulted Liu Zhensheng with a stick. Liu jumped up, and the stick hit a wooden pole used to tie horses. The villain grimaced in pain, and threw away the stick. "What're you waiting for? Just beat him!" The rest villains shouted. Before those villains took further action, Liu Zhensheng kicked the wooden pole, which immediately broke into two pieces. "Anyone who wants to the wooden pole can test me," Liu Zhensheng shouted. Scared by his marvelous kung fu, those villains ran away.

Later, some junior disciples of Huo Yuanjia came to Laoting and asked Liu Zhensheng to return to the Chin Woo Athletic Association in Tianjin. No matter how hard they pleaded, Liu refused.

At the time, Liu Zhensheng already established intimate friendship with local villagers in Hexinzhuang, where he married a local woman. Soon after their marriage, the couple gave birth to a child, and led a peaceful, happy life.

However, his wife died soon, which greatly struck Liu. From then on, the formerly optimistic man became silent and fell into deep sorrow.

To help Liu Zhensheng walk out of the grief, his mother-in-law and other relatives persuaded him to marry his widowed sister-in-law. After their marriage, they gave birth to a daughter, and laughter returned to the family. Liu Zhensheng shook off grief and embraced confidence once again about life.

Historical records reveal that Liu Zhensheng learned martial arts from Huo Yuanjia, and later formed the Yongle Three-Light Boxing by combining essence of other boxing genres. Besides boxing techniques, he was also skilled at fighting with spear, blade, sword, and whip.

攒力向左右一分，只听谭、张二人同声"啊"了一声，再看谭天华早已跌进炕脚，张大脚同时被扔到幔子上。张大脚站立不稳滚下幔子，跌得鼻青脸肿，夺路逃向院子。谭天华从炕脚滚下，跃起弹腿照着刘振声就是一脚，刘振声顺手牵羊，将谭天华扔到院子里。谭天华向着张大脚说声"撤"，谭、张二人夺命逃向大门。刘振声挥掌照定谭天华左臂就是一掌，可惜没能砸中谭天华，"啪"的一声，将大门墙砖深深砸出一个大洞。谭、张逃出大门，从此再也没敢来过乐亭。

刘振声与菩提岛潮音寺多有来往，留下了力断拴马桩艺镇群痞的一段佳话。

一日，刘振声又一次上岛到了潮音寺，寺僧以礼相见并即刻禀报住持。住持听说是刘振声前来，忙率僧众出迎，并将刘振声让至禅房用茶。说话间，沙弥慌忙来报，言说刘四儿等人在斋堂滋事，非要厨僧将他们在岛上狩猎的山鸡野兔做成荤食，百般解释，不依不饶。

住持听罢，满脸愁云，手捻佛珠，连说："阿弥陀佛，罪孽呀，罪孽！"刘振声不知事情究竟，忙问住持："请问住持，不知寺内何事？"住持听罢，长叹一声，这才把刘四儿等海痞横行码头，上岛胡作非为等诸事简要讲述。

刘四儿家居内陆，但常混迹海上鱼肉船民，渔家提起此人恨之入骨。上岛后，住持情知来者不善，便叫人把这伙不速之客敬若上宾，安置在后院精舍，一住数日，连日好饭好菜不说，另派人去内地购买佛家所用的美味珍馐。但这群赖皮非但不知宠辱，反而变本加厉，竟然不顾佛门斋戒，强令开荤，连日来闹得全寺人心惶惶，鸡犬难宁。

刘振声使人引领来到东院。刚一进院就听人声嘈杂，粗话骂詈，不堪入耳。及至近前，见一伙儿俗家人衣冠不整，一个个横眉立目，捋臂挽袖，直向厨僧发威。刘振声进屋后，抱拳问："各位兄弟，潮音寺乃佛门净地，不知何事如此动怒？"刘四儿等人听罢，不屑一顾地说："你是何人？管你屁事？"

面对刘四儿一伙，无事生非，欺凌佛门，刘振声怒火中烧，但想到佛家圣地，只好秉秉性子，劝道："诸位乃地面上人，如此无礼，就不怕世人笑话？""屁话！"一歹徒乘刘不备，手持棍子便伏身向刘振声腿部扫去。刘振声弓身跃起，未能击中，棍子落空"啪"地扫中旁边的拴马桩，只震得那人龇牙咧嘴松缩手将棍子扔在地上。众歹徒一见齐声呐喊："还愣着干什么？上！"没容众歹徒近身，刘振声大声喊道："哪个再敢无礼！"刘振声提起丹田之气，运起腿功"咔"的一声，顺势伸腿将身旁的拴马桩拦腰踢断，并呵斥道："哪个再敢妄为，木桩就是下场！"刘四儿一见，与众歹徒抱头鼠窜地向岛边逃去。

刘振声的行踪被天津"精武馆"的师弟们发觉后，曾来乐亭何新庄，找刘振声回天津"精武馆"支撑武馆门面，刘振声先是拒见，后婉言相辞，尽管师弟们跪地恳求，刘振声主意已决，始终未答应师弟们的请求。

原来，刘振声生性忠厚、刚直、开朗，在何新庄和乡民相处，建立了深厚的感情。在众人的撮合下，和村中一位姓于的姑娘结了婚。婚后，二人情投意合，全家三口从此过着平静而美满的生活。

天不遂人愿，时间不长，年轻的妻子因病猝然谢世。这一打击，对于刘振声无异于晴天霹雳。性格开朗的刘振声一度变得沉默寡言，成天在失落中打发日子。

刘振声的不幸遭遇牵动着各位亲朋的心，在众亲戚和岳母的一再劝说下，终于和寡居的妻弟媳结合。结婚后，爱女小彩霞诞生，给全家带来了欢乐，使刘振声重新振作精神，扬起了人生的风帆。

In Laoting County, Liu Zhensheng recruited dozens of disciples, of which the most famous included Yu Jilou, Yu Chengjie, Yu Chengming, He Qingrui, Cui Caizhang, Liu Xiaojun, He Yubang, Ma Xizhi, Liu Xiaosong, and Chen Shuqi.

Despite an accomplished martial artist, Liu Zhensheng remained extremely modest. After he lived in reclusion, he told little about his identity, martial arts origin, and life experience.

In 1960, Liu Zhensheng died for illness at the age of 77 in Laoting County. Among mementos that he left behind were a blade, a Buddhist bead necklace, and a letter of invitation from Zhang Zuolin.

15. General Luo Ruiqing Inspected Mortar Isle

In November 1964, General Luo Ruiqing, then secretary of the Secretariat of the CPC Central Committee, vice premier of the State Council, general secretary of the Central Military Commission, and chief of general staff of the People's Liberation Army, inspected the No.2 Company of the Tangshan Command Division garrisoning in Laoting County. Without informing local government, he took a car directly from Beijing to the North Harbor. Then, he inspected the defense fortifications in the forest farm on Xiangyun Island, and took a boat to inspect Puti Island.

据史料考评，刘振声师宗霍氏武功，综合各路拳法之妙，吸收武林众家之长，独创"永乐派三光门"。他所创的日、月、星三光拳法，诸如电光化翎拳、盖手拳、争手夺命拳、武祖拳、八面手等，出神入化，威震武林；他的三光本门枪法，诸如六合枪、黑风枪、五龙枪等枪法，以及各种套路的刀法、剑法、鞭法无不达到炉火纯青、出神入化的地步。

在乐亭，会聚他门下的弟子计有于继楼、于成杰、于成明、何庆瑞、崔彩章、刘小俊、何玉邦、马希之、刘小松以及关门弟子陈书琦等知名习武者数十人。

刘振声崇尚武德，谦虚谨慎，对自身武艺从不张扬。隐居后，对于自己的出身、经历和武宗，讳莫如深、守口如瓶。

1960年，刘振声病逝于乐亭，终年77岁。留下的遗物有：宝刀一口、佛珠一串以及张作霖的请帖一封。

十五　罗瑞卿大将巡视石臼坨

1964年11月，中共中央书记处书记、国务院副总理、中央军委秘书长、中国人民解放军总参谋长罗瑞卿大将，到乐亭县视察唐山军分区边防二连。罗瑞卿自带车辆，从京城出发，未经省市部门，直接赴北港码头。在祥云岛林场察看了碉堡工事后，乘船巡视了菩提岛。

Brilliance (the prelude), *Gazing at the Immense Ocean, October in Winter, Different Land*, and *Though the Tortoise Lives Long*. It has been believed that Jieshi Mountain mentioned in Cao's poems was already submerged in the sea, which should be the mountain submerged around today's Puti Island. Hereinafter is one of Cao's poems, *Gazing at the Immense Ocean*.

> Come east of Jieshi Cliff
> I gaze out across the ocean,
> Its rolling waves
> Studded with rocks and islets;
> Dense the trees and bushes here,
> Rank the undergrowth;
> The autumn wind is soughing,
> Huge billows are breaking.
> Sun and moon take their course
> As if risen from the sea;
> The bright galaxy of stars
> Seems sprung from the deep.
> And so, with joy in my heart,
> I hum this song.

II. Poetry and Prose
1. Poetry

(1) Tour to Xiamen [①]

By Cao Cao of the Han Dynasty

Tour to Xiamen, also known as *Tour to Longxi*, is a poetry series in the style of Yuefu Ballads. In 207, In 207, Cao Cao, a powerful warlord in the Three Kingdoms Period (220-265), passed Jieshi Mountain after he defeated Yuan Shao and Wuhuan, where he climbed onto the mountain and outlook the billowy sea. Impressed by the spectacular landscapes, he wrote a poetry series that consisted of five poems, including

① Extracted from No.14 Volume of *Records of Laoting County* (compiled in 1755 during the Qing Dynasty)

第二节 诗词赋序

一 诗词

（一）

步出夏门行①

（汉）曹操

《步出夏门行》为乐府体组诗，又名《陇西行》。曹操建安十二年（207年）北征乌桓亲率大军追歼袁绍残部。五月誓师北伐，七月出卢龙寨，九月班师，途经碣石时，他登山观海，面对洪波，触景生情，写下了这组壮丽的诗篇。全诗描绘了河朔一带的风土景物，抒发了作者的雄心壮志，反映了他踌躇满志、叱咤风云的英雄气概。组诗虽是曹操在戎马倥偬中写成，但统观全篇立意高远，笔力遒劲，气势磅礴，悲凉中带有苍劲之感。

全诗共五首，分别为序曲《艳》及《观沧海》、《冬十月》、《土不同》、《龟虽寿》四篇。据《曹操诗文选读》注释及学校课本教材介绍，碣石山已沉入大海下面，曹操当年所作《观沧海》中之碣石山应是沉入菩提岛一带沿海的碣石山。仅择与碣石有关的《观沧海》篇并加以注释。

> 东临碣石，以观沧海。
>
> 水何澹澹⁽¹⁾，山岛竦峙⁽²⁾。
>
> 树木丛生，百草丰茂。
>
> 秋风萧瑟，洪波⁽³⁾涌起。
>
> 日月之行，若出其中。
>
> 星汉⁽⁴⁾灿烂，若出其里。
>
> 幸⁽⁵⁾甚至哉，歌以咏⁽⁶⁾志⁽⁷⁾。

注释

（1）澹澹：水波涌动的样子。

（2）竦峙：竦通耸，高起。峙：直立。

（3）洪波：大浪。

（4）星汉：银河，也叫天河。

（5）幸：庆幸。

（6）咏：抒发。

（7）幸甚至哉，歌以咏志：每章最后都有以上这两句，是配合全诗加上去的，同正文无关。

译文

东行登上碣石山，观赏大海的景色。宽阔的海水，涌动着碧波，苍茫的碣石山，屹立在大海之中。山上树木丛生，各种花草繁密茂盛。每当飒飒秋风吹来，大海就会掀起惊涛骇浪。天穹的日月星辰，像从浩渺的大海中生出来的一样。哎呀，能看到这样景色真是太幸运了，用诗歌尽情抒发自己的思想感情吧。

①清乾隆二十年（1755年）《乐亭县志》卷十四。

79

(2) Watching the Sea [①]

By Yang Guang, historically known as Emperor Yang of

the Sui Dynasty

Although delighted to watch the blue ocean,

I remain a little disappointed for not seeing the legendary Golden

Terrace.

Rolling waves smash on banks,

While distant islands look blurry in clouds.

Against roaring billows,

Docile seagulls play with humans,

On the shore carpeted with lush trees and bushes.

The scenery is so beautiful,

That I need never travel afar

To admire the famous Gushe Mountain in Linfen.

① Extracted from No.14 Volume of *Records of Laoting County* (compiled

in 1755 during the Qing Dynasty)

（二）望海①

（隋）杨广

碧海虽欣瞩，金台⁽¹⁾空有闻。

远水翻如岸，遥山倒似云。

断涛还共合，连浪或时分。

驯鸥旧可狎⁽²⁾，卉木足为群。

方知小姑射⁽³⁾，谁复语临汾⁽⁴⁾。

注释

（1）金台：战国时期，燕国被齐国打败。燕昭王为了向齐国报仇，广招贤才，为才能平庸的郭隗筑黄金台。于是著名军事家乐毅以及邹衍、剧辛等来到燕国，燕国因而富强，终于打败了齐国。

（2）狎：亲近。

（3）小姑射：《庄子》："藐姑射之山有神人居焉。"山在北海（渤海）中，或许这就是石臼坨。

（4）临汾：今山西临汾有姑射山。

译文

虽然看到了碧蓝的大海感到高兴，但是燕昭王为招贤纳士而筑就的黄金台仅仅听说而没有亲见有些遗憾。在这里远望，海水翻腾，好像已涌到了岸上，而海中缥缈的山峦晃动就像浓云。连绵起伏的海浪时合时分，岸边海鸥温驯善良，与人接近，花草树木繁荣茂盛。我已被小姑射的美景陶醉了，哪还顾得上到临汾去寻求那里的姑射山呢？

①清乾隆二十年（1755年）《乐亭县志》卷十四。

(3) Watching the Sea with Your Majesty [1]

By Yu Mao of the Sui Dynasty

Tide surges up on the ocean.

Afar in clouds and billows,

Emerge ten mythical continents and three legendary islands.

Your Majesty,

Your brilliant poem even dwarfs all poetic classics.

Though lucky to accompany you in watching the sea,

I feel ashamed of my humble contribution to the country.

[1] Extracted from No.14 Volume of *Records of Laoting County* (compiled in 1755 during the Qing Dynasty)

（三） 奉和望海①

（隋）虞茂

清跸[(1)]临溟涨，巨海望滔滔。

十洲[(2)]云霭远，三山[(3)]波浪高。

长澜疑浩日，连岛类奔涛。

神游藐姑射，睿藻[(4)]冠风骚。

徒然随观海，何以效涓毫[(5)]。

注释

（1）清跸：皇帝车驾出行特意清扫道路。

（2）十洲：据《十洲记》（旧说为汉东方朔撰）载，东海中有十座仙山：祖洲、瀛洲、玄洲、炎洲、长洲、元洲、流洲、生洲、凤麟洲、聚窟洲。后又增加了沧海岛、方丈洲、扶桑、蓬丘、昆仑。

（3）三山：东海三仙山，即蓬莱、方丈、瀛洲。因形似壶，故也叫三壶。

（4）睿藻：华美、工巧的辞藻。（恭维皇上的话）

（5）涓毫：涓滴、丝毫，比喻很小或很少。

译文

随皇帝出驾观海，适逢海潮猛涨。瞭望大海，巨浪滔滔，远处是十洲仙山云霭缥缈。三仙山浪涛汹涌，浪花映着日光，仙岛相连，像大浪起伏。圣皇驾游射姑山的诗作华美工巧，胜过诗经楚辞，而我作为臣子，虽有幸随圣驾观海，但对皇帝没有点滴效荣，而深以为憾。

①清乾隆二十年（1755年）《乐亭县志》卷十四。

(4) Watching the Sea on a Spring Day

By Li Shimin, historically known as Emperor Taizong of

the Tang Dynasty

Putting on a robe,

I look afar at the immense ocean.

Lying against the handle of my chariot,

I feel intoxicated in the beautiful spring views.

The running river disappear at the horizon,

As though it flowed to heaven.

Hidden in haze are three legendary islands on the sea,

While spring breeze gently blows.

Piercing through waves,

The sun shines with dazzling light.

Colored clouds confuse wild geese,

Which then fly disorderly.

Despite my humble ambition,

I dare to shoot with bow.

Although with boundaries,

The ocean cannot be measured with a gourd ladle.

Although without a source,

The ocean cannot be emptied with a gourd ladle.

From time to time,

The ocean can turn into mulberry fields.

As Mount Zhifu reminds me of Emperor Wu of the Han,

Mount Jieshi reminds me of the First Qin Emperor.

Not as ambitious as them,

I merely wish a peaceful, harmonious society.

（四） 春日望海^{(1)①}

（唐）李世民

披襟眺沧海，凭轼玩春芳。

积流横地纪，疏派引天潢。

仙气凝三岭⁽²⁾，和风⁽³⁾扇八荒。

拂潮云布色，穿浪日舒光。

照岸花分彩，迷云雁断行。

怀卑⁽⁴⁾运深广，持满守灵长。

有形非易测，无源讵⁽⁵⁾可量。

洪涛经变野，翠岛屡成桑。

之罘思汉帝⁽⁶⁾，碣石想秦皇⁽⁷⁾。

霓裳⁽⁸⁾非本意，端拱⁽⁹⁾且图王⁽¹⁰⁾。

注释

（1）相传唐太宗李世民征高句丽，在石臼坨驻跸十九天，此诗为登岛时所作。

（2）三岭：据说海内有三神山，也叫三山、三岛、三壶，即蓬莱、方丈、瀛洲。

（3）和风：春风。

（4）卑：低下。

（5）讵：岂。

（6）之罘思汉帝：之罘，古齐国海中小岛。秦亡后，汉军虏齐王，齐贵族田横自立为齐王，带五百壮士逃入海岛。刘邦征召田横去洛阳，他带二门客赴召，在距洛阳30里处的驿馆自杀；二门客至洛阳，受到刘邦封赏后也自杀。消息传到海岛，五百壮士全部自杀，汉帝刘邦完成了统一大业。

（7）碣石想秦皇：秦始皇三十二年（前215年），到碣石山，派卢生寻找仙人，求长生不死之药。

（8）霓裳：用虹霓裁剪的裙子。

（9）端拱：垂手不做事，无为而治的意思。

（10）王：王道。我国古代政治哲学中指君主以仁义治天下的政策。

译文

穿上衣服到海边眺望大海，凭靠车轼欣赏美好的春光。遍地积水四溢，流向远方的天潢星。海上三仙山上凝结着仙气。和煦的春风吹向四面八方。朝阳映在海中，连潮水、海云也像上了红色。阳光透过海浪，放射出灿烂的光芒。海岸上的野花色彩绚丽。彩云迷惑了飞雁，以致雁阵行列中断。我个人并不是抱了自己天下称雄的大志，但我的作为也有深远的意义，就像箭上了弦，把弓拉满准备射向猎物。大海固然有一定形态，但是总不能用小瓢测量海水的多少。大海虽然没有源头，但海水岂能舀干！汹涌的大海有几度变成了沃野，翠绿的海岛也多次变成桑田。这时我似乎望见了之罘岛，于是想到了汉高祖灭亡了齐国，完成了大汉王朝统一的伟业，又似乎望见了碣石山，想到了秦始皇派人到海外寻找长生不死药的徒劳。我来这仙岛，不想得到白霓裳，没有汉高祖的雄心大志，更没有秦始皇的痴心妄想，而我所想到的只是努力建立一个无为而治，人民安居乐业的王道社会。

<hr>

① 明朝万历二十七年（1599年）《永平府志》卷九。

(5) A Response to Your Highness's Poem Watching the Sea on a Spring Day [①]

By Yang Shidao, a high-ranking official in the Tang Dynasty

On a spring morning,

I stood by the Bohai Sea,

With my campaign grown off.

What I see quite differs from Lulong and Shushen that I passed,

Which have been separated by the sea.

Against the setting sun,

The ocean merges the sky in distance.

On the immortal islands,

Hornless dragons drag chariots,

And huge tortoises form a bridge to the Dragon Palace.

As the mist thins out on Jieshi Mountain,

One can see wild geese hovering over Zhifu Mountain.

Unlike the Qin and Han emperors

Who came here in search of elixir,

Our king comes for a unification mission.

Our heroic warriors cross the Liao River.

What we desire from immortal abodes

Aren't white feather gowns,

But divine arrows that can help us defend the nation.

[①] Extracted from No.14 Volume of *Records of Laoting County* (compiled in 1755 during the Qing Dynasty)

（五） 奉和⁽¹⁾圣制春日望海^①

（唐）杨师道⁽²⁾

春山临渤海，征旅辍晨装。

回瞰卢龙塞，斜瞻肃慎⁽³⁾乡。

洪波回地轴，孤屿映云光。

落日惊涛上，浮天骇浪长。

仙台⁽⁴⁾隐螭⁽⁵⁾驾，水府泛鼋梁。

碣石朝烟灭，之罘归雁翔。

北巡非汉后⁽⁶⁾，东幸异秦皇⁽⁷⁾。

搴旗羽林客⁽⁸⁾，跋距少年场。

龙击驱辽水，鹏飞出带方⁽⁹⁾。

将举青丘缴⁽¹⁰⁾，安访白霓裳。

注释

（1）奉和：奉，敬辞。和：依照别人诗词的题材（内容）和体裁（形式）做诗词。

（2）杨师道：唐朝人，字景猷，贞观年间做过中书令、吏部尚书。善草隶、工诗。

（3）肃慎：古国名，今属吉林，一部分在俄罗斯境内。

（4）仙台：指神山。

（5）螭（chī）：古代传说中无角的龙。

（6）汉后：汉帝。汉武帝巡海上，曾至碣石。

（7）秦皇：秦始皇二十八年（前219年）东行，上邹峄山，登之罘，立石颂秦德。

（8）羽林客：羽林军，宫廷卫队。

（9）带方：古郡名，在朝鲜半岛。

（10）青丘缴（zhuó）：青丘，神仙住处。缴：系丝绳的箭。

译文

春天到了渤海边，脱下征衣来欣赏海上美景。回顾前此经过的卢龙关塞和肃慎地区，那些地区被大水隔绝，与眼前景物截然不同。孤岛射着云光，夕阳慢慢落入大海。汹涌的惊涛骇浪像是冲向长天。神山上隐藏着螭龙驾的车，无数巨鼋相连成为桥梁直通龙宫。碣石山上的朝烟渐渐幻灭，之罘岛上北归的大雁正在翱翔。我主为国家社稷统一强大而北巡、东幸。这与汉武帝、秦始皇来海上寻不死药不同。我们的队伍是英勇善战的羽林军和在战场上逞英雄的青年。他们飞快地渡过辽河，出征带方。我们只想从神府得到系丝绳的箭，用来保卫国家，访求白霓裳有什么用呢！

①清乾隆二十年（1755年）《乐亭县志》卷十四。

(6) Observing the Sea (Climbing onto Mortar Isle)

By Dugu Ji of the Tang Dynasty

Standing on Bohai Island,

I look towards Xianyang hundreds of miles in the west.

I wonder who could create such a picturesque island,

Which congregates a hundred valleys and boundless currents.

Watching afar, I see heaven and earth merge together at the horizon.

The sun looks so near

As though one could touch the legendary Fusang Tree where the sun rises.

In distance, Penglai Island inhabited by immortals emerges on the sea,

Reminding viewers of the Gold Terrace

Where King Zhao of the Yan recruited talents.

The First Qin Emperor made himself a joke by sending Xu Fu to look for elixir here.

All legends are just fancies, and

What do exist in reality are tide prints left on the piers of coastal stone bridges.

① Extracted from No.14 Volume of *Records of Laoting County* (compiled in 1755 during the Qing Dynasty)

（六）观海（登石臼坨）①

（唐）独孤及[1]

北登渤澥[2]岛，回首秦东门。

谁尸[3]造物功，凿此天池源。

溷洞吞百谷，周流无四垠。

廓然混茫际，望见天地根。

白日自中吐，扶桑[4]如可扪。

超遥蓬莱峰，想像金台存。

秦帝昔经此，登临翼飞翻。

扬旌百神会，望日群山奔。

徐福[5]竟何成，羡门[6]徒空言。

唯见石桥足，千里潮水痕。

注释

（1）独孤及：独孤，复姓。独孤及，唐洛阳人，曾任濠州、舒州刺史。徙常州刺史，谥宪。作品有《毗陵集》。

（2）渤澥：渤海。

（3）尸：空占着位置而不做事。

（4）扶桑：解释有三：一是传说中的神树，是太阳升起的地方。二是海中仙山之一。三是现代称日本为扶桑。

（5）徐福：或作徐市（fú），秦时琅琊方士，始皇时，徐市言海中有三神山，始皇派他带童男童女数千人入海寻仙人求长生不老药，后来他就没有回来。

（6）羡门：古代仙人，字子高，秦始皇东游海上就是去寻找羡门等仙。

译文

北行登上渤海岛，西望咸阳已远在千里之外。渤海岛风景秀丽，人没有创造自然的能力，景自天成，是开辟出了这方天池胜境般景象的根源。它就像一口巨大的山洞无边无际，吞没了上百个山谷。这里天空明朗，能望到天的尽头，甚至可以触摸到太阳升起处的扶桑神树。在这里可以远望蓬莱山，想象燕昭王招揽贤才的黄金台。这里既是神仙集会活动之处，所以秦始皇抱了与别人不同的寻找不死药的目的，派徐福带童男童女来此。这些幻想破灭了，给后人留下了笑柄。唯一真实存在的是当年桥基下留有的水痕。

---

①清乾隆二十年（1755年）《乐亭县志》卷十四，参照《全唐诗》校正。

(7) In Memory of Boyi and Shuqi [1]

By Wang Shipeng of the Song Dynasty

To escape from inhumane reign of King Zhou of the Shang,
Princes Boyi and Shuqi of the Guzhu State hid themselves by the Bohai Sea.
They finally achieved mortal perfection.
Although King Wu of the Zhou didn't adopt their expostulation,
Their loyalty and benevolence passed down over generations.

[1] Extracted from No.14 Volume of *Records of Laoting County* (compiled in 1755 during the Qing Dynasty)

（七）咏史怀夷齐[(1)][①]

（宋）王十朋[(2)]

避纣穷途北海滨，

归来端为有仁人[(3)]。

武王不听车前谏，

饿死西山志亦伸。

注释

（1）夷齐：伯夷、叔齐，商朝孤竹国两个王子，因互让王位而逃离本国，周武王得天下以后又"不食周粟"到首阳山"采薇而食"，最后饿死于此山。

（2）王十朋：宋乐清（今浙江省乐清市）人，字龟龄，号梅溪，官至太子詹事。作品有《梅溪集》。

（3）仁人：道德完美之人。

译文

为了躲避商纣王的残暴统治，孤竹国两个王子伯夷、叔齐互相推让王位而到了渤海之滨，最终二人成了完美之人。周武王姬发虽然没有听从他们劝谏，但他们的忠君爱民思想却得到了充分表现。

①清乾隆二十年（1755年）《乐亭县志》卷十四。

(8) Staying the Night by the Luanhe River [1]

By Nanlan Xingde of the Qing Dynasty

The Yusheng Star still twinkles before the arrival of dawn.

The Ancient Yuyang Road appears desolate in moonlight.

Stars glimmer against the weak hues of morning,

Just like surfs broken upon the sandy beach.

The sound of reed flutes emits from a desolated fort afar,

Provoking sorrow so deep that listeners cannot fall asleep.

Even purple mandarin ducks floating on the water

Become sleepless on the chilly night.

(9) Mortar Isle [1]

By Shi Menglan of the Qing Dynasty

A hub of water transportation,

Mortar Isle sees countless grain and trade ships shuttling around.

Locals cannot subsist on farming on their saline and alkaline fields,

But depend on grain transported from Northeast China. Extracted from No.4

Volume of the Interpretations of the Records of Laoting County

Appendix: A Brief Biology of Shi Menglan

In 1813, Shi Menglan was born at Dagang Village in Laoting County, Zhili Province (today's Hebei Province). His ancestor, Shi Kaiji, settled in Dagang Village during the Ming Dynasty, and the Shi family gradually became one of the four most celebrated and wealthy clans in Laoting. As a child, Shi Menglan was famous for his filial piety, and displayed a strong capacity in learning. In 1840, he passed the provincial-level imperial examination, and the emperor granted him a plaque with inscriptions meaning "Literary Champion." He attended five national imperial examinations, but all failed. Later, some officials recommended Shi Menglan to the post of magistrate of Chaocheng County, Shandong Province. But, Shi Menglan refused under the pretext of taking care of his mother.

Later, upon the invitation of Zeng Guopan, governor of

（八）菩萨蛮[(1)]·宿滦河[①]

（清）纳兰性德[(2)]

玉绳[(3)]斜转疑清晓，凄凄白月渔阳[(4)]道。

星影漾寒沙，微茫织浪花。

金笳[(5)]鸣故垒，唤起人难睡。

无数紫鸳鸯，共嫌今夜凉。

注释

（1）菩萨蛮：词牌名。

（2）纳兰性德：满洲正黄旗人，原名成德，字容若。康熙进士，官侍卫。善书能诗。作品有《饮水诗词集》、《通志堂经解》等。相传，他曾陪侍康熙皇帝到乐亭菩提岛和狼窝口一带巡视。

（3）玉绳：星名，共两星，在玉衡（北斗第五星）之北。

（4）渔阳：古郡名，唐渔阳郡在今蓟县、平谷一带。

（5）笳：胡笳，古代北方民族的一种类似笛子的乐器。

译文

玉绳星在天上运转，时间正到了清晨。凄冷的月光照着渔阳古道。寒沙上，星光荡漾在黎明前的熹微中，就像细碎的浪花。古代营垒上有人吹起了胡笳，那哀伤的旋律搅得人难以入睡。只有那些紫鸳鸯苦熬这漫长的寒夜。

①中华书局《饮水词笺校》。

邑人史梦兰诗

粮艘商舶聚丛丛

十九坨前水路通

丰歉、全家温饱仗关东

行囊无须问

Zhili Province, Shi Menglan became the "most celebrated lecturer" at Baoding Lianchi Academy. Soon, he quitted the job since he disliked the longstanding corruption in officialdom. He bought a piece of land at the foot of the Cuiping Mountain in Changli, and built the Zhiyuan Villa. After that, he spent the rest of his life on academic research in the villa. He devoted diligent efforts to writing monographs in various fields, ranging from literature, art, history, geography, folklore, and regional documents. His poems are "lyric masterpieces with unconfined freedom and realistic meaning." Shi Menglan was particularly good at writing folklores, and some historians once praised that his literatures showed "great concern about justice and morality." His works are of great artistic and historic value. Because of his unparalleled accomplishment in literature, Shi Menglan was dubbed "No.1 Scholar in Eastern Capital" and "Unrivaled Scholar in Zhili." His monographs include Commentary to the Analects, Study of Strange Clanships, Popular Ballads of Ancient and Modern Times, Supplementary to Old and Modern Sayings, Erer Library, History of Poetry of Four Dynasties, etc.

Throughout his life, Shi Menglan

stored up at least 300,000 volumes of books. In his Newsletter of Laoting, Li Dazhao, a revolutionary forerunner in China, praised that Shi Menglan was "knowledgeable and collected countless books."

Despite his reclusion, Shi Menglan concerned much about the fate of his motherland. During the Second Opium War, when the Anglo-French Allied Forced invaded Beijing and Tianjin, Sengge Rinchen, a chancellor of the Qing government, recruited militias in eastern Hebei Province to reinforce coastal defense forces. Hearing the news, Shi Menglan called on locals to join the army together with him. Due to his remarkable contribution, the Qing government granted him a fifth-grade official title.

In 1890, in view of Shi's literary and academic accomplishment and morality, Zhou Derun, education supervisor of Zhili Province, asked Emperor Guangxu to grant Shi Menglan a fourth-grade official title. In 1898, Xu Lifu, another education supervisor, advised the emperor to appoint Shi Menglan as headmaster of the Imperial Academy. The same year, Shi Menglan died in Zhiyuan Villa at the age of 85. Then, he was buried in the Capital Memorial Temple for Saints.

Shi Menglan left behind family precepts that read "Being frugal not for saving money but fortune; Being diligent just for asking nothing from others," with which he warned his descendants be frugal and virtuous. Shi Menglan had three sons. The oldest son, Shi Lütai, once acted as vice minister of civil affairs; The second son, Shi Lüsheng, passed the provincial-level imperial examination and was appointed as secretary of the Cabinet; The third son, Shi Lüji, passed the national imperial examination and consecutively acted as chief secretary of the Justice Ministry and supervisor of Liaoshen Route. A forerunner in China's modern industry, he once acted as general manager of Beijing Electric Lamp Company and head of Chinese delegation to Panama World Expo.

（九） 石臼坨[1]

（清）史梦兰

精艘商舶聚丛丛，十九坨前水路通。

斥卤[1]无须问丰歉，全家温饱仗关东。

注释

（1）斥卤：可煮盐而不能耕种之地。东方谓之斥，西方谓之卤。

附：史梦兰小传

史梦兰，字香崖，号砚农。清嘉庆十八年（1813年）生于直隶省（今河北省）乐亭县大港村。史家先人史开基于明万历年间，迁徙乐亭大港村落户，为乐亭当地名门富户四大家族之一。史梦兰，性至孝，自幼聪敏好学，无书不通，世人赞之："品端学粹，为世通儒。"

道光二十年（1840年）乡试得中举人，御赠竖匾，被敕之"文奎"，五次春闱未第，后朝廷以史馆誊录议叙选授山东朝城县知县，史梦兰以孝母为由，坚辞不就。

史梦兰应直隶总督曾国藩邀请，曾赴保定莲池书院讲学，在院期间属梦兰"最为出名"。不久，史梦兰因看不惯官场积弊，坚辞回乡，从昌黎碣石山的翠屏山麓购地一方，建成"止园"别墅。由此，史梦兰倾心治学，把毕生的精力投入了文学事业，他的后半生，就是在"止园"度过的。他奋进勤勉，敦行不怠，一生著述汗牛充栋。其内容涵盖文学、艺术、历史、地理、民俗、训诂、方志诸方面。纵观其著作，构合汉宋，博采古今诸名家之说；趋向宋儒，专言义理，旁参互征，不拘学派，表扬先哲，奖掖后进。"其为诗抒写性灵，不事雕琢……然非系世道人心而周于用者，不苟为也。"尤擅长乡野典故的撰写。前人评史香崖的著作："义理公私之辨，均关世道人心。"他的作品有着很强的艺术性和较高的参考价值。世人赞誉他的才华和造诣，冠以"京东第一才子"、"直隶一人"之美称。其著述计有《论语翼注》2卷，《叠雅》13卷，《史昉》8卷，《氏族考异》4卷，《舆地韵编》200卷，《全史宫词》20卷，《古今风谣》1卷，《古今风谣拾遗》6卷，《古今

译文

无数运粮船和商船聚在一起，石臼坨码头水路四通八达。盐碱地种粮，即使丰年也收获无几，全家温饱只能靠商船从关东运输过来的粮食。

谚拾遗》6卷，《异号类编》20卷，《尔尔书屋》1卷，《尔尔书屋诗草》8卷，《尔尔书屋文抄》2卷，另有《永平诗存》、《永平诗存续编》、《四朝诗史》、《畿府艺文考》等广传于世。

梦兰毕生重视图书购集，生前藏书不下30万卷。革命先驱李大钊在《乐亭通讯》一文中盛赞史梦兰："学识渊博，藏书最富，闻有《图书集成》一部。先生殁后，此物辗转易人。"

史梦兰虽然隐身世外，著书立说，以孝母教子为乐，但对民族荣辱、国家兴亡却时刻记挂在心。第二次鸦片战争期间，英法联军进犯京津，清廷派大臣僧格林沁在冀东一带招募乡勇团练，以加强沿海地区的防御力量。深明大义的史梦兰，闻讯后积极组织动员民众并亲自参加。因功绩显著，清廷褒奖史梦兰五品衔。

鉴于史梦兰的才学、人品及其在学术上的造诣与贡献，清光绪十六年（1890年），直隶学使周德润上奏光绪皇帝，加史四品卿衔。光绪二十四年（1898年），学使徐澧复再奏光绪帝，加封为国子监祭酒。同年，卒于"止园"，终年85岁，葬入畿辅先哲祠。

史梦兰以传世家训"惜衾惜衣非谓惜财缘惜福，求名求利但须求己莫求人"严律后人，后世子孙多能勤俭持家，洁身自好。史梦兰有子三人：长子史履泰，字安溪，廪贡生，户部员外郎；次子史履升，字旭东，光绪乙亥举人，内阁中书；三子史履晋，字康侯，光绪庚寅科进士，改刑部主事，累官辽沈道监察御史。后对于中国实业开发颇有建树，首任北京电灯公司总经办，在巴拿马曾主持过国际博览会。

---

① 《乐亭县志稿译编》卷四。

(10) Mortar Isle [1]

By Yang Zaiwen of the Qing Dynasty

My longtime dream hasn't comes true until today

When I mounted onto Mortar Isle.

White sands glimmer like snows in sunshine,

While surfs resound like thunder in sunny days.

Trade boats come and go, and

Fishermen cast nets.

Here, utopia already presents itself.

Why do we waste time seeking the fanciful Penglai Island?

Appendix: A Brief Biography of Yang Zaiwen

Yang Zaiwen, whose birth and death dates were unknown, was a native of Xinzhai Village, Laoting County. As a child, he showed a strong capacity in learning. At the age of 20, he passed the county-level imperial examination. Then, he was admitted into the Imperial Academy. He was a sensitive person, and suffered epilepsy since he was young. Later, he was appointed education supervisor of Xingtai County. He mourned so much for the death of his mother, which caused an outbreak of his former illness. Soon, he died in Xingtai County. Among the books he wrote is Poetry Collection of Chujing Thatched Cottage.

[1] Extracted from No.4 Volume of the Interpretations of the *Records of Laoting County*

（十）石臼坨[1]

（清）杨在汶

几载探奇兴，今偿素愿来。

旷沙明集雪，晴日走奔雷。

估客帆樯集，渔人网罟开。

仙源真世外，何必觅蓬莱。

译文

几年来一直想到石臼坨观赏奇景，今天才得偿夙愿。沙滩在阳光照耀下清白如雪，涛声轰鸣，像万里晴空上响着惊雷。商船云集，渔网撒开。这里简直就是一个世外桃源，何必再去寻找什么蓬莱仙境呢！

附：杨在汶小传

杨在汶，字鲁田，生卒年月不详，乐亭新寨人。天性机警，读书善悟自通，20岁补为县庠生，初应京兆试，得入取国子监太学俊秀（生员）。在汶少年清秀，风流自赏，体质素弱，且有痼疾。后以大挑二等，选授邢台训导，任未满即遭母丧，深切哀痛，使宿疾复发，逝于邢台任上。著有《锄经草堂诗草》一部。

[1]《乐亭县志稿译编》卷四。

商邱宋荦诗

沃焦秋更热，喷薄下滦河，眺望蛟龙窟，微茫十

九阮，地邻榆塞近，人说钓台多，侍侧中男在，双江

俟旧歌

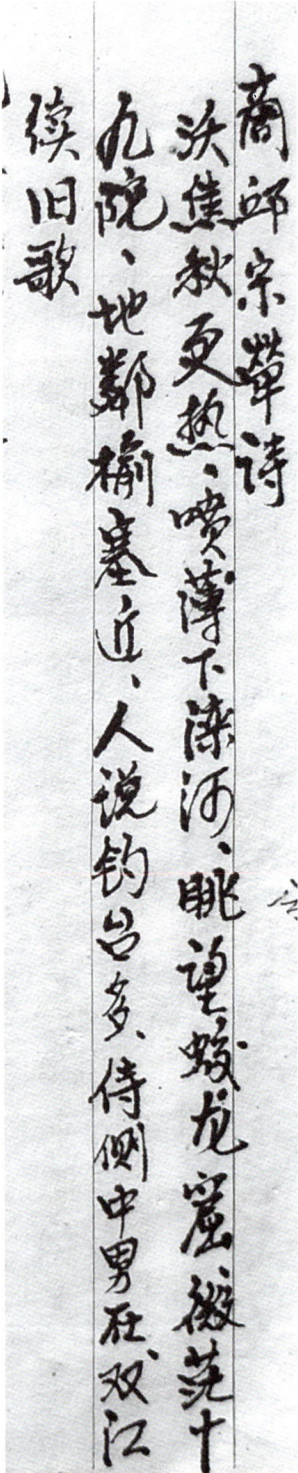

(11) Mortar Isle [1]

By Song Luo of the Qing Dynasty

The weather in Wojiao becomes even hotter with the arrival of autumn.

Against the scorching waves,

We boated downstream along the Luanhe River.

As we approached the coast,

A den of hornless dragons came into our field of vision.

Mortar Isle hid itself in mist.

I love this place not only for its frontier location,

But also because it offers an ideal place for angling.

Delighted to have my son aside,

I write this poem to honor this tour.

[1] Extracted from No.4 Volume of the Interpretations of the *Records of Laoting County*

（十一）石臼坨①

（清）宋荦[1]

沃焦[2]秋更热，喷薄下滦河。

眺望蛟龙窟，微茫石臼坨。

地邻[3]榆塞[4]近，人说[5]钓台多。

侍侧中男[6]在，双江续旧歌。

注释

（1）宋荦（luò）：清商丘人，字牧仲，号漫堂，又号西陂，为官累石，擢江苏巡抚，吏部尚书加太子少师。精鉴藏善画，诗与王士祯齐名。

（2）沃焦：山名，在东海南三万里。《玄中记》曰：天下之大者，东海之沃焦焉，水灌之而不已。这里可能指乐亭沿海。

（3）邻：应为怜（怜）爱。

（4）榆塞：边塞。《汉书》累石为城，树榆为塞。

（5）说："悦"的假借字。

（6）中男：次子。

译文

沃焦这个地方一到秋天天气就更加炎热。我们正是在这热气喷薄之下乘船驶向滦河下游。到了海边，能眺望到蛟龙的窟穴。在缥缈的雾气中，看见了石臼坨。我很热爱这个地方，因为它临近边塞，同时还因为这里有很多地方可以作为钓台尽情垂钓。令人惬意的是我的次子陪伴在身边。因而我写诗记下了这次游览的兴致。

① 《乐亭县志稿译编》卷四。

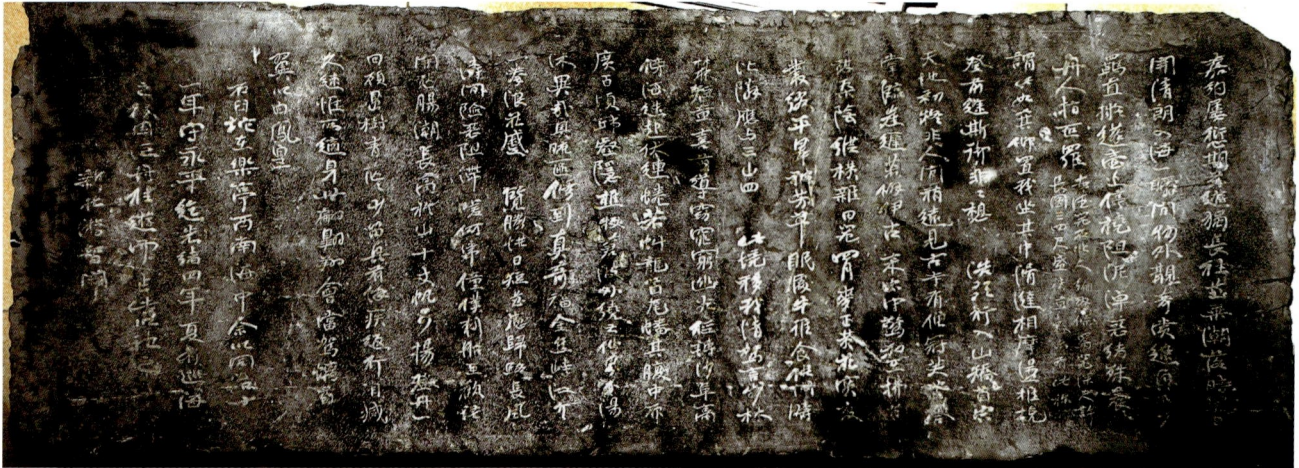

(12) A Travel to Mortar Isle

By You Zhikai of the Qing Dynasty

I had long planned to travel Mortar Isle with my friends. However, the tour was prolonged time and time again until I traveled alone on a sunny day when the tide retreated. As soon as I reached the coast, the marvelous sea views excited me. Then, I took a ferry towards Mortar Isle. Unfortunately, the ferry ran aground in muddy seabed. At the moment, the boatman pointed at a massive wine container that resembled an upturned dustbin and said it might carry us across the sea. Sitting in the container, we glided on the surface of the slippery mud. Though we found it difficult to stand steadily as the container shambled on the muddy surface, the special means of transport still amused us.

Disembarked on the island, I wandered around while singing all the way. The cloudless sky looked boundless, and the tranquil and picturesque landscapes made me misdeem I was on the fairyland. Not afar, an ancient temple emerged on the hilltop, from which monks wearing lotus crowns crept down, each holding their hands together. I had never visited the desolate island before. Everything was new to me. I touched mosses on the ground, and took rest under the shade of a mulberry tree, beside which were disorderly placed farming tools. In April, the wheat matured with golden color, with their ears swaying in the breeze. On overgrowing lawns, cattle replete with grass slept with satisfaction. Local residents introduced me to famous scenic spots on the island, which was as beautiful as the legendary islands of Fanghu, Penglai, and Yingzhou.

Delighted at the island's picturesque landscape, I roamed

（十二） 游石臼坨①

（清）游智开[1]

嘉约屡愆[2]期，兹游独长往。兼乘潮落时，风日开清朗。入海一瞬间，尘外觏[3]奇赏。逸兴不可羁，直拟蓬壶[4]上。停桡阻泥淖，恶绪殊养养。舟人指巨罗（本饮器名。北人编桑条为器，深尺许，长圆三四尺，盛诸杂物，亦有此称），谓此如箕仰。置我坐其中，滑汰[5]相磨荡。推挽登前途，斯御非非想。

浩歌行入山，矫[6]首空天地。初疑非人间，稍远见古寺。有僧冠芙蓉[7]，合掌临岩迟。荒僻伊古来，太守惊初至。拂苔憩桑阴，纵横杂田器。四月麦正黄，花实复丛缀。平皋被芳草，眠处牛谁食。借问畴比邻，应与三山四[8]。

此境移我情，驾言[9]步林麓。短童[10]喜前导，窈窕[11]穷幽谷。径转沙阜高，傍海迭起伏。连蜷[12]若虬[13]龙，首尾蟠[14]其腹。中原广百顷，邱墅隐樵牧。苍波外绕之，仙境分汤沐[15]。异哉奥[16]旷区，修到真仙福。金焦[17]峙江介[18]，一拳浪花蹙。

览胜惧日短，兼虑归路长。洪涛间险恶，阻滞嗟何常。僮仆刺船至，欢语开愁肠。潮长高于山，十丈帆可扬。登舟一回顾，岛树青茫茫。少留兴有余，疾返行自藏[19]。久速惟所适，身似翩翱翔。会当驾螭[20]首，翼以白凤凰。

注释

（1）游智开（1816—1899年），字子代，湖南新化人，成丰元年（1851年）举人。清同治十一年（1872年）至光绪四年（1878年）任永平知府，在此期间曾游览石臼坨并留下诗赋。

（2）愆（qiān）：错过，耽误。

（3）觏（gòu）：遇见，看见。

（4）蓬壶：传说海中的蓬莱、方壶仙山。

（5）滑汰（tà）：因泥泞而步行不稳。

（6）矫：抬起。

（7）芙蓉：指和尚戴的莲花冠。

（8）三山四：把石臼坨岛比喻为方壶、蓬莱、瀛洲三山之外的第四座仙山。

（9）驾言：传说。

（10）短童：未成年的孩子。

（11）窈窕：在此指深远貌。

（12）蜷：身体弯曲。

（13）虬：传说中一种有角的龙。

（14）蟠：盘曲卷伏。

（15）汤沐：沐浴。

（16）奥：深远隐蔽。

（17）金焦（蕉）：酒杯。喻石臼坨形似酒杯。

（18）江介：江畔。

（19）藏：通"藏"。

（20）螭：传说中一种没角的龙。

①本文录自乐亭文物管理所收藏游智开手书碑文。

on the forested hillside while my companions told me local folklores. Several children scampered ahead of us. Intoxicated in the aimless stroll, I didn't notice that we had crossed one and another secluded valleys. Sand dunes rolled up and down along the coast, which resembled a coiling dragon. On the vast plain in the heart of the island grew a hundred hectares of mulberry trees. When sea breeze gently skated over lush forests and grass, woodchoppers working the forests and cattle grazing on the prairie emerged from time to time. Deep blue waves flapped onto the rocky banks. What a marvelous island, just like an abode for immortals! It must a great fortunate for one to dedicate to coenobitism and seek immortality in such a remote, tranquil place. Standing on Mortar Isle, I tried to strike surfs with my hands when they flapped onto the banks to create heaps of vapor. Time flew by when I intoxicated myself in the beautiful scenery. Its remoteness from mainland, as well as fluky weathers and dangerous billows on the sea, often caused tourists stranded on the island. As I worried about my return trip, my attendants piloted a big ship to pick up me. Everyone burst into happy laughter when we finally met on the island. With a 30-meter-tall mast, our ship with could withstand surging billows as massive as hills. As we sailed out, we looked back up the island, on which a blurry figure of an old temple was hidden amidst lush trees. The excitement for traveling on the island still ran through my mind. Our ship galloped on the sea, and we hid in the cabin to avoid strong winds. The ship sailed so fast that I felt as if I flew above the boundless ocean. If I had another to sail on the sea, I would stand on the forehead of the dragon ship, just like a white phoenix flying freely on the sky.

You Zhikai (1816-1899), a native of Xinhua County, Hunan Province, passed the provincial-level imperial examination in 1851 and acted as governor of Yongping Prefecture from 1872 to 1878. He once visited Mortar Isle and left behind some poems.

① From stele inscriptions by You Zhikai in the collection of Laoting Cultural Heritage Office

译文

约好友去参观石臼坨，一次又一次地改变计划迁延时日，趁着大海落潮风和日丽的大好时机，自己决意作这次长途旅行。刚一进入大海，就遇见了新奇的景象。抑制不住自己放纵的游兴，驾起一叶轻舟直奔石臼坨。小船搁浅停在泥淖之中，愁绪袭人。驶船人指着一具筐箩说，这种器具就像是一个仰面朝上的簸箕，坐上去好极了。他们让我坐在其中，顺着泥泞光滑的水路，左摇右晃让人难以站稳脚跟，就这样连推带搡地向前行进，驾着这样的水上运输工具上岛，令人不由遐想联翩。

一路引吭高歌走进海岛，抬头仰望天空一望无际。使人像置身桃源仙境之中。不远的地方，建有一座古寺院。戴着莲花佛冠的和尚们，双手合十缓步走下山崖。这一偏僻荒凉的岛屿，从来没有到过，今天初次到这儿，处处令人新奇。用手抚开地上的藓类植物，坐在桑荫下稍事休息，在树旁横三竖四地摆放着不少农具。初夏四月，小麦泛着一片金黄，扬花结实的麦穗密密实实地随风摇曳。地面高低起伏，到处长满了青草，吃饱了青草的牛卧在地上甜睡着。向岛上的同乡们问过石臼坨的名胜景观之后，使人觉得这里就是幻境中的方壶、蓬莱、瀛洲之外的第四座仙山。

这里的景色令人感到心旷神怡，处处新奇，兴致使然，大家讲着传说故事走在林荫旁的山坡下。未成年的孩子们又跳又蹦地在前边引路，穿过一处又一处深远幽暗的谷地。路旁高高低低的沙丘起伏层叠紧依海岸，酷似一条头尾盘卷腹部的长龙。宽敞坦阔的海岛中部拓有桑田百顷，丘陵沟渠纵横，海风吹拂着茂密的草木，打柴的樵夫与放牧的牛羊隐蔽其间，时隐时现。深蓝色的大海波涛起伏紧围岛外，来到这里就像置身神仙盥洗梳妆的地方，好一个开阔深邃、神奇的地方啊！在这深远隐蔽的所在修行而成仙得道真是幸福啊！看着耸立在海边儿的石臼坨，不由自主地用拳击水，飞溅的浪花在水面上掀起一层层波纹。游览名胜总嫌时间不够用，再者是顾虑到归途的路程遥远，加之海上天气变化无常，大海惊涛险象环生，游人被阻海上那可是平平常常的事儿啊！正当愁绪扰人之际，书童和随从驾船而至，海岛相聚，大家笑逐颜开。沧海涨满潮水，汹涌澎湃的海浪像小山似的，十丈高樯的大船可扬帆远航了。登上轻舟，身行大海，回头一望，那岛上的黯然树木、寺院依稀可见。站在船头，眷恋地看了片刻仍是余兴盎然。由于船乘风势急驶大海，只好忍性躲进船舱隐藏身形。但在长时间快速前进的船内置身，自己仿佛生双翅膀，翩然飞翔在万里海疆。是啊！如有机会再次泛舟海上，我一定要驾驭在船前的龙头上，让自己像一只生有翅膀的白色凤凰那样自由自在地飞翔在海天。

2. Odes and Prologues

(1) Ode to Mortar Isle [1]

By Huang Yi of the Qing Dynasty

The ancient Haiyang County nestled deep in the heart of Jieshi Mountain by the Bohai Sea. In the astrocompass, Mortar Isle corresponds with the Green Dragon Constellation in the eastern hemisphere of the celestial globe. Embraced by the Bohai Sea, Mortar Isle is dozens of miles away from the mainland. Despite its desolation, it is a well-known sandy island far and near. The island resembles a stone mortar used to pound paddy rice, hence its name.

The seawater around Mortar Isle varies with the change of seasons, and even differs in different times of a single day. Billows surge up in autumn, while the waves turn gentler in springtime. The seawater becomes deep green in the moonlight, and glistens with red luster at sunrise. Big trade ships and small fishing boats shuttle on the sea, while magnificent halls and temples stand on the island. The spring water on the island tastes pleasantly sweet and cool, and local residents led simple lives and always displayed hospitality to visitors. There are relics left behind the ambitious Emperor Wu of the Han Dynasty, as well as legends of helmets and immortals. No words are enough to describe Mortar Isle's beautiful natural scenery and splendid cultural sights.

Lucky tourists may occasionally observe a fanciful mirage: The Dragon Palace glistens below the waves, while underwater residents gather pearls and gems. Colorful peaks tower amidst rippling waves, and dragons and sea snakes wander amidst coral trees. At the moment, Xi He, goddess of the sun, slowed her chariot that carries the sun, and Poseidon emerged with a gale of hurricane, along with all kinds of fish and shrimp spitting foams. Soon, the mirage transported by several hornless dragons sank in the sea.

As the sun crept in and darkness fell, the sky became cloudless, wild geese rested in reedy shoals, and folk songs emitted from fishing boats returning with harvest. Smoke from the kitchens of local households curled upwards, with the setting sun and desolate hills as the backdrop. Chime bells in temples sounded melodic but mournful, generating a sense of grief that made hornless dragons sink into the sea. A gale of hurricane swept across the graveyard, awakening the spirits of the deceased. The daytime and night views of Mortar Isle fairly differed. Perhaps many who never visited the island wouldn't believe what I said.

At dawn, the well platform got wet due to morning dew. Coastal land emerged when the tide retreated, leaving one and another ditches sculpted by waves on the beach. Then, I piloted a boat to fish on the sea. Anchoring in a secluded bay, I cast the net and luckily gained a good harvest, including weavers, oysters, crabs, and other marine species. Particularly, indigenous crabs feature milky meat and golden eggs. Salmon, octopus, clam, and spiral shell are also delicious food. In fact, the seafood that is supplied as "rare product" for wealthy urban families is fairly common on Mortar Isle. Although visitors will spread the fame of the beautiful Mortar, it still gains only a few opportunities for development due to its remoteness.

Nestling on the remote eastern coast, the beautiful island is rarely found in national geographic documents. In the past, only a few saints ever visited it. Historical records of the Liao and Jin dynasties reveal that warships ever cruised on the sea nearby the island, and fierce wars broke out there. Nowadays, the island has shaken off the shadow of warfare and resurrected with vibrant vigor with the arrival of spring. The beautiful legends about the picturesque island still remind people of our ancestors who ever visited here.

[1] Extracted from *Records of Laoting County* compiled by Hang Xiangting, a native of the county

二　赋序

（一）石臼坨赋①

（清）黄俏

维海阳⁽¹⁾之废县，为渤碣之奥区⁽²⁾。星戴箕尾⁽³⁾之度，野分析木⁽⁴⁾之隅。出镇海之郊门，距三舍⁽⁵⁾而有余。敞平原之百顷，环沧海以为居。地虽废壤，境实名墟。惟象形而若臼，乃肖像而名诸⁽⁶⁾。

秋涛汹汹，春水溶溶。夜月沉碧⁽⁷⁾，朝曦⁽⁸⁾浴红。贾舶渔舠⁽⁹⁾，出没乎其外；琳宫梵宇⁽¹⁰⁾，罗列乎其中。泉既甘而觉爽，村亦古而堪风。汉武雄心兮，寄遗踪于缥缈；羡门高蹈兮，传佳话于空濛。论白坨之胜概，靡笔舌而能穷⁽¹¹⁾。

若乃丽景乍开，波光甫⁽¹²⁾动，骊空⁽¹³⁾辉生，鲛人⁽¹⁴⁾采贡。縠文⁽¹⁵⁾叠处，矗彩巘⁽¹⁶⁾于洪涛，树影纷时，走龙蛇于颎洞⁽¹⁷⁾。由是羲辔⁽¹⁸⁾舒，飙轮运，海若⁽¹⁹⁾藏，天吴⁽²⁰⁾遁。鱼虾千种，喷沫争奇；蛟蜃百灵，潜逃效顺。

迨⁽²¹⁾至崦嵫⁽²²⁾日挂，海峤云收，雁栖苇泽，渔唱葭洲⁽²³⁾。十里平沙，半途青草，数家烟火，残照荒丘。梵磬⁽²⁴⁾悠扬兮，咽潜龙于海底；飘风震荡兮，出魑魅⁽²⁵⁾于陇头⁽²⁶⁾。斯又晦明风景之不同，举而绘之，悉海上之谬悠⁽²⁷⁾。

至若露濡银井，潮退江皋⁽²⁸⁾，临三岔之浅濑，驾一叶之轻舠。舟藏绝港⁽²⁹⁾，网撒长涛。长鲈兮得细鳞之美，子鱼兮美通印之褒。锼⁽³⁰⁾深房之牡蛎，持郭索⁽³¹⁾之巨螯。香凝石乳，腹满金膏。文鱼石拒，海蜇香螺，论白坨之土产，实珍异之为多。贡都门之豪贵，悉此地之余波。嗟嗟，地以人而显，亦以时而韬⁽³²⁾。瞰⁽³³⁾兹胜壤，僻在东皋，职方⁽³⁴⁾之所不载，圣哲之所罕遭。访辽金之故事，驾楼橹于层涛。虽宿兵于徼外⁽³⁵⁾，每辐辏而争鏖⁽³⁶⁾。春或有脚，地已不毛⁽³⁷⁾。寄传闻于胜岛，徒吊古兮空劳。

注释

（1）海阳：汉朝设置海阳县，包括今乐亭县。

（2）奥区：腹地。

（3）箕尾：天上星宿中的箕宿和尾宿各有两星。

（4）析木：在箕宿尾宿之间的星座为析木。古代帝王分诸侯国与天上星宿相对应，与燕相对应的是析木星座。乐亭与石白坨处在燕国境内。

（5）三舍：古代三十里叫一舍，三舍即九十里。

（6）诸：在这里相当于"之"。

（7）沉碧：深绿色。

（8）曦：阳光。

（9）渔舠：捕鱼的小船。

（10）梵宇：僧寺。梵，常称有关佛教的事物。

（11）穷：（说）尽。

（12）甫：刚。

（13）骊空：龙宫。骊，黑龙称骊龙，简称骊。

（14）鲛人：《述异记》：水居为鱼，眼泣则成珠。

（15）縠（hú）文：一种有皱纹的纱。文，通"纹"。

（16）巘（yǎn）：小山。

（17）颎洞：连绵，飞舞。

（18）羲辔：羲和所执笼头和缰绳。羲和为为太阳神驾车的人。

（19）海若：海神。

（20）天吴：水神水伯。《山海经》云：朝阳之谷有神曰天吴，是为水伯，八面八首八尾。

（21）迨：等到。

（22）崦嵫：日落处。

（23）葭洲：长着芦苇的小岛。

（24）磬：寺庙里常用的打击乐器，多为生铁铸就。

（25）魅：鬼怪。

①全文录自韩湘亭总纂《乐亭县志稿》。

Appendix: A Brief Biography of Huang Yi

Huang Yi (1723-1785), a native of Houguan County, Fujian Province, passed the provincial-level imperial examination in 1753, and then became a professor at Haidong Academy. Upon the invitation of Luo Siming and Yu Wenyi, governors of Taiwan, Huang Yi presided over the compilation of *Records of Taiwan* and annals of other Taiwanese regions. Before long, Records of Taiwan and annals of Zhuluo and Penghua were completed. Afterwards, Huang Yi joined hands with Zhuo Jichang, also a famous scholar, to compile Records of Fengshan. Huang Yi was a prestigious scholar at the time. When Li Guoliang, a native of Laoting County, acted as chief army commander of Fujian Province, he and Huang Yi swore to be blood brothers. When Li Guoliang returned hometown for his mother's funeral, Huang Yi accompanied him back to Laoting. During his one-year stay in Laoting, Huang Yi traveled around the county and left behind many poems and odes, including *An Ode to Mortar Isle*.

（26）陇（垄）头：坟墓。

（27）谬悠：荒诞无稽。

（28）皋：水边高地。

（29）绝港：不通向的港。

（30）锼：用工具取出。

（31）郭索：借指鲜活的螃蟹。

（32）韬：隐藏。

（33）睎：回顾。

（34）职方：掌天下地图的机构。

（35）徼外：边境以外。

（36）鏖：苦战。

（37）不毛：不长庄稼。

译文

古代的海阳县是渤海碣石山地区的腹地，按着星宿的分野，石臼坨对应着东方青龙星座的箕尾二宿及析木星座的一角。石臼坨距陆地有数十里。它是渤海环绕的万亩平川。虽说荒凉，却是一座著名的沙岛。因为它形似捣米的石臼，因而就以石臼给它命名了。

石臼坨四周的海水随季节不同而变化，而在一天的时间里也早晚各异。秋风吹来，波涛汹涌澎湃，春潮涨起，却水势大而平缓，夜间，月光下的海水是深深的碧绿；朝阳映照下的海水却又红色彤彤。大商船、小渔舟隐现在岛外；宏丽的殿阁，高大的僧寺矗立在岛中。岛上泉水甘洌，喝下去让人感到清爽，村子风气古朴，值得赞扬。这里有心怀壮志的汉武帝的遗踪，也流传着隐居不仕的古代仙人羡门的佳话。石臼坨美丽的自然胜景和和谐的人文景观是写不完、说不尽的。

有时会突然展现出美丽景色。波涛乍起，就能看到龙宫中发出光辉，鲛人采集珠宝，细浪里矗立着色彩明丽的山峰，树影婆娑中飞舞着连绵不断的龙蛇。于是羲和放缓了辔头，倏然间，狂风骤起，海神水伯遁形，各种鱼虾喷出水沫，表现出千奇百怪的姿态，蛟龙、蛤蜃表示归顺潜藏于海中。

到了日落西山，海空云消时，大雁到苇塘栖息，小船上唱起了渔歌。一边是平坦的沙滩，一边是碧绿的草地，袅袅

炊烟冉冉升起，残阳斜照着荒丘。寺庙里磬声悠扬缠绵，连蛟龙也感到忧伤而潜入海底。翻江倒海的狂风把鬼魅也吹出了坟头。这些又是石臼坨白天和夜间风景的差异。把这一些景象描绘出来，也许会让人认为是无稽之谈吧。

等到朝露打湿了井台，潮水后退露出了高地，到退潮留下的小河沟，驾一叶小渔舟驶向大海，把小舟藏在外界不相通的港汊，将渔网撒入大海，就会得到特大的惊喜：小鳞的鲈鱼味道鲜美，子鱼更是令人赞不绝口。钩出藏于壳内的牡蛎肉，捉住一贯横行的螃蟹。螃蟹肉（石条鱼）像冷凝的乳汁，它腹内满是蟹黄，其他如文鱼、章鱼、海蛤、香螺，无一不是吃后齿颊留香的佳肴。谈到石臼坨的海鲜，大多都是珍贵奇特的。那些作为上品供给城市富贵人家的水产，其实都是这里物产中的末流而已。唉！石臼坨会因人们的赞誉而声名显扬，但也因为缺少机遇而不为人所知。

再回顾这片美好的土地，位置偏僻，在大海的东岸，国家图籍不曾记载，历代圣贤也很少到达，访察辽代、金代往事，知道那时大海中曾经航行过战船。虽然军队驻扎在边境以外，却曾各路兵马聚在一起进行鏖战。春光毕竟会运转前进，大地已经变得多姿多彩。这美丽的岛屿存在过美好的传说，但也仅仅是凭吊古人而已。

附：黄佾小传

黄佾（1723—1785年），字乐绪。福建省侯官人。乾隆十八年（1753年）中举，掌教于海东书院。是时台湾道觉罗四明、知府余文仪，准备修撰各志，请黄佾执掌其事。黄佾协助修撰《台湾府志》等志书，时间不长，《台湾府志》及诸罗、彰化二志先后告成，相继又与举人卓肇昌共同参校《凤山志》。他是当时较有名气的一位学者。乐亭县武状元李国梁任福建陆路提督时，与黄佾结为金兰之好。李国梁奔母丧回乡期间，黄佾也来乐亭为义母守孝一年，遍游乐亭山水，写下许多诗赋，《石臼坨赋》为其中篇章。

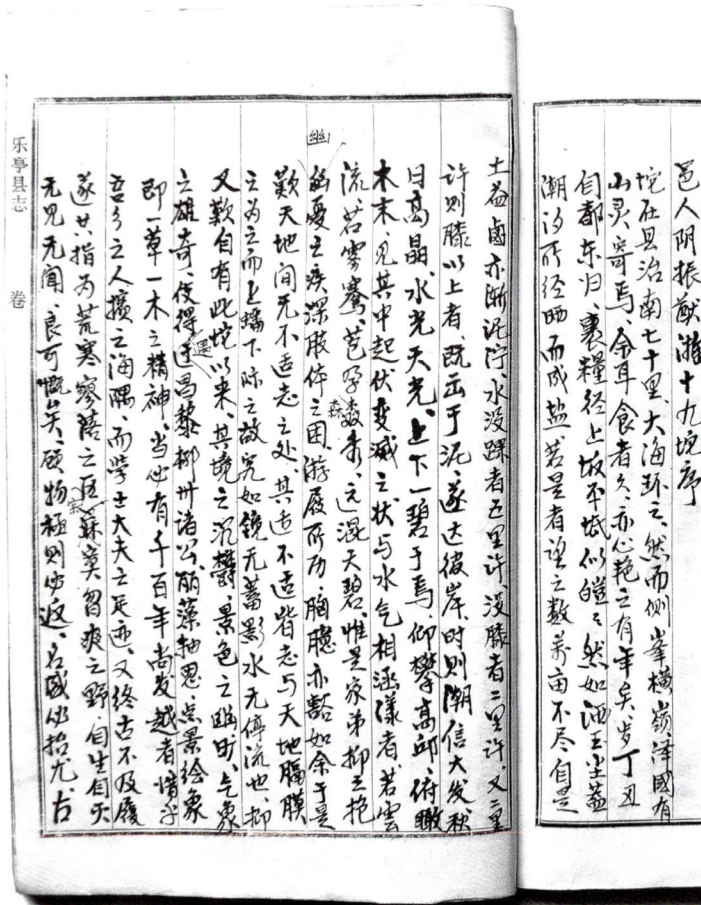

(2) Prologue to Tour of Nineteen Isle [1]

By Yin Zhenyou of the Qing Dynasty

Nineteen Isle (also named Mortar Isle) lies 35 kilometers southwest of the county seat of Laoting. Encircled by the ocean, the island features rolling hills and is known far and near for its picturesque landscapes. Over many years, I dreamed of a visit to the famous island.

In 1757, I returned to Laoting from the capital. As soon as I arrived home, I packed some solid food and headed for Nineteen Isle. Viewed from the distance, the island featured a gentle, flat terrain and looked like a sandy shelter for sailors. Its white beach seemed like a carpet of snow. Perhaps this

（二）游十九坨序①

（清）阴振猷

坨在县治南七十里，大海环之，然而侧峰横岭泽国有山灵寄焉。余耳食者久，亦心艳之有年矣。

岁丁丑自都东归，裹粮径上坂⁽¹⁾平坻⁽²⁾似。皑皑然如洒玉尘⁽³⁾，盖潮汐所经晒而成盐，若是者望之数万亩不尽。自是土益卤，亦渐泥泞，水没踝者五里许，没膝者二里许，又二里许，则膝以上者。既出淤泥，遂达彼岸。时则潮信大发，秋日高晶，水光天光，上下一碧于焉。仰攀高丘，俯瞰木末，见其中起伏变灭之状，与水气相涵漾⁽⁴⁾者，若云流，若霞骞⁽⁵⁾，苞孕森秀，远混天碧。

惟是家弟抑之，抱幽忧之疾，深肢体之困。游屐所历，胸臆亦豁如余。于是叹天地间无不适志之处。其适不适皆志与天地隔膜之为之，而上蟠下际⁽⁶⁾之故，究如镜无蓄影，水无停流也。

抑又叹自有此坨以来，其境之沉郁，景色之幽旷⁽⁷⁾，气象之雄奇，使得遇昌黎、柳州诸公，丽藻抽思，点景绘象，即一草一木之精神，当必有千百年尚发越者。惜乎！吾乡之人摈之海隅，而学士大夫之足迹，又终古不及履。遂共指为荒寒寥落之区，寂寞罟爽⁽⁸⁾之野，自生自灭，无见无闻，良可慨矣。

顾物极则必反，名盛必招尤。古今名迹指不胜屈，当其发山水之精华，蜚声名于词客，凿幽缒（锤）险，莫避雕搜，遂不瞬目间而已变洁净场成污秽土，则此坨之嶔奇⁽⁹⁾历落，与其洋溢乎庸耳俗目，曾不若听蜑（蜑）人⁽¹⁰⁾估客之奇迹，犹未至杀风景。凿混沌⁽¹¹⁾其闷胧抑塞⁽¹²⁾之故，安知非地示昭鉴，百灵呵护，绝不著纪录于人世间而沐日浴月，呼翕（噏）⁽¹³⁾乾坤，自抒海外之灵异，以留为终古之胜也。是则重可慨也。

注释

（1）坂：山坡。
（2）坻：水中的小洲或高地。
（3）玉尘：雪。
（4）涵漾：广阔的大泽碧波涌动，与泽面的水气相映照。
（5）骞：飞。
（6）上蟠下际：充塞天地，无所不在。
（7）幽旷：深奥而开朗。
（8）寂寞罟爽：冷寂，不为人知。
（9）嶔奇：形容高峻的石白坨品格特异，与众不同。
（10）蜑（dàn）人：船民、渔夫。
（11）混沌：天地初开时无所知的意思。
（12）抑塞：泛指拥塞荒僻。
（13）呼噏：呼吸。

译文

石白坨在乐亭县的西南，距县城70华里。坨的四周被大海环绕着，坨上峰峦丘陵纵横，因这个海岛有灵性，所以远近闻名。我听说这个岛屿的盛况很久了，多年来一直在心里向往着这里。

丁丑年（1757年）我从京城回到乐亭，带着干粮择路直往十九坨海岛，远远望去，全岛山坡地势平坦，酷似大海中一个可供休息居住的小洲。白花花的地面，就像覆盖着一层积雪。大概是涨潮、落潮海水过后经日晒而形成了一层盐。这样的地表远看要有好几万亩。从足下开始，滩涂含的盐分越来越多，所以道路也越来越泥泞了。有5里多水没脚踝，2里多没膝盖骨，再走2里就要没到膝盖以上了。走出这段泥泞的地区，就到了对面的海岸。当时正涨大潮，秋季的太阳高悬天穹鲜艳明亮。浩瀚大海，水天一色，光洁如玉。仰望高丘，攀缘绝顶，再往下看去，那片片丛林忽隐忽现，与云

①原文录自韩湘亭总纂《乐亭县志稿》。

was because seawater crystallized into salt in the sun, which stretched for thousands of hectares. As the tide retreated, the offshore seabed emerged to form a belt of muddy land that linked to Nineteen Isle. Along the belt, I walked towards the island. The farther I went into the sea, the deeper the seawater was until it grew thigh-high. Fortunately, I crossed the sea and reached the island before the flood tide. The autumn sun is hung high in the sky. At the horizon, the blue sky and the immense ocean merged together. Climbing onto a lofty hill, I overlooked the entire island: Lush forests were shrouded in dense clouds, which extended as far as the remote horizon where the blue ocean and azure sky met.

Before mounting onto the island, my brother looked depressed. However, a stroll of the island cheered him up, who became as delighted as I. Inspired by such spectacular landscapes, I concluded that no matter how insignificant they were, no aspiration and ambition were unsuitable only if one had a deep insight of the real meaning of life. In fact, all ambitions would eventually become reflections on the mirror, and the truth was eternal just like water never stopping running. How regretful it was!

More regretfully, the island's lush vegetation, spectacular landscape, and marvelous environment were never found in literary works of historically famous poets and writers like Han Yu and Liu Zongyuan. With their marvelous knowledgeableness and writing skills, they would have left behind a number of poetic masterpieces and historic relics for later generations to admire on the island. However, the truth is that our fellow men just neglect the coastal island, and no prestigious literati, scholars, and officials ever left their footprints there. For this reason, the beautiful island has always been described as a desolate, lonely place over ages. What a pity it is!

However, anything always has two sides. Fortune often comes along with misfortune. For instance, countless scenic resorts and historic sites attracted men of letter with their renown, who left behind numerous inscriptions carved on rocks and stones. If this happened to Mortar Isle, its untouched tranquility would be devastated, and the island would become a dirty place. It would be better for tourists merely to hear local fishermen and merchants tell local folklores. Perhaps it is the blessing of Mother Nature that Mortar Isle could maintain its desolation and seclusion from the very beginning, thus making itself an eternal offshore resort. If this is true, what a fortune it is!

Appendix: A Brief Biography of Yin Zhenyou

Yin Zhenyou (1788-1851) was a native of Xinzhai Village, Laoting County. When he was young, his parents died, and he was adopted by his uncle Yin Qi. As a child, he was weak but studious. At the age of 15-16, he became crazy about reading love tragedies. His tutor often admonished him not to read such novels, but he didn't listen. After he passed the county-level imperial examination, he realized outstanding performances in the following examinations. Soon, he passed the provincial-level imperial examination, but failed in national imperial examinations after several attempts. Later, he was appointed as education supervisor of Fuzhou, where he received great respect from local students. Six years later, his father died, and Yin returned to his hometown to keep mourning. After that, he became education supervisor of Pingxian County, where he soon died. Yin was noted for his outstanding literary capacity. The books and monographs he wrote include *Notes of Family Education*, *A Brief Record of Qianxing*, *Records of Celebrated Women*, and *Poetry Collection of Yiaiwu Cottage*.

① Extracted from *Records of Laoting County* compiled by Hang Xiangting, a native of the county

蒸霞蔚的水汽相互辉映，其景象就像那天空随风流动着的白云，熠熠飞舞的彩霞，涵蕴着丛生茂盛的林荫，隐约消逝于远方的碧海蓝天。

只是临上坨之前，家弟的心情非常郁闷，老是打不起精神头来，经过在坨上的一番游历，心情豁然开朗，倏忽变得和我一样怡悦。为此不禁使我感叹人生天地间，并没有什么所谓适合不适合自己的志愿，因为不管适合不适合都是志愿，只不过是你自己对于世事还没有达到洞悉彻悟的境界罢了。应该说这样的情况充塞天地间，无所不在，其实就像镜子里留不下影子，水不会永远停止流动一样。

然而更加令人感叹的是，自有这个坨以来，这样茂郁秀美的环境、深奥广阔的景色、新奇壮美的境况，如能使之遇到像韩愈、柳宗元这样的诗文大家，推满腹之经纶、溢华丽之辞藻，神思遐想、状景写物，那么这里的一草一木的深层蕴涵，必定会有世世代代抒发不尽的诗情画意、描写不完的历史陈迹。可惜的是，我们故乡的人们，随意把它抛弃在海边，因而那些文人、学者、职官的足迹永远到不了这里。于是被说成是荒凉、冷寂不为人知的地方，从而历尽沧桑，默沉隔世，真是令人感慨万千啊！

不过事物的规律是物极必反，如果它声名过于彰显，必然招致过失。从古至今名胜古迹数不胜数，然而当这些历史遗迹以其灵山秀水的精神和魅力声名昭著之时，文人骚客必将慕名而至。是时，发古之幽情，述今之险奇，竭尽才华，不讳雕琢袤集加以涂饰，就会一眨眼的工夫将洁净的石臼坨变成脏乱不堪的地方。石臼坨清纯脱俗卓而不群的风貌与其充斥、传播于平庸的世人，不如让他们听听渔民和商贩们的奇闻逸事还不至于败人清兴。追索天地初开以来的石臼坨之所以如此壅塞荒僻，谁能知这不是天地神灵显照呵护，使之不事张扬，于是才保守下历史原貌，从而经受日月之精华，吞吐天地之万灵，自然倾泻挥发沧海之外的灵秀珍奇，用以留作永世长存的名胜古迹。如果真是这样，更是令人无限感慨！

附：阴振猷小传

阴振猷（1788—1851年），字子翼。乐亭县新寨人。幼年父母双亡，被伯父阴琦收养。身体瘦弱，酷爱读书。十五六岁时，喜读哀艳之文，私塾先生常规劝他不再读这类文字，矢志不移。中秀才后，每次考试，均获优等。丙子年中举，后几次参加会试，未能中进士。后被朝廷任命为复州学正。训诲生徒，文行兼重，很受复州士子爱戴。在复州任职六年，父死回家守孝，守孝期满，又被选为平县训导，到任时间不长，死于任上。其人文才很好，著有《庭训笔记》、《前行纪略》、《女子奇行传》、《亦爱吾庐诗集》等。

(3) A Brief Record of Mortar Isle

By Han Xiangting

Some apotheosize Jetavana Vihara where the Buddha preached as a paradise inhabited by gods; Some admire the legendary Penglai, Fangzhang, and Yingzhou Islands, which are believed to abodes for immortals on the Bohai Sea; Legend goes that during the Jin Dynasty, a fisherman entered a utopia by chance, but no one of later generation has the same luck; The mythical Jade Abode of the Western Empress couldn't be reached even though one rode the eight mythical horses of King Mu of the Zhou Dynasty.

Compared with those mythical places, however, Mortar Isle is something real on the Bohai Sea. It isn't a legendary island carried by mythical tortoises, but a product of Mother Nature. Near the shore of southwestern Laoting, the island is accessible even without the need of taking a boat. Sea breeze blow white sails on the ocean, while various species of birds rest or hover on the beach. The colorful clouds on the sky and the glimmering waves on the sea set off each other, composing a natural landscape painting. Bathing in the morning glows, the entire island appears like a fanciful mirage. When morning dewdrops glisten in the sun, Mortar Isle looks as beautiful as the Crystal Dragon Palace.

At dawn, monks recited Buddhist sutras while beating bells, which reverberate together with the sound of waves on the sea. At night, the fishing lanterns light up the sea, which appear like bright stars dotted on the sky. The columns of the Sakyamuni Hall of Chaoyin Temple are carved with two lifelike dragons, while the statues of 500 Arhats in the Arhat Hall demonstrate various postures in the glows of the Eternal Lamps. The crops and fruit growing in the west courtyard of the Chaoyin Temple already mature. Staying in the temple, tourists can admire the moon while sipping a cup of tea at night. Besides serving

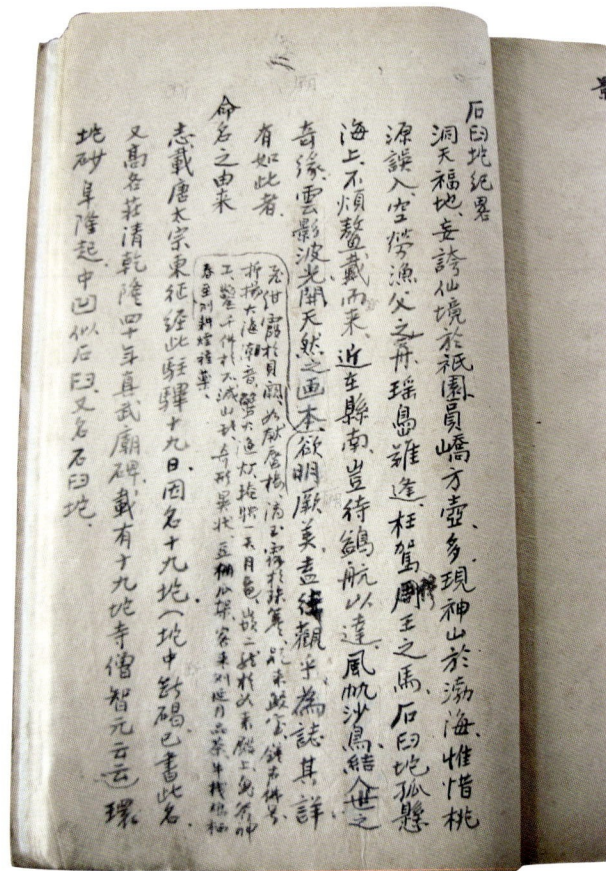

the Buddha, monks also graze cattle and raise chickens on the island, and grow medical herbs in springtime. For a deep insight of its beautiful landscapes, one can personally visit the island.

① Extracted from *Records of Laoting County* compiled by Hang Xiangting, a native of the county

（三）石臼坨纪略[1]

韩湘亭

洞天福地[1]，妄夸仙境于祇园[2]；圆峤方壶[3]，多现神山于渤海。惟惜桃园误入，空劳渔父之舟；瑶岛[4]难逢，枉驾穆王之马[5]。石臼坨孤悬海上，不烦鳌[6]戴而来；近在县西南，岂待鹢[7]航以达。风帆沙鸟，结人世之奇缘；云影波光，开天然之画本。飞绀霞[8]于贝阙[9]，如献蜃楼；滴玉露于珠盘，疑来鲛室[10]。钟声佛号，抑扬大海潮音；蟹火鱼灯，掩映一天月色。嵌二龙于如来殿[11]上，鬼斧神工；凿千佛于不灭山[12]头，奇形异状。豆棚瓜架，客来则延月品茶；牛栈鸡栖，春至则耕烟种药。欲明厥美，盍往观乎？

注释

（1）洞天福地：神仙居住的名山胜境。

（2）祇园：见楹联诠释"金刚殿楹联"注（7）。

（3）圆峤方壶：海中仙山，在渤海东，泛指东海蓬莱、方丈、瀛洲三山。

（4）瑶岛：瑶池，西王母居住的宫阙。

（5）穆王之马：传说中周穆王驾车用的日行万里的八匹骏马。

（6）鳌：海中大龟或大鳖。

（7）鹢：水鸟名。形如鹭而大。羽色苍白，善高飞。古代在船首以彩色画鹢鸟之形，后借指船。

（8）绀霞：绀，青红色，俗称天青。

（9）贝阙：阙，门。贝阙，用贝壳建成的门观。

（10）鲛室：鲛与蛟通。蛟室，蛟人居住的地方。这里指海中的龙宫。

（11）如来殿：此处指潮音寺供奉释迦牟尼的大雄宝殿。

（12）不灭山：此处指长明灯照耀下的潮音寺后殿山墙。

译文

人们总是爱把佛祖讲经说法的祇园赞誉为神佛居住的胜境。人们更是赞美传说时常隐现于渤海之中的蓬莱、方丈、瀛洲那三座仙山。晋时渔夫误入的胜境桃花源，后人根本无处可寻。而西王母居住的瑶池仙境，就是驾驭周穆王那日行万里的八匹骏马也难以找到。

与这些仙境相比，孤悬渤海之中的石臼坨岛却真真实实地存在着。它不是由神话中海里的大龟驮涌而来，它的生成是大自然造化之功。它就在乐亭西南渤海湾的近岸处，人们不用坐船就可登临。海风吹拂着岛边船只的白帆，各种鸟儿在沙滩上起起落落，好像与人间结下奇缘。天空的彩云与海水的波光交相辉映，似展开的一幅天然画卷。天空中天青色的霞光把海岛上如门观殿堂的贝壳，照耀得像海市蜃楼般美轮美奂。苍穹中的露珠滴落下来，把石臼坨打扮得似龙宫般美丽。

清晨，僧人们礼佛诵经的钟声佛号，与大海的涛声一起传扬；夜晚，渔民们捕鱼捉蟹的灯火，与碧空的星月相辉映。潮音寺如来殿的明柱上，镶嵌有两条栩栩如生的巨龙，雕刻之精可谓鬼斧神工；罗汉堂后山墙青石上的五百罗汉，在长明灯的照耀下千姿百态，神采奕奕。潮音寺西院那豆棚瓜架上果实扬手可摘，来岛的游客在此小住可邀月品茶。岛上的僧人养牛养鸡，一到春天则耕耘种药。人们若想详细地领略石臼坨的美景，何不亲自登岛一观了却雅兴呢？

---

[1]原文录自韩湘亭总纂《乐亭县志稿》。

Appendix: A Brief Biography of

Han Xiangting

Han Xiangting (1886-1960), alternatively named Zuozhou, was born into a farmer's family in Yinhao Village, Laoting County. As a child, he was famous for his cleverness and studiousness. Before the imperial examination was abolished at the end of the Qing Dynasty, he was admitted as a *gongsheng* (candidate in provincial-level imperial examination. As the founder and first headmaster of the Yantuo West District Primary School, he was noted for his remarkable virtuousness and contribution to education throughout the county. He once acted as magistrate of Guangping County in southern Henan Province under the control of the Japanese puppet government. During his tenure, he was so merciful that he never executed any criminals. He also compiled *Records of Guangping County*. After he returned to his hometown, Han was appointed as president of Laoting Detention Center. During the period, he kept close touch with CPC secret organizations, and did all he could do to resist Japanese invaders. In 1951, Han underwent a trail on Chinese traitors. In view of his deeds, Han was released on the site although the rest six traitors were all executed.

In 1930, the government of Laoting County ever invited Han to participate in the compilation of *Records of Laoting County*. In 1952, he was invited to revise the *History of Laoting County* in the Republic of China Period.

Han was noted for his knowledgeableness and versatility. He was good at poetry, calligraphy, and particularly seal cutting. At the time, he was ranked among the most famous scholars in Laoting County, together with Hui Yitang and Yan Bonian.

Throughout his life, Han compiled and published a number of literary works. Besides poems and short stories he published on newspapers and regional annals (including *Records of Guangping County* and *Records of Laoting County*), he also published *Collection of Poetry and Seal Cuttings*, *Poetry Collection of River Reflection Tower*, *Collection of Xiaolang Garden*, *Annals of Past Dynasties*, *Research of Topographic Names of Past Dynasties*, *Records of Seal Cutters*, *A Brief History of Militarists*, *An Encyclopedia of Culture and Education*, *Research of Long-living People*, *Selected Collection of Shaoling Poetry*, *Records of Famous Physicians*, and *Strange Stories*.

附：韩湘亭小传

韩湘亭（1886—1960年），名作舟，乐亭县迎好村人。出身农家，自幼聪慧好学，清代废除科举前，在乡试中曾考中副贡。韩湘亭是严坨西区高小的创建人，第一任校长。他以治学严谨，育才有方，学行端庄，知名全县。日伪时期，在河北省南部的广平县曾做一任县长，他体恤百姓有政声，广平任上从未处决过犯人，并主持纂修了广平县志。回乡后，乐亭日伪政权为利用他的德望拉拢他出任乐亭"感化院长"。但是，韩湘亭主动与我党地下工作者保持联系，为抗日斗争做了力所能及的工作。

1930年，当时的县政府曾聘请韩湘亭主参与编纂乐亭县志。1952年韩湘亭受乐亭县人民政府聘请，对民国县志稿重行修订。

韩湘亭学识渊博，多才多艺。善诗文、长书法，真草隶篆无一不精，尤擅金石雕刻。在乡与惠易唐、严柏年等同为乐亭著名文人。

一生著述颇丰，除散见于书报的短篇诗文及其主纂参与的二志《广平县志》、《民国乐亭县志稿》外，还有《诗品印集》、《江影楼诗草》、《小阆园外集》、《历代世系年谱》、《历代郡县地名考》、《文字记名录》、《印人志》、《兵家小史》、《文教大统录》、《寿人考》、《少陵诗选》、《医家统考》、《词选》及《故事奇闻》等多种。

Chapter IV: Stele Inscriptions

Stele Inscriptions of the Chaoyang Nunnery [①]

About 25 kilometers southwest of the county seat of Laoting lies a mortar-shaped island, hence its name Mortar Isle. A renowned scenic spot in Laoting County, the island features tranquil environment, sweet spring water, and hundreds of hectares of mulberry trees, as well as billowy sea. Although hearing my friends talk about the island many times, I've never had a chance to visit it. This March, Master Ruiguang, who took charge of Buddhist documentary in the county government, and Master Huichen, abbot of Chaoyang Nunnery, came to see me, inviting me to writing a piece of stele inscription for the temple.

"Although Chaoyang Nunnery has long been a famous resort on Mortar Isle," Master Ruiguang said, "but few know its history and what painstaking hardship its founder endured to construct the temple. A sacred Buddhist land, Mortar Isle concentrates many temples such as Guanyin Nunnery and Dragon King Temple, of which Guanyin Nunnery is the largest. Master Zhiyuan, the eighth-generation descendant of the Linji Sect, once learned Buddhism from the same teacher with me. Later, he became Huichen's teacher. When he was young, Zhiyuan converted to Buddhism on Mortar Isle, and hadn't since left the island. He led disciples to grow crops and saved every coin. With the grains they harvested, they not

第四章　碑刻与碑记

一　朝阳庵碑记①

乐邑滨于海，其西南五十余里，有坨在海中，其形如臼，故名石臼坨。境幽而地广，泉甘而土肥。桑田数十顷，与洪波相上下，盖邑之名区也。余尝闻诸友朋而未获一览其观。岁戊午三月，僧会司⑴瑞光偕其住持⑵慧辰，以重修观音庵，请书于石。

瑞师之言曰："石臼之胜，人知之久矣，而其兴衰之故，创造之劳，有不可以不详者。坨之中，梵宫⑶鼎峙，而观音庵为最。住僧智元，余之法兄即慧辰之师也。自幼时，落染⑷于此。足不履城市，苦志参修，自摅⑸其力，播植艺获⑹，积株粒而存之，量所入以给僧众终岁之用，而以其余为祠宇修补之资。迄今六十余年，广积囊资，于乾隆二十四年创修佛殿两座，费金千金有余。至六十年，积蓄倍常⑺，志在修整未逮⑻，适遭恶徒慧林抢劫之变。幸蒙府县断明，枷杖递籍，遂令还俗，仍给告示，严禁晓喻，抄铭碑阴⑼，以杜后患。"

斯时也，智元已示寂矣。其徒慧辰续其衣钵尽所有，以终其志。自丙辰三月，至今告成，佛殿六楹，廊房六间，门宇墙垣，无不焕然一新。而又恐后之无以继也，窃欲述其颠末，以贻将来。

余慨曰："有是哉！智师之能守也。世之游方者，奔走富贵之门，不过为一身之衣食计耳。合其师徒，不布施，不经谶⑽，株积寸累，未尝借檀越⑾之力，可不谓知道者欤！"

夫茫茫沧海中，而有桑田，是亦天地之秀灵，非人力所能逾也；又得贤师徒，修整废坠，以大其规模，则观音之庵可以久不敝矣。

余欣慕有年，会当⑿身历其地，以极海外之大观而并颂智元贤师徒之功于不朽云。

清乾隆五十一年举人　李中淑

注释

（1）僧会司：县设专掌佛教事的机构。

（2）住持：僧院主僧。

（3）梵宫：泛称佛寺。

（4）落染：指佛教信徒离家到寺院做僧尼。

（5）摅（shū）：舒展发挥的意思。

（6）艺获：种植收割庄稼。

（7）倍常：比平常有了更多的积蓄。

（8）逮：成功，达到。

（9）碑阴：碑的背面。泛指碑刻。

（10）经谶（chèn）：迷信预言，附会吉凶。

（11）檀越：施主。

（12）会当：应该。

译文

乐亭县濒临大海，其西南50多里海中有一个岛屿，因形状像个石臼，所以取名叫石臼坨。那里的环境幽雅，面积宽广，泉水甘甜，土质肥沃，有桑田几千亩，与波涛汹涌起伏的大海遥相呼应，是乐亭一处有名的景区。我曾听朋友们谈起过这个岛屿，但是始终没有机会到那里去看看。戊午年三月，县衙里掌管僧录的瑞光同朝阳庵的住持慧辰来找我，让我为重新修建的寺院写篇碑文。

瑞光师父说："石臼坨岛上朝阳庵这处名胜，人们很早就知道了，但这座寺院的兴建与衰落以及这次修建的种种劳苦艰辛，应该详详细细地告诉世人知道。石臼坨为佛教圣地，岛上观音庵、老爷龙王庙等庙宇错落而建，其中以观音庵的规模最大。临济宗八代传人智元是我的法兄，他就是

①原文录自韩湘亭总纂《乐亭县志稿》。

only fed themselves, but also earned money used to refurnish their temple. Over six decades, they saved a great amount of wealth in this way. In 1759, they invested a large amount to build two halls. In 1795, the temple's wealth doubled, so the monks decided to further expand their temple. However, their money was robbed by Huilin, an evil monk. Fortunately, the county government investigated the case and punished Huilin in light of laws. Then, Huilin was secularized and sent back to his hometown. The government placarded a post to declare its official attitude toward the event. Meanwhile, the event was carved on a stone stele for the purpose of precaution."

"At the time," he added, "Monk Zhiyuan died, and his disciple, Huichen, succeeded the post as the abbot. Then, Huichen invested all of their savings to fulfill his teacher's unfinished wish. From March 1795 to March 1798, the project was completed, and six halls and six side rooms were added to the temple. I tell you the story because I fear it will be forgotten by later generations."

The story deeply impressed me. "Master Zhiyuan demonstrated his loyalty and piety towards Buddhism in this way," I exclaimed. "Some monks travel around to beg alms from wealthy families in the name of practicing Buddhism. But in fact, their real purpose is to feed themselves. Zhiyuan and his disciples never made money through begging alms or practicing superstition activities, but accumulated wealth through saving every piece of coin. Their virtuous deeds deserve wide respect and praise, don't they?"

In the immense ocean, the island growing mulberry trees must be a blessed child of Mother Nature because such a miracle is beyond the capacity of mankind. Thanks to the tireless endeavor of Zhiyuan and his disciples, the once-desolate Guanyin Nunnery already resurrects and has been further expanded. We believe the temple will be an eternal pilgrimage destination over ages.

I have admired famous resorts on the island for many years. I wish one day I will have a chance to personally visit the refurnished Guanyin Nunnery and other historic sites on the island so that I can learn more about the outstanding achievements realized by Zhiyuan and his disciples.

Li Zhongshu, a scholar of the Qing Dynasty

Appendix: A Brief Biography of Li Zhongshu

Li Zhongshu (1766-1840), a native of Chengnanguan, Laoting County, was noted for his righteousness and filial piety. In 1786, he passed the provincial-level imperial examination. In 1801, he was appointed as a county magistrate, but he didn't take office for certain reason. In 1802, he became a jinshi after passing the national imperial examination, and was once again appointed as a county magistrate. He didn't take the post again. Later, he was elected a professor of Daming Prefecture. After his mother died, Li returned to his hometown to observe mourning for his mother. Then, he kept watch of father in sickbed for which he didn't pull off his clothes for a sleep for three months. His father said, "An old saying goes that a prolonged illness of parent might create an impatient son, but it isn't true to my son." After the death of his father, Li stayed home for mourning. The magistrate of Laoting County invited him to act as a lecturer in local academy. During the period, Li was elected a professor of Zhengding Prefecture. In 1840, he died at the tenure.

His works included Analytical Study of the Map of Liyuan, References of Birthdays of Ancient People, Huaixi Poetry, and Dialogues on Shifo Nunnery.

① Extracted from *Records of Laoting County* compiled by Hang Xiangting, a native of the county

慧辰的师父。智元幼年皈依佛门，在石臼坨落发修行，从没
离开过这里。他们发挥自己的力量，种植庄稼，铢积寸累，
聚少成多，积蓄财力。对每年的收获，量入为出，除供给僧
众食用之外，剩余资金全部作为修补寺院的费用。至今六十
多年的时间，积蓄了大量的财富。于乾隆二十四年，建造了
两座佛殿，耗资超过千金。到乾隆六十年，财富成倍增长，
立志再造佛殿，佛殿工程尚未实施，寺院的财富遭到恶徒慧
林的抢劫，可幸的是此事引起府县重视，查明案情，做出判
决，使慧林受到了应有的惩罚，之后派差人把他送回原籍，
强令还俗。同时衙门张贴布告，申明官府态度，并把这件事
刻在了石碑上，以警告后人，杜绝此类事件的再次发生。"

　　就在这个时候，智元和尚去世了。他的徒弟慧辰接任
了寺院住持，秉承师父的遗愿，动用所有的积蓄，终于圆满
完成了智元师父的未竟事业。从乾隆六十年三月开始，到嘉
庆三年三月完成了全部工程。前后共建造正殿六间，廊房六
间，整座寺院焕然一新。唯恐后人因不清楚这件事的历史，
不能从中引出教训，把前人所开创的佛门善事传承下去，所
以我把这件事的始末说了一遍，为的是把它留给后世，引以
为戒啊！

　　这件事引起我无限感慨："是啊，高僧智元对于佛门的
事业真是守诚敬业啊，多见那些世上游僧，为了募化施舍信
游奔走在豪门富户，不过也就是为了自己的衣食住行罢了。
而朝阳庵的智元师徒，他们不到处乞求施主施舍、编造附会
进行迷信活动去敛财，而是一滴一点地积蓄财富，这种高洁
的行为难道不应该让世人知道吗？"

　　在这茫茫无际的大海之中能有桑田，已经是天公的灵
秀之功，这是人力不可以达到或超越的。如今，岛上这座已
将荒废的寺院，又得到智元师徒的修复，并且扩大了它的规
模，由此观音庵必将世代香火鼎盛，永不凋敝啊！

　　我对石臼坨岛的各处名胜已是仰慕多年了，日后应该找
机会到岛上仔仔细细地看看焕然一新的观音庵与各处的历史
景观，以便更加翔实地颂扬智元师徒的不朽之功。

附：李中淑小传

　　李中淑（1766—1840年），字致轩，号陶山。为人
正直，性至孝，乐亭城南关人。乾隆丙午年（1786年）中
举，嘉庆辛酉年（1801年）大挑一等，选为知县，因故
未任。壬戌年（1802年）中进士，被任命为知县，再次未
任。后被选用为大名府教授。母丧回家守孝，侍候卧病不起
的父亲，累月不脱衣裳。其父常对人说："人言久病床前无
孝子，今吾以病之知孝子矣。"父亲死后，中淑在家守孝，
乐亭知县聘其为书院讲席，诲人不倦。服丧期满，选为正定
府教授，道光二十年（1840年）病逝于任。

　　著有《历元地舆考辨》、《古人生辰备鉴》、《明文新
机》、《槐西诗话》、《石佛庵问业》等。

2. A Brief Record of Chaoyang Nunnery [1]

Nineteen Isle, also known as Mortar Isle, features dense plants that shelter the blue sky. The sea surrounding the island boasts surging billows, and was as deep as a hundred meters. Eddy currents form massive swirls underwater, which look dark green and horrible. For this reason, few people dared to come to this place before.

In 1573 during the Ming Dynasty, a monk named Xianguang mounted onto the island, where he logged trees and reclaimed wasteland to build Chaoyang Nunnery. Since then, the temple received constant pilgrimage and became a sacred Buddhist sanctum of the Linji Sect by the Bohai Bay. With the passage of time, the temple became desolate when it was passed down to Monk Zhiyuan, the eighth-generation abbot of the temple. To resurrect the temple, Monk Zhiyuan saved every penny he could and finally accumulated enough money to build two halls. Before the project was completed, however, Monk Zhiyuan died. In 1828, his disciple, Huichen, finally completed the project and fulfilled Monk Zhiyuan's

二 朝阳庵记略^①

十九坨，或曰石臼，草树蒙茸⁽¹⁾，蔽亏天地，其外杀绿洋水险恶，深可数十丈。盘盂⁽²⁾下陷，暗暗作黝绿色，不可以目。以故人迹罕到。明万历初，显光上人，伐榛莽，铲茅筏⁽³⁾，始建庵于此。代有嗣人，而鹿野坛场⁽⁴⁾与临济宗⁽⁵⁾风，大阐海澨⁽⁶⁾。及八代智元，发洪愿力，鸠工饬材⁽⁷⁾，事未葴⁽⁸⁾而圆寂⁽⁹⁾。道光纪年之戊子，其法嗣慧辰，慨然于师志之未就，悉鼎新之。既讫，以碑属焉。

余窃维释迦坐四禅天，现一切相，开十丈眉，说万种法，直将断⁽¹⁰⁾三千大千世界⁽¹¹⁾，掷过恒河沙国界外。区区兰若⁽¹²⁾一幻相，而曰"即此是佛"。此亦如涅槃经所云："象之形如箕，如臼，如芦菔⁽¹³⁾根者，同一盲而已矣。"第庄生有言："道恶在，恶不在。"通斯义者，其视甓⁽¹⁴⁾瓦蝼蚁，曾不异其视圣贤。彼之期而后可，是亦作胶柱⁽¹⁵⁾之鼓者也。然则朝阳庵一祇树林⁽¹⁶⁾也，十九坨一灵鹫峰也，偃月半环一华藏界⁽¹⁷⁾也，瀛海四围一功德水也。垺金粉数笔，即应身法身⁽¹⁸⁾之具足⁽¹⁹⁾也，焚柏子一粒，即摄身摄意之分香也。荒寒寂寞之区，杳冥⁽²⁰⁾汩没⁽²¹⁾之所。盼饰⁽²²⁾秘仪，搞张大乘⁽²³⁾，于以庄严宝相光普人天。

于乎！允⁽²⁴⁾矣。皇兮，大哉！抑吾于此，且重有感焉。胜国⁽²⁵⁾自中叶以还，淀迤海、盖，海氛甚恶，沿岸食毛⁽²⁶⁾之地，俱伏在荓之戎。大圣人出，狐鼠伏，而四海一，男女织耕，老死不知外事。极之寒丘穷野，至此一天犹得以耕雨锄风，含哺鼓腹⁽²⁷⁾，鼓钟击磬，梵呗祝釐⁽²⁸⁾。夫亦孰知皆重熙累洽⁽²⁹⁾之功德，休养生息，涵濡⁽³⁰⁾于数百年之深也。余之至止此也，登高丘，望远海，鲸波平漾，飓风恬然。睇四山⁽³¹⁾，则嗔恚泥开⁽³²⁾；仰虚空，则愚痴云散，则遍阎浮提⁽³³⁾百千万亿之总总林林者，披梵夹⁽³⁴⁾，溯根因，岂必待兜率陀天⁽³⁵⁾而始见一茎草化为丈六金身⁽³⁶⁾也哉！

清嘉庆二十一年举人　阴振猷

注释

（1）蒙茸：覆盖着茂盛的草树。

（2）盘盂：海水漩流形成深窟。

（3）榛莽、茅筏：泛指茂密的野草丛林。

（4）鹿野坛场：佛教徒念经说法举行祭祀的场所。

（5）临济宗：佛教宗派之一。明代朝阳庵寺僧即属该派。

（6）澨（shì）：水涯。

（7）鸠工饬材：招工匠，买建材。

（8）葴（chǎn）：圆满、完备。

（9）圆寂：和尚去世。

（10）断：掌管。

（11）三千大千世界：佛教语。以须弥山为中心，四周以铁围山为界称一小世界，一小世界的千倍叫小千世界；小千世界的千倍叫中千世界；中千世界的千倍叫大千世界。因为三次用千倍之，故称作三千大千世界。

（12）兰若：僧人居所。

（13）芦菔：萝卜。

（14）甓：砖。

（15）胶柱：守旧，不能见机行事。

（16）祇树林：佛说法的地方。

（17）华藏界：莲花世界的简称。

（18）应身法身：泛指佛的身形。

（19）具足：具备满足。

（20）杳冥：昏暗。

（21）汩没：海水急流，忽然不见。

（22）盼（xì）饰：涂绘装饰。

①全文录自韩湘亭总纂《乐亭县志稿》。

unfinished wish. After the temple was reconstructed, Huichen asked me to write this stele inscription.

In my imagination, Buddha Sakyamuni showed in varied majestic forms at four-dhyana heavens, with extended light emitting from his eyes, and recited thousands of Buddhist sutras, in order to deliver all lives in the world to the paradise. Although it appeared as an abode for monks, the temple is actually an embodiment of the Buddha. Nirvana Sutra records such a story: Once upon a time, a group of blind men wished to know what an elephant looks like, but they could do nothing but feel it with their hands. Those who touched the elephant's ear declared that the elephant was like a dustpan, those who touched one of the elephant's leg concluded that the elephant resembled a stone mortar, those who touched its tooth said the elephant was just like a long radish. The reason is that those blind men didn't see the truth. Zhuang Zhou, a philosopher in the Warring States Period, ever said, "The truth is hard to be found although it is always there." In the eyes of some observers, saints have nothing different from bricks, stones, and insects. In fact, those who insist on seeking one certain conclusion don't know the truth that there are always alternatives. Chaoyang Nunnery is merely a place to preach Buddhist doctrines; Mortar Isle is just an abode for monks; The crescent-shaped Moon Isle is the Holy Land inhabited by the Buddha; The sea around Nineteen Isle that subsists local people is water of eternal virtue. Although it is simple to paint Buddhist statues with golden powder in Chaoyang Nunnery, and the three embodiments of the Buddha realize perfection in this way. Burn a cypress seed that symbolizes piety, and invite the Buddha into Chaoyang Nunnery for pilgrims to worship. So, it is a great achievement to build temples on the desolate Nineteen Isle, paint statues of the Buddha, and publicize Mahayana doctrines, so that the majestic power of the Buddha can shine on the entire world.

Oh, this is true! The Buddha shows endless mercy and wisdom. Standing on the island, I cannot help but exclaim. "How great he is!" During the Ming Dynasty, the coastal areas of Bohai Bay, from Caofeidian in the west to Guandongzhou in the east, were overgrew with seaweeds and featured a harsh social environment. Locals subsisted on farming and fishing, and bandits and pirates hid in lush forests. Thanks to sage monarchs of the Qing Dynasty, their stateliness warded off the evil, and the area around Mortar Isle has become a land of peace. Nowadays, locals lead a utopian life: Men cultivate crops in fields, while women weave at home. Throughout their lives, they know little about the outside world. Despite its infertility and remoteness, the land offers a shelter for local farmers and fishermen to live on their own labor, without worrying about their subsistence. Accompanied by morning bells and evening drums, monks recite Buddhist sutras and pray for blessings for people. In fact, it is the blessings of the Qing rulers that people can live in peace over centuries. During my stay on the island, I climbed onto a mountain to watch the immense ocean: Perilous billows became placid, and hurricanes ceased on the sea. My spirit cheered up as the legendary Fanghu, Penglai, and Yingzhou Islands entered to the field of my vision. When I saw the immense ocean and sky, all worries that used to haunt my mind disappeared. All lives who attempt to seek the truth through reading Buddhist sutra should visit Mortar Isle, a holy land of Buddhism, so that they needn't travel far to the Western Paradise for a glimpse of the majestic embodiments of the Buddha.

Yin Zhenyou, a scholar of the Qing Dynasty

① Extracted from *Records of Laoting County* compiled by Hang Xiangting, a native of the county

（23）摛（chī）张大乘：摛，舒展。摛张大乘即指传扬大乘佛法。

（24）允：实在，诚信。

（25）胜国：指前朝。

（26）食毛：古代毛和苗读音相同，毛也称苗。禾苗，泛指五谷。

（27）含哺鼓腹：吃饱喝足，无忧无虑的意思。

（28）梵呗祝釐（xī）：梵呗，吟咏佛经。釐同禧。祝釐即祝福。梵呗祝釐即诵念佛经为众生祝福的意思。

（29）重熙累洽：国家接连几代太平安乐。

（30）涵濡：恩德深厚，泽被尘世。

（31）四山：指方壶、蓬莱、瀛洲三山，及被视为仙山的石臼坨。

（32）嗔恚泯开：嗔，怒。恚，愤恨。指愤恨消逝。

（33）阎浮提：阎浮，树名。提，意为洲。俗指中华及东方各国。

（34）梵夹：佛教经卷。

（35）兜率陀天：指弥勒菩萨说法的地方。

（36）丈六金身：指佛像。

译文

十九坨，也叫石臼坨。岛上茂密的草树遮天盖地，几乎不见蓝天沃土；岛的外围，深绿色的海水波涛汹涌，深可达数十丈，且盘旋曲流变成深窟，隐隐现出黑绿的颜色，阴森森的，看后惊心动魄。为此，从前很少有人来到这个地方。

明朝万历初年，一名法号显光的高僧来到岛上，伐林木，锄荒草，在这里始建朝阳庵。由此，显光和尚卓锡朝阳庵，世代香火不断，使南岳临济宗教派在渤海湾沿岸佛教圣地兴盛起来。世事沧桑，传至八代住僧智元，该寺已废。为重修此寺院，他发奋图新，积铢累寸，招工匠，购建材，相继创修了佛殿两楹。可是工程尚未完备，住持智元就去世了。道光八年（1828年），智元的徒弟慧辰，对于师父未竟的事业无限感慨，于是发奋把后期工程全部焕然一新。寺院建成后，他请求我为这座寺院写篇碑文。

我私下里想，世尊释迦牟尼仪像威严地在四禅天佛地，显现各种法相，眉宇现出十丈毫光，诵说着数以万计的佛经法典，以佛的愿力将世上的芸芸众生全都超度到恒河沙国界外的极乐世界去安享幸福。这个规模并不算大的僧人居

住处，亦不过是世间虚幻的一事相，而说这就是佛。这就像《涅槃经》中所讲众盲人摸象的故事那样，有的盲人摸到象的一只耳朵，就说象像一个簸箕；有的摸到象的一只脚，就说象像石臼；摸到一颗牙齿，则又说象的形象就像一根又肥又白的萝卜。所以出现上述种种说法，因这些人都是盲人而已。战国人庄周亦曾说：大道在，而又不在。以这些哲理观察事物的人，看砖瓦石块蝼蛄蚂蚁与看圣贤无异。如果要求必定得有最后结论才行，这就变成了拘泥守旧不知变通的人。说实在，朝阳庵也就是一个佛家传教说法的地方；石臼坨也就一处僧人居住之所；酷似仰面半环新月的月坨岛，也就像是佛居住的莲花净土；十九坨四围的大海施惠于民，可以说它是具有无限功德之水。在朝阳庵为佛塑画金身，虽只是简练地涂抹彩绘，但佛的三身也就圆满完备了。焚化一粒柏子，也就是虔诚，是把佛请到了朝阳庵，供那些信徒们焚香膜拜。所以在十九坨荒凉昏暗的地方，创建寺院为佛涂绘庄严的神像，传扬大乘佛法，以使佛陀威严仪态风貌，普照着天上人间。

哎，确实如此啊！无限仁慈智慧的佛，真是太伟大了！我登上海岛驻足在这里，又别有一番感慨在心中。明朝中期以来，地域潮湿、漫长水草的渤海湾沿岸，西起曹妃甸，东到关东州的金、复、海、盖一带，社会环境非常险恶。这一以农渔为生的地区，在草木茂密荒芜的去处，潜伏着海匪强盗。自大清朝的圣明帝主出世，石臼坨一带，在其盛威的震慑之下，滨海的邪恶社会势力全都潜伏起来了，石臼坨也变成了四海一统的升平世界，就像世外桃源一般，男耕女织，其乐融融，一辈子都很少知道外边的事情。拼力登上这贫瘠的荒山野岭，在这别有风情的天地，得以顶风冒雨，勤劳农渔，不愁吃不愁穿，心无疑虑；寺院的僧人暮鼓晨钟，诵念佛经，为众生祈求幸福。唉！可是谁知这都是大清朝接连几代为民创下的福音，使平民百姓得以休养生息，给以数百年深厚的恩德啊！我逗留在这里，登上石臼坨高高的所在，远望着那苍茫的大海，天际的惊涛骇浪变得那么平静，海上呼啸的大风变得那么安详。翘望幻境中的方壶、蓬莱、瀛洲，及拭目石臼坨这些仙山，心情顿时豁然开朗，烦恼愤恨竟皆除尽；仰望着旷远浩瀚的海天，心里那些想不开的事情，全都消失得一干二净。那么，遍人世间的黎庶众生，颂扬经卷佛法，求索事物的因果根源，当阅过石臼坨这一佛家圣境，又何用再到弥勒菩萨的佛国世界去瞻仰佛变幻万象的伟岸化身呢！

3. Stele Inscriptions of Chaoyang Nunnery [1]

Archeological research reveals that Mortar Isle has a long history. Its name was already confirmed when Li Shimin, an emperor of the Tang Dynasty, stayed on the island for 19 days during his military expedition to ancient Korea. Far from the mainland, the island was desolate and saw few visitors. Previously, there was only a temple on the weedy island, in which was enshrined a statue of the Avalokitesvara Bodhisattva. During the reign of Emperor Qianlong, bandits ran amuck in Laoting County, and the island became their base camp. To eliminate the threat of bandits, Yu Chenglong, then county magistrate of Laoting, had to burn the temple. Soon after social order was restored, Yu called on people to donate money used to rebuild the temple. Totally, six halls were constructed. Of the three halls in front, the left one was used to worship the Devil-Taming King, the right one used to worship the Dragon King, and the middle one used to worship the Maitreya Buddha. The three rear halls were used to enshrine the Avalokitesvara Bodhisattva. As more temples were built and more Buddhist statues were erected, the numbers of pilgrims also saw an increasing growth. At the time, devils often invaded the island. After the Sanjing Rite and the Niangniang Worship Ceremony were held here, the island began to see more visitors and Buddhist activities and resume its peace. This was, on one hand, because of pilgrims' devoutness to the Buddha; on the other hand, due to the endless power of the Avalokitesvara Bodhisattva. Following the wish of his forerunners, Monk Zhiyuan added three new halls to the temple. In the middle hall was enshrined a statue of the Avalokitesvara Bodhisattva. After the temple was refurnished, I was invited to write this stele inscription. Due to my limited knowledge of Buddhism, I just simply recorded what I heard and saw.

Almost all people know the Avalokitesvara Bodhisattva is an important figure in Buddhism, but few are clear about his origin and cultivation. Legend goes that the bodhisattva is smart and embraces a heart of mercy. He practices Buddhism in Putuo Mountain, and has a deep insight of Buddhist doctrines. He often preaches at the Purple Bamboo Forest. He gained endless power when he became the bodhisattva. He often held a vase with a willow branch. He variably displays as male or female, and few can spot him unless he shows by himself. His blessings cover the entire world. He always gives a hand to people in need no matter where they pray for help. There are numerous stories about how he helps people in need. Thus, people have worshipped the bodhisattva for hundreds of years. Mortar Isle is a remote, desolate place. There are no Confucian

三　朝阳庵碑记[①]

　　粤稽石臼坨由来久矣。自唐王东征，厥名已立。地势荒凉，人迹罕到，其中只有茅庵一座，观音大士一尊。嗣后于翁职宰乐亭，以海寇故，不得已遂焚其庵。后复捐资首倡而修大殿六间。前三间左塑伏魔大帝，右塑龙神，中塑弥勒；后三间遂为大士祠堂，以镇海内。厥后诸佛相继而登，自是人踪渐觉烦多，而游魂冤鬼往往作祟。兹因三经会与娘娘会屡次上坨超度，庶乎稍安。虽众会人等之诚心，实借观音大士之法力也。僧智元踵前之故事，又新修大殿三间，塑观音大士一尊，以表佛门无边之法力也。欲竖碑以志，揥[(1)]笔于余，余愧才陋学浅，不能道佛门寔[(2)]事，惟即耳所习闻者，偶述一二。

　　盖闻观音大士，佛门中显著者也，其生平出处不可得而详，而其行事大要以清净为本、慈悲为怀者也。慧心慧性，修道于普陀中；参妙参玄，谈禅于紫竹林下。迨功成行满，遂具无边法力。注净水于瓶底，洒甘露于枝头。倏为男倏为女，变化无方；忽而隐忽而现，杳冥难寻。感应遍乎天下，咸灵及于遐荒，一切救厄扶困、拯危恤急之事不可尽述，此所以俎豆[(3)]千秋，声名百代者也。夫坨偏隅也，圣教之所不及，而菩萨能化之，亦僻壤也。王化之所力，菩萨能感之，是菩萨之妙用，不惟有功于佛门，且兼以补圣教、赞王化也。是以鱼翁舟子戴菩萨之慈悲，感神圣之默佑，周不教服，爰作庙宇用志矣。尊左边护法，则有妙道真君，右边护法，则有伏魔大帝。丛林既成，竖碑以志，余述所闻，不知有当于一二否？

诰封

邑庠生　　安汝林

通议大夫　安于德

儒学教谕　陈永清

　　拜撰并书

乾隆夏五穀旦立

石　工　李超李玉　刊

注释

（1）揥：扛抬泥土的器具。

（2）寔（shí）：此处指不能说清深奥佛事之意。

（3）俎豆：一是俎和豆，古代祭祀、宴会时盛肉类食品的两种器皿。二是引申为祭祀崇奉之意。

译文

　　据考证，石臼坨海岛历史悠久。自唐王李世民东征高句丽经此驻跸十九天，石臼坨这个名字已经确立。此地远离陆地，荒凉偏僻，人们很少来到这里，野草遍岛的石臼上，只有修建平实的庙宇一座，塑绘一尊观音菩萨圣像。乾隆间，乐亭内地盗贼猖獗，时常逃到海边岛屿藏匿，县令于成龙职宰乐亭稽寇屡逸，不得已焚毁此庵。事过不久，境内社情平靖，于公首先向社会倡议捐资重修庙宇。计建成前后大殿六间，前殿三间，左供伏魔大帝，右供龙王老爷，居中供奉弥勒佛；后三间，为观音菩萨祠堂，以靖安海域和内陆。自此

---

① 因年代久远，风雨浸蚀，数处碑文缺损，有些文字为共同斟酌补入。此碑文源自朝阳庵遗址石碑。

schools, but the Avalokitesvara Bodhisattva can teach people there. He ever gave a hand to the emperor on the island, so the emperor supported to worship the bodhisattva there. The construction of Chaoyang Nunnery on the island was not only a benevolent deed of Buddhists and a supplement to Confucianism, but also demonstrated the emperor's love of people. Since then, all local fishermen and boatmen could bathe in the blessings of the Avalokitesvara Bodhisattva. So, who will behave evilly? The Avalokitesvara Bodhisattva is the main patron of Chaoyang Nunnery, who is accompanied by the Miaodao True God (or Erlang God) and the Devil-Taming King (or Guan Yu). This stele inscription is written to commemorate the establishment of the Buddhist temple. Please correct any errors in above text that I wrote.

Appendix: A Brief Biography of Chen Yongqing

Chen Yongqing (whose birth and death dates were now unknown) was a native of Laoting County. When he was young, he was noted for his filial piety. In 1735, he passed the provincial-level imperial examination, and was then admitted as a gongsheng in 1737. He attended six national imperial examinations, but all failed. During the early reign of Emperor Qianlong, he acted as an education supervisor in Luxian County (today's Luquan City, Hebei Province). During his tenure, Chen devoted himself to rejuvenate local cultural and education undertakings. Besides teaching students, he also took measures to prevent corruption and encourage the good. Thanks to his tireless efforts, the county's education sector witnessed an increasing improvement. When he retired, locals held his clothes while bursting into tears, attempting to persuade him to stay. Chen was particularly expert at the Eight-Part Essay. He was crazy about study, and didn't give up reading even in scorching summer and chilly winter. He often dedicated much energy to correct the schoolwork of his students until he thought them perfect. Historical records reveal that he had "many publications," but few of them were passed down.

① For centuries of weathering, parts of the stele inscription already faded away. Therefore, some words were supplemented upon conjecture. This text is based on a stone stele found at the site of Chaoyang Nunnery.

地随着寺庙的不断修缮，各种神像相继塑绘，随着香火日益兴盛，朝拜者越来越多，但与此同时，邪魔外祟时常作怪。今因三经会与娘娘会上岛的人也越来越多，通过各种佛事活动超度，这才日趋平静下来。之所以如此，一是僧众对佛的虔诚，而实际上是借观音菩萨的无边法力呀！僧人智元遵循先辈的遗愿，新修大殿三间，中塑观音菩萨像，以此显示佛法无边。寺院修缮完毕，为竖碑以记，撰写碑文找到我的名下，抱愧无才，无力说清佛门的这件事。我只能是把所见所闻的事情加以简单表述而已。

人们听说观音菩萨在佛教中名望很高，对他的出身和教养却不太清楚。只知他弘法济世，以清净为本、以慈悲为怀。他心性聪慧，修行在普陀山中，对佛教的理法有着精细研悟，常在紫竹林读经讲法。当他修炼成正果成了菩萨，具有了无边的法力，他手持净瓶和杨柳枝，常将瓶中的清水洒在杨柳枝上。他一会儿变成男子，一会儿变成女子，一会儿隐身，一会儿现身，难以见到他的。但他恩惠遍于天下，显灵及于四方。对俗人的所做所想则都能知道，不管俗人在什么地方求助，他都能给以救援。他救苦救难、扶困济危的事儿数不胜数。因此千百年来，人们一直虔诚地供奉他。石臼坨是个偏僻荒凉的地方，这里没有儒家的学堂，而观音菩萨却能在此教化人，在这荒凉的地方助了皇上一臂之力。这道理观音很明白，皇上也支持在此供奉观音。因此在石臼坨修建朝阳庵，不仅有功于佛门，也补了儒教之不足，是对皇上爱民之心的赞美。从此以后，不论是打鱼的人，驶船的人，都可以感恩于观音的慈悲胸怀，得到观音的护佑，谁还敢做坏事呀！故作朝阳碑记。朝阳庵中，主神为观音菩萨，左边胁侍神妙道真君（二郎神），右边的护法神是伏魔大帝（关羽），参禅修法之地修建成了，立碑以记，我写的以上文字，尚请方家指正。

附：陈永清小传

陈永清（生卒年月不详），字济周，乐亭人。少年时，以孝友闻名乡里。童年入学，考试第一名。由选拔登雍正乙卯（十三年）科举人。又中乾隆丁巳科（二年）明经榜（贡生）。六次赴京会试不中，乾隆初，出任获鹿县（今河北省鹿泉市）教谕。到职后，即以振兴文教为务。躬身试教，亲自定甲乙，黜退腐败，嘉奖优良，一县之文风大为改变而且越来越好。去官之日，竟有牵衣流涕而不愿其离去者。永清对于精深八股文一道，视同性命，虽盛夏严冬仍手不释卷。命题作文，诸生作有不合题者，呕心沥血给予修正，以达完美而后止。志书有载："平生著作甚多"，但鲜见流传于世。

4. Stele Inscriptions for the Buddhist Hall
of Guanyin Temple [1]

Editor's Note: Although it was discovered later than many other stone steles on Puti Island, the Stele Inscription for the Buddhist Hall of Guanyin Temple is of great archeological value, and bears testimony of the past prosperity of Buddhist temples on the island. Regretfully, some characters carved on the stone stele are already unrecognizable after centuries of weathering. But, the majority of its inscriptions remain so that later generations can still figure out what the stone stele records.

It is said that deities could be found both in heaven and on earth. According to the Book of Changes, "one can naturally conquer the whole world when he understands the secret law of heaven." Therefore, many ancient monarchs held grand ceremonies to worship deities for the purpose to avoid earthly disasters. However, divine doctrines are too profound to be understood by secular people. So, secular doctrines have won popularity as a way to educate ordinary people since ancient times. Built in the Qing Dynasty, the Guanyin Temple originally consisted of a front hall, a Buddhist hall, and a kitchen. After years of weathering, it became dilapidated. Then, some Buddhists refurnished it, but the temple once again fell into deterioration. Therefore, local Buddhist believers hired artisans and bought building materials to refurnish the ancient temple. After the reconstruction project was completed, I was appointed to write this stele inscription. Impressed by the kindness of those contributors, I visited the temple. Everything seemed better than I imagined, so I had no more to say.

[1] Extracted from stone stele on the site of Chaoyang Nunnery

四　观音庙佛堂碑记[1]

按:《观音庙佛堂碑记》是菩提岛石碑中发现较晚且极有研究价值的碑刻。它进一步佐证了石臼坨海岛历史上"梵宫鼎峙"的寺院兴替旧貌。令人遗憾的是,随着年代悠远,风雨浸剥,碑上许多文字已经残缺难辨。所幸此碑少数文字虽已无从查明,但大部文字尚存。卷中权且留下如许缺损,以待后贤研究完善。

碑额　永垂不朽

地域　直隶永平府乐亭县

观音庙佛堂碑记

盖闻天有天神地有地示[1]易曰观天之神道而天下服以故先王之制祀典也能御大蕾[2]则祀□

迷而神道远伊古以来厥典维彰我□□□□□

观音庙一座前有大殿后有佛堂日久年深风雨颓□圮经重修迄今佛堂火房又复残缺众善士

以凭有其举之莫敢废也于是鸠工庀材残者□

新工成告竣嘱予作文以记之予嘉众善士好□昭来兹至庙中神圣之灵感前人之述备矣予

儒学生员××××　　　　××

本邑膳生员×××　　　　××

大清道光三十年岁次庚戌秋七月

注释

(1)示:(qí):神。

(2)蕾:灾害。

译文

听说,天上有天上的神仙,地下有地下的神仙。《易经》说:"仰观天的神秘法则,则天下就在不知不觉中信服。"所以历代帝王设祭祀天地神灵的礼仪,是认为能抵御人间的灾难才行祭祀。然而,理不可知,目不可见,令人不知所以然的所谓神法却远离世俗,因此自古以来总是那些教化民众的常法显现于民间。我(朝在此兴建)一座观音庙,前面为大殿,后边为佛堂与火房,年深日久,风雨剥蚀已经破败不堪。虽已经过善士们重新修葺,可是随着时间推移,目前再次破旧不全,因之众善士不忍见其残状,才有此次的举动。于是找工匠,购置建材,使旧庙焕然一新,完工之后,找我写篇碑文,以作纪念。我欣赏众善士的好生之德来到这里,到庙堂一看,众前贤在神灵的感应下各方面的事情比我想象的更加完备,我也就没更多的话要说了。

①此碑文源自朝阳庵遗址石碑。

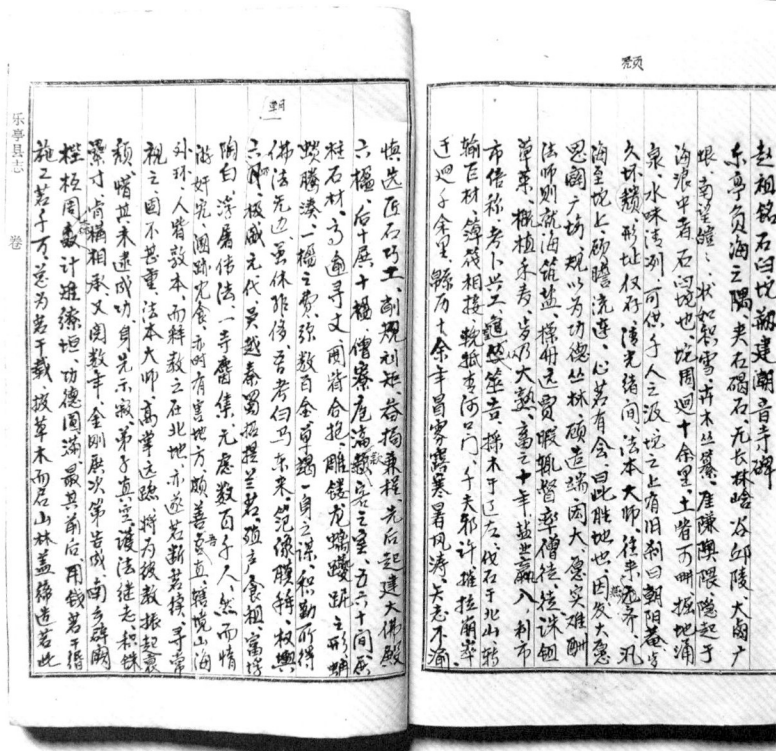

5. Stone Stele in Commemoration of the Establishment of Chaoyin Temple [1]

Situated on the shore of the Bohai Sea, Laoting County faces Jieshi Mountain on right. There are no forested valleys and hills, but a vast expanse of saline and alkaline land that appears like snow. Viewed from distance, Mortar Isle seems floating on the sea waves. With a circumference of more than five kilometers, the island boasts tillable fields, as well as sweet spring water enough for 1,000 people to drink. Once upon a time, the ancient Chaoyang Nunnery on the island was almost dilapidated due to centuries of weathering. During the reign of Emperor Guangxu of the Qing Dynasty, Master Faben traveled far from Hebei and Shandong provinces to the island. He checked out the island and concluded this might be a Buddhist holy land. So, he swore to himself that he would build an immense Buddhist temple here. However, it wasn't easy to fulfill the pledge. To raise funds, he then produced salt on the coast and then transported it elsewhere by boat. In spare

五 创建潮音寺碑[1]

乐亭负海之隅，夹右碣石。无长林谽[1]谷丘陵，大卤广垠，南望皑皑，状如积雪。卉木丛篆，崖隒[2]隩[3]隈[4]，隐起于海浪之中者，石白坨也。坨周迴十余里，土皆可耕。掘地涌泉，水味清冽，可供千人之汲。坨之上有旧刹曰朝阳庵，岁久坏颓，形址仅存。清光绪间，法本大师，往来齐燕，汎海至坨上。顾瞻流连，心若有会，曰此胜地也。因发大愿，思辟广场，规以为功德丛林。顾造端阔大，愿实难酬，法师则就海筑盐，操舟远贾。暇辄督率僧徒，诛鉏[5]草莱，稴[6]植禾麦，岁乃大熟。畜之十年，盐业赢入，利市倍称。考卜兴工，龟从筮吉。采木于辽左，伐石于北山。转输巨材，箁筏相接，挽抵青河口门，千夫邪许，摧拉崩崒[7]，迂回千余里，绵历十余年。冒雾露寒暑风涛，矢志不渝。慎选匠石巧工，削规园矩，备揭[8]兼程。先后起建大佛殿六楹、后佛殿十楹、僧寮[9]庖湢[10]、款客之室五六十间。殿柱石材，高逾寻丈，围皆合抱。雕镂龙螭[11]夔跜[12]之形，蚺惔[13]腾凑。一楹之费弥数百金，单竭一身之谋，积勤所得，佛法无边，虽休非侈。吾考白马东来[14]，范像膜拜。权舆[15]六朝[16]，极盛元代。吴越秦蜀，招提[17]兰若[18]，殖产食租，富埒[19]陶白。浮屠传法，一寺麇集，无虑数百千人。然而惰游奸宄[20]，阇[21]迹冗食，亦时有害地方。颇善吾直辖境，山海外环，人皆敦本，而释教之在北地，亦遂若断若续，寻常视之，固不甚重。法本大师，高瞻远瞩，将为彼教振起衰颓，惜其未逮成功，身先示寂。弟子真空，护法继志，积铢累寸，旨构相承。又阅数年，金刚殿次第告成。南乡辟阙，桠柤[22]周森。计雉缭垣，功德圆满。最其前后，用钱若干缗。施工若干万，总为若干载。披草木而启山林，盖缔造若此之艰也。坨三面距海，北通潮流。岗垄洼隆，皆生杂树。远望天际风驷[23]沙鸟、摩荡起伏、烟云变幻，亦奇观也。忆予方壮，来游坨上，初识法师一贫衲耳，安知其成就至此。法师戒律谨严，雅性慈善，尝出巨款施赈凶荒。又于曹妃甸洋面募建灯塔，遄利航行。居恒不尚说法，专注实践，盖于彼教宗派又殊已。法师名醇诚，法本者人之称之以其字，俗姓郭，家世京兆宁河北塘人。民国六年一月，即夏历丙辰十二月四日，居于寺中，趺跏[24]怛化[25]。

诰封朝仪大夫选用直隶州判赵祖铭篆文
诰封奉政大夫翰林院庶吉士葛毓芝书丹
中华民国十六年五月　谷旦

注释
（1）谽（hān）：山岭大谷。
（2）隒（yǎn）：层叠的山崖。
（3）隩：水涯深曲处。
（4）隈：弯曲的地方；角落。
（5）鉏：同"锄"。
（6）稴：稠密。
（7）崒（zú）：高耸而险峻。
（8）揭：抬土的器具。
（9）寮：小屋、茶寮。
（10）湢：浴室。
（11）螭：没有角的龙，古建筑上的装饰。
（12）夔跜（kuí ní）：动貌。
（13）蚺惔（rán tān）：兽吐舌貌。
（14）白马东来：指东汉明帝时，天竺僧人摄摩滕、竺法

---

① 原文录自韩湘亭总纂《乐亭县志稿》。

PUTI ISLAND A FAIRYLAND ON EARTH

time, he led other monks to reclaim weedy fields and grow crops. Their labor was rewarded by a good harvest that year. After ten years of endeavor, they earned considerable profits from salt trade. Then, they chose an auspicious day to begin the construction of the temple, for which they bought timber from eastern Liaoning and stone from Beishan. Those building materials needed to be transported by reedy rafts to the estuary of the Daqing River. In fact, their transportation cost more than a decade of painstaking efforts. While singing work songs to synchronize their movements, nearly 1,000 logged forests to cut a road through mountains. Even chilly waves couldn't stop them. Then, they hired experienced artisans, drafted blueprints, and prepared all tools needed. Eventually, a temple with six front halls and ten rear halls, as well as 60 dwelling rooms and living facilities like kitchens and bathrooms, was completed. Each of the stone pillars in its main hall measured nearly four meters high and could get an adult's arms around. The pillars were carved with lifelike dragons flying in clouds. Each hall cost hundreds of taels of gold. It was unbelievable for a monk to complete such a massive project with his own efforts. Perhaps this was because he was blessed by the Buddha. The temple looked magnificent, but not luxurious. Upon my investigation, the Buddhism was first spread to China during the Eastern Han Dynasty, when a white horse carried Buddhist sutras to the East, then flourished during the Wei and Jin dynasties, and reached its zenith in the Yuan Dynasty. At the time, numerous temples were constructed in Wu, Yue, Qin, and Shu areas. Those temples earned great wealth that could rival Fan Li and Bai Gui (both famous wealthy merchants in ancient China) through making loans and exploiting tenants. Each temple gathered nearly 1,000 monks, of which those lazy and evil persons loafed on their jobs and even tyrannized local people. Fortunately, people in Zhili Province are all unsophisticated and devout. Historically, the Buddhism also witnessed many ups and downs in North China. A foresighted monk, Faben

pledged to resurrect the Buddhism. However, he died before his dream came true. His disciple, Zhenkong, succeeded his unfinished wish. Upon years of endeavor, all halls of the temple were completed one after another. The temple faces south and is encircled with high walls. Totally, its construction cost large amounts of money and manpower, as well as tireless endeavor of many years. It was an arduous work to build a temple in such a desolate place. Mortar Isle is embraced by seawater in three directions all year round. At flood tide, seawater surged in its north side to completely separate the island from the mainland. Various species of trees grow on the island's hills and marshes. Looking at the distance, one can see boats sailing on the sea and birds hovering in the sky. What a wonderful view! I remembered when I first met Master Faben during a tour around the island many years ago, I didn't thought the poor monk could realize such a tremendous achievement.

Master Faben strictly followed Buddhist disciplines, but demonstrated great benevolence by donating large amounts of money for disaster relief. He once constructed a lighthouse to guide boats cruising on the sea near Caofeidian. He didn't preach much, but took active actions in helping others. Perhaps this was because the majority of local people believed in the Zen Sect. Originally named Guo Chuncheng, Master Faben was a native of Beitang, Ninghe County. In January 1917, he passed away in the Chaoyin Temple.

① Extracted from *Records of Laoting County* compiled by Hang Xiangting, a native of the county

132

兰应邀来洛阳，是用白马驮经书而来，从此佛教在东土传开。

（15）权舆：开始。

（16）六朝：指三国时吴、东晋、宋、齐、梁、陈。

（17）招提：寺院的别称。

（18）兰若：寺庙。

（19）埒（liè）：相等、相同的意思。

（20）奸宄：坏人。由内而起叫奸，由外而起叫宄。

（21）溷（hùn）：混乱。

（22）梐枑（bì hù）：，设在官衙前遮拦人马的栅栏。

（23）飒：帆的异体字。马行貌。

（24）趺跏：盘腿坐。

（25）怛化：怛（dá），死亡。

译文

乐亭县靠着大海的一角，右边是碣石山。没有长林山谷和丘陵，但盐碱荒地广阔，向南一望白花花的，就像积雪。草木丛生，崖叠水曲，隐现在海浪之中的，就是石白坨。坨周长十余里，土地都可以耕种，挖地就有泉水，水味清凉，可供千人饮用。坨上有古寺叫朝阳庵，年代久远已经毁坏倒塌，仅存轮廓遗址。大清光绪年间，法本大师，往来河北、山东之间，乘船来到坨上，观察了一段时间，心中有所领悟，说这是佛家圣地呀。因此他发下宏愿，想开辟出一块地方，建成诵经礼佛的禅林。考虑到工程浩大，誓愿难以实现，他就在海边筑池晒盐，驾船到远处去经商。有空闲就率领僧众，铲除野草，密植谷麦，当年就获大丰收。积蓄了十年，盐业大有收益，商业利润倍增。于是就占卜选吉日开工。从辽东采购木料，从北山选购大石，辗转运输这些巨大的材料，苇筏相接，拉运到大清河口，上千民工喊着号子伐木开山，克服艰难险阻，往返上千里，费时十多年。冒着雾露寒暑风浪，也决心不贰。慎重地选挑能工巧匠，定好规矩制度，备齐工具加快进程。先后建起大佛殿六间、后佛殿十间，僧房厨浴、待客室五六十间。大殿石柱的石料，有一丈多高，围都合抱。上面雕刻的龙螭栩栩如生，翻云吐雾。一间的费用高达数百金，单尽一个人的智慧，勤劳积蓄，真是佛法无边，虽然修建得这么壮美，也并非奢侈。我考证佛教

自东汉由白马驮经传到东土，塑像礼拜。应为传播开始于魏晋南北朝，极盛于元代。那时吴越秦蜀各地广建寺庙，寺院放贷吃租，财富可以比过范蠡和白圭。佛经传法，一寺之中聚集了不下千八百人。然而那些坏人懒汉，也在其中鬼混白吃，有时更为害地方。所幸我们直隶辖境，山海外环，人们都朴实本分。然而佛教在北方，亦就若断若续，这在平常人看来固然不太重要。法本大师，高瞻远瞩，打算为佛教振起颓势，可惜没等到成功，却先圆寂了。弟子真空，护法继志，一分一寸地积累，宗旨做法一脉相承。又过了多年，金刚殿逐个建成。向南开门，栅栏周严，高墙环绕，功德圆满。总计前后，用钱若干缗，用工若千万，共用若干年。斩草木而开山林，建寺是如此艰难哪。石白坨三面临海，北面只有涨潮时有水，坨上高岗和低洼地，都长着各种树木。远望天际风帆沙鸟，摇荡起伏，烟云变幻，也是奇观哪。回想我刚成年时，来坨上游玩，初次认识法本大师的时候，他不过是个穷和尚，哪里知道他会有这么大的成就。法本大师戒律严谨，性情高尚慈善，曾经拿出巨款，赈济救灾。又曾经在曹妃甸洋面募建灯塔，便利海船航行。大师平常不尚说法，专重实践，可能是这里的禅宗和自己不同的缘故吧。法本大师名叫醇诚，法本是人们以字称呼他，俗家姓郭，祖籍京畿宁河县北塘人。民国六年（1917年）一月，即夏历丙辰年十二月四日，在潮音寺中盘坐圆寂。

Appendix: Brief Biographies of Zhao Zuming and Ge Liuzhi

Zhao Zuming (1856-1928), a native of Fantuo, Laoting County, passed the provincial-level imperial examination in 1870. Though a proud and aloof person, he was crazy about reading. At the time, the imperial examination system hadn't been abolished yet, but Zhao dared to publicly criticize the Eight-Part Essay adopted by the system. He often encouraged later generations with new thoughts and science imported from the outside world. Upon the invitation of Peng Xiangcheng, then governor of Zhili Province, Zhao became the headmaster of Lianchi Academy in Baoding Prefecture. Later, he was appointed by Lian Jia, then governor of Hubei Province, as secretary of the Governor's Mansion responsible for the compilation of confidential documents. After the 1911 Revolution, Zhao returned to his hometown and spent his rest life cultivating flowers and drinking. He left behind two books, Collection of Shequ Garden and Maigu Records.

Ge Liuzhi (1861-1942), a native of Gezhuang Village, Laoting County, was noted for his knowledgeableness and versatility. He was expert at Confucian classics, especially the Book of Changes. In 1885, he passed the provincial-level imperial examination, and then passed the national imperial examination in 1895. After that, he was admitted into the Hanlin Academy for further study. Then, he was appointed general secretary of the Ministry of Justice. As an uncorrupted and righteous official, he never fawned on his seniors and led a poor but spiritually-comfortable life. At that time, many provincial governments manufactured coins without the court's permission. Upon the emperor's decree, Ge was responsible for investigating Fujian and Guangdong Provinces and searched 8,000 taels of illegal silver coins. The principal criminal tried to bride Ge with the same amount, but he refused. "Now many people suffer from shortage of food and clothes," Ge scolded. "Why not use the money to help people in need rather than bride me? You just increase your guilty by doing so." Ge won high applause from both the court and ordinary people for his uprightness and incorruptness. After the 1911 Revolution, he quitted his job and returned to his hometown, where he helped reinforce river courses and relieve natural disasters. His book included the *Literary Records of Buyuan*. In 1942, he died at the age of 85.

附：赵祖铭、葛毓芝小传

赵祖铭（1856—1928年），字式如，亦号什如。乐亭县樊坨人。同治九年（1870年）考取恩贡。为人孤高跌宕，无书不读，很有文才。当时科举制度尚未废止，他就诋毁八股文。常以世界上的新思想、科技鼓励后辈。曾被直隶总督彭项城聘请，主持保定府的莲池书院。以后又被湖北总督连甲聘为总督府秘书。总督府的奏牍军书等机要文件皆出于公之手笔。1911年辛亥革命，公归乡里，以养花饮酒自娱。著有《涉趣园集》、《迈古录》二卷流传于世。

葛毓芝（1857—1942年），字养泉，乐亭城西葛庄人。敏学多才，为文下笔万言，见者无不倾倒。通达经学，尤精易学。光绪十一年（1885年）中举，光绪二十年（1894年）中进士，授翰林院庶吉士，学业期满，授刑部主事。为官清廉，足不入权贵之门，守贫自安。是时各省设炉制钱，均不合朝廷规定。葛毓芝奉旨查办福建、广东二省，查出侵冒炉银达八千余两，主造者惧怕治罪，以这八千两白银行贿于他。葛毓芝义正词严地对当事人说："目前正遇灾荒，老百姓缺衣少食，把这些钱拿来贿赂于我，怎比得上把它悉数充公，赈济灾民，你如果这样做不更是触犯国法罪上加罪吗？"这一消息传出后，民众欢声雷动。葛毓芝不为利益所动的廉洁言行，受到朝野上下的称赞。辛亥革命后，卸职归乡，为家乡修河、赈灾，做过许多善事。著有《补园文存》行于世，1942年病世，享年85岁。

6. Gravestone for Monks Jing'an and Puji of the Linji Sect

The Shrine for Linji

Sect Monk Jing'an (Shenming) of Chaoyang Nunnery on Mortar

Isle of Laoting County

The Shrine for Monk Puji (Ruling)

Erected by Haichan and Haiyin

On June 18, 1924

① The gravestone was erected by Haichan and Haiyin, both monks of the Linji Sect on Mortar Isle, to commemorate their forerunners Jing'an and Puji. According to Buddhist routines, their secular names are also carved on the gravestone.

六　临济宗派寺僧静安普济墓碑[1]

临济宗派

乐亭石臼坨朝阳庵由唐至今

圆寂先祖上神下明静安老和尚之龛

圆寂先师上如下凌普济和尚之龛

徒孙　海禅　海印

中华民国十三年六月十八日立

---

[1]这通石碑是石臼坨临济宗派寺僧海禅、海印为怀念朝阳庵由唐至
今的师爷十代和尚静安，师父十一代僧人普济所立，碑文沿佛教习
俗撰写，把俗名以上下二字相嵌。

Chapter V: Religious Sites

I. The History of Chaoyang Nunnery

Puti Island has two religious structures: One is the Chaoyang Nunnery (also called Guanyin Nunnery) that was first built during the reign of Emperor Wanli of the Ming Dynasty; The other is the Chaoyin Temple that was constructed during the reign of Emperor Guangxu of the Qing Dynasty. Throughout history, the Chaoyang Nunnery underwent several ups and downs.

Records about the nunnery are clearly found in local historical books. According to *Records of Laoting County*, its founder was Zenist Master Xianguang from the Linji sect of Buddhism. A stone stele unearthed at the site of Chaoyang Nunnery, which was erected in 1924, reads that "forefathers of the Linji Sect died in the Chaoyang Nunnery on Mortar Isle in Laoting County since the Tang Dynasty."

After the Buddhism was introduced to China, eight major sects emerged one after another, of which the Zen sect cast great influence on traditional Chinese culture throughout history. The Zen sect deemphasizes theoretical knowledge, but advocates "direct self-realization" through meditation and dharma practice.

According to Buddhist records, during the Southern and Northern Dynasties (420-589), Bodhidharma, the founder of the Zen sect, traveled afar from India to China. In the Shaolin Temple on Songshan Mountain, he engaged in ten years of silent meditation to research Zen doctrines. In 622 during the Tang Dynasty, Hongren, the fifth-generation patriarch of the Zen sect, organized a debate for the purpose to choose his successor. His oldest student, Shenxiu, chanted a poem that reads, "The body is a Bodhi tree, and the mind a standing mirror bright. At all times polish it diligently, and let no dust alight." His another student, Huineng, responded with another poem that reads, "Bodhi is no tree, nor is the mind a standing mirror bright. Since all is originally empty, where does the dust alight?" So, Hongren thought Huineng had deeper understanding of Buddhism, and appointed him as the successor. As the sixth-generation patriarch of the Zen sect, Huineng opened the most brilliant page in the history of the Zen sect and even brought significant and far-reaching influence to the development of Buddhism.

In 845, the Tang rulers launched a campaign aiming to crack down the Buddhism, which is historically known as "Huichang Calamity." During the period, Buddhist temples around the country were mostly demolished, all Buddhist statues were destroyed, and monks were forced to resume secular life. Because the Zen doctrines were typically spread mouth-to-mouth and easy to learn, the Zen sect survived the calamity and gradually became the majority of Chinese Buddhism. Some even deem it as a synonym of Chinese Buddhism.

Then, the Zen sect was divided into "five schools and seven houses." During the period of Huichang Calamity, the military commander of Zhengding, Hebei Province, was a devout Buddhist believer, so local Buddhist establishments didn't see many deteriorations. In 854, Yixuan, a monk of the Zen sect, came to the Linji Temple in Zhengding. He then settled there to spread Buddhism, and founded the Linji Sect, a subdivision of the Zen sect.

In 1368, Zhu Yuanzhang founded the Ming Dynasty in Nanjing. In his youth, he once acted as a monk. After he ascended the throne, the emperor began to support Chinese Buddhism, rather than Tibetan Buddhism supported by the Yuan rulers. Yao Guangxiao (1335-1418), an important consulter

第五章　宗教名胜

第一节　朝阳庵的兴衰与变迁

菩提岛有两处宗教建筑，一是创建于明朝万历年间的朝阳庵（也称观音庵），二是始建于清朝光绪年间的潮音寺。伴随着国运的盛衰，朝阳庵几起几落，兴衰变迁。

朝阳庵的历史脉络，史志有较明确记载。据《乐亭县志》记载，朝阳庵的创建者是佛教禅宗临济派显光上人。在朝阳庵遗址上现存有一块刻立于1924年的石碑，碑文中写着"临济宗派乐亭石臼坨朝阳庵由唐至今圆寂先祖"。

自佛教传入中国后，相继产生了八个较大的宗派分支，其中对中国传统文化产生较大影响的是禅宗门派。禅宗以"不立文字，教外别传；直指人心，见性成佛"为修行方法，通过"顿悟"，达到"立地成佛"。

根据佛教教内的说法，南北朝（420—589年）时，禅宗初祖菩提达摩从古印度来到中国，在嵩山少林寺面壁十年，传习禅法。唐高宗龙朔二年（662年），禅宗第五代祖师弘忍考问弟子，以便选定继承人。弟子神秀写道："身是菩提树，心如明镜台，时时勤拂拭，莫使惹尘埃。"弟子慧能则诵吟出："菩提本无树，明镜亦非台，本来无一物，何处惹尘埃。"弘忍法师认为慧能悟性更深，于是将衣钵传给了慧能。慧能成为禅宗第六代祖师之后，开启了禅宗的辉煌兴盛，对佛教产生了重大而深远的影响。

唐朝晚期武宗李炎时期，发生了排斥佛教的"会昌法难"（845年），当时全国大多佛教寺院被拆，金银佛像被毁，僧人被强制还俗。禅宗因为"不立文字"，所依经典不多，修行简易便捷，因而继续得以传承，并逐渐成为汉传佛教的主流，甚而成为中国佛教的代名词。

禅宗在发展过程中，又产生了"五宗七家"诸流派。"会昌法难"时，河北正定地区的节度使是一位虔诚的佛教徒，因此正定一带佛教没有受到大的冲击。唐宣宗李忱人中八年（854年），禅宗僧人义玄辗转来到正定临济寺院开始弘扬佛法，正式形成临济宗派。

1368年，朱元璋在南京称帝，正式建立明王朝。朱元璋早年曾经出家当过和尚，他当上皇帝后，不像元代那样支持藏传佛教喇嘛教，而主要支持传统汉传佛教。明朝永乐皇帝朱棣的重要谋士姚广孝（1335—1418年），是一位禅宗临济门派僧人（法名道衍），他半官半僧，执掌管理全国佛教。禅宗在慧能大师后极盛于唐宋，而到了明代临济宗的发展又超过其他禅宗宗派，与道衍和尚对朝政的影响是不无关

of Emperor Zhu Di, was a monk from the Linji Sect. His religious name was Daoyan. He also acted as an official responsible for the administration of Buddhism affairs around the country. The Zen sect reached its zenith during the Tang and Song dynasties. In the Ming Dynasty, the Linji Sect exceeded other subdivisions of the Zen sect largely because of Monk Daoyan's influence in the court.

Early in the reign of Emperor Wanli (1573-1620), Master Xianguang mounted onto today's Puti Island, where he "cut weeds and reclaimed wasteland" to build a temple. Then, he settled there to spread Buddhist doctrines.

In 1618, Nurhachi, the founder of the Qing Dynasty, led an army of 20,000 warriors and declared war against the Ming Dynasty. In 1644, the Qing army captured Beijing, and then the Qing Dynasty was officially founded.

Years of warfare made many people homeless, and bandits began to wreak havoc. Early in the reign of Emperor Kangxi (1654-1722), Yu Chenglong was appointed as magistrate of Laoting County. He took immediate measures to crack down bandits, who then retreated to Puti Island and took the Chaoyang Nunnery as their hideaway. Yu then ordered to burn down the temple. After that, he "raised funds to rebuild the temple."

In the middle of the reign of Emperor Kangxi, Monk Zhiyuan, the eighth-generation descendant of the Linji Sect, spent more than six decades raising money to add two halls to the Chaoyang Nunnery in 1759. In 1795, he raised more money and planned to further expand the temple. However, Huilin, one of his disciples, robbed the money. Through investigation, local government "expelled Huilin back to his hometown and ordered him to assume secularization." Stricken by the accident, Master Zhiyuan soon died, and his disciple Huichen succeeded the abbot's post. In 1798, six halls and six side rooms were added to the temple, which thus took a totally new look.

In 1885, Monk Faben of the Caodong Sect, another major subdivision of the Zen sect, came to Puti Island from Caofeidian. At the time, the Chaoyang Nunnery was already on the verge of dilapidation. Faben then swore to "resurrect the Buddhist temple." Monk Jing'an, then abbot of the Chaoyang Temple, persuaded other monks from the Linji Sect to give up sectarian bias and accept Faben as their new abbot. After that, Faben led other monks to reclaim wastelands, grow crops, raise funds through trades, and exploit stone and timber. After more than ten years of preparation, a new, magnificent monastery, Chaoyin Temple, was erected on the island.

Early in the Republic of China period, Monk Puji, a student of Jing'an, led monks of the Chaoyin Temple to settle in the Chongfu Temple in today's Shibei Village, Matouying Town, which is popularly called the Lower Chaoyang Nunnery.

According to *Records of Laoting County* compiled in 1945, "in the northeast of Mortar Isle stands an ancient pagoda that houses two urns, one erecting straightly and the other unturned. In the corridor of the west chamber of the rear hall lies a stone stele carrying inscriptions by You Zhikai, a governor of ancient times. There are two historic sites of the Chaoyang Nunnery: One is under the mulberry tree southeast to the Chaoyin Temple, and the other is 250 meters north to the Chaoyin Temple. So far, broken stone steles can still be found in overgrown weeds."

朝阳庵中静心经堂
虔诚膜拜颂经扬
修行顿悟禅宗秋
胸宽体健解虑肠

（落款）因水清朝阳庵□□初夏平和室主璧朝□书於广皇蜀琢□斋

系的。

明万历（1573—1619年）初年，临济宗显光上人登上人迹罕至的菩提岛，"伐榛莽，铲茅筏"，建庵传法。

明万历四十六年（1618年），清太祖努尔哈赤亲率两万八旗劲旅，拉开同明军正式作战的大幕，直至崇祯十七年（1644年）攻入北京建立清王朝。

由于处在明清朝代更替之际，连年战乱使百姓居无定所，盗贼匪徒横生不断。清康熙初年，于成龙任职乐亭县令时，大力捕盗缉贼，盗贼匪寇逃入菩提岛朝阳庵藏居。盛怒之下，于成龙下令烧毁了朝阳庵，后来又"首倡捐资而修"。

清康熙年（1662—1722年）中期，临济宗第八代传人智元经过60多年"广积囊资"，在乾隆二十四年（1759年）建造了两座佛殿。到乾隆六十年（1795年）时，智元积累了更多的财力，准备继续扩大朝阳庵，不料弟子慧林看到师父积聚的巨大财富，心生不轨，发生了"恶徒慧林抢劫之变"。报经官府后，很快查明真情，慧林被"枷杖递籍，勒令还俗"。经此变故，智元法师圆寂，其弟子慧辰继承师父衣钵，至嘉庆三年（1798年）建起佛殿六间，廊房六间，整座寺院焕然一新。

清光绪十一年（1885年），曹洞宗僧人法本从曹妃甸来到菩提岛。曹洞宗也是禅宗较有影响的支派，有"临天下，曹一角"之说。法本登岛时，朝阳庵已渐显衰落，"惟经营无人，榛芜未辟"，他"因发大愿，思辟广场，归以为功德丛林"。当时的朝阳庵住持临济僧静安以"佛法万宗终归于佛祖"劝说弟子摒弃门派之见，接受异宗法本代为住持。法本从此率领僧众垦荒种粮，航海经商，伐石采木，经过十数年的筹备，终于建成规模宏大的新寺院——潮音寺。

民国初年，静安的徒弟普济率朝阳庵僧人，移居位于今天马头营镇石碑村的崇福寺，设为朝阳庵的下院。

据1945年成书的《乐亭县志稿》记述石臼坨古迹："一、坨东北有古塔一，中置二缸，一仰一覆。后殿西耳房廊下，有前郡守游智开手书卧碑。二、朝阳庵故址有二，一处在潮音寺东南的大桑树下，另一处在潮音寺正北半里。均遗迹宛然，并有断碑，没草荒中。"

II. Monk Faben and Chaoyin Temple

Originally named Guo Chuncheng, Monk Faben was a native of Beitang, Tianjin. He was born into a poor fisherman's family in 1839, and died on January 16, 1917. As a child, he was hired as a sailor to fish along the coastal areas of the Bohai Sea, including Liaoning, Hebei, and Shandong. One time, his boat wrecked due to hurricane on the sea near Caofeidian. All sailors aboard died except for him. He then swore to build a lighthouse at Caofeidian to avoid similar tragedies.

At 19, Faben fled home to escape the marriage arranged by his parents, and converted to Buddhism at an old temple in northern Beijing. He then became a practitioner of the Caodong Sect. To fulfill his pledge, he came to Caofeidian and became the abbot of a local temple. Then, he spent four years raising money around the country and finally constructed a lighthouse at Caofeidian. Since then, he kept watch on the lighthouse day and night to guide local fishermen on the sea.

After centuries of weathering and tide erosion, the Caofei Hall erected in the Tang Dynasty gradually sank in water. Faben then decided to rebuild it elsewhere. He heard that Laoting County's Mortar Isle, which was only dozens of miles north from Caofeidian, was a Buddhist holy land. He then led his disciples to visit the island. As soon as they set foot on the island, they were immediately intoxicated in its picturesque landscapes: The crowns of skyscraping bodhi trees stretched like huge umbrellas, lush grass carpeted the ground, fishing boats shuttle in and out to the accompaniment of the sound of shell trumpets, and wild birds sang on the golden and silver beaches. "Legend goes that three legendary islands, Penglai, Fangzhang and Yingzhou, lie on the East Sea," Faben said to himself. "Mortar Isle must one of them. It is a perfect location for the construction of Buddhist temples." As they went deeper, a dilapidated temple entered into their sight. A plaque on the collapsed gate carried three characters translated as "Chaoyang Nunnery." Heaps of ruins lied in overgrown weeds. The singing of a crow in a nearby old tree added a dreary atmosphere. All monks couldn't help mourning for the dilapidated temple. Suddenly, an idea hit Faben: Why not rebuild the temple?

He consulted local fishermen about the origin of the temple. He learned that the temple was first constructed in the Ming Dynasty and received constant pilgrimages until years ago. In recent years, the temple became increasingly desolate, and its monks had no capacity to refurnish it and then moved to the Chongfu Temple in inland area.

This further made Faben confirm his decision to reconstruct the temple. The first thing he then did was to visit the Chongfu Temple to call on Monk Jing'an, former abbot of the Chaoyang Nunnery. He told Jing'an about his decision to rebuild the temple, and said he was willing to acknowledge Jing'an as his teacher although they belonged to different sects. Jing'an had long heard the story how Faben endeavored to build the lighthouse at Caofeidian, and was deeply moved by his benevolent deeds. Moreover, the Linji Sect would regain its prosperity if the temple was rebuilt. So, Jing'an granted the site of the former Chaoyang Nunnery to Faben, who then acquired the right to rebuild the temple. After he returned to

第二节　法本与潮音寺

　　法本，俗姓郭，名醇诚，天津宁河北塘人，道光十九年（1839年）生，故于1917年1月16日。法本生于一个穷苦的渔民家庭。刚进童年就跟随家人受雇于船主，以船为家，往返于辽宁、河北、山东之间的渤海沿线进行近海捕捞。一次随船出海作业，在曹妃甸海区遭遇狂风，触沙沉船，船上的人均葬身大海，只他一人幸免于难。于是，他矢志要在曹妃甸建立一座灯塔，以解船民遭遇风险之虞。

　　法本19岁时，因不满父母为他说亲，逃婚到京北红螺山古台寺受戒出家，成为曹洞宗正宗传人。之后，为实现建立灯塔的夙愿，辗转来到曹妃殿卓锡住持，潜心虔修。为在甸上建立灯塔，他托钵远游，到处募化，历时四年，终于用募化到的资金在曹妃甸建起一座灯塔。从此，他日夜守候在灯塔旁，为过往渔民解难消灾。

　　潮汐起落，世事沧桑，由于连年风雨侵蚀和海潮的冲击，建于盛唐时的曹妃大殿，渐次浸于水下，岌岌可危，重新修复无望。法本决定择地另辟功德丛林。久闻曹妃甸北望数十里的乐亭海域有个石臼坨，是个佛教圣地，他就带领僧徒，乘船迤逦向石臼坨而来。来到坨前，上岸放眼望去，眼前不由一亮：啊，此处和曹妃甸相比，简直是另一番天地！只见坨上菩提婆娑如巨伞迎宾，芳草萋萋似锦毯铺地，海螺声声催渔舟竞发，金银滩头听百鸟争鸣，法本师徒立即被岛上秀丽奇绝的自然风光所吸引，他们看了一景又一景，走到一处迷一处，法本想：人都说东海有蓬莱、方丈、瀛洲三个神仙海岛，我看这石臼坨就是其中一个仙岛了，这里才是建造功德丛林的最佳境地！法本师徒越看越有兴致。他们继续

前行，眼前隐约出现一座庵院，走到近前，那庵院却已是断壁残垣，在倒塌的山门上有写着"朝阳庵"三字的匾额。举目四顾，只见庵堂、殿阁颓败不堪，荒草遍地，人去寺空，枯藤老树，寒鸦凄厉，让人感到无限凄凉！众僧目睹如此惨状，不由扼腕长叹。然而此时唯有法本心中却是一亮，重修此庵之念蓦然浮现心头。

　　他向休憩的渔民仔细询问了此庵的来龙去脉，得知此庵建于明朝万历初年，历经明清都有剃度的和尚在此虔修，一直是香火不断，只是近些年，庵院颓败，无力修复，众僧不能在此居住，只得迁至内地的石碑崇福寺。

　　法本听罢暗下决心：重修朝阳庵！但因寺院权属之故，不能草草行事，只得亲自寻踪到石碑崇福寺，去拜见朝阳庵原住持静安。法本来到崇福寺，相见后，对静安说明要重修朝阳庵之意，并愿认静安为异宗师。此时，静安已是暮年老衲，但对法本的为人早有耳闻，特别是曾被他燃指化缘，在曹妃甸上修建灯塔解航船之险等义举深深感动。这次，对重修朝阳庵又怀有一片诚心，且庵院修好后，临济宗又能传承

Mortar Isle, Faben conducted a geographic reconnaissance of the island together with his disciples. They reached a consensus that the new temple should be built on the vaster land south to its former site. Then, they began to draft the blueprints of the new temple.

Faben was then committed to visiting governmental departments, charity organizations, and wealthy merchants, but his purpose wasn't to raise money, but win their recognition and support.

In 1889, the construction of Chaoyin Temple commenced under the supervision of Faben. To raise money, Faben led other monks to reclaim wastelands and build salt fields near the estuary of the Daqing River, for which they hired experienced workers from former salt fields. Then, the transported salt products with boats and sold them to the north. Thanks to the tireless efforts of Faben, the government loosened its restriction on their salt business. In this way, they earned considerable profits, which laid financial foundation for the construction of the new temple.

To raise more money, Faben learned from local merchants and took advantage of the favorable geographic location of Mortar Isle and the convenient water transportation of Laoting County to construct docks on the coast and build gigantic ships that could carry nearly 100 tons of grain, salt, seafood, and textile products each. He then recruited sailors to organize a fleet to trade cargos in such cities as Tianjin, Tangu, Qingdao, Yantai, Dalian, and Yingkou. Faben even hired professional managers to help him run business, and established shops at Daqing Harbor, Laoting, Matouying, and areas along the Luanhe River. It is unbelievable that a Buddhist could establish such an impressive commercial kingdom. In the Stele Inscriptions in Commemoration of the Establishment of the Chaoyin Temple on Mortar Isle, Zhao Zuming said that Faben "didn't emphasize theoretical research but practice, and perhaps this is because the doctrines of his sect are different." With an enterprising spirit, Faben made every effort to raise funds and gather building materials for the construction of the temple. He purchased timber from the Greater Higgan Mountains, Liaoning and Chengde that were a thousand miles away, and exploited Beishan Mountain to gather stones

香火，他感到非常欣慰，当即表示甘愿将朝阳庵旧址传于法本，为此法本取得了建寺权。他回到石臼坨后，就和徒弟们认真对石臼坨上的地形进行了勘测，认为寺院的位置应向南移到一处宽敞地带，以扩大寺院规模。决策后立即对新建寺院重新进行了规划设计。

法本为取得建寺主动权，频频奔走于邑内各级官衙、慈善殿堂、商贾豪富之家，其目的不是去布施募化，而主要是为了在建寺过程中，求得官府、社会贤达的首肯和支持。

光绪十五年（1889年），法本主持的潮音寺工程破土动工。法本一面亲率僧众对石臼坨进行规模空前的开发垦种；为了筹集资金，利用海水资源，在大清河口一带海域修

建盐池，并从原石碑场招来有经验的老盐工"就海煮盐"，晒成盐后，再从当地渔民那儿雇用船只运往塞北出售，形成盐业生产、销售一条龙。在他的不懈努力下，官府放宽了限制，使盐业生产很快形成了规模，获取了巨大的经济效益，奠定了建寺的资金基础。

为扩大资金来源，法本还借鉴乐亭人上关东经商经验，充分运用石臼坨的地域环境和乐亭的河海运输条件，在海边建船坞，请工匠，先后排成了大木鱼、二木鱼、三木鱼三条负载数千石粮食、盐、海产品、丝织品等的大型商船。大船排好后，他招聘水手，组成经商运营船队，来往于口外、天津、塘沽乃至延伸到山东的青岛、烟台，辽宁的大连、

that measured "three meters high." He hired laborers to carry timber and stones out of mountains, and then shipped them thousands of kilometers back to Laoting. Light materials were directly transported to Mortar Isle, and heavy ones arrived at Daqing Harbor first and were then re-transported to the island. Those stones and timber were so massive and heavy that they couldn't be transported with cattle-driven carts. So, transporters had to pour water on the roads in winter and then slip them on frozen surfaces. It is said that it cost a whole winter to transport a single stone used as a pillar. As all building materials arrived at the estuary of the Daqing River, they were then transferred to Mortar Isle by boat. Then, they were unloaded and delivered to the construction site with animal power and manpower. During the period when the temple was under construction, building materials like stones, timber, and bricks piled up at the Daqing Harbor. Passersby were impressed by seeing so many boats busy transporting building materials to the island.

To ensure the temple's architectural magnificence and superb workmanship, Faben hired seasoned artisans far and near and kept a close watch on project quality in the course of construction. He often inspected the construction site to give instructions. After 27 years of painstaking efforts, the temple finally took shape, for which Faben devoted considerable endeavor until his last breath.

In 1917, although he was on the sickbed, Faben still concerned much about the construction of the Chaoyin Temple. He often met his disciples to discuss on the construction project. On the dawn of the 4th day of the 12th lunar month, Faben summoned all disciples to declare his last wish. With tears in their eyes, his disciples pledged that they would fulfill his unfinished wish. Satisfied at their response, Faben chanted Buddhist sutras with them and then died. That year, he was 79 at age. Not only monks in the Chaoyin Temple but also local residents, especially those fishermen who ever benefited from Faben's help, mourned for his death. They

flooded from every corner to Mortar Isle to attend Faben's funeral. Although absent from the funeral, Ge Yuzhi, a famous scholar and one of Faben's old friends, sent a pair of elegiac couplets to express his grief and condolence.

After the death of Faben, his disciple, Zhenkong, led other monks and spent 17 years to complete the construction project in 1933. After the completion of the temple, Shi Lüjin, the third son of Shi Menglan (who was dubbed "No.1 scholar in eastern Beijing"), wrote couplets for columns of the temple's front gate, and Han Xiangting, a famous local scholar, was invited to write couplets for the front hall, rear hall, and other structures. Faben's long-cherished wish was eventually fulfilled. When the temple was finished, abbots of many other temples, as well as local officials, merchants, and aristocrats, came to celebrate its completion. The construction lasted 44 years. All structures of the new temple were exquisitely decorated. The front gate consisted of three rooms, and a plaque carrying inscriptions translated as "The Sound of Sea Tide" was hung under its eaves. Inside the first floor building were the colored statues of the Four Guardian Warriors, which looked magnificent and differed in postures.

Then was the Tathagata Hall (or Great Hall). Also called "Zhuanjiao Temple," it was a pavilion-like structure with three rooms. Inside the hall were the statues of Sakyamuni, Manjushri, and Samantabhadra, which were flanked by the Eighteen Arhats. All colored statues were exquisite and lifelike. The floor of the hall was paved with stone planks, which could reflect the sound of bells and drums. Hence, the temple was also nicknamed "Echo Temple."

The rear hall consisted of five rooms. On the stone wall inside the hall were carved the Three Saints of Western Paradise and the 500 Arhats, which varied in postures but looked similarly majestic.

On each side of the rear hall were eight rooms for monks to live. There were also two side halls, each with three rooms,

营口等地。在商业经营中，他雇用了乐亭富有经商经验的精英们进行管理，并先后在大清河口岸、乐亭、马头营及滦河沿线设立经营商号。如此经营规模，让人很难想象，这是一个佛门弟子所能从事的事业。正如当时邑人赵祖铭撰写石臼坨《创建潮音寺碑》中对法本作出的评价："居恒不尚说法，专注实践，盖于彼宗教派又殊已。"富有干事创业精神的法本，一面千方百计筹集建寺资金，采集建寺物料，一面着手实施土木工程。他不远千里从大兴安岭、辽宁、承德等地去采购上等木材，还由北山碣石筹集"高逾寻丈，围皆合抱"的巨大石材。在伐木、采石过程中，指挥雇用的民夫翻山越岭将物料移至山下，然后分装上船，远涉千余里甚至几千里，超重的运抵大清河口岸，轻便的直接运往石臼坨。那体积庞大的青石、木料因十分沉重无法用畜力拖拉，只好在冬季冰封大地时，在地面上泼水使之结冰，然后再组织人力

推动木料、巨石在地上慢慢滑行，逐段搬运，据说，仅一块楹柱的石料就需要整整一个冬季才能完成。其运料之难可见一斑。建寺所用的物料运抵大清河口后，然后再分批倒运到石臼坨海岸，全凭人、畜推、拉、牵、曳运往潮音寺建筑工地。建寺期间，清河口岸，石木砖瓦堆积如山，船来舟往，车水马龙，行人见之，无不瞠目结舌、诚服感叹。

为建设高标准寺院，大兴土木建筑工程，法本从邑内外精选工匠。在建设过程中，从难从严要求工程质量。为此，经常亲自到现场监督，提出自己的意见。历经漫长27个年头的昼夜施工，寺院建设工程已粗具规模。他为潮音寺的建设付出了大量心血，直到生命最后一息。

1917年已卧病在床的法本仍十分关注潮音寺建设，经常在床前召集弟子们商讨建寺事宜。农历十二月初四拂晓，已气息奄奄的他招来全寺僧人，还对身后建寺事宜进行了叮嘱，众徒含泪合十发誓决心完成师父建寺夙愿。法本听后，感到无限欣慰，之后，与众僧念《大悲咒经》毕，飞升示寂，享年79岁。法本趺坐示寂，不仅是潮音寺僧众万分悲痛，就连邑内百姓特别是当年受过法本救助的沿海民众也悲痛伤感不已，纷纷结队到石臼坨上致哀送行。昔日故友前清翰林葛毓芝未能亲临现场，还专门派人送来挽联，以示哀悼。

as well as such facilities as a sutra hall, a guestroom, and a bathing room. All of those structures were in a compound "encircled by solid walls."

On each side of the compound was a moon-shaped gate that led to an independent courtyard. The east courtyard was where hired laborers and servant monks lived and worked, which housed all kinds of living facilities such as mills, warehouses, kitchens, sesame oil mills, and tofu workshops, as well as domestic animals like cattle, sheep, chickens, and dogs. Surrounded by quickset hedges, the west courtyard covered 0.7 hectares, in which grew all sorts of vegetables, fruits, and ornamental plants.

In the north part of the temple, a zigzagging path led to three chambers that were gracefully furnished. This was where monks examined patients and gave medicine for free. In ancient times, the temple offered free accommodation and catering services for those who came to pay pilgrimage, ask for medical treatments, consult fortunetellers or do sightseeing, no matter how long they stayed. Therefore, the Chaoyin Temple received countless pilgrims each year, and its fame was widely spread in areas east to Beijing.

After the completion of the temple, Buddhist activities began to flourish on Mortar Isle. Countless inspectors, scholars, and migrant monks flooded to the island to pay homage to the temple. At its apex, the temple had more than 100 resident monks. Under the influence of his teacher's edification, Monk Zhenkong practiced a strict management of Buddhist activities. At the time, the sound of drums and bells reverberated over the temple shrouded by the smoke of burning incense sticks, and the chanting of Buddhist sutras echoed together with the roaring of billows on the sea. The island on the Bohai Sea was thus reputed as a Buddhist holy land.

Throughout his life, Monk Faben insisted on the motto: To nurture the myriad forms of life and practice benevolence and kindness. To raise funds for the construction of the temple, he didn't beg from the wealthy, but make money through persistent struggle and sweaty labor. He regards helping others as the most important thing. In the spring of 1910, as he engaged all energy to the construction of the temple, a severe famine hit Laoting's coastal areas. Many people were starved. Thus, Faben suspended the construction project and allotted 3,000 strings of coins and 320 *dan* (a unit of dry measure in ancient China) of grain to help people in need. His benevolent deed enabled thousands of people to survive the famine.

So far, it has been a century since Master Faben passed away. During the period, the Chaoyin Temple that consumed his lifelong endeavor was devastated due to warfare and social chaos. Due to the development of local tourism, the temple was restored in recent years.

Although time flies away, Master Faben will never be forgotten by later generations for his respectful virtuousness and persistent devotion to Buddhism, as well as his painstaking struggle for the construction of the Chaoyin Temple.

法本圆寂后，徒弟真空牢记师父的嘱托，率寺内众僧继其遗志，齐心协力建设寺院，矢志不渝，历经17年艰辛，终于在1933年完成后续工程，并请京东第一才子史梦兰（字香崖）三子史履晋为山门两旁楹柱题写了长幅楹联，请邑内文人韩湘亭为正殿、后殿，各楹柱题写了楹联。法本的夙愿终得实现。在潮音寺建筑工程竣工时，永平、乐亭官场、佛门住持、邑内外贤达、商界显贵都前来庆贺。全部工程共历时44年，所建各殿，无不雕梁画栋，金碧夺伦，流光溢彩。计有：山门，即金刚殿三间，门檐下，横悬"大海潮音"四字匾额，殿内两厢分塑增长、广目、多闻、持国四大金刚彩绘塑像，造型伟岸，神态各异。

第二层为"如来殿"（大雄宝殿）三间，全殿呈亭子状，又名"转角寺"。殿内居中供奉佛祖释迦牟尼、文殊、普贤华严三圣，堂内旁列十八罗汉，造型各异，彩绘精细，栩栩如生。该殿因地铺青石，寺内回音洪亮，又有"回音寺"之称。

后殿五间，石壁上镂有西方三圣、五百罗汉，风采各具，肃穆庄严。

后殿两旁各建有僧房八间，东西配殿六间，经堂、客舍、厨房、浴池，无所不备。殿院坐落整齐，"墀基围墙既坚且备"。

从中院出月亮门，是自成体系的东西跨院。东院为雇工、劳僧杂作之所，碾、磨、仓、厨、香油坊、豆腐坊，凡生活用具无所不有，牛、羊、鸡、犬各有栖处；西院面积有10亩之多，沿园边插树为篱，院内菜圃花丛、豆棚瓜架，种植各种蔬菜、瓜果和花木。

寺院北面，斜径通幽，建有精舍三间，室内窗明几净，布置幽雅，这是大师本着"救人一命，胜造七级浮屠"的佛家理念，对来自各地求救无门的病患者施医舍药之所。在当时，凡来坨上拜佛、还愿、求医、问卜、观光、游览在此居住者，不拘时间多寡，吃、住、医、养全由寺内开销，并以佛家礼仪相待。由是，石臼坨上的潮音寺香火鼎盛，闻名京东。

潮音寺建成后，坨上的佛事空前兴盛，官方巡检、文人墨客、僧侣云游和来石臼坨上参禅的人更是络绎不绝，

III. Couplets in the Chaoyin Temple

The Plaque on the Front Gate of the Vajra Hall

On the huge plaque hung on the front gate of the Vajra Hall are four gilded characters translated as "The Sound of Sea Tide."

In Buddhist sutras, the "sound of sea tide" is a metaphor of the preaching of Bodhisattva Avalokitesvara. According to ancient classics, "the flood tide on the sea sounds just like the preaching of Bodhisattva Avalokitesvara, hence the metaphor."

Couplets Hung on the Columns of the Vajra Hall:

Both the four guardian warriors that look angry and the six bodhisattvas that appear amiable intend to eliminate distress and help the kind ascend to heaven, so the meaningful Buddhist doctrines should be passed down from generation to generation; Both white lotuses and green stones that are used to decorated the Chaoyin Temple symbolize the Pure Land of the West in Buddhist sutras, which faces the billowy ocean in the south and adds a solemn, majestic atmosphere to the holy Puti Island (Originally named Mortar Isle, as mentioned hereinafter.)

Couplets Hung on the Columns of the Tathagata Hall:

Nestling in the Bohai Bay that connects to the Pacific, the magnificent Chaoyin Temple can shine blessing on immense oceans throughout the world; Due to their devout spirit that benefits the Republic, Faben and his disciples will be remembered forever just like auspicious multicolored clouds.

鼎盛时期，寺内僧众曾达百人之多。法本弟子真空遵承师教，在管理日常佛事时严谨不怠。屹立在石臼坨上的潮音寺，终日里暮鼓晨钟，香烟缭绕，僧笳佛号不绝于耳，与大海潮音，渔灯蟹火遥相呼应，宝岛佛寺，渤海明珠，被世人誉为佛教圣地。

法本是佛门弟子，一贯奉行普度众生，行善济世的佛门信念，但他干事创业，不是仅凭募化筹集资金，而是凭着自己的毅力和智慧去开创、用劳动的汗水去换取，在遇到重大问题需要决策时，他心中却有一个孰轻孰重的砝码。宣统二年（1910年）春，在他千方百计筹集到资金，全身心投入建设潮音寺的关键时刻，时值青黄不接，由于上年歉收，乐亭沿海发生了严重的饥荒，土地荒芜，饿殍遍野，其情景惨不忍睹，而法本大师却看在眼里，痛在心上，他心想，建潮音寺，是兴佛事，佛事即善事，怎能眼睁睁地看着百姓遭难，而只顾建寺不管他们的疾苦呢？为此，他决定修改建寺计划，暂时缓建部分工程，毅然从建寺资金中抽出制钱三千缗米三百二十石赈济沿海贫民。此项义举，使数以千计的饥民渡过了饥馑，得以活命。

光阴荏苒，潮音寺住持法本大师跏趺圆寂已近百年。经他殚精竭虑，倾注毕生心血和汗水所兴建的潮音寺，在战火硝烟和社会动荡的年代，却连连遭到厄运，大部变成墟址瓦砾，而随着旅游事业的发展，近年才得以维修重建，以飨游人。

历史烟云虽悄然逝去，但法本大师那"志操孤洁，梵行清贞，苦力虔修，深入佛海"的佛门操守及建设潮音寺的艰辛创业精神，却流芳后世，永远为人们所敬仰。

第三节　潮音寺楹联诠释

"金刚殿"山门匾额：

"金刚殿"山门前额有巨幅横匾，上书"大海潮音"四个镏金大字。

"大海潮音"，取佛家语"海潮音"之意。喻观音菩萨说法之声音也。古籍载："海潮音至者壮，又潮依而至，与观世音菩萨应时机而说法相似，故以为喻。"其意为：宏伟雄壮的海潮声，总是伴随着汹涌澎湃的大潮而至，它好像是观音菩萨应时机在说法。"大海潮音"，其意源此。

"金刚殿"楹联：

佛法本无边努目低眉[(1)]度[(2)]娑婆[(3)]众生苦恼胥成极乐界[(4)]；

菩提[(5)]应不住白莲[(6)]青石看海天万顷庄严满布祇陀园[(7)]。

注释

（1）努目低眉：《谈薮》："薛道衡游钟山开善寺，谓小僧曰：'金刚何为怒（一作努，下同）目？菩萨何为低眉？'答曰：'金刚怒目所以降伏四魔，菩萨低眉，所以慈悲六道。'"

（2）度：佛事剃度，意即度其离俗出生死。

（3）娑婆：梵语音译。意译"堪忍"。为释迦牟尼佛教化的世界，泛指大千世界。

（4）极乐界：佛家所云之极乐世界，乃阿弥陀佛所居之国土也。其国众生无有众苦，但受诸乐，故名极乐。佛家修净业者，以往生极乐世界为旨。

（5）菩提：梵语，通达、觉悟之意。略分为三种：声闻菩提；缘觉菩提；诸佛菩提。这里指诸佛菩提，谓诸佛于因中发善菩提心也。诸佛在因地中自发菩提心，复劝众生发菩提心，习大乘经义与得解脱。

（6）白莲：梵名分陀利，即白莲华。此处喻人间稀有生于西土之白莲也。

（7）祇陀园：一作祇园，祇树给孤独园之略称。故事

Couplets Hung on the Columns of the Rear Hall:

1. After he arrived at the remote Mortar Isle, Master Faben led monks to cut weeds, reclaim wastelands, and carry out marine trades. Their painstaking efforts were rewarded when the Chaoyin Temple was finally completed, which turned the once-unmanned island into a Buddhist holy land.

The lighthouse built by Master Faben at Caofeidian shine on the immense ocean all year round. From then on, the Chaoyin Temple that aims to publicize the Eastern Buddhist doctrines will definitely be closely associated with the boundless universe.

2. Master Faben reconstructed a Buddhist temple on the remote Mortar Isle, where he engaged in Buddhist meditation and preaching. All evil snakes gradually disappear on the island for fear of the power of Buddha;

Sailing boats anchored at Mortar Isle, which is now a Buddhist holy land. All fish and dragons from rivers, seas, and ponds come to listening to the chanting of Buddhist sutras.

3. Reclining against the Luanhe River, the one thousand arhats in the Chaoyin Temple bathed in the pure moonlight

一燈萬里法今東法接寰瀛

孤嶼千年到此西方開樂國

源自释迦牟尼佛在王舍城说法时，被古印度侨萨罗国舍卫城豪商给孤独长者得知，想请释迦牟尼来舍卫城弘扬佛法，欲购祇陀太子的园林献佛说法。祇陀太子开玩笑说："你如果能够用金子铺满我的园林，那么，我就把这个园地卖给你。"给孤独长者真的按祇陀太子所言，用金子把园子铺满。这桩交易遂达成了协议。园地虽为给孤独长者所买，但林木却仍属祇陀太子所有，因此史称这块园林为祇陀给孤独园。潮音寺"金刚殿"楹联取其义弘扬佛法之地。

译文

佛家通达、觉悟的法理，恢弘无垠，怒目的金刚降伏四魔，低眉的菩萨慈悲六道，都是为了超度众生，使其苦恼尽除，全都飞升到极乐世界。佛家法理道、觉之大义，应当世代相传，弘扬广大；具有象征佛家西方净土的白莲与青石装饰下的潮音寺，南向仰望碧波滔滔的大海，其庄严肃穆的氛围，布满了整个佛家圣地菩提岛。

因该岛原名石臼坨，为其历史氛围，下文仍沿用石臼坨旧名。

"如来殿" 楹联：

涌座太平洋泽普五洲功德(1)水；

现身共和国光垂万劫(2)吉祥云。

注释

（1）功德：佛教用语，指行善念佛等事。

（2）万劫：佛家称世界从生成到毁灭的一个过程为一劫，万劫就是万世的意思，言时间之幽深漫长。

译文

气势雄伟的潮音寺，坐落在和太平洋汹涌波涛相接的渤海湾里，它的泽惠将永远普照着紧连世界五大洲的浩瀚大海。法本师徒献身共和国的精神，及其照人的风采，像吉祥的五彩云霓那样悠久绵长，永垂万世。

"后殿" 楹联

1.孤屿千年到此西方(1)开乐国(2)；

一灯万里从今东法(3)接寰瀛(4)。

注释

（1）西方：泛指西天，即佛祖释迦牟尼所居之国土。

（2）乐国：佛教名词，极乐世界之简称。或称为净土。佛经说，这是阿弥陀佛成道时依着愿力而建立的，远在西方十万亿佛土以外的世界，是佛教徒所向往的地方，俗称西天。

（3）东法：指东方佛教经义。

（4）寰瀛：地球水陆之总和，亦作瀛寰。泛指地域无限宽广的世界。

译文

孤悬海天千年的石臼坨，法本长老来到这里之后亲率僧众，披荆斩棘，拓垦种植，远航交易，托钵募化，历尽千辛万苦，终于建成了功德丛林潮音寺。把个野草丛生、杳无人迹的海岛开拓成为一块佛教圣地。

法本大师建于曹妃甸的终年不熄的灯塔，永照着万里海疆，由此开始，弘扬东方的佛教大法的潮音寺，必将和广袤无垠的世界紧紧地连接在一起。

2.海岛孤悬长老安禅(1)制蛇蝮(2)；

河舟四集菩提说法到鱼龙。

注释

（1）安禅：禅，禅那略写，思维静虑之意。安禅谓身心宴然入于禅定，即佛事静坐、坐禅也。

（2）蛇蝮：泛指各种蛇类。

译文

孤悬海天的石臼坨岛，法本长老在此重起功德丛林，思维静虑、虔心潜修、弘扬佛法，岛上各种蛇类慑于佛家法力相继隐隐退却。

来自四方河流的帆樯，聚集于佛教圣地石臼坨前，连同

153

over ages; Facing the Bohai Bay, the Buddhist temple received Master Faben, who crossed the sea with his fleet just like Dharma cruised to China by a ferry.

4.The ruins of the Chaoyang Nunnery on Mortar Isle regained life like a booming pure flower of the Buddhism thanks to the painstaking efforts of Master Faben and his disciples; Mortar Isle embraced by immense ocean has amazingly become a Buddhist holy land covered with green.

Couplets of the Sutra Hall

The percussion of wooden fish used to warn people can be sent northwards to the picturesque Xiangyu Island;

The sound of golden chime bells used to inspire enlightenment can be heard as far as the southern Crescent Isle.

阿舟四集菩提说法到鱼龍

海岛孤怒長老安禅制蛇蝮

河、江、海、涵的鱼龙都慕名前来聆听普度众生的佛家法典。

3.背指滦河罗汉[1]千身印空月；

前临溟海达摩[2]一叶渡慈波。

注释

（1）罗汉：梵语，阿罗汉之略称。佛教称断决了一切嗜欲，解脱了烦恼的僧人。

（2）达摩：高僧名，禅宗东土之初祖。天竺香至王第三子。梁大通元年（527年）泛海至广州。武帝遣使迎至建业（今南京），因和武帝言语不契，遂渡江去魏，至嵩山少林寺，终日面壁，凡九年。修行示寂，武帝闻之亲自撰文刻碑于钟山。唐代宗时谥佛号圆觉大师。

译文

背向滦河的潮音寺，这里的千身罗汉，世代映照着寺前光洁的明月。孤悬溟海的功德丛林，南仰浩瀚的渤海湾，法本大师的船队，像高僧达摩孤舟泛海来中原那样，冲波泛浪慈航普度在慈祥的大海里往来游弋。

4.地是旧莲塘[1]放出如来[2]花十丈；

天临孤竹国[3]化成般若[4]翠千寻。

注释

（1）莲塘：喻佛教圣地。

（2）如来：佛教名词，为释迦牟尼的十种称号之一。

"如"谓如实。"如来"即从如实之道而来开示真理的人。佛常用以自称。

（3）孤竹国：古国名，在今冀东、辽西一带，国都在今卢龙。存在于商、西周、春秋时。

（4）般若：梵语，意译智慧。佛教指如实了解一切事物的智慧。

译文

原本是朝阳庵废墟的石臼坨，经法本大师率领僧众开发兴建，荒原萌绿，枯林逢春，再次开放出高大净洁的佛教之花。地处孤竹的石臼坨的浩瀚苍穹，蓝天碧洁，在这里神奇地化成了弘扬佛家智慧的千寻翠绿。

"经堂联"

觉世木鱼[1]声悠悠北渡祥云岛；

参禅[2]金磬[3]响历历南闻半月坨。

注释

（1）木鱼：佛家法器，为团圆之鱼鳞形，礼佛时叩之。

（2）参禅：佛家语，禅定中参究真理曰参禅。

（3）磬：寺观中铸铜铁为钵形，拜佛则击之谓磬。

译文

警彻世人的木鱼声，悠悠北渡，飘向北方风光秀丽的祥云岛；参修佛法时敲击金磬的声响，连远在南方的半月坨都清晰可闻。

IV. The Origin and Filiations of the Zen Sect on Puti Island

All Buddhist temples on Puti Island belong to the Zen sect, a branch of Buddhism that was founded by Dharma.

According to Buddhism thesaurus, the Zen sect derived its name from the Sanskrit word "dhyana" that means "meditation" or "meditative state." Its founder, Dharma, was an Indian monk. During the Liang and Wei Dynasties, he came to China to spread Buddhism, and his practice method emphasized meditation and sudden enlightenment. The origin of the Zen sect is ascribed to the Flower Sermon. It is said that Gautama Buddha gathered his disciples one day for a Dharma talk. The Buddha silently held up a flower, and one of his disciples, Mahakasyapa, silently gazed at the flower and broke into a broad smile. He was then acknowledged as the first ancestral founder. Dharma was considered the first-generation ancestral founder of the sect in the East. He fell into meditation for nine years in the Shaolin Temple, where he taught a special transmission outside scriptures, with no words or letters. The sect was passed down through Huike (the second ancestor), Sengcan (the third ancestor), Daoxin (the fourth ancestor), and Hongren (the fifth ancestor). Hongren had two disciples: Huineng and Shenxiu. The branch of the Zen sect that Huineng advocated mainly prevailed in the south, hence its name "South Branch," while that advocated by Shenxiu prevailed in the north, hence its name "North Branch." Then, the South School was divided into the Nanyue and Qingyuan genres. The Qingyuan genre was later subdivided into Guiyang, Caodong, Linji, Yunmen, and Fayan sects. In the Song Dynasty, the Linji Sect was further divided into Yangqi and Huanglong branches. By the time, the Zen sect had been divided into the Five Schools and Seven Branches. Its Chinese name, Chan, began with the Tang Dynasty.

The Linji Sect emphasizes that everyone can reach the Buddha, and advocates a realization of spiritual purity through acknowledging the "emptiness" of the secular world and warding off all differences in the real world. It features a quick and even violent transmission of Buddhist doctrines.

The Caodong Sect deems that one needn't struggle to seek the Buddha because he was always in one's heart, and advocated sudden enlightenment, but not acquiring self-realization through meditation year after year. The teacher usually teaches his students through examples, but not empty talks.

The Chart of the Pedigree of Buddhist Monks on Puti Island

(No records before the Ming Dynasty) Xianguang, eighth generation of the Linji Sect — Zhiyuan — Huichen (unknown for the following several generation) — Jing'an — Puji

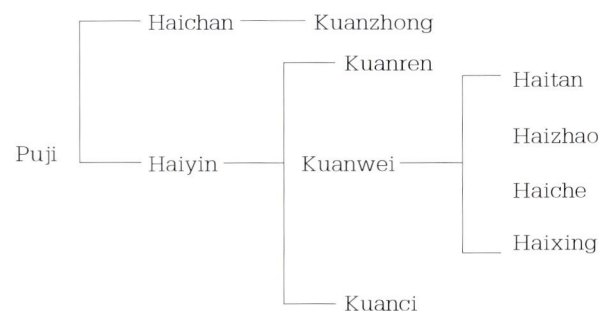

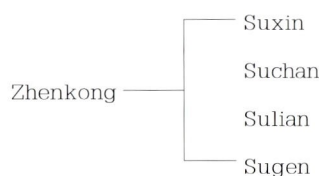

```
                        ┌─ Haichan ──────── Kuanzhong
                        │              ┌─ Kuanren
                        │              │            ┌─ Haitan
         Puji ──────────┤              │            │
                        ├─ Haiyin ─────┤ Kuanwei ───┤ Haizhao
                        │              │            │
                        │              │            ├─ Haiche
                        │              │            │
                        │              │            └─ Haixing
                        └─ Kuanci
```

```
                       ┌─ Zhenjie
                       │  Zhenkong (originally a hired laborer
                       │  engaged in temple construction for 30
                       │  years, and Faben then recruited him as
                       │  his disciple)
                       │
Faben from             ├─ Zhenwu
Caodong Sect           │
                       ├─ Zhenming
                       │
                       ├─ Zhenfu
                       │
                       ├─ Zhenxiang
                       │
                       ├─ Zhenxiu
                       │
                       └─ Zhensheng
```

```
                       ┌─ Suxin
                       │
                       ├─ Suchan
Zhenkong ──────────────┤
                       ├─ Sulian
                       │
                       └─ Sugen
```

第四节　菩提岛禅宗门派源系

菩提岛宗教系禅宗门派，其初祖为达摩。

据佛教辞典禅宗条释：禅宗，以禅那为宗，故名。禅那或译思维修，或译静虑，为思维真理静息念虑之法，原为三学六度之一。初祖达摩，天竺人，梁魏之世来支那传佛心宗。其法唯静坐默念，发明佛心，凝工夫而已。其外相一等于禅那，故称为禅宗。所谓禅宗非三学六度之一分禅，于是而如来禅，祖师禅之称起。以经论所说，六度所摄之禅为如来禅，达摩所传之心印为祖师禅。故由彼宗之本义言之，则与其谓为禅宗，毋宁目为佛心宗为适当。释尊在灵山会上拈花，迦叶破颜微笑，为第一祖。二十八传至达摩为东土初祖。在少林寺面壁九年，是教无言之心印于无言也。慧可得其心印为二祖。僧璨为三祖。道信为四祖。弘忍为五祖。弘忍之下有慧能、神秀二大师。慧能之禅行于南地，故称南宗；神秀之化盛于北地，故称北宗。而北宗不免如来禅之迹，南宗得祖师禅之神髓。六祖慧能之下生南岳、青原两系。南岳传于马祖；青原传于石头。马祖之下独盛，转传而分沩仰、曹洞、临济、云门、法眼之五家。至宋朝，临济之下又附杨岐、黄龙之二流。总是五家七宗。按禅宗之称，始于李唐。

临济宗强调人人皆有佛性"即心即佛"。主张通过取得对世俗世界"空寂"的认识，"离一切相"，在心识中断除所有是非、善恶、有无等差别的绝对世界，以达到与清静无为的真如佛性相契合的精神境界。宗风特点是"全机大用，棒喝齐施，虎骤龙奔，星驰电掣"。

曹洞宗认为无须四处去求佛，佛在性中，心即是佛，觉悟不假外求，得道靠顿悟，用不着以打坐息想、起坐拘束其心地终年修行来渐悟。宗风特点是"家风细密，言行相应，随机利物，就语接人"。其师徒相接，不多言多说，玩弄禅机，而是应机接人，方便开示，以事显理，敲唱为用，以理

事圆融来指导践行，劝学者行解相扶，自在解脱。

菩提岛寺僧传承一览表

（明代以前无详）临济宗显光八代到智元—慧辰（慧辰以下几代不详）—静安—普济

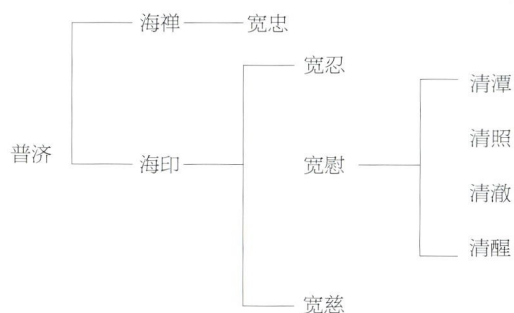

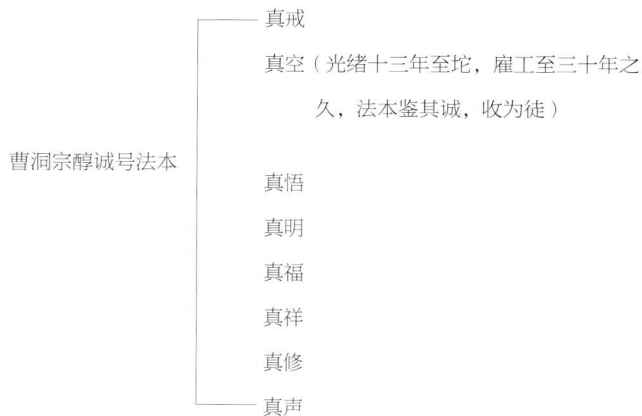

V. Buddhist Statues in the Chaoyin Temple

The reconstructed Chaoyin Temple on Puti Island is similar to its original, which mainly consists of the Front Hall (including the front gate), the Great Hall (or Tathagata Hall), and the Rear Hall.

1. Front Hall

In the Front Hall is enshrined the statues of the Four Guardian Warriors, popularly known as the Four Heavenly Kings in China. The Sanskrit classic, Abhidharma-mahavibhasa-sastra, records that the four warriors are "more than 300 meters high." Thus, all of their statues are typically tall and magnificent. According to Indian Buddhist legends, they respectively live on the four peaks of Mount Sumeru to protect the world. The four peaks are formed with gold, silver, emerald, and agate, respectively. Their statues are often found in the gate hall of many Chinese temples. This is because they serve as gate guardians for the Jade Emperor in Chinese mythology. Each of them holds a utensil that respectively symbolizes "wind, tune, rain, and smoothness." Among the Four Heavenly Kings, Vaisravana (or Duowen in Chinese) is most admired in China because he is regarded as the god of wealth and a patron of all treasures around the world in Brahmanism and Hinduism.

(1) Chiguo Heavenly King of the East

Called Dhrtarastra in Sanskrit, he wears a white armor and holds a lute that symbolizes "tune."

(2) Zengzhang Heavenly King of the South

Called Virudhaka in Sanskrit, he wears a blue armor and holds a sword that symbolizes "wind."

(3) Guangmu Heavenly King of the West

Called Virupaksa in Sanskrit, he wears a red armor, with one of his arm circled with a dragon or snake that symbolizes "smoothness."

(4) Duowen Heavenly King of the North

Called Vaisravana in Sanskrit, he wears a green armor and holds an umbrella that symbolizes "rain."

第五节　潮音寺供奉佛像

菩提岛潮音寺原建及复修大体相同，即前殿（含山门）、大雄宝殿（如来殿）、后殿三层。其间供奉诸神依次为。

一　前殿

前殿的殿堂内塑有四天王神像，俗名四大金刚。这四座神像，民间为什么称他们为金刚呢？《娑婆论》谓："盖其身长百丈。"故今凡塑金刚像，皆伟岸高大。印度佛教传说称他们是须弥山腰，犍陀罗山东、南、西、北四峰各护一方天下之王。这四座山四宝所组成，东面黄金，西面白银，南面琉璃，北面玛瑙。在中国，各寺院多在门殿塑其像，皆因他们还是玉帝属下的守门天将。四位天王手中各拿着不同的物件，分别职掌风、调、雨、顺。

在四大天王中，毗沙门天王（多闻天王）在中国崇拜最盛，因他是婆罗门教、印度教的财神，是世上一切财富的守护者。

（一）东方持国天王　　**（二）南方增长天王**　　**（三）西方广目天王**　　**（四）北方多闻天王**

名多罗吒，俗名魔礼寿，身着白色法衣，手拿琵琶，职掌调。

名毗琉璃，俗名魔礼青，身着青色法衣，手拿宝剑，职掌风。

名毗留博叉，俗名魔礼红，身着红色法衣，手绕缠一龙（或说蛇、蜃），职掌顺。

名毗沙门，俗名魔礼海，身着绿色法衣，手中拿着一把伞，职掌雨。

2. Great Hall (or Tathagata Hall)

The Great Hall is used to worship the Three Saints of Hua-yen, namely Sakyamuni, Manjusri, and Samantabhadra.

(1) Sakyamuni Buddha

Sakyamuni is also known as Gautama Buddha. According to *Biography of Sakyamuni Buddha*, there were six other Buddhas, including Vipasyin, Visvabhu, Krakucchanda, Kanakamuni, Kasyapa, and Gautam, who were enlightened before Sakyamuni. Of countless Buddhas, however, only Sakyamuni is considered the founder of Buddhism.

Some historical records reveal that Sakyamuni was born in the 26th year during the reign of King Zhao of the Zhou Dynasty, and died in the 53rd year during the reign of King Mu of the Zhou. However, recent archeological research testifies that he was actually born in the 7th year during the reign of King Ling of the Zhou, and died in the 33rd year during the reign of King Jing of the Zhou. The two statements have a time gap of 462 years.

It is said that Sakyamuni was born in Lumbini, Kosala, in central India. He was originally named Siddhartha. His father, King Suddhodana, was the lord of Lumbini, and his mother, Queen Maha Maya, died seven days after she delivered Sakyamuni. The infant was then raised up by his aunt. Legend goes that when Sakyamuni was born, a dragon spitted cold water and another warm water to bathe him. As soon as he was delivered, Sakyamuni pointed to the sky with one hand and the earth with another and announced loudly that he would be "the only supreme ruler of both heaven and earth." At the age of 19, Sakyamuni married Princess Yasodhara, who later gave birth to a son, Pahula. At the age of 29, during one of his outing tours, Sakyamuni met some sick and dead people, which inspired him to overcome ageing, illness, and death by living as an ascetic. One night, he rode a horse to flee from the palace to Ramagrama, where he converted to Buddhism. He initially went to Rajagaha, where he became a student of Udaka Ramaputta and began to practice self-mortification through meditation. Later, he seated under a pipal tree (now known as Bodhi tree), and vowed never to arise until he found the truth. After seven days of meditation, he finally attained enlightenment through an inspiration of a bright star. At the time, he was already 35 years old. (In some Buddhist classics, Sakyamuni is thought to convert to Buddhism at 19 and attained enlightenment at 30.) Then, he spent 49 years traveling around to spread Buddhist dharma. Later, he died for a trauma on his back at the age of 79.

The ten foremost disciples of Sakyamuni included Mahakasyapa, Ananda, Sariputta, Mahamoggallana, Anuruddha, Subhoti, Mahakaccana, Punna, Upali, and Rahula. They compiled what Sakyamuni preached into 12 volumes of sutras, which were then re-compiled into 42 chapters. Since then, Buddhism has been widely spread till today.

二　大雄宝殿（如来殿）

大雄宝殿供奉华严三圣。

（一）释迦牟尼

释迦牟尼，一名如来佛。在他之前已有六佛。《魏

书·释老志》载：一曰毗婆尸，二曰尸弃，三曰毗舍浮，四曰拘留孙，五曰拘那舍牟尼，六曰迦叶（此迦叶，非释迦之徒摩诃迦叶）。释迦之后称为佛者，数以千计，释教之奉为佛祖者，唯有释迦牟尼。

释迦牟尼，其生卒年代，北传佛教推断为公元前565—

前486年；南传佛教则为公元前624—前544年或公元前623—前543年。

释迦牟尼出生于古印度北部迦毗罗卫国（今尼泊尔境内），名悉达多。他的父亲是迦毗罗卫国国王，名曰净饭王。母亲摩耶夫人，生下释迦七日即与世长辞，由其姨母波阇波提扶养成人。传释迦刚降生于世时即有异象，一龙吐冷水，一龙吐温水，沐浴其身，降生坠地即作狮子吼。一手指天，一手指地，周行七步，目顾四方，大声叫道："天上地下，唯我独尊。"19岁释迦为太子时，纳拘利城主善觉王之女耶输陀罗为妻。生有一子，名罗睺罗。29岁时偶乘车出游，见衰病及死者，深悟世间之无常，遂决意出家。十二月十八日夜半，乘马潜出王城，入东方兰摩国，削发为沙门。随即到王舍城边阿兰若林，就郁陀罗伽仙求道，遂修习诸种禅定。后至优楼频罗村圣毕钵罗树（菩提树）下，敷草，结跏趺坐，深发愿誓，说："不成正觉，终不起此坐。"时经七日，至二月八日夜，忽然看到一颗巨大的明星而大悟，得一切神智，于是成大觉世尊，为人天之大导师。时年35岁（诸佛经中亦有19岁出家，30岁成道之说）。于是周游四方，化导群类，在世行道49年。后因背疾剧作，北首而卧（按《太平御览》：后世绘卧佛像即由此始），于拘尸那城娑罗双树间，求生不得，求死不得，至二月十五日去世。应世79年。

释迦之大弟子共有十名，即摩诃迦叶、阿难、须菩提、舍利、弗迦游、延目、乾连、阿难连、优婆离、罗睺罗。追述释迦所说，缀以文字，集经十二部，后编为四十二章，佛教由此兴盛传至今日。

(2) Manjusri Bodhisattva

Manjusri means "virtuous and auspicious" in Sanskrit. Manjusri is one of the four major bodhisattvas of Chinese Buddhism (the other three are Samantabhadra, Avalokitesvara, and Ksitigarbha). It is said that Manjusri and Samantabhadra are the left and right servants of Sakyamuni Buddha, and they are collectively known as the Three Saints of Hua-yen. Manjuri is noted for his transcendent wisdom, hence his nickname "Bodhisattva Great Wisdom." He is typically depicted as a bodhisattva wielding a flaming sword in his hand, representing the realization of transcendent wisdom which cuts down ignorance and duality. He is also depicted as riding a lion that could ward off evil with its ferocious roaring.

(3) Samantabhadra Bodhisattva

Samantabhadra, also known as Vishvabhadra, is one of the four major bodhisattvas of Chinese Buddhism (the other three are Samantabhadra, Avalokitesvara, and Ksitigarbha). Samantabhadra helps Sakyamuni spread Buddhist dharma, and is collectively called the Three Saints of Hua-yen together with Sakyamuni and Manjusri. Samantabhadra is not subject to limits of time, place, or physical conditions, but an embodiment of natural clarity with unceasing compassion.

3. Rear Hall

The Rear Hall is used to enshrine the Trinity of Western Paradise:

(1) Amita Buddha

Amita Buddha is the principal Buddha of the Pure Land of Ultimate Bliss. His Sanskrit name, Amitabha, literally means "infinite light."

According to Sutra of Observing Immensurable Life, in remote antiquity, a king named Amitabha renounced his throne and converted to Buddhism. He then resolved to become a Buddha and create the Pure Land in the utmost west with his infinite merits. So, Amitabha is thought as the founder of the Pure Land Sect. By the power of his vows, Amitabha has made it possible for Buddhist believers to be reborn into this land, hence his nickname "Guide Buddha." Amita Buddha is often shown as flanked by Avalokitesvara and Mahasthamaprapta Bodhisattvas, and they are collectively known as the Trinity of Western Paradise.

（二）文殊菩萨

文殊菩萨，音译文殊师利或曼殊室利。意译妙德、妙吉祥。又译妙首、普首、濡首、敬首。曼殊是妙之意，室利是吉祥之意，简称为文殊。为中国佛教四大菩萨（文殊菩萨、普贤菩萨、观音菩萨、地藏菩萨）之一。文殊菩萨和普贤菩萨为释迦牟尼佛的左、右胁侍，他们合称为"华严三圣"。文殊菩萨智慧、辩才第一，为众菩萨之首，被称为"大智文殊菩萨"。文殊菩萨的形象，通常是手持慧剑，骑乘狮子，比喻以智慧利剑斩断烦恼，以狮吼威风震慑魔怨。

（三）普贤菩萨

普贤菩萨，音译三曼多跋陀罗菩萨、三曼陀菩萨。又作遍吉菩萨。我国佛教四大菩萨之一。普贤菩萨辅助释迦佛弘扬佛道，且遍身十方，常为诸佛座下的法王子，他和释迦牟尼、文殊菩萨合称为"华严三圣"。故普贤行愿品言："普贤行愿威神力，普现一切如来前。"又言："十方如来

有长子，其名号曰普贤尊。"普贤菩萨，不但能广赞诸佛无尽功德，且能修无上供养，能做广大佛事，能度无边有情，其智慧之高，愿行之深，唯佛能知。

三　后殿

后殿供奉西方三圣。

（一）阿弥陀佛

为西方极乐世界之教主。又作阿弥多佛、阿弭跢佛、阿弭鄲佛。略称弥陀。

阿弥陀佛成道之本缘，据《无量寿经》卷上载，过去久远劫世自在王佛住世时，有一国王发无上道心，舍王位出家，名为法藏比丘，于世自在王佛处修行，熟知诸佛之净土，历经五劫之思虑而发殊胜

(2) Avalokitesvara Bodhisattva

Avalokitesvara, literally meaning "Lord who looks down upon voice [of human beings]," is one of the four major bodhisattvas in Chinese Buddhism. The bodhisattva is often depicted as an amiable female holding a vase with a willow branch, who rescues people in need with her infinite wisdom and magic power. It is said that the bodhisattva would show up to rescue victims from calamities only if they chanted her name. Avalokitesvara and Mahasthamaprapta are servants flanking Amita Buddha, and they are collectively known as the Trinity of Western Paradise.

The bodhisattva is variably depicted as male or female. No matter in which forms, Avalokitesvara is always dedicated to helping secular people.

(3) Mahasthamaprapta Bodhisattva

Mahasthamaprapta (literally meaning "arrival of the great strength"), also known as Mthuchen-thob in Tibetan language, is the right companion of Amita Buddha. Together with Amita Buddha and Avalokitesvara Bodhisattva (the left companion of Amita Buddha), he composes the Trinity of Western Paradise. According to the *Compassionate Lotus Sutra*, King Cakravartiraja had four sons: The oldest son became Avalokitesvara Bodhisattva, the second son Mahasthamaprapta Bodhisattva, the third son Manjusri Bodhisattva, and the youngest son Samantabhadra Bodhisattva. Later, King Cakravartiraja attained enlightenment and became Amita Buddha, and Avalokitesvara and Mahasthamaprapta became his left and right companions.

Mahasthamaprapta is ranked second amongst all bodhisattvas who are expected to become a Buddha. According to *Sutra of Observing Immensurable Life*, Mahasthamaprapta can "dispel three evils (namely, hell, ghost, and beast) with his power of wisdom," hence his name. The light of wisdom stored in the treasure vase on his head can shine on all beings in the world, and enables all beings to escape wars and disasters and gain infinite power.

Thus, Mahasthamaprapta is considered a bodhisattva with supreme wisdom. According to *Sutra of Observing Immensurable Life*, wherever he visits, both sky and earth will shake. He is always dedicated to protecting all beings from evils.

之四十八愿。此后，不断积聚功德，而于距今十劫之前，愿行圆满，成阿弥陀佛，在离此十万亿佛土之西方（十万亿指十恶业并非真实距离，意思是造十恶业就离极乐世界越来越远，西方也不是真实的方向，西方是指安稳、安养的意思），报得极乐净土。迄今仍在彼土说法，即净土门之教主，能接引念佛人往生西方净土，故又称接引佛。阿弥陀三尊像通常以观音菩萨及大势至菩萨为其胁侍，而与此二尊并称为西方三圣。

（二）观音菩萨

观音菩萨，又作观世音菩萨、观自在菩萨、光世音菩萨等，从字面解释就是"观察（世间民众的）声音"的菩萨，是四大菩萨之一。他相貌端庄慈祥，经常手持净瓶杨柳，具有无量的智慧和神通，大慈大悲，普救人间疾苦。当人们遇到灾难时，只要念其名号，便前往救度，所以称观世音。在佛教中，他是西方极乐世界教主阿弥陀佛座下的上首菩萨，同大势至菩萨一起，是阿弥陀佛身边的胁侍菩萨，并称"西方三圣"。

观音菩萨有时是男相，有时则是女相，因观世音是普度众生，救苦救难的菩萨，无所谓男相女相，可现各种面相法身适时在人间行法。

（三）大势至菩萨

大势至菩萨，是阿弥陀佛的右胁侍者，又称大精进菩萨，简称为势至，与阿弥陀佛、观音菩萨（阿弥陀佛的左胁侍）合称为"西方三圣"。《悲华经》中说过去有个转轮圣王，大太子是观音菩萨，二太子是大势至菩萨，三太子是文殊菩萨，四太子是普贤菩萨。后来转轮圣王修行成佛，即西方极乐世界阿弥陀佛，观音和大势至成为父亲的左右胁侍。

大势至菩萨，梵语称"摩诃那钵"，现今在极乐世界，为第二顺位递补佛位的菩萨。《观无量寿经》载，他"以智慧光普照一切，令离三涂（指地狱、饿鬼、畜生'三恶趋'）得无上力"，因此称为大势至菩萨。根据《观无量寿经》记载：大势至菩萨以独特的智慧之光遍照世间众生，使众生能解脱血光刀兵之灾，得无上之力量，威势自在，因此，大势至菩萨被认为是光明智慧第一，所到之处天地震动，保护众生免受邪魔所害。

4. The Eighteen Arhats

Arhats refer to monks who attained enlightenment. In Buddhist tradition, arhats are only inferior to buddhas and bodhisattvas. They typically emerge as statues accompanying the Buddha in the great halls of temples.

When Buddhism was first introduced to China from India, there were only sixteen arhats, and their names mainly derived from *Record on the Duration of the Law as Spoken by the Great Arhat Nadimitra* translated by Monk Xuanzang of the Tang Dynasty. According to the book, before his death, Sakyamuni ordered the sixteen arhats to "stay in the secular world to protect the dharma." The book also elaborates the names and dwelling places of the arhats. Along with the spread of Buddhist sutras translated by Xuanzang, the sixteen arhats also prevailed across China.

During the period of the Five Dynasties (907-960), the worship of arhats began to prevail, and the former sixteen arhats were expanded to the Eighteen Arhats. Some conjecture that the two newly-added arhats are Nadimitra and Xuanzang, while others assert that they are Dharmapala and Cloth-Bag Monk. In the Qing Dynasty, Emperor Qianlong nominated the two additions as Taming Dragon and Taming Tiger. Then, the Eighteen Arhats were confirmed in China.

(1) Pindola the Bharadvaja, popularly known as Long-Eyebrow Arhat, is the head of the Eighteen Arhats. Typically, he is portrayed as a silver-haired man with extended eyebrows. His statues are often found at dinning halls in Chinese temples.

(2) Kanakavatsa, popularly known as Happy Arhat, is a prominent preacher and dedicates himself to the realization of happiness of all beings.

(3) Kanakabharadraja, popularly known as Bowl-Raising Arhat, preached while raising a bowl to receive happiness and jubilance.

(4) Nandimitra, popularly known as Pagoda-Raising Arhat, is the last disciple of Buddha. He is often depicted as an arhat enlightening humans with Buddhist doctrines through preaching while holding a pagoda in hand.

(5) Nakula, popularly known as Meditating Arhat, attained the truth of the universe through meditation, and is then committed to spreading it amongst all beings.

(6) Bodhidruma, literally meaning "saint" in Sanskrit, is an attendant of Buddha. Popularly known as River-Crossing Arhat, he can acutely cross the river of annoyance. According to *Surangama Sutra*, he takes charge of bathing affairs. Thus, his statues are often enshrined at bathing rooms of Chinese temples.

(7) Kalika, popularly known as Whisk Arhat, is an

四 十八罗汉

罗汉，是修行得道的高僧，为梵语音译"阿罗汉"的简称，在佛教中的地位次于佛与菩萨。在寺院的造像中，他们往往在大雄宝殿内，作为陪衬人物环护在佛的两旁。

罗汉从印度传入中国时为十六尊，称"十六尊者"。其名称来源主要出自唐代高僧玄奘翻译的《大阿罗汉难提密多罗所说法住记》（简称《法住记》）。据该书记载，释迦牟尼佛涅槃（逝世）前，以"佛法"叮嘱十六罗汉，要他们"常住世间，护持正法"，该书还详细记载了十六罗汉的名称和所住地方，随着唐僧玄奘所取的佛经的流传，十六罗汉的形象在中国也应运而生。

五代时对罗汉的尊崇开始风行，并有所发展。由十六罗汉发展为十八罗汉。有人推论说，增加的两人，一是《法住记》的述说者庆友尊者，另一人就是《法住记》的译者玄奘和尚。还有说是达摩多罗和布袋和尚的。清乾隆年间，由皇帝钦定"降龙"和"伏虎"两罗汉，十八罗汉在中国确定下来。

第一位：宾度罗跋啰惰阇，俗称长眉罗汉，十八罗汉之首。他的典型形象是头发皓白，有白色长眉。俗称"长眉罗汉"，中国禅林食堂常常供他的像。

第二位：迦诺迦伐蹉尊者，俗称喜庆罗汉，杰出的布教师，随机说教，方便说法，让众生得欢喜。

第三位：迦诺迦伐厘情阇尊者，俗称托钵罗汉，是一位慈悲平等托钵化缘的行者。借托钵福利世人，予众生种植福德，并为他们讲说佛法，以身教、言教度化众生。

第四位：苏频陀尊者，俗称托塔罗汉，是佛陀所收的最后一名弟子。他手托佛塔，怀记佛陀的教法，并启化众生广植福德以成就佛道。

第五位：罗距罗尊者，俗称静坐罗汉，于禅坐中冥思世界宇宙的真理，证悟后说法度众。

第六位：跋陀罗尊者。跋陀罗，意为"贤者"，是佛的一名侍者。俗称过江罗汉，过江似蜻蜓点水，洒脱自在，超越烦恼无边的苦海。据《楞严经》称，他主管洗浴之事，所以近世禅林浴室中常供他的像。

第七位：迦理迦尊者，俗称拂尘罗汉，是佛的一名侍

attendant of Buddha. With a benevolent heart, he cleans away annoyance for all beings with his whisk.

(8) Vijraputra, popularly known as Goodness Arhat, once preached dharma to Ananda and encouraged him to practice Buddhist doctrines.

(9) Gobaka, popularly known as Open Heart Arhat, has his heart open, which inspires all beings will be Buddha if they keep a pure heart shall keep their hearts clear and practice benevolence. Gobaka means "pariah" and "castrated man" in Sanskrit, so he might be from underclass or a eunuch.

(10) Panthaka, popularly known as Raising Hand Arhat, derived the name from the fact that he often raises his hands and gives a stretch after meditation.

(11) Rahula, popularly known as Thinking Arhat, converted to Buddhism when he was a child. He devoted painstaking effort to Esoteric practice. Rahula, literally meaning "impediment and obstacle," was the only son of Sakyamuni. It is said that on the night when Sakyamuni converted to Buddhism, his second wife got pregnant. Six years later, when Sakyamuni attained enlightenment, Rahula was born on a night with lunar eclipse, hence his name. At the age of 15, Rahula converted to Buddhism and became one of the ten most famous disciples of Buddha.

(12) Nagasena, popularly known as Ear-Scratching Arhat, is famous for keeping deaf to annoyances, hence his name. He was born after the death of Buddha. At the age of seven, he converted to Buddhism, and once answered questions raised by King Milinda.

(13) Angida, popularly known as Cloth-Pack Arhat, is immune to all annoyances. He has a comprehensive heart that can contain all things in the world, and enjoys a life of freedom.

(14) Vanavasa, popularly known as Plantain Arhat, often meditated under a plantain tree, no any annoyance and hullabaloo in the world could disturb him.

(15) Asita, popularly known as Deer-Riding Arhat, once rode a deer to the imperial palace to persuade the king to learn Buddhist doctrines. He is an attendant of Buddha.

(16) Pantha the Younger, popularly known as Doorman Arhat, was dumpish and had short memories before he converted to Buddhism. He attained enlightenment when cleaning dust on the ground, through which he realized that practicing Buddhist dharma can clean annoyances in his heart.

(17) Taming Dragon Arhat. In the time when the term "Eighteen Arhats" first appeared, Qingyou was considered Taming Dragon Arhat. During the Song Dynasty, people venerated Mahakassapa, the oldest disciple of Buddha, as Taming Dragon Arhat. In the Qing Dynasty, Emperor Qianlong personally nominated Mahakassapa as Taming Dragon Arhat.

(18) Taming Tiger Arhat, known as Pindola in Buddhist sutras, often heard the roaring of a tiger outside the temple where he practiced Buddhism. He knew the tiger was hungry, and then gave half of his food to the tiger. At the beginning, the tiger didn't listen to him. Eventually, he struggled to tame it, and the tiger often came to temple to play with him. So, later generations called him Taming Tiger Arhat.

者，以清净慈悲心，用拂尘去除众生的烦恼。

第八位：伐阇罗弗多罗尊者，俗称劝善罗汉，曾为多闻第一的阿难说法，鼓励他要行解并重，在佛道上精进修行。

第九位：戍博迦尊者，俗称开心罗汉，袒露其心，启示众生若能常保持心地的清净，不造恶业，努力行善，自身便是佛，自心即是佛心。戍博迦，有"贱民"、"男根断者"之意，可见其出身不高，或为宦者。

第十位：半托迦尊者，俗称探手罗汉，因打坐后常举起双手伸懒腰而得此名。

第十一位：罗睺罗尊者，俗称沉思罗汉，幼年出家，是佛教僧团中最初的沙弥，修忍辱行，以密行居首。罗睺罗，意译"复障"、"执目"，他是释迦在俗时所生唯一的儿子，据说佛出家之夜，释迦在俗时的第二夫人耶输怀胎，六年后佛成道之夜月食时降生，故名，15岁出家，为佛的十大弟子之一。

第十二位：那伽犀那尊者，俗称挖耳罗汉，以论耳根清净闻名，故称为挖耳罗汉。那伽犀那，意译"龙军"，习称"那先比丘"，生于佛灭后，7岁出家，曾在舍竭国答国王弥兰陀之问。

第十三位：因揭陀尊者，俗称布袋罗汉，断除一切烦恼，不受毁誉得失心及外境的影响，凡人间是非善恶之事皆包容于心，如同布袋容纳而欢喜自在。

第十四位：伐那婆斯尊者，俗称芭蕉罗汉，出家后常在芭蕉树下修行，世间的喧嚷烦恼不能侵挠他的心。

第十五位：阿氏多尊者，俗称骑鹿罗汉，曾乘鹿入皇宫劝谕国王学佛修行。阿氏多，是佛的一名侍者。

第十六位：注荼半托迦尊者，俗称看门罗汉，又名周利槃陀。未出家时，愚笨善忘；以扫地上的尘垢，悟出要实践佛法来清除心中的贪瞋痴。

第十七位：降龙罗汉，开始出现十八罗汉时，降龙罗汉为庆友，宋代降龙罗汉的名号归到佛的十大弟子中的大弟子迦叶身上。清朝乾隆年间，乾隆皇帝钦定降龙罗汉为迦叶。

第十八位：伏虎罗汉，佛教名称为宾头卢尊者。他修行出家的寺门外常闻到虎啸，他认为这只老虎肯定饿了，便将自己的饭食分一半喂这只老虎。这是一只威势逼人的猛虎，面对宾头卢并不领情，时时作威。他便软硬兼施，猛虎终于被他驯服了，并常来寺院和他玩耍。故世人称其为"伏虎罗汉"。

5. Five Hundred Arhats

On the rear wall are reliefs of the Five Hundred Arhats.

According to Buddhism in China, as soon as he was born, Sakyamuni began to preach 500 disciples, who are collectively called Five Hundred Arhats. During the Southern Song Dynasty, Master Daosu confirmed the names of the Five Hundred Arhats.

The names of the Five Hundred Arhats are as follows:

001. Ajnata-kau-hdmya	002. Aniruddha	003. Youxian Wugou
004. Subhadda	005. Kalodayin	006. Wenshengdeguo
007.Ganchanzangwang	008. Shichuangwugou	009. Fanboti
010. Yintuodehui	011. Jianaxingna	012. Posupandou
013. Fajiesile	014. Youloupinluo	015. Fotuomiduo
016. Natijiaye	017. Nayanluoti	018. Fotuonanti
019. Weitiandijia	020. Geituoduohua	021. Youpojuduo
022. Sengjiayeshe	023. Jiaoshuochangzhu	024. Shangnahexiu
025. Dharmapala	026. Gayakayapa	027. Dingguodeye
028. Zhuangyanwuyou	029. Yichiyinyuan	030. Kanadeva
031. Poxieshentong	032. Jianchisanzi	033. Akouloutuo
034. Kumarada	035. Dulongguiyi	036. Tongshengjishou
037. Piluozhizi	038. Fasumiduo	039. Jatisena
040. Sengfayeshe	041. Beichashijian	042. Xianhuashouji
043. Yanguangdingli	044. Jiayeshena	045. Shadibiqiu
046. Bozhetipo	047. Jiekongwugou	048. Buddhamitra
049. Funayeshe	050. Jiayetianyan	051. Buzhushijian
052. Xiekongdiyi	053. Luoduwujin	054. Jingangpomo
055. Yuanhushijian	056. Wuyouchanding	057. Wusuohuishan
058. Shijiehuishan	059. Zhanchandexiang	060. Jinshanjueyi
061. Wuyesujin	062.Mokechali	063. Wuliangbenxing
064. Yinianxiekong	065. Guanshenwuchang	066. Qianjiebeiyuan

五　五百罗汉

后墙浮雕五百罗汉。

据《中国的佛教》一书所记，释迦出生时，便有随他听法传道的五百弟子，称"五百罗汉"。南宋时期的高道素为五百罗汉落实了名号。

五百罗汉名录如下：

001.阿若憍陈如尊者	002.阿泥楼尊者	003.有贤无垢尊者
004.须跋陀罗尊者	005.迦留陀夷尊者	006.闻声得果尊者
007.旃檀藏王尊者	008.施幢无垢尊者	009.梵波提尊者
010.因陀得慧尊者	011.迦那行那尊者	012.婆苏盘豆尊者
013.法界四乐尊者	014.优楼频螺尊者	015.佛陀密多尊者
016.那提迦叶尊者	017.那延罗提尊者	018.佛陀难提尊者
019.未田底迦尊者	020.给陀多化尊者	021.优婆鞠多尊者
022.僧迦耶舍尊者	023.教说常住尊者	024.商那和修尊者

067. Quluonashe	068. Jiekongdingkong	069. Chengjiuyinyuan
070. Jiantongjingjin	071. Sadavilapa	072. Qiantuokeli
073. Jiekongzizai	074. Mokezhuna	075. Jianrenfeiteng
076. Bukongbuyou	077. Zhoulipante	078. Qushabiqiu
079. Shizibiqiu	080. Xiuxingbuzhu	081. Pilindgavagsa
082. Molibudong	083. Sanweiganlu	084. Jiekongwuming
085. Qifonanti	086. Jingangjingjin	087. Fangbanfazang
088. Guanxingyuelun	089. Anazhanti	090. Zhichensanwei
091. Mokejuchi	092. Pizhizhuanzhi	093. Shandinglongzhong
094. Luowangenwei	095. Jiebinfuzang	096. Shentongyiju
097. Jushoujuti	098. Fawangputi	099. Fazangyongjie
100. Shanzhu	101. Chuyou	102. Daren
103. Wuyouzizai	104. Miaoju	105. Yantu
106. Jinji	107. Leide	108. Leiyin
109. Xiangxiang	110. Matou	111. Mingshou
112. Jinshou	113. Jingshou	114. Zhongshou
115. Biande	116. Canti	117. Wuda
118. Fadong	119. Ligou	120. Jingjie
121. Masheng	122. Tianwang	123. Wusheng
124. Zijing	125. Budong	126. Xiuxi
127. Tiaoda	128. Puguang	129. Zhiji
130. Baochuang	131. Shanhui	132. Shanyan
133. Yongbao	134. Baojian	135. Huiji
136. Huichi	137. Baosheng	138. Daoxian
139. Diwang	140. Mingluo	141. Shiguang
142. Shantiao	143. Fenxun	144. Xiudao
145. Daxiang	146. Shanzhu	147. Chishi
148. Guangying	149. Quanjiao	150. Shansi
151. Fayan	152. Fansheng	153. Guangyi

025.达摩波罗尊者　　026.伽耶迦叶尊者　　027.定果德业尊者

028.庄严无忧尊者　　029.忆持因缘尊者　　030.迦那提婆尊者

031.破邪神通尊者　　032.坚持三字尊者　　033.阿口楼驮尊者

034.鸠摩罗多尊者　　035.毒龙皈依尊者　　036.同声稽首尊者

037.毗罗胝子尊者　　038.伐苏蜜多尊者　　039.阇提首那尊者

040.僧法耶舍尊者　　041.悲察世间尊者　　042.献花授记尊者

043.眼光定力尊者　　044.伽耶舍那尊者　　045.莎底比丘尊者

046.波㝿阇提婆尊者　047.解空无垢尊者　　048.伏陀蜜多尊者

049.富那夜舍尊者　　050.伽耶天眼尊者　　051.不著世间尊者

052.解空第一尊者　　053.罗度无尽尊者　　054.金刚破魔尊者

055.愿护世间尊者　　056.无忧禅定尊者　　057.无作慧善尊者

058.十劫慧善尊者　　059.旃檀德香尊者　　060.金山觉意尊者

061.无业宿尽尊者　　062.摩诃刹利尊者　　063.无量本行尊者

064.一念解空尊者　　065.观身无常尊者　　066.千劫悲愿尊者

067.瞿罗那含尊者　　068.解空定空尊者　　069.成就因缘尊者

070.坚通精进尊者　　071.萨陀波仑尊者　　072.乾陀诃利尊者

073.解空自在尊者　　074.摩诃注那尊者　　075.见人飞腾尊者

076.不空不有尊者　　077.周利盘特尊者　　078.瞿沙比丘尊者

079.师子比丘尊者　　080.修行不著尊者　　081.毕陵伽蹉尊者

082.摩利不动尊者　　083.三昧甘露尊者　　084.解空无名尊者

085.七佛难提尊者　　086.金刚精进尊者　　087.方便法藏尊者

088.观行月轮尊者　　089.阿那邠提尊者　　090.指尘三昧尊者

091.摩诃俱𫄷尊者　　092.辟支转智尊者　　093.山顶龙众尊者

094.罗网恩惟尊者　　095.劫宾覆藏尊者　　096.神通亿具尊者

097.具寿具提尊者　　098.法王菩提尊者　　099.法藏永劫尊者

100.善注尊者　　　　101.除忧尊者　　　　102.大忍尊者

103.无忧自在尊者　　104.妙惧尊者　　　　105.严土尊者

106.金髻尊者　　　　107.雷德尊者　　　　108.雷音尊者

109.香象尊者　　　　110.马头尊　　　　　111.明首尊者

112.金首尊者　　　　113.敬首尊者　　　　114.众首尊者

115.辨德尊眷　　　　116.羼提尊者　　　　117.悟达尊者

118.法灯尊者　　　　119.离垢尊者　　　　120.境界尊者

154. Zhiyi	155. Modi	156. Huikuang
157. Wusheng	158. Tanmo	159. Huanxi
160. Youxi	161. Daoshi	162. Mingzhao
163. Pudeng	164. Huizuo	165. Zhuhuan
166. Nansheng	167. Shande	168. Baoya
169. Guanshen	170. Huawang	171. Deshou
172. Xijian	173. Shansu	174. Shanyi
175. Aiguang	176. Huaguang	177. Shanjian
178. Shangen	179. Deding	180. Miaobi
181. Longmeng	182. Fusha	183. Deguang
184. Shanjie	185. Jingzheng	186. Shanguan
187. Dali	188. Dianguang	189. Baozhang
190. Shanxing	191. Luoxun	192. Cidi
193. Qingyou	194. Shiyou	195. Mansu
196. Chantuo	197. Yuejing	198. Datian
199. Jingzang	200. Jingyan	201. Boluomi
202. Junahan	203. Sanweisheng	204. Pusasheng
205. Jixiangzhou	206. Boduoluo	207. Wubianshen
208. Xianjieshou	209. Jingangwei	210. Chengwei
211.Posizha	212. Xinpingdeng	213. Bukebi
214. Lefuzang	215. Huoyanshen	216. Poduoduo
217. Duanfannao	218. Bojuluo	219. Lipoduo
220. Humiaofa	221. Zuishengyi	222. Xumidong
223. Meidejia	224. Mishasai	225. Shanyuanman
226. Botoumo	227. Zhihuidong	228. Zhanshanzang
229. Jiananliu	230. Xiangyanchuang	231. Ashibi
232. Monibao	233. Fudeshou	234. Lopomi
235. Shezhedu	236. Duanye	237. Huanxizhi
238. Qiantuoluo	239. Shajiatuo	240. Xumiwang

121.马胜尊者	122.天王尊者	123.无胜尊者
124.自净尊者	125.不动尊者	126.休息尊者
127.调达尊者	128.普光尊者	129.智积尊者
130.宝幢尊者	131.善慧尊者	132.善眼尊者
133.勇宝尊者	134.宝见尊者	135.慧积尊者
136.慧持尊者	137.宝胜尊者	138.道仙尊者
139.帝网尊者	140.明罗尊者	141.室光尊者
142.善调尊者	143.奋迅尊者	144.修道尊者
145.大相尊者	146.善住尊者	147.持世尊者
148.光英尊者	149.权教尊者	150.善思尊者
151.法眼尊者	152.梵胜尊者	153.光曜尊者
154.直意尊者	155.摩帝尊者	156.慧宽尊者
157.无胜尊者	158.昙摩尊者	159.欢喜尊者
160.游戏尊者	161.道世尊者	162.明照尊者
163.普等尊者	164.慧作尊者	165.助欢尊者
166.难胜尊者	167.善德尊者	168.宝涯尊者
169.观身尊者	170.华王尊者	171.德首尊者
172.喜见尊者	173.善宿尊者	174.善意尊者
175.爱光尊者	176.华光尊者	177.善见尊者
178.善根尊者	179.德顶尊者	180.妙臂尊者
181.龙猛尊者	182.弗沙尊者	183.德光尊者
184.散结尊者	185.净正尊者	186.善观尊者
187.大力尊者	188.电光尊者	189.宝杖尊者
190.善星尊者	191.罗旬尊者	192.慈地尊者
193.庆友尊者	194.世友尊者	195.满宿尊者
196.阐陀尊者	197.月净尊者	198.大天尊者
199.净藏尊者	200.净眼尊者	201.波罗密尊者
202.俱那含尊者	203.三昧声尊者	204.菩萨声尊者
205.吉祥咒尊者	206.钵多罗尊者	207.无边身尊者
208.贤劫首尊者	209.金刚昧尊者	210.乘昧尊者
211.婆私吒尊者	212.心平等尊者	213.不可比尊者
214.乐覆藏尊者	215.火焰身尊者	216.颇多堕尊者

241. Chishanfa	242. Tiduojia	243. Shichaosheng
244. Zhihuihai	245. Zhongjude	246. Busiyi
247. Mizhexian	248. Nituojia	249. Shouzhengnian
250. Jingpoti	251. Fanyitian	252. Yindiguo
253. Jueshengjie	254. Jingjinshan	255. Wuliangguang
256. Budongyi	257. Xiushanye	258. Ayiduo
259. Suntuoluo	260. Shengfenghui	261. Manshuxing
262. Aliduo	263. Falunshan	264. Zhonghehe
265. Fawuzhu	266. Tiangusheng	267. Ruyilun
268. Shouhuoyan	269. Wubijiao	270. Duojialou
271. Lipoduo	272. Puxianxing	273. Chisanwei
274. Weidesheng	275. Lidesheng	276. Mingwujin
277. Anaxi	278. Pushengshan	279. Biancaiwang
280. Xinghuaguo	281. Shenglongzhong	282. Shinanshan
283. Fujiaye	284. Xingchuanfa	285. Xiangjinshou
286. Monaluo	287. Guangpuxian	288. Huiyiwang
289. Xiangmojun	290. Shouyanguang	291. Chidayi
292. Zangluxing	293. Dezizai	294. Fulongwang
295. Duyeduo	296. Qinmoli	297. Yifasheng
298. Shipoduo	299. Chantimo	300. Wangzhudao
301. Wugouxing	302. Aboluo	303. Shengguiyi
304. Chandingguo	305. Butuifa	306. Sengjiaye
307. Damozhen	308. Chishanfa	309. Shoushengguo
310. Xinshengxiu	311. Huifazang	312. Changhuanxi
313. Weiyiduo	314. Toutuoxin	315. Yixichang
316. Dejingwu	317. Wugoucang	318. Xiangfumo
319. Asengjia	320. Jinfule	321. Dunwu
322. Zhuotuopo	323. Zhushijian	324. Dongdaoshou
325. Ganlufa	326. Zizaiwang	327. Xudana

217.断烦恼尊者	218.薄俱罗尊者	219.利婆多尊者
220.护妙法尊者	221.最胜意尊者	222.须弥灯尊者
223.没特伽尊者	224.弥沙塞尊者	225.善园满尊者
226.波头摩尊者	227.智慧灯尊者	228.旃檀藏尊者
229.迦难留尊者	230.香焰幢尊者	231.阿湿卑尊者
232.摩尼宝尊者	233.福德首尊者	234.利婆弥尊者
235.舍遮独尊者	236.断业尊者	237.欢喜智尊者
238.乾陀罗尊者	239.莎伽陀尊者	240.须弥望尊者
241.持善法尊者	242.提多迦尊者	243.水潮声尊者
244.智慧海尊者	245.众具德尊者	246.不思议尊者
247.弥遮仙尊者	248.尼陀迦尊者	249.首正念尊者
250.净菩提尊者	251.梵音天尊者	252.因地果尊者
253.觉胜解尊者	254.精进山尊者	255.无量光尊者
256.不动义尊者	257.修善业尊者	258.阿逸多尊者
259.孙陀罗尊者	260.圣峰慧尊者	261.曼殊行尊者
262.阿利多尊者	263.法轮山尊者	264.众和合尊者
265.法无住尊者	266.天鼓声尊者	267.如意轮尊者
268.首火焰尊者	269.无比较尊者	270.多伽楼尊者
271.利婆多尊者	272.普贤行尊者	273.持三昧尊者
274.威德声尊者	275.利德声尊者	276.名无尽尊者
277.阿那悉尊者	278.普胜山尊者	279.辨才王尊者
280.行化国尊者	281.声龙种尊者	282.誓南山尊者
283.富伽耶尊者	284.行传法尊者	285.香金手尊者
286.摩拿罗尊者	287.光普现尊者	288.慧依王尊者
289.降魔军尊者	290.首焰光尊者	291.持大医尊者
292.藏律行尊者	293.德自在尊者	294.服龙王尊者
295.阇夜多尊者	296.秦摩利尊者	297.义法胜尊者
298.施婆多尊者	299.阐提魔尊者	300.王住道尊者
301.无垢行尊者	302.阿波罗尊者	303.声皈依尊者
304.禅定果尊者	305.不退法尊者	306.僧伽耶尊者
307.达摩真尊者	308.持善法尊者	309.受胜果尊者
310.心胜修尊者	311.会法藏尊者	312.常欢喜尊者

328. Chaofayu	329. Demiaofa	330. Shiyingzhen
331. Jianguxin	332. Shengxiangying	333. Yingfugong
334. Jiechenkong	335. Guangmingdong	336. Chibaoju
337. Gongdexiang	338. Renxinsheng	339. Ashiduo
340. Baixiangxiang	341. Shizizai	342. Zantanyuan
343. Dingfuluo	344. Shengyinzhong	345. Lijingyu
346. Jiushe	347. Yuduoluo	348. Fuyechu
349. Luoyuxi	350. Dayaozun	351. Shengjiekong
352. Xiuwude	353. Xiwuzhu	354. Yuegaizun
355. Zhantanluo	356. Xindinglun	357. Yanluoman
358. Dingshengzun	359. Sahetan	360. Zhifude
361. Xunacha	362. Xijianzun	363. Weilanwang
364. Tipochang	365. Chengdali	366. Fashou
367. Supintuo	368. Zhongdeshou	369. Jingangzang
370. Qujiali	371. Yuezhaoming	372. Wugoucang
373. Chuyiwang	374. Wuliangming	375. Chuzhongyou
376. Wugoude	377. Guangmingwang	378. Xiushanxing
379. Zuoqingliang	380. Wuyouyan	381. Qugaizhang
382. Zimingzun	383. Heluntiao	384. Jingchugou
385. Quzhuye	386. Cirenzun	387. Wujinci
388. Satuonu	389. Naluoda	390. Xingyuanchi
391. Tianyanzun	392. Wujinzhi	393. Bianjuzu
394. Baogaizun	395. Shentonghua	396. Sishanshi
397. Xixinjing	398. Mokenan	399. Wuliangguang
400. Jinguanghui	401. Fulongshi	402. Huanhuakong
403. Jingangming	404. Lianhuajing	405. Junayi
406. Xianshouzun	407. Ligengluo	408. Tiaodingzang
409. Wugoucheng	410. Tianyinsheng	411. Daweiguang
412. Zizaizhu	413. Mingshijie	414. Zuishangzun

415. Jingangzun

416. Juanmanyi

417. Zhongwubi

418. Chaojuelun

419. Yueputi

420. Chishijie

421. Dinghuazhi

422. Wubianshen

423. Zuishengchuang

424. Qiefa

425. Wuaixing

426. Puzhuangyan

427. Wujinci

428. Changbeimin

429. Dachenzhang

430. Huoyanming

431. Zhiyanming

432. Jianguxing

433. Shuyunyu

434. Budongluo

435. Puguangmingyan

436. Xinguanjing

437. Naluode

438. Shizizun

439. Fashangzun

440. Jingjinbian

441. Leshuoguo

442. Guanwubian

443. Shizifan

444. Poxiejian

445. Wuyoude

446. Xingwubian

447. Huijingang

448. Yichengjiu

449. Shanzhuyi

450. Xincheng

451. Xingjingduan

452. Depuha

453. Shizihua

454. Xingrenci

455. Wuxiangkong

456. Yongjingjin

457. Shengqingjing

458. Youxingkong

459. Jingnaluo

460. Fazizai

461. Shizijia

462. Daxianguang

463. Mokeluo

464. Yintiaomin

465. Shiziyi

466. Huaimojun

467. Fenbieshen

468. Jingjietuo

469. Zhizhixing

470. Zhirenci

471. Juzuyi

472. Ruyiza

473. Dazhimiao

474. Jiebinna

475. Puyanguang

476. Gaoyixing

477. Defozhi

478. Jijingxing

479. Wuzhenchang

480. Poyuanzei

481. Mieequ

482. Xinghaitong

483. Fatong

484. Minbuxi

485. Shezhongxin

486. Daodazhong

487. Changyinxing

488. Pusaci

489. Bazhongku

490. Xunshengying

491. Shujieding

492. Zhufashui

493. Dedingtong

494. Huiguangzeng

495. Liugenjing

496. Baduluo

497. Sisaduo

498. Zhutujia

499. Boliluo

500. Yuanshizhong

313.威仪多尊者	314.头陀信尊者	315.议洗肠尊者
316.德净悟尊者	317.无垢藏尊者	318.降伏魔尊者
319.阿僧伽尊者	320.金富乐尊者	321.顿悟尊者
322.周陀婆尊者	323.住世间尊者	324.灯导首尊者
325.甘露法尊者	326.自在王尊者	327.须达那尊者
328.超法雨尊者	329.德妙法尊者	330.士应真尊者
331.坚固心尊者	332.声晌应尊者	333.应赴供尊者
334.劫尘空尊者	335.光明灯尊者	336.执宝炬尊者
337.功德相尊者	338.忍心生尊者	339.阿氏多尊者
340.白香象尊者	341.识自在尊者	342.赞叹愿尊者
343.定拂罗尊者	344.声引众尊者	345.离净语尊者
346.鸠舍尊者	347.郁多罗尊者	348.福业除尊者
349.罗余习尊者	350.大药尊尊者	351.胜解空尊者
352.修无德尊者	353.喜无著尊者	354.月盖尊尊者
355.旃檀罗尊者	356.心定论尊者	357.庵罗满尊者
358.顶生尊尊者	359.萨和坛尊者	360.直福德尊者
361.须那刹尊者	362.喜见尊尊者	363.韦蓝王尊者
364.提婆长尊者	365.成大利尊者	366.法首尊者
367.苏频陀尊者	368.众德首尊者	369.金刚藏尊者
370.瞿伽离尊者	371.月照明尊者	372.无垢藏尊者
373.除疑网尊者	374.无量明尊者	375.除众忧尊者
376.无垢德尊者	377.光明网尊者	378.修善行尊者
379.坐清凉尊者	380.无忧眼尊者	381.去盖障尊者
382.自明尊尊者	383.和伦调尊者	384.净除垢尊者
385.去诸业尊者	386.慈仁尊尊者	387.无尽慈尊者
388.飒陀怒尊者	389.那罗达尊者	390.行愿持尊者
391.天眼尊尊者	392.无尽智尊者	393.遍具足尊者
394.宝盖尊尊者	395.神通化尊者	396.思善识尊者
397.喜信静尊者	398.摩诃男尊者	399.无量光尊者
400.金光慧尊者	401.伏龙施尊者	402.幻化空尊者
403.金刚明尊者	404.莲花净尊者	405.拘那意尊者
406.贤首尊者	407.利亘罗尊者	408.调定藏尊者

409.无垢称尊者	410.天音声尊者	411.大威光尊者
412.自在主尊者	413.明世界尊者	414.最上尊尊者
415.金刚尊尊者	416.蠲慢意尊者	417.众无比尊者
418.超绝伦尊者	419.月菩提尊者	420.持世界尊者
421.定花至尊者	422.无边身尊者	423.最胜幢尊者
424.弃恶法尊者	425.无碍行尊者	426.普庄严尊者
427.无尽慈尊者	428.常悲悯尊者	429.大尘障尊者
430.光焰明尊者	431.智眼明尊者	432.坚固行尊者
433.澍云雨尊者	434.不动罗尊者	435.普光明焰尊者
436.心观净尊者	437.那罗德尊者	438.师子尊尊者
439.法上尊尊者	440.精进辨尊者	441.乐说果尊者
442.观无边尊者	443.师子翻尊者	444.破邪见尊者
445.无忧德尊者	446.行无边尊者	447.慧金刚尊者
448.义成就尊者	449.善住义尊者	450.信澄尊者
451.行敬端尊者	452.德普洽尊者	453.师子化尊者
454.行忍慈尊者	455.无相空尊者	456.勇精进尊者
457.胜清净尊者	458.有性空尊者	459.净那罗尊者
460.法自在尊者	461.师子颊尊者	462.大贤光尊者
463.摩诃罗尊者	464.音调敏尊者	465.师子臆尊者
466.坏魔军尊者	467.分别身尊者	468.净解脱尊者
469.质直行尊者	470.智仁慈尊者	471.具足仪尊者
472.如意杂尊者	473.大炽妙尊者	474.劫宾那尊者
475.普焰光尊者	476.高逸行尊者	477.得佛智尊者
478.寂静行尊者	479.悟真常尊者	480.破冤贼尊者
481.灭恶趣尊者	482.性海通尊者	483.法通尊者
484.敏不息尊者	485.摄众心尊者	486.导大众尊者
487.常隐行尊者	488.菩萨慈尊者	489.拔众苦尊者
490.寻声应尊者	491.数劫定尊者	492.注法水尊者
493.得定通尊者	494.慧广增尊者	495.六根净尊者
496.拔度罗尊者	497.思萨埵尊者	498.注荼迦尊者
499.钵利罗尊者	500.愿事众尊者	

Chapter VI: Ten Sights on Puti Island

Puti Island boasts a profound history and primitive but enthralling landscapes. In 2000, on the basis of its historic heritages like Chaoyang Nunnery and Chaoyin Temple, the island further expanded its tourism resources along with the rapid development of local tourism industry. Based on local historical records and folklores, Puti Island has constructed many cultural sights, which not only add a historic aroma to the island, but also provide tourists with more enjoyments. Hereinafter are the ten most famous sights on Puti Island.

I. Zhubi Pavilion

Standing on Zhubi Pavilion, one can overlook the entire island with lush trees, blooming flowers, and singing birds. Along with the development of Puti Island in recent years, the pavilion was built to commemorate the Tang emperor Li Shimin, who stayed on the island (then called Mortar Isle) during his military expedition to ancient Korea.

Legend goes that the Tang emperor and his troops continued smashing into the enemy territory during the military expedition till they reached Yannan. In the Yannan Battle, the enemy ambushed 50,000 soldiers in a dense forest. As the Tang army passed by, the ambushed enemy suddenly assaulted and defeated the Tang army. The Tang troops then retreated southwards, and the enemy chased. As they arrived at the Daqing River, the retreatment route was cut by the torrential Daqing River. They had to flee south along the river to its estuary on the coast, where the water level was only ankle-high. However, all soldiers who attempted to cross the river were stuck in silt. Then, their chasers almost reached the river estuary. Li Shimin sighed, "God! Shall I die here?" At the moment, countless crabs climbed onto the beach and set a bridge with their bodies. Delighted at the miracle, the emperor ordered his troops to retreat to Mortar Isle via the crab bridge. As they mounted onto the island, the enemy already arrived at the opposite end of the crab bridge. "Crabs, please dismantle the bridge," Li Shimin shouted in hurry. However, those crabs crowded together and couldn't disperse immediately. "Crabs, sidle away!" Li Shimin ordered. Following the emperor's order, the crabs sidled and the bridge immediately disappeared. The enemy couldn't cross the sea, and had to retreat. Then, Li Shimin stayed for a short time on Mortar Isle. Inspired by the story, later generations built the pavilion on the island.

第六章 菩提岛十景

菩提岛历史悠深，古朴神奇。除原存朝阳庵、潮音寺等历史景观外，随着近年旅游事业的发展，2000年对相对丰富的景观资源进行了拓展。在深入挖掘海岛文化的基础上，本着以史为鉴，借助口碑文学的原则，先后为菩提岛营建多处人文景观。这些溢自历史长河的名胜，带着史海陈迹与新时代的气息，不仅为开发中的菩提岛增辉添色，也为众多来自各地的游人带来了更多情趣。经筛选，撷取驻跸亭、菩提树、和尚井、讲经台、菩提山门、正觉湖与观音台、盼王桑树、鸳鸯树、许愿树、三日同辉十景入卷，分别介绍如下。

一 驻跸亭

登上菩提岛驻跸亭，放眼全岛，绿荫如盖，花草叠翠，飞鸟婉鸣，令人心驰神往。这一人文景观是近年随着菩提岛的开发为纪念唐王李世民东征高句丽曾驻军石臼坨而兴建的。

相传，当年唐王李世民御驾东征，一路旗开得胜，但在燕南战役中，因敌军搬来数万援兵，排兵布阵隐蔽在燕南林木之中，待唐兵赶到，呼啸而起，唐军伤亡惨重，溃军南逃，敌兵乘胜追击。唐王溃军逃到大清河河畔，水流湍急，几次抢渡均未成功，便沿河南进，到了海口，水浅没踝，唐王率兵涉水过河，但下水军卒均被陷淤泥之中，此时，敌兵已以排山倒海之势向河边追来。唐王李世民一筹莫展，仰天长叹："苍天啊！难道我李世民命该休矣？"是时，海中众多的螃蟹闻讯赶来，乘势架起一座蟹桥，唐王一见欣喜若狂，急忙催动坐骑率师争进，马踏蟹桥登上海岛。回头看，见敌兵正欲踏桥追赶，唐王忙道："众位神蟹，赶紧散开，撤掉蟹桥！"众蟹前挤后拥，疏散不开。唐王忙传口谕："众位神蟹，赶快横向爬开呀！"螃蟹听后，立刻横向爬开，蟹桥转眼不见，敌兵见河水阻路无计可施，只好败兴退却。后来，人们为了纪念唐王曾在此小住，在岛上修建了"驻跸亭"。

II. Bodhi Trees

The Bodhi tree, called Pippala in Sanskrit, is a species of plant endemic to India. Legend goes that Sakyamuni, the founder of Buddhism, attained enlightenment under a Bodhi tree. Historical records reveal that in 502, Indian monk Zhiyao Sanzang introduced Bodhi trees from India and planted them in front of the Guangxiao Temple in Guangzhou. Gradually, Bodhi trees began to take roots in Guangdong, Guangxi and Yunnan Provinces. More than 2,500 years ago, Sakyamuni, originally named Siddhartha Gautama, was a prince of Kapilavastu Kingdom (in today's Nepal) in the north of ancient India. When he was young, he gave up his identity as the heir and converted to Buddhism in order to help people get rid of illness, pain, and death. Legend goes that he finally attained enlightenment and became Buddha after 49 days of meditation under a Bodhi tree. Therefore, the Bodhi tree is considered holy by Buddhists.

In China, there is also a prevalent story concerning the Bodhi tree.

It is said that Huineng, the sixth-generation patriarch of the Zen sect, was born into a poor family. When Huineng was a child, his father died. To help his mother and support the family, Huineng often went to mountains to chop firewood for sale. One day, when he sold firewood in the market, Huineng encountered Hongren, the fifth-generation patriarch of the Zen sect, preached there. Huineng then listened to his preaching. "Where're you from?" Hongren asked him. "Lingnan," Huineng replied.

"People from Lingnan have no knowledge about Buddhism," Hongren said.

"People may come from south or north, but Buddha from nowhere." Huineng argued.

Hongren knew the boy would be somebody in future, and thus recruited Huineng as his student. In the temple, Huineng worked at the mill. Years later, Hongren knew it was time to find an heir amongst his disciples. He then ordered each of his disciples to write a Buddhist hymn. His oldest student, Shenxiu, wrote a poem that reads, "The body is a Bodhi tree, and the mind a standing mirror bright. At all times polish it diligently, and let no dust alight." Huineng responded with another poem that reads, "Bodhi is no tree, nor is the mind a standing mirror bright. Since all is originally empty, where does the dust alight?" Later, Hongren visited the mill where Huineng worked, and knocked the stone mortar three times with his stick. Huineng understood his teacher's hint, and then visited Hongren's bedroom at mid-night. There, Hongren passed down the gown that represented succession to Huineng, who then became the six-generation patriarch of the Zen sect.

二　菩提树

菩提树，原产印度，梵语原名为"毕钵罗树"（Pippala），相传佛教的创始人释迦牟尼在菩提树下悟道成佛。据史籍记载，梁武帝天监元年（502年），印度僧人智药三藏从西竺引种菩提树于广州光孝寺坛前。从此我国广东、广西、云南等地开始有菩提树生长。

2500多年前，佛祖释迦牟尼原是古印度北部的迦毗罗卫王国（今尼泊尔境内）的王子乔答摩·悉达多，他年轻时为摆脱生老病死轮回之苦，解救受苦受难的众生，毅然放弃继承王位和舒适的王族生活，出家修行，寻求人生的真谛。经过多年的修炼，在菩提树下禅定四十九日，战胜了各种邪恶诱惑，获得大彻大悟，终成佛陀。所以，后来佛教一直都视菩提树为圣树。

在中国，菩提树也有一段脍炙人口的故事。

相传，禅宗六祖慧能从小丧父，家徒四壁，长年以上山打柴养母。一日入市，见五祖弘忍市井诵经，便近前聆听大师讲经说法。弘忍见状便问："汝从何处来？"答曰："岭南。"弘忍说："岭南人无佛性！"慧能辩道："人既分南北，佛性岂不也分南北吗？"五祖知面前少年乃异人，便收他为徒，使入碓房春米。时经八月，五祖知授法衣时间已至，便让徒弟们各自书一首得法偈语。上座神秀所书偈曰："身是菩提树，心如明镜台，时时勤拂拭，莫使惹尘埃。"慧能见后也书一偈："菩提本无树，明镜亦非台，本来无一物，何处惹尘埃。"五祖阅后，潜入碓房，问道："你春的米白吗？"慧能答道："白米经筛。"五祖用手杖击碓三下而去。慧能心领神会，即以三更进入老师的禅房，于是五祖弘忍传授衣法，慧能成为合法的佛门继承人，是为六祖。

III. Fuhe Spring

Puti Island abounds in freshwater resources, and its spring water tastes "as delicious as sweet wine." Fuhe Spring, popularly known Monk's Well, was dug by Monk Faben and his disciples. Although it is less than two meters deep, the well never dries even in drought years.

The phenomenon is attributed to the special geography of Puti Island. The island resembles a gigantic mortar, with its edges protruding upwards and its center sunken. Such a terrain is easy to withhold rainwater. Meanwhile, the island can turn seawater into underground freshwater due to the filtration of its sandy soil. Historically, Faben and other monks dug several wells on the island. With the passage of time, Monk's Well is the only one preserved today.

IV. Preaching Terrace

Situated in the southeast of the Chaoyin Temple on Puti Island, the Preaching Terrace features lush trees and a tranquil environment. It was where Monk Faben preached Buddhist sutras to his students. So far, only a round stone platform remains.

V. The Front Gate of Puti Island

Built along the terrain, the gate is 6.6 meters high and 19 meters long, which symbolizes the island's former name Nineteen Isle. Carved atop the gate are three characters translated as "Puti Island" written by Zhao Puchu, former president of China Buddhism Association. On the front side of the gate are the couplets written by Chen Ziheng, chairman of the Chinese Society for Hard Pen Calligraphers, which mean "Fishing lamps and moonlight set off each other, and temple drums and bells echo together with the roaring waves." On the opposite side are couplets written by Zhao Puchu, which mean "A fairyland on earth composed with sails and dunes; A jade abode for immortals built with clouds and billows."

三 和尚井

　　菩提岛淡水资源十分丰富，掘地成泉，"独甘如醴"。法本和尚当年带领僧众开凿的这口和尚井（又名福和泉），井深不到两米，水质清澈，取之不尽，大旱之年，从未干枯。

　　这一现象是由菩提岛的特殊地理环境所决定的。菩提岛地形四周高，中间低平，环岛沙丘隆起，状若石臼，地下水主要靠天然降水来补给。雨季，雨水不能外溢，海岛沙性能涵水、滤水。滤出的淡水，多埋在1米多深的地下，其含量十分丰富。法本和尚率僧众在岛上曾掘成多口水井。历史沧桑，风雨剥蚀，多处水井无存。目前所见的和尚井，是岛上仅存的最完整的一口古井。

四 讲经台

　　讲经台，位于菩提岛潮音寺的东南处，绿树成荫，环境

幽雅。目前尚存一圆形石台，系法本和尚在此讲经时所用。当年，法本等众僧常聚集于此讲经说法。

五 菩提山门

　　东低西高，依地势而建。门高6.6米，长19米，寓"十九坨"之意。山门正中上方镌刻着中国佛教学会原会长赵朴初先生手书"菩提岛"三个大字，正面为中国硬笔书法家协会主席陈子恒先生书写的"蟹火渔灯掩映一天月色，晨钟暮鼓抑扬大海潮音"。另一面为赵朴初先生的墨迹，内容是：风帆沙岛皆人间奇境，云影波光造玉宇琼阁。

VI. Zhengjue Lake and Kwan-yin Terrace

Zhengjue Lake is a freshwater lake on the island. There, fish swim in clear water, and reeds sway in breeze. It is an ideal place to angle by boat. On the islet in the middle of the lake stands an earth terrace, which is named Kwan-yin Terrace. An 81-step staircase leads to a statue of Kwan-yin, or Goddess of Mercy, atop the terrace, where one can overlook the entire island.

VII. Emperor-Greeting Mulberry Tree

South to the east gate of the Tathagata Hall in the Chaoyin Temple is growing a huge mulberry tree with a tall trunk and an extended crown. It burgeons in spring and bears fruits in summer, which don't fall all year round.

It is said that when the Tang emperor, Li Shimin, stayed temporarily on Mortar Isle, he was surprised at the mulberry tree thriving on the sea island. "The tree must be blessed, so its fruits must be rare treasures on earth," the emperor sighed. "I would be lucky to taste them if the tree fruited in autumn. How regretful it is!" The tree nodded in breeze as though it understood what the emperor said. That year, the tree began to fruit in summer, and its fruits didn't fall until deep autumn when the emperor returned to the island after victory.

VIII. Mandarin Duck Trees

Situated at the east corner of the Chaoyin Temple, the Mandarin Duck Trees are two thriving mulberry trees entwining together. Legend goes that the two trees are incarnations of a couple of lovers. Once upon a time, a boy worked together with his parents in a local wealthy family, where he fell in love with his employer's daughter. As they grew up, the girl's parents arranged an engagement with the son of another wealthy family. But, the girl couldn't erase the boy she loved from her heart. Due to their extremely different family background, however, their love was not blessed at that time. As her arranged wedding draw near, the girl fell into deep sorrow. On the night of her wedding, the girl eloped with her lover. Her parents sent servants with sticks to chase them. As the couple of lovers reached the coast, they found no way to escape and then jumped into the sea while tightly hugging each other. Day after day, year after year, their tragic love story was spread farther and farther. Then, a miracle happened: Two entwining trees grew on the island. People believed they were incarnations of the couple of lovers, and then named them Mandarin Duck Trees.

六 正觉湖与观音台

正觉湖为岛上的淡水湖，泛舟碧波，随风荡漾，鱼儿嬉戏，芦苇摇曳。坐船垂钓，虽无"寒江独钓"之雅致，却有"独钓湖心一抹青绿"之异趣。湖心岛为一土筑高台，名曰"观音台"，沿九九八十一级台阶拾级而上，可拜谒观音大士，鸟瞰菩提全岛。

七 盼王桑

潮音寺如来殿东便门南，长有一棵硕大的桑树，枝干挺拔，树冠如盖，入春发芽生叶，盛夏果实累累，压弯枝头，经年不落。

相传，此奇观源自唐王李世民驻跸石臼坨，踏春观景时，见坨前生有一株桑树。唐王以为，石臼坨地处溟海之中，能生如此葱郁之奇树，乃天地灵秀之造物也，所结果实，定是果中之珍，世间极品。想至此，面对奇树叹曰：

"此果再好，可惜季节不对，如果能结果深秋，供朕品尝多好！"唐王道罢，桑树会意地点了点头。自此，夏季长果后，轮替递生，直至深秋，顶凌不落，直待唐王回师再次登岛笑贡御前。

八 鸳鸯树

鸳鸯树位于潮音寺东不远的路旁拐角处，为菩提岛一处自然奇观，该树是两棵同根相拥的古桑，根系发达，枝繁叶茂，无花无果。相传，这两棵树是一对真心相爱的恋人的化身。故事的情节是：男孩的父母在女孩家里做长工，男孩和女孩青梅竹马，两小无猜。到了婚嫁年龄，女孩的父母托媒与一富家子弟定了亲，而女孩的心里却只有与她一起长

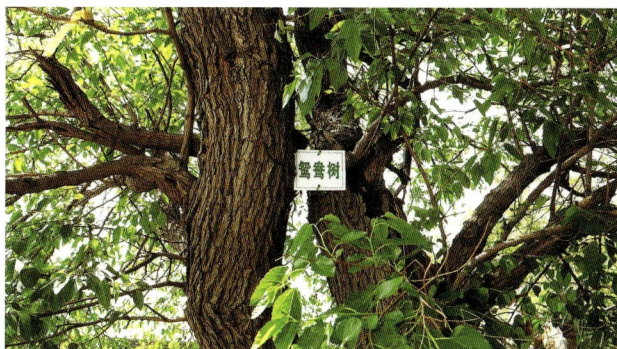

大的男孩。在当时，这种门不当户不对的婚事是封建观念所不容许的。到了出嫁的日子，女孩以泪洗面，心里眷恋着男孩；男孩野外独处，神舍难分。女孩出嫁的晚上，乘机逃了出来，找到等候她的男孩一起奔向沿海荒岛。家人发现后，立即派来持棍携棒的家丁追了上来。赶到海边，前临滔滔大海，后随如狼似虎的打手，女孩和男孩走投无路，相拥搂抱投入大海。潮汐起落，岁月悠悠，人们一直在怀念着这对为追求真爱而献身的恋人。奇迹发生了，不知哪年哪月，海岛上长出了这株连理树，传说这就是当年那女孩和男孩生死相爱的化身，因而人们把它称作"鸳鸯树"。

IX. Wish Tree

The Wish Tree is a silk tree planted by Monk Faben in the Chaoyin Temple. It features a coiling, sturdy trunk, an extended crown, and strong fragrance when flowering. It is said that when Faben arrived at the island, he vowed under the tree to devote all his life to Buddhism. One evening, auspicious clouds floated breeze. Avalokitesvara Bodhisattva flew over the island and saw the Mandarin Duck Trees. He feared that monks in the temple might go to wrong roads in the course of practicing Buddhism, and then threw down a seedling of a silk tree. Faben understood the bodhisattva's kind warning, and planted the seedling in the temple. As he knelt down before the newly-planted tree, its twin leaves marvelously closed. Faben then knew the tree was incarnation of Avalokitesvara Bodhisattva. Thus, he sat under the tree and chanted sutras to display his devoutness. When darkness fell, Faben continued chanting as if he didn't notice the passage of time. Everything around him was silent except for the roaring waves. When the sun climbed up the next morning, Faben stopped chanting and stood up. At the moment, the tree blossomed with flowers. Faben thus knew his devoutness finally moved the bodhisattva.

X. Three Suns Shine Together

On the first and fifteenth days of each month in lunar calendar, people can see the spectacular scene that the sun shines together with its two reflections on the sea. Such a marvelous sight must be a favored bliss of Mother Nature.

九　许愿树

　　许愿树，也叫绒花树，又名合欢树，位于潮音寺院内，系法本栽植，树干虬曲强壮，树冠硕大，花香四溢。相传，当年法本刚到海岛的时候，曾经在这棵树下许下了"深入佛海，终生虔修"的心愿。一天傍晚，祥云浮动，凉风习习，观音菩萨巡视云头，途经菩提岛上空，偶见潮音寺东部的那棵鸳鸯树，心中泛起波澜，唯恐皈依佛门寺僧心生业障，便扔下一棵绒花树苗以作警世。法本见后，深知菩萨佛意良苦，便在潮音寺院内将那棵绒花树苗亲手栽下，双手合十，跪拜在地。刹那间，绒花羽状对生树叶立刻合拢。法本大惊，自知观音菩萨已将自己附于绒花树身，便急忙打坐诵经，心中默念经文。时间移逝，夜色已深，但法本却全然不知，唯四周沉没静寂，大海抑扬潮音。太阳从东方冉冉升起，法本起身归寺，就在这时，满树绒花，悄然绽放。法本一见喜出望外，心知观音菩萨已信己诚。

十　三日同辉

　　每逢初一、十五，潮汐低平，驻足菩提岛能见到天上的太阳与海中的两个倒影互相辉映呈三日同辉的壮观景象。自然造化的菩提奇景让人大开眼界，叹为观止。

Chapter VII: Plants on Puti Island

Puti Island covers an area of only 4.4 square kilometers, but there are three kinds of soil within its territory. The east and north parts are sandy soil, the central and south parts are loams, and the southwest and coastal areas are moist salinized soil. Due to its unique geographic environment, soil diversity, and humid marine climate, the island is an ideal habitat for plants, with 98 percent of its space covered with vegetations. There, one can find plants endemic to both northern and southern China, as well as both coastal and mountainous botanic species. Even some species never found in Laoting's mainland, such as Bunge hackberry, oriental bittersweet, and Korean moonseed, flourish on the island. Among the 571 species of terraneous plants of Laoting County, 333 species can be found on the island.

Its unique geography, climate, and soils bestow the island a botanic diversity. Most species were transported here by migrant birds except for those introduced by humans, wind, or oceanic currents. The island offers an ideal habitat for birds, and in return birds carried seeds of more botanic species. The island nurtures birds, and birds enrich the island.

So far, the island has become a kingdom of plants and a paradise for birds in North China.

The rich plant species on the island can be approximately divided into ligneous plants, herbaceous plants, and medical herbs.

I. Ligneous Plants

Ligneous plants mainly include forest trees and fruit trees. A recent survey shows that the island grows 46 species of trees, including Laoting's indigenous trees like poplar, willow, elm, heaven tree, Chinese toona, silk tree, hibiscus, mulberry, locust tree, apricot, pear, jujube, peach, and plum tree, as well as species that are rarely seen in Laoting such as gingko, Bunge hackberry, lespedeza, Loblolly pine, ash tree, paper mulberry tree, ampelopsis, and bower vine. Among them, the most famous species include:

第七章　菩提岛上的植物

菩提岛全岛面积只有4.4平方公里，却分布着三种土壤类型。岛上东部、北部为沙土，中南部为壤土，西南部和靠近沿海地带为盐化潮土。由于其独特的地理环境和多种土壤类型，加之湿润的海洋气候，冬无严寒，夏无酷暑，全岛草木丛生，植被覆盖率达98%。这里既有北方生长的植物，又有南方生长的植物，既有沿海生长的植物，又有山区生长的植物，甚至乐亭陆地没有的植物如小叶朴、南蛇藤、木防已等，在岛上生长茂盛，乐亭陆地内共有植物102科，267属，571种，而岛上即有植物56科、158属、333种。

石臼坨独特的区位环境、气候环境和土壤环境造就了石臼坨植物的多样化。这些物种，除了人工引进、风力、海水传播而来以外，大部外来物种是由于大量的候鸟南北迁徙传播而来的。岛为鸟创造了栖息的条件，鸟为岛增加了植物资源，是岛养育了鸟，是鸟发展了岛。

因此，石臼坨成了北方植物的宝库，也是鸟类的天堂。

岛上众多的植物资源，大致可分为木本植物、草本植物和药用植物。

一　木本植物

木本植物主要指林木和果树，资源普查时统计，全岛有树种46种，其中有乐亭当地树种，如杨、柳、榆、樗、香椿、合欢、木槿、桑、槐、杏、梨、枣、桃、李，也有乐亭不常见的银杏、小叶朴、五加皮、胡枝子、火炬、白蜡、构树、蛇葡萄、凌霄等。其中较为出名的树有：

Bodhi tree, also known as Bunge hackberry, is a deciduous arbor belonging to the genus hackberry located in the ulmaceae family. As a rare botanic species on Mortar Isle, it blossoms in spring and bears stone fruits. Around 1949, there were 5-6 Bodhi trees behind the Chaoyin Temple, each with a trunk diameter of 50 centimeters. All of them were destroyed during the Cultural Revolution period, except for the one in front of the temple's dinning hall, whose trunk is now 48.4 centimeters in diameter. Today, most Bodhi trees are no more than 20 centimeters in trunk diameter. Their leaves have effect to cure cold, flu, erysipelas, and diarrhea. It is said before 1949, when a plague hit Laoting, monks saved many patients with the leaves of those trees.

Gingko, also known as maidenhair tree, is a genus of deciduous, dioecious arbor with fan-shaped leaves and egg-like seeds. Before 1949, there were three gingko trees that dated back to the Ming Dynasty, each with a trunk 30 centimeters in diameter. A survivor of the fourth glacial epoch, gingko is thus dubbed "living fossil." People believe that its leaves can prevent apoplexy,while its fruit can cure asthma and relieve leucorrhea and spermatorrhoea. Unfortunately, all big gingko trees on the island already disappeared, and only small ones survive.

Kwan-yin willow, also known as five-stamen tamarisk or rain forecaster, is an arbor belonging to the family tamarisk. It blossoms in summer, and its flowers feature reddish panicles. According to *Encyclopedia of All Things*, tamarisk shows signs before the arrival of rain, hence its nickname "rain forecaster." Meanwhile, it is reputed the "saint of trees" because it doesn't wither even in frost and snow. Its branches and leaves have effect to cure exanthema and rheumatism. Most of those trees grow in the west of the island. The biggest is found by Nanxia Pond, which measures 3.2 meters in height and 15 centimeters in diameter.

菩提树（原名小叶朴，又名棒棒木），榆科，朴属，落叶乔木。叶基有三大脉，春季开花，核果球形。是石臼坨的珍贵树种，新中国成立初期潮音寺后有五六株大树，直径都在50厘米以上。"文革"前后被毁，现只在木板房餐厅前保留一株，直径48.4厘米，人们把它称为"菩提树"，现在不满20厘米的幼树甚多，成为石臼坨一大景观。此树枝叶可以入药，治风寒、流行性感冒、丹毒、痢疾等，据说新中国成立前乐亭沿海流行瘟疫时，僧人曾以此树枝叶熬汤，遍施患者，救人甚多。

观音柳，又名柽柳、三眠柳、雨师、西河柳。柽柳科。小乔木，鳞片状叶，夏季开花，花小型，淡红色，圆锥花序。蒴果。《博物志》载：天之将雨，柽先知之，故名雨师。又云：负霜雪而不凋，乃木之圣者。以枝叶入药，性平味甘咸，能透发痧疹，祛风湿。岛西部较多，南虾池旁，最大一株直径15厘米，树高3.2米。

银杏树，又叫白果、公孙树。银杏科。落叶乔木。叶扇形，雌雄异株，种子卵形。新中国成立前有三株直径1.5尺的银杏树，据说是明朝栽植的。银杏树是第四纪冰川以后孑遗的树种，向有"活化石"、"活文物"、"活历史"、"活标本"之称，人们说它："叶似扇，果似蛋，叶子防中风，果子治肺喘，女人疗带下，男治遗精多小便。"可惜的是大树已经被毁，只剩小树了。

Albizia, also known as silk tree or mimosa, is a dioecious arbor of the family Fabaceae. It blossoms in summer, and its flower features reddish capitulum. Its leaves open in the daytime, and close at night. In ancient China, couples often admired the tree to pray for lasting love. People also worshipped the tree to pray for wealth and dignity. It likes sunshine and can endure drought and barrenness. Its barks can calm mood, rejuvenate blood circulation, and cure insomnia and wrench. Its flowers can also be used as medicine, with effect similar to its barks.

Apricot is the commonest species among all trees on the island. Around 1949, there were 20-30 big apricot trees. The apricot is an arbor belonging to the family Prunus. It blossoms in spring and fruits in summer. Its fruits are sweet and juicy. At the end of the Qing Dynasty and the beginning of the Republic of China period, a plague hit the coastal area in southern Laoting. Local monks granted medicine to patients, and asked each cured person to plant an apricot tree on the island. Before long, an apricot forest took shape on the island. Therefore, later generations used the term "apricot forest" to imply hospitals. Today, the island still preserves an old apricot tree that dates back more than 70 years, which remains flourishing. It is proven that almonds have detoxifying effect and can moisten the lung and relieve cough.

合欢树，也叫绒花树、夜合花、芙蓉树。豆科。落叶乔木，羽状复叶，夏季开花，花淡红色，头状花序，荚扁平。其叶子白天张开夜间成对相合，因而叫合欢，夫妻祈求百年好合，多有拜谒此树的。祈求荣升富贵的也有拜谒此树的，因它又叫绒花（华）树。此树喜光、耐干旱、耐瘠薄。皮叫合欢皮，可入药，性平、味甘、安神、解郁、活血，治气郁、胸闷、失眠、跌打损伤。花也能入药，功能与皮相似。

奉居庐山，为人治病不求索谢，只求种杏一株。未几，杏树成林，杏熟买杏者将谷一担换杏一担。故后人称医家为杏林。现在岛上还保存一株大树，至少有70年，仍然枝繁叶茂。杏仁可入药，解毒、润肺、止咳。

杏树，是岛上人工栽植最多的一个树种，新中国成立之初有大树二三十株。杏树为蔷薇科，落叶乔木，春季开花，夏季成熟，杏果甘甜多汁。岛上杏树独多，其原因是清末民初乐亭南部沿海一带发生瘟疫，寺内僧人施舍药物，不取分文，病愈者可在岛上栽植杏树一棵。学习汉董

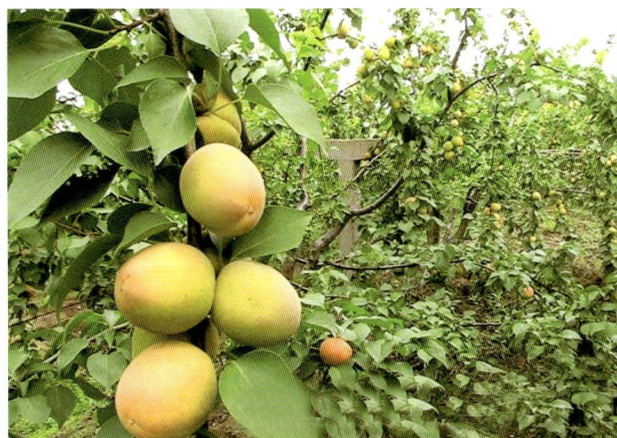

Euonymus is nicknamed Devil's Arrow in China. According to *Compendium of Materia Medica*, euonymus looks like arrow or spear, hence its nickname. It is a dioecious shrub with elliptical twin leaves. It blossoms with cymes in early summer. Both its branches and stems can be used as medicine, with effect to relieve catamenia, night sweat, bellyache, and skin flare. Euonymus trees usually grow in dunes on the island. The biggest one lies southwest to the Chaoyin Temple and measures 4.9 meters in height and 21 centimeters in diameter.

Sour jujube, also known as wild jujube, is a dioecious arbor belonging to the family Rhamnaceae-suanzao. It features elliptical leaves and small, yellowish flowers with cymes. Its fruits are nearly round-shaped. The immature fruits are green, and mature ones turn dark red. It blossoms in early summer and fruits in autumn. It prefers warm, dry habitats, but marshes and wetlands are not suitable for the plant to grow. Both its fruits and seeds have effect to calm mood and nurture the liver and can cure neurasthenic, insomnia, and palpitation. Sour jujubes are scattered around the island. In a temple is a jujube tree with a trunk of 20.5 centers in diameter, which is 4.5 meters tall and has a canopy stretching for 13.8 square meters. Today, it remains lush and fruitful.

Crape myrtle, also known as itch tree, is a dioecious arbor with slippery trunk and elliptical leaves. A species of the family loosestrife, it blossoms in summer, and its flower has six petals and is reddish, purple, or white in color. When grabbed, its branches will shake as if it was tickled, hence its name "itch tree." It root and leaves have effect to rejuvenate blood circulation and relieve gores.

卫矛，一名鬼箭羽。《本草》载：齐人谓箭羽为卫。枝叶犹如箭羽，又有矛刀之状，故名。卫矛科。落叶灌木。叶对生，椭圆形，初夏开花，聚伞花序，果实分四个分果，种子有红色假种皮。枝和茎可供药用。主治妇女崩中下血，腹满汗出，中恶腹痛，祛百虫，消皮肤风毒肿。岛内沙丘上多有生长，潮音寺西南有一株直径21厘米、高4.9米的大树。

紫薇，亦名百日红、痒痒树。千屈菜科。落叶小乔木。树干光滑，叶椭圆形，全缘。夏季开花，花瓣6枚，淡红紫色或白色。其树用手抓挠，枝叶颤动，因而又叫痒痒树。其根叶可以入药，有活血化瘀的功效。

酸枣，又名野枣。鼠李科。落叶乔木。卵状叶，聚伞花序，花生于叶腋内，花小，黄绿色，有花盘，多蜜。果近圆形，鲜嫩时青色，成熟后紫红色。夏初开花，秋季果熟。适于较温暖干燥的环境，不适于低洼和涝地。果和果仁均能入药，具有养心安神、补肝益气功效，主治神经衰弱、虚烦不眠、惊悸等。岛内分布较多，有一株直径20.5厘米、树高4.5米的大树，树冠占地13.8平方米，而且枝繁叶茂，连年丰收。

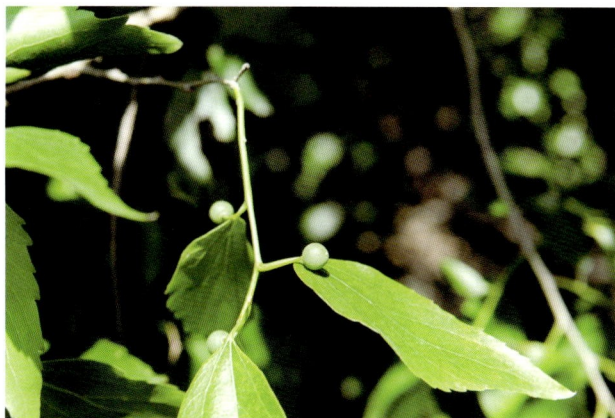

Birch-leaved pear is a dioecious arbor belonging to the family Rosaceae. Its diamond-shaped leaf has edge like saw teeth. Its flower is white and has 2-3 columns. Its fruit appears nearly ball-shaped and taste sour. The plant can tolerate drought and barrenness. There are many birch-leaved pear trees on the island. To the northeast of the Chaoyin Temple once grew an old birch-leaved pear with a trunk of 40.7 centimeters in diameter, which already died.

Mulberry is an arbor belonging to the family Morus. It has egg-shaped leaves with sharp edges. The mature fruits are purple or white and taste sweet. Its leaves, fruits, roots, and barks can all be used as medicine. Mulberry trees are scattered around the island. To the southeast of the Chaoyin Temple grow twin mulberry trees, which measure 7.5 meters tall and 61.4 centimeters in trunk diameter. The west one of the twin trees has a trunk of 36.4 centimeters in diameter, while the east one has a trunk of 33.4 centimeters in diameter. The two trees entwine together, hence their nickname Mandarin Duck Trees.

Acacia, also known as thorn tree, is a genus of arbor belonging to the family Fabaceae. Its elliptical leaves are compound pinnate in general, and its branches are typically thorny. In early summer, it blossoms with white, fragrant flowers. When being ripe, its seeds are dark brown. It grows fast, prefers sunshine, and tolerates drought and barrenness. There is an acacia forest in the west of the island, of which the biggest measures eight meters high, with a trunk of 41.4 centimeters in diameter and a canopy extending 52.8 square meters. In summer, when they are in full blossom, a strong fragrance will please the visitors.

杜梨树，又名棠梨。蔷薇科。落叶乔木。叶片菱状卵形，叶缘有锯齿。叶片和花序都有茸毛。花白色，花柱2—3个，果实近球形，褐色有斑点，小而酸。耐干旱，耐瘠薄。岛上较多，是梨树的较好砧木，潮音寺东北有一株直径40.7厘米的大树，目前已经死亡。

桑树，桑科。乔木。叶卵形，有锯齿，果实为聚花果，即桑葚，成熟时呈紫色或白色，味甜，叶、果、根、皮均可入药。岛内分布较广，潮音寺东南方有一株直径61.4厘米，高7.5米的大桑树，主干分为两个，西干直径粗36.4厘米，东干粗33.4厘米。两枝状似搂抱，人称鸳鸯树。

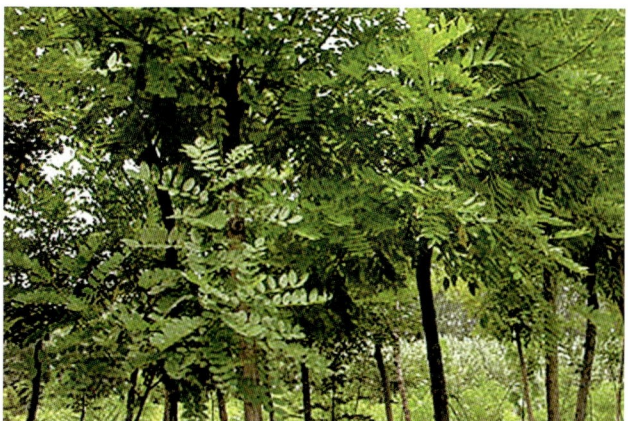

刺槐，又名洋槐。豆科。落叶乔木。小枝有针刺，奇数羽状复叶，小叶对生，全缘，椭圆形。初夏开白色花，有芳香，总状花序下垂，种子有扁状荚。成熟时深褐色，种子呈扁豆状。生长快，喜光，耐干旱瘠薄。岛上西部有刺槐林，最大的一株直径粗41.4厘米，高8米。树冠占地52.8平方米。夏日槐花盛开，白花一片，芳香扑鼻，沁人心脾。

II. Herbaceous Plants

Totally, the island has 277 species of herbaceous plants belonging to 144 genus in 53 families, including species found in Laoting's mainland like Indian lovegrass, wiregrass, crabgrass, barnyardgrass, roegneria kamoji ohwi, creeper, salsola collina, kochia scoparia, Ipomoea nil, shepherd's purse, Japanese thistle herb, common cephalanoplos herb, setaria viridis, and Ixeris polycephala, as well as species endemic to Jieshi Mountain area like American milletgrass, themeda japonica, old world bluestem, Zoysia grass, and cleistogenes hancei. Such rare species as Ranunculus chinensis, cochinchinese asparagus, China pink, allium tenuissimum, silene conoidea, Chinese sesban, trefoil rattlepod, and orobanche coerulescens are also found on the island, of which the most uncommon species include:

Cogon grass is a perennial grass belonging to the family Poaceae. The stem is flat, the leaves are long and pointed, with white, hairy tassel. The species thrives on the island, accounting for 30 percents of total grass-covered areas on the island. The tallest may reach one meter. When they grow tassels, a wide expanse of whiteness sways like waves in breeze. Its roots and tassels can be used as medicine, with effect to relieve bleeding and facilitate emiction.

Giant reed is a perennial grass belonging to the family Poaceae. It generally grows to 2-3 meters and features knotty, creeping rootstock, cane-like clumps, ligules truncate and erecting panicles. According to History of the Song Dynasty, when Ouyang Xiu, an eminent scholar at that time, was four years old, his father died. His mother raised him up and personally educated him. Because they were so poor to afford paper and brush pens, his mother then taught him to write on the ground with giant reed stems. Later, Ouyang Xiu was admitted into the Hanlin Academy. The story has since been widely spread.

Reed is a perennial grass belonging to the family Poaceae. Typically, it grows to 2-3 meters and features round, knotty stem, needle-like leaves, and hairy tassel. It prefers marshes and wetlands. Its stems can be used to weave mats. Reeds are found in the south of the island and by the Duanhe River. Each leaf of the reeds growing on the island has wrinkles. Legend goes that when Empress of Heaven traveled the remote island, she pissed in the reeds. A reed leaf happened to cut her skin. This irritated her, who then clutched the leaf. Since then, all native reeds have wrinkles on their leaves.

二 草本植物

　　全岛有草种53科、144属、277种。其中有乐亭陆地的草种，如画眉草、牛筋草、马唐草、稗草、鹅冠草、地锦、猪毛菜、地肤、牵牛、荠菜、大蓟、小蓟、狗尾草、苦荬菜等；也有碣石山上的草种，如粟草、黄背草、白羊草、结缕草、北京隐子草等。特别是一些不常见的较弱种群，如茴茴蒜、天门冬、石竹、细叶韭、麦瓶草、问荆、野大麻、假苜蓿、列当等在岛上也可以找到。较特殊的有：

　　白茅，禾本科。多年生草本。茎扁，叶互生，长而细，穗白色有茸毛，根长而有节。在岛上生长旺盛，面积最大，约占草面积30%，最高植株超过1米，比内地生长的高出很多，抽穗以后，白茫茫一片，经风吹过白穗起伏，犹如海水波浪。其根穗可以入药。性甘、寒，有凉血止血、利尿功效，用于热症吐血、咳血、尿血。

　　荻草，禾本科。多年生草本。根状茎有鳞片，叶片线状披针形，秋季抽生扇形花序，小穗多数成对生于各节，株高2—3米，在岛上多分布在沙丘的低洼处，据《宋史》载：

欧阳修4岁而孤，其母郑氏，守节自誓，亲教子读书，家贫无纸笔，教以荻画地学书，后为翰林学士，故有"修母画荻教子，谁不称贤"的成语。

　　芦苇，禾本科。多年生草本。圆径有节，叶披针形，穗有茸毛，株高2—3米，多生于低洼的湿地，茎秆可编织席子，岛内广场南部以及断河两侧多有生长。岛上生的苇叶片片都有一块皱褶。传说是王母游人间大地，来到荒岛，忽觉得腹内鼓胀，忙蹲下小解，情急被苇叶扎了一下，怒气顿生，顺手狠狠掐了一把，那苇叶上就被掐成一块皱褶。

Sedge is an annual grass belonging to the family Cyperaceae. Typically, it grows to 30-40 centimeters and features triangle stem, long and sharp leaves, and yellowish flowers. The grass is commonly found in the island's marshes. Its roots smell fragrant, which have effect to smoothen the liver, relieve pain, and reduce dyspepsia, resentment, and breast gall caused by depression.

American milletgrass is a perennial grass belonging to the family Poaceae. It features needle-shaped leaves, erecting panicles, and flat tassels with gray green flowers. Typically, it blossoms in summer and prefers sandy environment.

Suaeda glauca, popularly known as salty clover, is an annual grass belonging to the family Chenopodiaceae. It features red or green stems, thick and succulent leaves, and tiny black seeds. It flowers in autumn, and its stem taste salty, hence the name "salt clover." In ancient time, coastal residents ate them to survive famines. The grass is commonly found in western coast of the island.

粟草，禾本科。多年生草本。叶片条状披针形，叶片常翻转，上下颠倒，圆锥花序，小穗背腹扁，灰绿色，含一小花，夏季开花，岛上沙地生长较多。

莎草，莎草科。一年生草本。茎三角形，株高30—40厘米，叶细长而硬，夏日茎顶生三叶，开黄褐色小花。岛上低洼湿地生长较多，根有香味，又叫香附子。可以入药，用于疏肝理气、止痛和情志抑郁所致的消化不良、胸膈痞闷、心腹疼痛、乳房胀痛等。

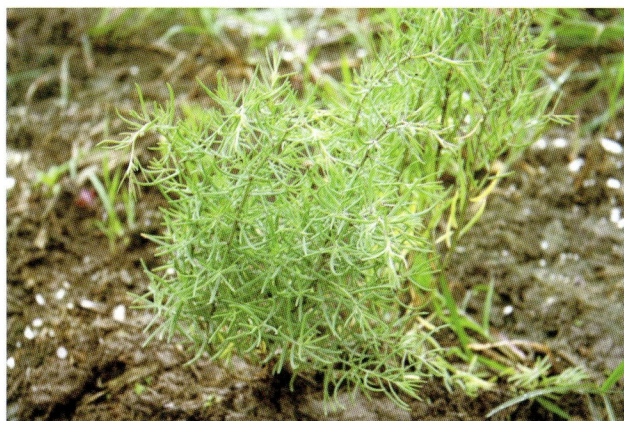

碱蓬，俗名盐蒿。藜科。一年生草本。茎红色或绿色，肉质叶片，秋季开花，子小，黑色，全株含盐，味咸，故名盐蒿。过去糠菜半年粮时，是沿海度荒的主要野菜。岛上多生长在西部靠近海水的盐碱地。

III. Medical Herbs

A survey shows that the island grows 109 species of medical herbs, including betilla striata, cogon grass, blackend swallowwort, polygonatum sibiricum, marguerite, medlar, saposhnikovia divaricata, limonium sinense, dandelion, giant reed, Japanese thistle herb, common cephalanoplos herb, gingko, sour jujube seed, almond, peach nut, wormwood, snake plant, calamus, China pink, honeysuckle, mint, rib grass, caltrop, sedge, algae, mulberry, yam, lily, fennel, peony, ginger, lotus seed, Chinese foxglove, job's tears, towel gourd, cockscomb, jimsonweed, jujube, mulberry leaves, gingko leaves, euonymus, and jacaranda. The most famous species include:

Hemerocallis fulva, also known as orange daylily, is a perennial herbaceous plant belonging to the Hemerocallis family. It has spindle-shaped, succulent root, long leaves with a range on the back, and flowers growing atop the stem. Each bears 6-12 funnel-like flowers in summer and autumn, orange-red or yellow in color. The plant is commonly planted in gardens. In ancient times, it was called Worry-Forgetting Grass or Male-Benefiting Grass. It is said that the grass can help people ward off anxieties and help pregnant women bear boy babies. Its leaves, flowers, and roots can be used as medicine. The flowers and leaves have effect to smoothen the five internal organs, cheer up spirit, brighten the eyes, relieve red urine, and encourage digestion. The roots are effective in curing emmeniopathy and jaundice.

Indian hemp, also known as rosebay hemp or red hemp, is a species of perennial herbaceous plant or shrub in the Apocynaceae family. The tender branches contain white latex, and the leaves resemble willow's leaves. It features red stems and pink or purple flowers with cymes. The plant prefers sunshine and can tolerate drought, alkali and chilliness. It is effective in relieving hypertension, and can cure headache, megrim, and insomnia. The medical herb can be taken with water just like drinking tea. Meanwhile, it can be taken together with self-heal, uncaria macrophylla, and marguerite.

三 药用植物

药用植物，经资源普查时调查岛上药用植物109 种，有白及、白薇、海巾黄精、白菊、枸杞、防风、补血草、五加皮、列当、苍耳、地丁、马齿苋、蒲公英、荠菜、漏卢、徐长卿、隐子草、杭子稍、猫眼、合掌消、天门冬、獐矛、白刺、柽柳、菟丝子、无根藤、白茅、大蓟、小蓟、萝藦果、白果、鹅绒藤、益母草、黄芩、菖蒲、马蔺、薤白、罗布麻、酸枣仁、杏仁、桃仁、合欢皮、茵陈、艾蒿、青蒿、菱陵菜、翻白草、地锦、地肤、鹤虱、牵牛、风花菜、问荆、野大麻、车前子、结缕草、半夏、紫苏、桑白皮、桑葚、夏枯草、金银花、薄荷、瓜蒌、蒺藜、荆芥、萱草、芦根、知母、葶苈、马兜铃、柴胡、香附子、木贼、麻黄、百合、茴香、山药、海藻、芍药、丹皮、鹅不食、生姜、天花粉、莲心、地黄、地骨皮、马勃、莱菔子、小茴、薏苡、瞿麦、扁蓄、丝瓜络、鸡冠花、槐花、曼陀罗、大枣、桑叶、银杏叶、朴树叶、卫矛、紫薇。其中岛上较为出名的有：

罗布麻，亦称夹竹桃麻、红麻、红柳子、茶叶花。夹竹桃科，多年生草本或半灌木。嫩枝含白色乳胶液，叶柳叶状，茎红色，花粉红或紫色，芳香，聚伞花序，喜光耐旱，耐碱，耐寒。全草入药，性味甘苦，微寒，是降血压的良药。兼治头痛、头晕、失眠等症。可以单味服用，以水泡汁代茶饮，也可配夏枯草、钩藤、野菊花等。

萱草，又名金针菜。百合科。多年生宿根草本。根肉质肥大，长纺锤形，叶丛生，狭长，背面有棱脊。花生在茎顶端，花序开花6—12 朵，夏秋间开花，花漏斗状，橘红色或黄色。庭院多有栽植。古人称为忘忧草，又称宜男草，传说见到萱草可以忘忧，孕妇佩戴可以生男。萱又是母亲的代名词，父母健在称"椿萱并茂"。叶、花、根均可入药。叶花安五脏，令人欢乐无忧，轻身明目，治小便赤涩，消食，利清热。根，治沙淋，下水气，退黄疸。

Bluestem joint fir belongs to the Equisetaceae family. The stems are knotty and leafless. Both the roots and stems can be used as medicine, which taste a little bitter. They can be taken in fresh or with honey, and have effect to relieve cold, fever, headache, and running nose.

Green shiso is an annual herbaceous plant in the Lamiaceae family. The leaves and stems are effective in curing cold, dyspepsia, and chest stuffiness. If taken together with ginger, they can relieve toxicosis caused by fish and crabs.

Saposhnikovia divaricata, popularly known as mountainous celery, is a species of perennial herbaceous plant in the Umbelliferae family. It features crossed branches and feather-like leaves. The plant blossoms in summer, with umbrella-shaped flowers. The roots have effect to cure cold, fever, and headache. If taken together with pinellia pedatisecta, angelica dahurica, and gastrodia elata, they can cure tetanus.

紫苏，唇形科。一年生草本植物。其叶、茎入药，7—9月采收。性辛、温，治感冒风寒，亦可用于脾胃气滞、胸闷，与生姜为伍可解鱼蟹中毒。

麻黄，木贼科。形似木贼，有节无叶。其根、茎入药。性辛、味微苦，生用或蜜炙，发汗解表。用于外感风寒、恶寒发热、头痛鼻塞。

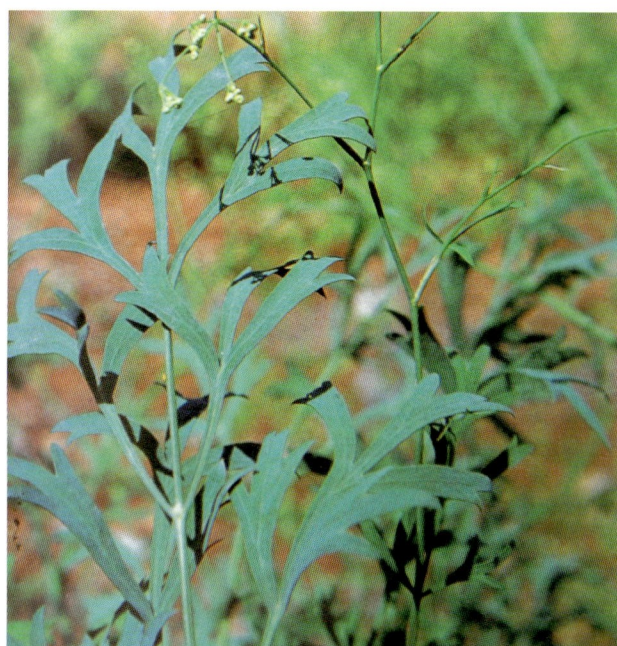

防风，又名山芹菜。为伞形科多年生草本植物。基分枝呈双权式。基生叶三四羽状分裂，最终裂片狭窄。夏开花，白色，复伞形花序，双悬果，根入药，性辛、甘。用于感冒发热、恶寒、头痛，与天南星、白芷、白附子、天麻合用可治破伤风。

Xanthium sibiricum is an annual herbaceous plant in the Asteraceae family. The triangle leaves have long stalks, with toothed edges and floss on both sides. The flowers blossom in spring and summer, with capitulums. The fruits have tiny thorns and are a little toxic, which can be used as medicine to relieve stuffed nose and rheumatism. If taken together with magnolia liliiflora and angelica dahurica, they can cure hick and sticky nasal discharge.

Lycium chinense, popularly known as Chinese wolfberry, is a species of perennial shrub in the Solanaceae family. Its stems have short thorns, and its leaves are egg-shaped. The plant blossoms with light purple small flowers in summer and autumn. Its red, egg-shaped fruits have effect to nurture the kidney and stimulate estrus. Therefore, an old Chinese saying goes that "a man who leaves his wife shall never eat Chinese wolfberry." Its roots can also be used as medicine to relieve fatigue, fever, night sweat, and emptysis.

Artemisia capillaris, also known as capillary wormwood, is a species of perennial herbaceous plants in the Asteraceae family. The leaves have pale white flosses, and the flowers feature cone-shaped capitulums. It blossoms with yellow flowers in autumn. Tender branches and leaves have effect to curing rheumatic fever, jaundice, and deep-colored urine. As a local saying goes, "capillary wormwood should be gathered in the second lunar month, sweet wormwood in the third month, and motherwort in the sixth and seventh months; Instead, they can only used as firewood."

苍耳，菊科。一年生草本植物。叶有长柄，叶片宽三角形，边缘有不规则锯齿，两面有伏毛，春夏开花，头状花序，果实有刺，果可入药，性辛、苦、温。有小毒。用于通鼻窍，祛风湿，与辛夷、白芷为伍可治鼻渊。

枸杞，俗名狗奶子。茄科。多年生灌木。茎丛生，有短刺，叶卵形。夏秋季开淡紫色小花。浆果卵圆形，红色，果入药，名枸杞子，味甘，性平。补肾益精、壮阳，民谚有："离家千里，勿食枸杞症。"根入药名地骨皮，清热、凉血，主治虚劳发热、盗汗、咯血等。

茵陈，又名绵茵陈、茵陈蒿。菊科。多年生草本。多分枝。茎生叶，二面羽状全裂，裂片丝状，有灰白色茸毛。头状花序密集成圆锥形花丛。秋季开花，花黄色，嫩茎叶入药。性微寒，味苦，清热利湿，主治湿热黄疸、体热尿赤等症。乐亭民谚有：二月茵陈，三月蒿，六月七月益母草，下霜以后当柴烧。说的是二月（农历）采茵陈，三月采青蒿，六月、七月采益母草。错过时机不能入药。

211

Periploca sepium, also known as Chinese silk vine, is a species of deciduous shrub in the Asclepiadaceae family. It features needle-like leaves and light purple or reddish flowers. The roots and barks can be used as medicine to curerheumatism and strengthen bones and muscles.

Amytornis textilis, also known as thick-billed grass, is a species of perennial herbaceous climber in the Rubiaceae family. It has yellow-red root, square-shaped stem with upturned thorns, and heart-shaped leaves. The plant blossoms with small, yellow flowers in autumn, and its fruits are red. Its roots can be used as medicine to cool blood, relieve breeding, and rejuvenate blood circulation, with effect to cure haematemesis, hematuria, and menstrual flood.

Inula caspica, also known as Eurasian caspica, is a species of perennial herbaceous plant in the Asteraceae family. Some branches and leaves are cross-grown, and its leaves are elliptically shaped. It blossoms with golden flowers in summer and autumn, which have effect to smoothen breath and reduce phlegm. Its stem, popularly known as golden boiling grass, has the similar effect.

北五加皮，又名杠柳。萝藦科。落叶缠绕灌木，含乳汁。叶对生，广披针形，全缘。夏季开花，聚伞花序，花内淡紫红色，有毛。果近圆柱状，微曲而尖，两果相对。根皮可入药。性温，味辛，祛风湿，壮筋骨。用于风寒湿痹、腰腿疼痛、筋骨拘挛等症。

茜草，又名血茜草、血见愁。茜草科。多年生攀缘草本。根黄红色。茎方形，有倒生刺。叶4枚轮生，叶片心脏形。秋季开小黄花。果红色，有棱。根可入药。性寒，味有微苦，有凉血、止血、祛瘀功效。治吐血、咯血、便血、血崩、尿血等症。

旋复花，亦称欧亚旋复花。菊科。多年生草本。茎上部分枝，叶互生，长椭圆形，基部包茎，头状花序，生于枝顶，夏秋季开花，花金黄色。花序入药，性微温，味苦、辛咸。功效：下气降逆、化痰。旋复梗，名金沸草，药用与花同。

Allium macrostemon, popularly known as spicy garlic, is a species of perennial herbaceous plant in the Liliaceae family. It has egg-shaped, hollow bulk with several semi-round leaves on the base light purple flowers on the top. Its roots and stems have effect to cure cordio- anesthesia and diarrhea.

Semen cuscutae, popularly known as diarrhea extractor, is a species of annual herbaceous plant in the Convolvulaceae family. Its orange-yellow stem is soft and thin, and often sticks to other plants. It blossoms with small white flowers in summer. Its seeds have effect to replenish the liver and kidneys, and can cure impotence, spermatorrhea, and pregnant unrest.

Pharbitis nil, popularly known as morning glory, is a species of annual herbaceous climber in the Convolvulaceae family. The leaves are almost heart-shaped. It blossoms with blue, light purple or white flowers in autumn. Its seeds are effective in treating constipation, edema, diarrhea, and bellyache. It is said that once upon a time, a cowboy suffered a severe bellyache caused by ascariasis, but he got cured after eating pharbitis nil, hence its nickname "cowboy's flower."

Equisetum hyemale is a species of perennial herb in the Equisetaceae family. It has hollow, green stems with pointed tops, and yellow-brown roots. Its stems have effect to expel heat and improve eyesight, which can cure trachoma and nebula.

薤白，俗称辣辣蒜。百合科。多年生草本。鳞茎狭卵形。基生叶数枚，半圆柱线形，中空。伞形花序，顶生，花淡紫色。根茎入药，称薤白，性湿，味苦辛。功效：通阳散结，主治心痹痛、泻痢等症。

牵牛，俗称喇叭花。旋花科。一年生缠绕草本。叶互生，近心脏形，一般三裂，秋季开花，花冠漏斗形，蓝色、淡紫色或白色。蒴果球形，种子三棱形，有褐色短毛。种子淡黄色的称"黑丑"，淡黄白色的称"白丑"。入药，性寒，味苦，有毒。功效逐水通便，杀虫，消积，主治水肿胀满，二便不通，痰饮喘满，虫积腹痛等。传说，过去牧牛人得蛔虫病，疼痛难忍，吃了牵牛子病愈，牵牛来谢，因名牵牛。

菟丝子，俗名牛吸涎。旋花科。一年生缠绕寄生草本。茎细柔，呈丝状，橙黄色，随处生吸盘，附着在寄主植物上。叶退化。夏季开花，花细小，白色，簇生于茎侧，蒴果扁球形。种子入药，性平，味辛甘，功效补益肝肾，主治肾虚、阳痿、遗精、小便频数、腰膝疼痛、胎动不安等。

木贼，俗名节节草。木贼科。多年生草本。茎节中空绿色，无叶片，根茎黄褐色，通常不分枝，枝端有毛笔头状顶尖。茎入药。性平，味甘苦。功效：散风、清热、明目，主治迎风流泪、翳膜遮睛等症。

ChapterVIII: Animals on Puti Island

I. Birds

On the southernmost tip of the northern mainland bordering the Bohai Sea, Mortar Isle faces Shandong Peninsula on the opposite side of the sea. The island's lush forests and grasslands offer sufficient food for birds. Every autumn, migrant birds from Siberia, Mongolian Grassland, and northeastern China temporarily stop on the island to replenish food and prepare their cross-sea flights. In spring, they also pass by the island on their flights to north. Many birds, both migrants and residents, take the island as their breeding habitat. Therefore, numerous birds are found here in spring and autumn, including some rare species like white stork, black stork, red-crowned crane, whooper swan, short-tailed albatross, and golden eagle. The island has thus become a must-see destination for bird observers from both home and abroad.

Statistics show that the island has 409 species of birds, of which 68 species are under state first-class or second-class protection. They are divided into swimming birds, wading birds, singing birds, scansorial birds, terrestrial birds, and predatory birds.

1. Swimming Birds

Swimming birds refer to birds that inhabit and seek food in water. There are myriad species of swimming birds on the island, including geese, gulls, and swans. The species observed from 1979 to 1989 include bean goose, swan goose, brand goose, lesser white-fronted goose, smew, fulvous whistling duck, spot-billed duck, green-winged teal, Eurasian widgeon, garganey, ruddy shelduck, red-crested pochard, Baer's pochard, tufted duck, common merganser, harlequin duck, long-tailed duck, common goldeneye, mallard, facated duck, Baikal teal, pintail, mandarin duck, white-winged scoter, greater scaup, whooper swan, whistling swan, short-tailed albatross, black-footed albatross, horned grebe, black-necked grebe, great crested grebe, sea cormorant, seagull, skua, slaty-backed gull, black-legged kittiwake, roseate tern, black-napped tern, bridled tern, sooty tern, common black-headed gull, Caspian tern, common tern, little tern, herring gull, common moorhen, marbled murrelet, rhinoceros auklet, common coot, Von Schrenck's bittern, red-throated loon, black-throated loon, Swinhoe's storm petrel, white-throated loon, etc.

第八章　菩提岛上的动物

第一节　鸟类

石臼坨岛，位于北方大陆靠近渤海的最南端，隔海与山东半岛相望，岛上有丰茂的林地、草场和充足的鸟类食物，每年秋季南下迁徙的鸟类从西伯利亚、内蒙古大草原及我国东北地区飞往南方，这里是补充食物、习练越海的桥头堡，春季归来这里又是跨海的第一站。还有好多候鸟、留鸟在这里繁衍后代。因此，每逢春秋两季这里鸟类成群。许多在世界上存量极少的鸟类如白鹳、黑鹳、丹顶鹤、大天鹅、短尾信天翁、金雕等，在这里都可以见到，成了国内外观鸟爱好者必到之处。

据统计，岛上生存和季节生存的鸟类达409种，其中属于国家一、二级保护鸟类的就有68种。按一般分类，有游禽、涉禽、鸣禽、攀禽、陆禽和猛禽。

一　游禽

游禽，是指在水中取食和栖息的鸟类的总称。游禽的种类繁多，在岛上可以见到的包括雁鸭类、鸥类、天鹅类等。从1979年到1989年观察到的有：豆雁、鸿雁、黑雁、小白额雁、斑头秋沙鸭、树鸭、斑嘴鸭、绿翅鸭、赤颈鸭、白眉鸭、赤麻鸭、翘鼻麻鸭、红头潜鸭、青头潜鸭、凤头潜鸭、红胸秋沙鸭、普通秋沙鸭、丑鸭、长尾鸭、鹊鸭、赤膀鸭、绿头鸭、罗纹鸭、花脸鸭、针尾鸭、鸳鸯、斑脸海番鸭、斑背潜鸭、大天鹅、小天鹅、短尾信天翁、黑脚信天翁、角鹏鹏（pì tī）、黑颈鹏鹏、凤头鹏鹏、斑嘴鹈鹕、海鸬鹚、海鸥、贼鸥、灰背鸥、三趾鸥、粉红燕

The commonest species on the island include mallards and seagulls, and there are also rare species like swans and mergansers. In spring and autumn, those birds fly in groups, and the largest group has a population of more than 100 individuals. In the past, hunters set traps in the Duanhe River with a bended one-meter-long tree branch and a loop on the top. When a mallard swam at night, its neck would be struck in the loop, and then the branch sprung up. In this way, the hunter could catch mallards alive. In summer, mallards lay eggs in bushes. Previously, one needed only an hour to search 20-30 eggs in weeds. The number of eggs that one can find has now reduced.

Large seagull communities are also found on the island. During flood tides and ebb tides, flocks of seagulls hover over the sea. When local fishermen transported fish onto the shore, seagulls will dive to snatch fish from their baskets. Thus, the birds become fat especially in spring and autumn. A local saying goes that "robbers get fat, while waiters lose weight."

Among the rare species that call the island home is the whooper swan. It belongs to the Anatidae family and can grow to 1.5 meters. The bird features a long neck, white feathers, a beak with a black tip and a yellow base. It prefers to inhabit coastal and riverside areas and marshes. Its staples are aquatic plants, and it also eats shell, fish, and shrimp. It flies acutely and quickly, and is under state second-class protection in China. A Chinese slang goes that a toad daydreams to eat swans, which means impossible desire.

鸥、黑枕燕鸥、褐翅燕鸥、乌燕鸥、红嘴鸥、红嘴巨鸥、燕鸥、白额燕鸥、银鸥、黑水鸡、水鸡、斑海雀、刀嘴海雀、骨顶鸡、紫背苇鳽、黄斑苇鳽、红喉潜鸟、黑喉潜鸟、水葫芦、燕鸻、黑叉尾海燕、瑟嘴鸭、白喉潜鸟、鸥嘴燕鸥。

　　岛上较多的有野鸭、海鸥，珍贵的有天鹅。野鸭有绿头鸭、秋沙鸭，春秋季成群结队，最大群有时上百只，过去人们在断河里下套，用1米长的树条，顶部拴套，卡在树条中部，做套贴近水面，野鸭夜间游到，脖子闯入套内，树条直起套住鸭脖，便得一只活野鸭。夏季鸭在岛上草丛里产蛋，游人拨草找蛋，一个中午可找20—30枚。现在有所减少。

　　种群大的还有**海鸥**，每逢涨潮落潮，海鸥云集，盘旋鸣叫，渔人担鱼上岸，海鸥从筐里抢鱼，春秋季节海鸥个个肥胖，所以民谚说，肥了抢食的（海鸥），瘦了等食的（老等）。

　　珍稀鸟有**大天鹅**，亦叫鹄。鸭科，天鹅属。体长1.5米以上，颈极长。羽毛纯白色，嘴端黑色，嘴基黄色。好群居于沿海、河流、沼泽地带。主食水生植物，兼食贝类、鱼、虾，飞行快速而高，为国家二级保护动物。俗语有癞蛤蟆想吃天鹅肉——异想天开。

Mandarin duck is considered the most beautiful species in the Anatidae family. An adult mandarin duck is 40-60 centimeters long and 450-600 grams heavy. The male and female differ in colors. The male features colorful feathers, a red beak, a bronze-colored neck, a beautiful crest, and an emerald forehead, with a white eye-ring and stripe running back from the eyes. It has yellowish feathers on its wing, while two white belts extend on its chest. It has milky abdomen and tails, and yellow-brown feet. The female is characterized by gray brown furs, but has no beautiful crest and feathers like the male. The mandarin duck prefers to live in lakes, rivers, and reedy waters, and is good at swimming and diving. They often swim in pairs. The bird mainly feeds on fish, frogs, and insects, as well as plant leaves and seeds. As a species under state second-class protection in China, the mandarin duck lives in China, Japan, and North Korea. During breeding periods, mandarin ducks are often seen playing on water or flying in the sky in pairs. In traditional Chinese culture, therefore, the bird symbolizes love and fidelity. It is said that if one of the mandarin duck couple died, the spouse will also die for love.

鸳鸯，雁形目，鸭科，鸳鸯属。是鸭科最美丽的一种水禽。体长40—60厘米，体重450—600克，雌雄异色。雄鸟羽色艳丽，喙呈暗红色，枕部为铜绿色，头部有美丽的冠羽，额部和头顶中央呈翠绿色，头两侧具有白色眉纹，延至颈部。上体羽为暗褐色，缀以铜绿色的闪光，翅上有一对栗黄色立帆状羽，下颏、喉部为栗色，上胸铜紫色，有光泽，下胸和两侧为绒黑色，具有两条白色带斑，腹部和尾下为乳白色，脚为黄褐色。雌鸟体羽为灰褐色，无漂亮的冠羽和帆羽。鸳鸯生活在湖泊、河流、芦苇丛生的水域，善于游泳和潜水，常成对活动。鸳鸯为杂食性，以鱼、蛙、昆虫为主，兼食植物叶、种子等。主要分布在我国、日本和朝鲜等地，是我国二级保护动物。鸳鸯是一种深受人们喜爱的鸟，在繁殖期间，雌雄成对，形影不离，朝夕相处，日夜相伴，有时在水里并肩嬉戏，有时在天空比翼双飞，情意绵绵，所以，人们把它作为爱情的象征。民间传说鸳鸯之间的爱情忠贞不渝，一旦匹配成对，便从一而终，如果对方死去，另一方也会跟着殉情。

2. Wading Birds

Wading birds refer to birds living in shallow water and marshes. Typically, they have long legs and extended bodies and toes, so they are suited to walk in water rather than swim. They often rest on one leg and seek food in shallow water or silt, which mainly include egrets, storks, and cranes.

The waders that can be found on the island include Siberian crane, scaly thrush, black-faced spoonbill, white spoonbill, striated heron, white-naped crane, hooded crane, red-crowned crane, common crane, bustard, red-necked phalarope, northern lapwing, grey-headed lapwing, grey plover, common ringed plover, little ringed plover, Kentish plover, Mongolian plover, greater sand plover, oriental pratincole, solitary snipe, Swinhoe's snipe, common snipe, red-breasted stint, green sandpiper, sanderling, greater painted snipe, Eurasian oystercatcher, marsh sandpiper, common greenshank, Terek sandpiper, turnstone, pied avocet, Temminck's stint, long-toed stint, sharp-tailed sandpiper, curlew sandpiper, broad-billed sandpiper, black-winged stilt, water rail, whimbrel, Eurasian curlew, Far Eastern curlew, red phalarope, spotted redshank, common redshank, common greenshank, wood sandpiper, Baillon's crake, ruddy-breasted crake, Swinhoe's yellow rail, ibis, black stork, black-crowned night heron, intermediate egret, cattle egret, purple heron, grey heron, sandpiper, grey sandpiper, red sandpiper, and red-waisted stint.

Previously, rare white storks and black storks were commonly found on the island, which locals call "wagou." They belong to the Ciconiidae family, and look like cranes, with long beaks, extended wings, and short tails. They prefer to live by water, and feed on fish, shrimp, shell, and snakes. They are often found whistling loudly while flying in the sky. The birds can forecast weathers. As an old saying goes, it will be cloudy if they whistle in the morning, sunny if they whistle in the evening, and rainy if they whistle at midnight. Su Songpo, a prestigious scholar in ancient China, ever described their whistle sounded like an old man coughing while laughing. Currently, they are under state first-class protection in China.

The red-crowned crane is a species in the Gruidae family. It grows to one meter and is characterized by white feathers, with the part above its neck in black, and a red crown. It has long, thin legs and feet without webs. When in flight, its legs stretch straightly. It is often found dancing gracefully and bursting into melodic singing. Its staples include plants and insects, as well as frogs and mussels. Legend goes that immortals often take red-crowned cranes as their ride, hence its nickname "celestial crane." Currently, the species is under state first-class protection in China.

二 涉禽

涉禽是指那些适应在浅水或沼泽地生活的鸟类。它们的腿细长，身和脚趾也较长，适于涉水行走，不适合游泳，休息时常一只脚站立，主要从浅水或污泥中觅食。有鹭类、鹳类、鹤类等。

在岛上可以观到的有：白鹤、栗头虎斑鸦、黑脸琵鹭、白琵鹭、绿鹭、白枕鹤、白头鹤、丹顶鹤、灰鹤、大鸨、红颈瓣蹼鹬、凤头麦鸡、灰头麦鸡、灰斑鸻、金鸻、剑鸻、金眶鸻、环颈鸻、蒙古沙鸻、铁嘴沙鸻、普通燕鸻、孤沙锥、大沙锥、扇尾沙锥、红胸滨鹬、黑腹滨鹬、白腰草鹬、三趾鹬、彩鹬、蛎鹬、黑尾鹬、泽鹬、小青脚鹬、翘嘴鹬、翻石鹬、反嘴鹬、青脚滨鹬、红腹滨鹬、长趾滨鹬、尖尾滨鹬、弯嘴滨鹬、流苏鹬、勺嘴鹬、阔嘴鹬、黑翅长脚鹬、普通秧鸡、中杓鹬、白腰杓鹬、大杓鹬、灰瓣蹼鹬、鹤鹬、红脚鹬、青脚鹬、林鹬、白脚草鹬、针尾沙鹬、小田鸡、红胸田鸡、花田鸡、大麻鸡、白鹳、黑鹳、夜鹭、中白鹭、牛背鹭、大白鹭、草鹭、苍鹭、黑冠虎斑鸦、夕鸡、草鹬、灰鹬、红鹬、黑腹浣鹬、红腰滨鹬。

珍稀的 **白鹳、黑鹳**，过去在这里经常出没，当地人叫哇勾。属鹳科，体形较大，形状像鹤，嘴直大，翼长而尾短，白色为白鹳，黑色为黑鹳，生活在水边以鱼、虾、贝类、蛇等为食。常在高空鸣叫，能预报天气，民谚有：早哇阴，晚哇晴，半夜哇勾到不了天明（降雨）。鸣叫声音洪亮，苏东坡云：有如老人咳且笑者是此鸟也。现在为国家一级保护动物。

丹顶鹤，鹤科。大型鸟类，体长可达1米，全身羽毛白色，颈部以上有黑色羽毛，顶部红色，两翅有黑条纹，腿细长，脚趾没有蹼，后趾位比前三趾高，飞行时颈伸直，两腿后伸，行动大方，节奏分明，舞姿潇洒，鸣声悦耳，常以植物或昆虫、蛙类、蚌类为食。被人们称为仙鹤，是传说中神仙骑乘的坐骑，国家一级保护动物。

The Asian dowitcher is a rare species in the Scolopacidae family. An adult features brown feathers with thin stripes, a long, straight beak, and long legs. The bird often searches food in shallow water, and its staples include fish, shrimp, clam, and insect. According to the *Strategies of the Warring States*, when the Zhao State planned to declare war against the Yan, Su Dai, a famous strategist at that time, told a fable story to King Hui of the Zhao: Today, when I crossed the Yi River, I saw a clam shining in the sun, with its shell opened. A dowitcher tried to eat the clam, and the clam closed its shell to clip the bird's beak. The dowitcher said, "you'll die if no rain falls today and tomorrow." The clam replied, "you'll die if I don't let you go by the end of tomorrow." As the two fought each other, a bypassing fisherman caught them both. With this story, Su Dai persuaded King Hui to reconsider his plan.

The grey heron is a large wader in the Ardeidae family. An adult measures 80-90 centimeters long, and has a white beak, yellow eyes, a pale grey neck decorated with 2-3 long black stripes, and a grey tail. The bird often lives in coastal shallow water and feeds on fish, frogs, and mussels. It dislikes living in flocks.

The bustard is a large wader in the Otididae family. An adult can grow to one meter in length, and is characterized by a grey neck, a yellow-brown back with black stripes, and a pale white abdomen. Bustards are often found running in flocks on waterside lawns. Its staple is plants, and it also eats fish, frogs, and insects. Currently, it is under state first-class protection in China.

The albatross is a large marine bird in the Diomedeidae family. An adult female grows to one meter and features hollow nostrils, a white body, a yellowish neck, and brown wings and tail. It feeds on fish, shrimp, and mussels, and is under state first-class protection in China.

半蹼鹬，鹬科。是鹬中稀有品种，体形中等，褐色，密缀细斑纹，喙细长而直，喙尖稍弯，腿长，适于涉行浅水，常在涨潮落潮时在浅水觅食，主食小鱼、虾、蛤类、昆虫等。民谚有鹬蚌相争，渔人得利。出自《战国策·燕策》赵伐燕，苏代对惠王曰：今者臣过易水，蚌方出曝，而鹬啄其肉，蚌合而钳其喙，鹬曰：今日不雨，明日不雨，即有死蚌，蚌曰：今日不出，明日不出，即有死鹬，两者不肯相舍，渔人得而并擒之。

苍鹭，又名青庄、老等。鹭科，大型涉禽，体长80—90厘米，全身白色喙，虹膜黄色，跗趾特长，头侧枕部黑色，颈羽灰白，有2—3条纵长黑纹，尾灰色，多活动在近海浅水中，主食小鱼、蛙类、蚌类，不善群居。

大鸨，又名地鸨，鸨科。大型水鸟，体长可达1米，颈部淡灰色，背部黄褐色且有黑色斑纹，腹部灰白色，常群集在草地上，善奔驰，杂食性，以植物为主，兼食蛙类、鱼类、昆虫等。为国家一级保护动物。

信天翁，信天翁科。大型海鸟，雌性可达1米。鼻孔呈孔状，左右分开，体呈白色，颈部略带浅黄，两翼和尾端褐色。生活在水边，以鱼、虾、蛙类为食。为国家一级保护动物。

225

3. Terrestrial Birds

Terrestrial birds mainly live on lands. Typically, they feature sturdy physiques and round-tipped wings, which are unsuited for long-range flights. Their beaks are often short and firm, and their legs strong and powerful with hooked claws, which are suitable for walking on the ground and digging for foods. Their staples include leaves, fruits, and seeds. Among ordinary terrestrial bird species are grouse, common pheasant, monal pheasant, and long-tailed pheasant. The commonest species on the island is ring-necked pheasant.

The ring-necked pheasant, popularly known as pheasant, belongs to the Phasianidae family. An adult male measures 0.9 meters long and features colorful plumage, with an obvious white ring around its neck. The female is smaller and features a shorter tail and grey brown plumage with spots. The bird prefers to live in overgrown weeds and feeds on cereals, berries, seeds, and insects. It is good at walking and cannot fly for a long time. The bird can be bred by humans. Its meat tastes delicious, and its tail feathers can be used as ornaments.

三 陆禽

陆禽主要在陆地上栖息。体格健壮、翅膀尖圆形，不适于远距离飞行，嘴短而坚硬，腿、脚壮而有力，爪钩状，适于陆地上奔走及挖土觅食。陆禽，主要以植物的叶子、果实、种子等为食，属于陆禽的主要禽种有：松鸡、马鸡、虹雉、长尾鸡等，在岛上主要有环颈雉。

环颈雉，通称野鸡，雉科。雄鸡长近0.9米，羽毛艳丽，颈下有显著白环纹。足后有距。雌鸡较小，尾也较短，无距，全身沙褐色，有斑点。喜栖于蔓生草莽中，以谷类、浆果种子和昆虫为食。善走，而不能久飞。可人工饲养，肉鲜美，尾羽可做饰品。

4. Singing Birds

There are many species of singing birds. They vary in sizes, of which small ones include chiffchaff, zosterops and tit, and large ones include crow and pied magpie. They mainly feed on insects and seeds. Most singing birds are expert in constructing nests. For instance, larks build their nests with soft grass and animal furs; orioles weave their nests with cattle or horse's tail hair; and chiffchaffs construct ball-like nests with leaves and weed roots. During the breeding season, those birds eat tremendous numbers of insects, which are good for agricultural production. The common species on the island include sooty flycatcher, red-billed blue magpie, emberiza fucata, oriental tree pipit, water pipit, Passeriformes, Pechora pipit, red-throated pipit, Daurian partridge, yellow bunting, calcarius lapponicus, Tristram's bunting, sparrow, yellowbird, goldfinch, rosefinch, fringillidae, marsh tit, greater tit, brambling, red crossbill, bullfinch, white-winged crossbill, hawfinch, yellow-billed grosbeak, pine bunting, yellowhammer, reed bunting, Pallas's bunting, red-necked bunting, little bunting, rustic bunting, yellow-throated bunting, yellow-browed bunting, black-faced bunting, chestnut bunting, meadow bunting, pine bunting, Siberian rubythroat, bluethroat, snowy-browed nuthatch, Eurasian nuthatch, grey-backed thrush, white-browed thrush, Japanese thrush, dusky thrush, common stonechat, Siberian thrush, rufous-tailed robin, white-throated rock thrush, reed oriole, rusty-rumped warbler, dusty warbler, yellow-streaked warbler, Radde's warbler, yellow-browed warbler, yellow-rumped warbler, Arctic warbler, Eastern crowned warbler, wren troglodytes, throstle, Bohemian waxwing, Japanese waxwing, white-eye zosterops, chestnut-flanked white-eye zosterops, tiger shrike, brown shrike, northern shrike, jackdaw, large-billed crow, carrion crow, rook corvus, collared crow, red-billed chough, azure-winged magpie, pied magpie, ashy drongo, black drongo, blue-winged pitta, ashy minivet, oriole, lark, Mongolian lark, horned lark, crested lark, barn swallow, rock swallow, red-rumped swallow, house martin, rock pigeon, oriental turtle dove, Eurasian collared dove, yellow-legged buttonquail, partridge, yellow-throated fantail, Asian paradise flycatcher, Japanese paradise flycatcher, white-faced wagtail, yellow wagtail, grey-headed yellow wagtail, forest wagtail, yellow-rumped grey wagtail, brown flycatcher, white flycatcher, etc. The most special species include:

The grey wagtail, popularly known as Shuidiandian in China, belongs to the Motacillidae family. An adult measures 18 centimeters long. The male is black from its upper body to rear waist, with white spots under its wings, and the rest parts are grey white. The bird often searches insects by water, and its quivers up and down when it stands in stillness. It sings when flying and shakes when standing. According to the *Book of Poetry*, a grey wagtail will sing for help from others when its nest is destroyed, so the bird is often used as a metaphor of brotherhood.

The skylark, popularly known as Wole, belongs to the Alaudidae family. An adult measures 15 centimeters long and features dark brown in upper, with light brown edges on its wings and tail. The outermost tail feathers are white. It also has a white lower part and light brown chest with black spots. Its eyes are lead-colored, and its feet are brown. Its staple is seeds, and it also eats insects. In summer, skylarks lay eggs in their nests hidden in bushes, and each adult female can deliver 3-5 eggs one time.

四 鸣禽

鸣禽的种类很多，以善于鸣唱为特点。外形大小差异较大，小的如柳莺、绣眼鸟、山雀，大的如乌鸦、喜鹊。其食性也较复杂，主要以昆虫、植物种子为主。鸣禽的营巢大都精巧，如云雀、百灵多以细草或动物的毛发编织而成，黄鹂则以牛马尾吊在树枝上，柳莺用树叶、草根做成球状巢。它们在繁殖季节大量捕食昆虫，有利于农业。岛上多见的有：北掠鸟、灰掠鸟、乌鸫、红嘴蓝鹊、赤胸鹀、树鹨、水鹨、田鹨、北鹨、红喉鹨、斑翅山鹨、硫黄鹀、铁爪鹀、白眉鹀、麻雀、黄雀、金翅雀、白腰朱雀、山麻雀、极北朱顶雀、沼泽山雀、银喉山雀、大山雀、朱雀、北朱雀、燕雀、红交嘴雀、红腹灰雀、白翅交嘴雀、锡嘴、黑尾蜡嘴雀、白头鹀、黄雄鹀、芦鹀、苇鹀、红颈苇鹀、小鹀、田鹀、黄喉鹀、黄眉鹀、灰头鹀、栗鹀、三道眉草鹀、红点颏、蓝点颏、黑头鹀、普通鹀、红肋蓝尾鸲、灰背鸫、白眉鸫、乌灰鸫、斑鸫、黑喉石䳭、红腹蓝矶鸫、白眉地鸫、红尾歌鸲、蓝鸲、红尾鸲、白喉矶鸫、芦莺、小蝗莺、矛斑蝗莺、大苇莺、双眉苇莺、褐柳莺、棕眉柳莺、巨嘴柳莺、黄眉柳莺、黄腰柳莺、极北柳莺、冕柳莺、鳞头树莺、北蝗莺、苍眉黄莺、黑眉苇莺、淡脚柳莺、戴菊、鹟鹩、画眉、太平鸟、小太平鸟、绣眼鸟、红肋绣眼鸟、虎纹伯劳、红尾伯劳、灰伯劳、寒鸦、大嘴乌鸦、小嘴乌鸦、秃鼻乌鸦、白颈鸦、红嘴山鸦、灰喜鹊、喜鹊、灰卷尾、黑卷尾、蓝翅八色鸫、灰山椒鸟、黄鹂、云雀、蒙古百灵、角百灵、凤头百灵、蚁列、家燕、岩燕、金腰燕、毛脚燕、灰沙燕、原鸽、山斑鸠、灰斑鸠、黄脚三趾鹑、鹌鹑、石鸡、红尾斑鸫、黄喉鹀、北领雀、云鹨、煤山雀、姬鹟、寿带、黄眉姬鹟、紫寿带、白脸鹡鸰、黄鹡鸰、灰头黄鹡鸰、山鹡鸰、黄腹灰鹡鸰、鹡鸰、三色鹡、灰鹡、乌鹡、白鹡、灰鹡、红骨顶。较有特点的有：

灰鹡鸰，俗名水点点。鹡鸰科。体长约18厘米，雄鸟上体至后腰均为黑色，翼表底里有白斑，其他部分灰白色，常在水边觅食昆虫。行止时尾上下颤动，有"飞则鸣，行则摇"的特点。"鹡鸰失所，飞鸣求其同类。"常以鹡鸰比喻兄弟友爱，急难相助。《诗经·小雅》："脊令在原，兄弟急难。"

云雀，俗名窝勒。雀形目，百灵科。体长15厘米左右，上体黑褐色，翅尾外缘淡棕色。最外侧一对尾羽白色。下体白色，胸部淡棕色，并有黑色斑点。眼睛铅黑色，脚褐色。食物以植物

种子为主，兼食昆虫，常与百灵混杂在一起。夏季在岛上草丛做巢产卵，每窝产蛋3—5枚。

The lark, popularly known as Bailingzi, belongs to the Alaudidae family. It features a streamline body, which enables it suited for flight. It has well-developed feathers, which help it fly high. Its abdomen, back, and chest are covered with thin furs, which help it resist chilliness. Its tail feathers are comparatively short, which enable it to change directions quickly in flight. It has a short neck that moves agilely. Its strong toes are suited for walking, and its short but sturdy beak suited for pecking seeds. An adult extends 22 centimeters in length. The male has reddish plumage on the crest, neck, and forehead, as well as a light brown back and dark brown wings and tail. The edges of its wings are grey white, and a black stripe encircles its neck like a necklace. The chest is rounded with a white ring and flanked by two black brown stripes. The lark sings loudly and is expert in imitateing the sound of other animals. It is often found singing while dancing. In coastal areas of Laoting County, the most famous lark subspecies is the Mongolian lark, which looks comparatively larger and is noted both at home and abroad for its beautiful plumage, loud singing, and stunting imitation capacity. The lark feeds on seeds and insects. It can tolerate drought, but dislikes moist. As an old Chinese saying goes, "the lark never cross the Yangtze River to south." Larks are often found living together with skylarks on the island.

The oriole, also known as yellowbird, belongs to the Icteridae family. Du Fu, a noted poet of the Tang Dynasty, wrote the bird in his poem that reads "Two orioles sing in weeping willows, while a flock of egrets fly into the sky." An adult oriole extends 25 centimeters. The male is totally bright yellow, while the female has some green. Black stripes are seen on two sides of the head, while the central parts of the wings and tail are also black. It mainly feeds on insects, and also eats fruits, particularly mulberries on the island. In summer, orioles breed in their nests in the trees. Typically, their exquisite nests are tied onto the trees with 4-6 horse tail hairs, which look like cradles. Each female lays 2-4 eggs one time.

The brown shrike, popularly known as tiger shrike, belongs to the Laniidae family. It has no colorful plumage, but melodic singing. So, people often use it to teach other birds singing. An adult grows to 18 centimeters, and has a grey brown body with pale brown lower part, and a black, hooked beak. It feeds on all kinds of insects. Brown shrikes construct nests in the trees, and each female lays 4-6 eggs one time.

百灵鸟，俗名百灵子。雀形目，百灵科。它的躯体呈流线型，便于飞翔。主、副羽发达，便于高飞。腹背和胸长满薄羽，能抵御寒冷，尾羽较短，在飞翔时能够很快改变方向。颈部稍短，但转动灵活。脚趾粗壮，善于行走，嘴较短，但圆钝，适于啄食植物种子。全身长约22厘米。雄鸟头顶、后颈及额部羽毛呈红褐色，背部大部为浅棕色，翅和尾部为深褐色，大翅边缘为灰白色，围绕喉部下方横贯一条黑带，很像一条项链，胸后有一条白圈，腹部沙白色，胸部两侧布有黑棕色条纹。百灵鸟叫声洪亮，善于模仿其他动物的叫声和物体活动的声音，唱起来成套，还能边唱边舞，十分令人喜欢。最著名的是乐亭沿海一带的蒙古百灵，体形较大，羽色美丽，叫声洪亮，而且善于模仿，在国内外享有盛名。百灵鸟以植物种子为食，有时也吃些昆虫，习惯于干旱，不习潮湿，所以有"百灵不过江"（长江）的说法。在岛上常与云雀在一起。

黄鹂，又名黄柳、黄莺、黄雀。雀形目，黄鹂科。唐朝诗人杜甫曾有"两个黄鹂鸣翠柳，一行白鹭上青天"的诗句。黄鹂体长25厘米。雄鸟全黄有光，雌鸟黄中带绿，头部两侧有黑纹，翼和尾部中央呈黑色。主要食物以昆虫为多，也吃各种果子。特别爱吃岛上的桑葚。夏季在岛上大树做巢繁殖，巢用马尾4—6根系在树枝上，将巢吊起来，十分精巧，犹如摇篮一般，每窝产蛋2—4枚。

红尾伯劳，俗名虎伯拉。雀形目，伯劳科。红尾伯劳虽不华丽，但歌声动人。常被人们架养做"教师鸟"，为其他歌鸟呼口。成年鸟约18厘米，全身灰褐色，下体棕白色，嘴黑色，有钩，主食各种昆虫，是吃害虫的能手。在岛内树上做巢，每窝产卵4—6枚。

5. Scansorial Birds

Scansorial birds refer to those species expert in climbing. Their specially-structured feet help them hold things tightly. For instance, woodpeckers, kingfishers, parrots, hoopoes, and nighthawks are all scansorial birds. The common scansorial birds on the island include green barbet, grey-capped woodpecker, ruddy-bellied woodpecker, spotted woodpecker, hoopoe, kingfisher, red kingfisher, blue kingfisher, nighthawk, cuckoo, Hodgson's hawk cuckoo, white-throated needletail, house swift, and common swift.

The kingfisher, popularly known as fish angler, belongs to the Alcedinidae family. It features a big head and a small body, with a short tail and a sturdy, straight beak. It has emerald forehead and neck, a brown green body, white cheeks and throat, and dark brown feathers. Typically, it perches by water and feeds on small fish.

The hoopoe, popularly known as mountain monk, belongs to the Upupidae family. An adult extends 30 centimeters and has an erecting crest. Its neck and chest have similar color to the crest, but lighter. The lower part of its back and its shoulders are dark brown, with grey brown spots. Its tail is black, with white spots. In summer, hoopoes construct nests and lay eggs in hollows of trees or walls. It mainly feeds on insects.

The woodpecker is a species of scansorial bird in the Picidae family. Its strong and sharp beak is suited for pecking wood, and its long, flexible tongue has short hooks on the tip, which is thus suited for hooking worms in wood. It has a wedge-shaped tail with thick, strong bones, which enables it to support the body when pecking trees. Thus, it is reputed as "forest doctor." The black-necked green woodpecker is comparatively larger and features a green back and a dark grey belly. The spotted woodpecker is smaller and features a white-and-black spotted back and red legs. Typically, woodpeckers construct their nests in wood, and breed in summer.

五 攀禽

　　善于攀缘树木或物体的鸟叫攀禽。它们的脚构造特殊，能有效地用爪抓握物体。如专吃林木害虫的啄木鸟，生活在水边的翠鸟，学人说话的鹦鹉，以及戴胜、夜鹰等，都属于攀禽。岛上见到的有：绿啄木鸟、星头啄木鸟、棕腹啄木鸟、斑啄木鸟、戴胜、翠鸟、赤翠鸟、蓝翠鸟、夜鹰、布谷鸟、棕腹杜鹃、白喉针尾雨燕、白腰雨燕、小白腰雨燕、楼燕。

　　翠鸟，俗称钓鱼郎。翠鸟科。体长约15厘米，头大体小尾短，喙强壮而直，额、枕部羽毛均为苍翠绿色，身羽棕黄色，颊和喉白色，飞羽黑褐色。常栖息在水边，俯冲啄食小鱼。

　　戴胜，俗名臭咕咕、山和尚。戴胜科。体长约30厘米，具有显著的羽冠，颈和胸等与羽冠同色而较淡，下背和肩部羽黑褐色，杂有棕白斑、尾羽黑色，中部亦有白斑。尾脂腺能分泌臭液。夏季在树洞或墙洞营巢产卵。主食昆虫。

　　啄木鸟。啄木鸟科，树栖攀禽。喙强直尖锐，可用于凿开树木，舌细长，能伸缩，尖端有短钩，适于钩食树木内的蛀虫。尾呈楔形，羽轴粗硬，啄木时支架身体。有森林医生的美名。岛上有黑枕绿啄木鸟，体形较大，背部绿色，腹部暗灰色。斑啄木鸟，体形较小，背部有黑白花，腿上羽为红色。啄木鸟，凿树洞为巢，夏季产卵孵化。

6. Predatory Birds

Typically, predatory birds are comparatively larger and ferocious, and hunt for flesh with the help of their sharp beaks and talons and strong wings. They are roughly divided into two genera: Falconiformes and Tytonidae. Local raptors include goshawk, condor, kite, honey buzzard, Eurasian sparrow hawk, pied harrier, northern harrier, western marsh harrier, peregrine falcon, Merlin falcon, Eurasian hobby falcon, red-footed falcon, lesser kestrel, buzzard, rough-legged buzzard, grey-faced buzzard, upland buzzard, common buzzard, Steller's sea eagle, golden eagle, white-tailed sea eagle, osprey, owl, brown hawk owl, long-eared owl, short-eared owl, and scops owl.

The northern goshawk, also known as hare hawk, is a large raptor in the Accipitridae family. An adult male can grow to 50 centimeters and features a dark brown head. The upper part of its body is grey, and the lower part grey white, with grey spots. Its wings have black stripes. The female is comparatively larger. The bird inhabits forest meadows and hunts for hares, rats, pigeons, and turtledoves. It can be domesticated to be hunting falcon. Currently, it is under state second-class protection.

The red-footed falcon, popularly known as locust hawk, belongs to the Falconidae family. An adult male measures 30 centimeters long, and has a dark grey body, with its crissum, fur under tail, and two legs in orange-yellow. It often hovers above to prey on insects.

六 猛禽

猛禽一般体形较大，主吃肉食，性格凶猛，嘴和爪锐利，翅膀强大有力，善于捕捉动物，主要包括两大类，一是隼形目，一是鸮形目。在岛上可见到的有：苍鹰、秃鹫、鸢、蜂鹰、雀鹰、鹊鹞、白尾鹞、白头鹞、松雀鹰、游隼、灰背隼、燕隼、红脚隼、黄爪隼、红隼、矛隼、鵟、毛脚鵟、灰脸鵟、大鵟、普通鵟、鸡鵟、虎头海雕、金雕、白尾海雕、鱼鹰、猫头鹰、鹰鸮、长耳鸮、短耳鸮、红角鸮。

苍鹰，也叫兔鹰，鹰科。大型食肉鸟，雄性体长约50厘米，除头黑褐色外，上体为苍灰色，下体为灰白色，密布暗灰色斑点，羽有黑色干纹。雌性体形较大。主要生活在林间草地，捕食兔、鼠、鸽子、斑鸠等。经人工驯服可以供狩猎用。为国家二级保护动物。

红脚隼，俗名蚂蚱鹰。隼科，雄性体长约30厘米，通体呈暗灰色，肛周、尾下和两腿橙黄色。常在田野上空盘旋，能扇动两翼悬在高空不动，主要捕食昆虫。

The golden eagle is a large raptor in the Accipitridae family. An adult male measures one meter in length. The underage has brown-yellow neck and head and white wings except for the outermost three feathers. Its body is dark brown, and its tail pale white, with a black tip. The adult has no white wings and tail, but features a brown crest and feeds on hares, turtledoves, and pheasants. Historical records show that in 1952, a golden eagle preyed on a lamb grazing in Jiatan. Currently, it is under state first-class protection.

The buzzard, popularly known as old leopard, belongs to the Accipitridae family. It looks like the northern goshawk, except that its beak is shorter and its tail longer. It has a brown and light purple body, and often hovers in the sky to prey on rats, snakes, chickens, and dead animals. It prefers to live in flocks in autumn. Sometimes, 10-20 buzzards perch in the same tree. Previously, local hunters used to hunt buzzards on Xiangyun Island. They set a trap on the ground, with a smaller, living bird as the prey. When the bird tried to catch dead rats or fish set by the hunters, buzzards in the sky would be attracted to dive down. Then, the hunters who hid 50 meters away pulled a rope tied on the trap to catch them.

The owl belongs to the Strigidae family. It has a cat's head, with wide, round eyes, and hooked beak and claws. Typically, it has brown plumage and preys on rats at night. A survey shows that an owl can prey on nearly 1,000 rats each year. Currently, it is under state second-class protection.

金雕，鹰科，大型食肉禽，雄性体长可达1米。未成年时头颈棕黄色，两翼飞羽除最外侧3枚外，基部均缀有白色，身体全部为暗褐色，尾羽灰白，端部黑色。成鸟翼和尾均无白色，头顶羽色为全褐色，性猛力强，以捕食野兔、斑鸠、野鸡为主。1952年一只金雕曾把贾滩上正在放牧的幼羊叼走。为国家一级保护动物。

鵟，俗名老豹子、鹰科。与苍鹰略同，唯嘴稍短，尾较长，全身褐色微紫，常在上空作大回旋飞行，以鼠、蛇、鸡或腐肉为食，秋季喜群居，有时一棵树竟栖10—20只。过去祥云岛有一专猎老豹的，在草地上拴一"豹油子"，前方放一木板，板上放死鼠或小鱼，豹油子吃不到，油子前方设置网片，猎人在50米外藏身。看到空中过老豹，拉动木板，豹油子展开两翅抢吃食物，空中老豹立即俯冲来抢，再拉网网住。

鸮，又名猫头鹰、夜猫子，鸱鸮科。头部似猫，眼大而圆。喙、爪呈钩形。羽毛多为褐色。夜间活动，主要捕食鼠类，是灭鼠的能手。据调查，一只猫头鹰一年可捕食鼠类近千只。是重点保护的益鸟，列为国家二级保护动物。

II. Marine Animals

Several rivers, including Luanhe and Daqing, flow into the sea via the coasts of Laoting County, which bring rich food supplies for marine animals and make the offshore area an ideal breeding habitat for fish. Totally, there are living more than 200 species of fish, shrimp, crab, and shellfish. Local fishery industry has an annual output of 130,000 tons. The four most famous categories of seafood are horse crab, oriental prawn, silverfish, and Bohai flatfish.

A famous kind of seafood around the world, the horse crab native to eastern Hebei Province is big and delicious. It is particularly tasty in early spring before it lays eggs or in late autumn. No one will forget the delicacy once he tries it, which can rival the famous Suzhou hairy crab in taste.

The oriental prawn native to the Bohai Sea is noted for its thin shell and extended body. An adult grows to 150-200 grams. It is delicious and nutritious, and all other species of shrimps, such as lobsters, grass shrimps, and white shrimps, can parallel its taste.

The silverfish native to the Bohai Sea is scaleless and fleshy, which tastes tender and has no unpleasant odor. It is known as the only species of fish that is edible without the need of cooking with oil.

The Bohai flatfish is a subspecies of the flounder and resembles a bottle in shape. It tastes tender and delicious. A local saying goes that among all native seafood, the flatfish is ranked first, the butterfish second, and the mandarin fish third.

In addition, local seafood also includes mantis shrimp, dried shrimp, Venus clam, common clam, and oyster.

第二节 鱼虾类

乐亭渤海沿岸是滦河、清河等河的入海口，腐殖质丰富，海水肥沃，是各种鱼类繁殖产卵区域，有各种鱼虾、蟹贝200多种，年产量13万吨，其中最出名的要属乐亭四大名鲜，即三疣梭子蟹、东方对虾、无鳞银鱼、渤海鲆鱼。

冀东三疣梭子蟹，个大肉硬黄多，味道鲜美，为世界名蟹，早春产卵前和晚秋口味极佳，吃上一只，将终生难忘，可与苏州大闸蟹媲美。

渤海东方虾，皮薄枪长，三四两一只，味道鲜美，营养丰富，是虾中的极品，它的味道，为龙虾、青虾、白虾所不及。

冀东渤海无鳞银鱼，无鳞无刺，体青肉肥，鲜而不腥，肥而不腻，是唯一可以不用油烹调即可食用的鱼。

冀东渤海鲆鱼，是比目鱼的一种，体似瓶形，肉质细嫩，味道鲜美，为渤海鱼中的上品，素有一鲆二鲭三鳎板之说。

此外，还有体大肉多的琴虾（琵琶虾），渤海产的金钩海米，味道鲜美的青蛤、蛤蜊，鲜嫩的牡蛎等。

III. Other Animals

There are also many domestic animals, wild beasts, and insects calling Mortar Isle home. Almost all native inland animal species can be found on the island, including domestic animals like cattle, horse, donkey, mule, pig, sheep, chicken, duck, cat, and dog, wild animals like fox, badger, hare, weasel, snake, rat, hedgehog, and pheasant, and insects like hornet, cicada, mantis, moth, fly, mosquito, midge, snail, earthworm, frog, toad, cricket, dragonfly, butterfly, mole cricket, bollworm, centipede, and scorpion.

The snake is the commonest wild animal on the island. So, locals once called it "Snake Island." All native snakes, varying in shapes and colors, are nontoxic. They live in weeds, trees, riverbanks, and even human residences. Typically, they hide in their nests during the daytime and go out to search food at night. In summer afternoons, particularly, they come out to enjoy the cool independently or in groups. Sometimes they are found entwining together on roadsides, under trees or in bushes. In the 1980s and 90s, snakes were often seen creeping out of brick wall cracks and relaxing at noon in the halls of the dilapidated Chaoyin Temple. Visitors to the island might be careful for fear to tramp on snakes. Sometimes snakes sneaked into human residences and climbed onto the beds, and people would be scared when carelessly touching them. In fact, local snakes are harmless.

Why did the island have so many snakes? Perhaps this was largely because ancient Chinese rulers made the island a grain storage and transportation base, which stimulated the rapid development of rat populations. Then, rat-eating animals like snakes, weasels, and owls began to flourish. In recent years, however, less and less living room has been left to snakes along with the increase of developers and tourists on the island. Today, the population of snakes on the island has been much less than before.

第三节 其他动物

石臼坨上的畜禽草虫类动物很多，凡是陆地上有的基本都有，如毛属的养殖的有牛、马、驴、骡、猪、羊、鸡、鸭、猫、狗等畜禽，野生的如狐狸、獾、兔、黄鼠狼、蛇、鼠、刺猬、野鸡等。虫属的有蜂、蝉、蟑螂、蛾、蝇、蚊、蠓、蛤蟆、蜗牛、蚯蚓、螳螂、蟋蟀、蝈蝈、蜻蜓、蝴蝶、蝼蛄、蝙蝠、蛴螬、蜻蛉、蚰蜒、蛇、蝎、蜥蜴等。

石臼坨上最多的动物就是蛇了，从前，当地人又将其称为"蛇岛"。这里的蛇都是无毒的。其形状有大的、小的、粗的、细的、畸形的；颜色有黄的、绿的、黑的、花的，传说还有白的，有的活动在草丛中，有的盘绕在树下枝头，有的隐蔽在房前屋后，也有的游弋在河岸水边。平时，它们潜伏在各自的活动区域里，大多是昼伏夜出。特别是炎炎夏日，它们也难耐酷暑，在午后都爬出洞来歇凉，有的单个，有的三三两两，有的聚集成群，或仰卧或盘绕在路边、树下、房舍和茂盛的青草阴凉处，可以说遍地皆是，在20世纪八九十年代时，残破的潮音寺大殿里，在中午时，那歇凉的蛇都从砖墙的缝隙里探出头来，滴溜溜地瞪着小眼睛，煞是有趣。凡是上坨的人，如在此时出游，在行路时就要十分小心，如踩上躺倒在路上的蛇，那被踩的蛇因疼痛猛地盘卷翻身，胆小的就会吓一大跳。夜里活动的蛇有时也爬到房舍里，爬到炕上和人在一起歇息，当人们睡觉醒来时，用手一摸，凉飕飕，胆小的也会吓得一惊甚至出一身冷汗。其实，蛇对人并没有歹意。

石臼坨上的蛇为什么多呢？究其原因，可能主要是当年历代统治者在这里屯积储粮筑仓和转运，有粮即有鼠，鼠多了，自然就有蛇、黄鼠狼、猫头鹰等捕鼠动物，以至后来逐渐繁殖增多。只是，随着近年来人们大量的上坨建设、旅游，蛇的生存空间越来越小，因之，比过去也越来越少了。

Chapter IX: Hot Springs on Puti Island

Nestling in immense ocean, Puti Island boasts lush forests and a heaven-given favorable environment. Upon careful investigation and exploitation, geologists have found abundant terrestrial heat and hot spring resources on the island.

Hot springs serve as an ideal way for modern people to seek refreshment, relieve strains, and even treat illness. The history of hot springs used as a recreational method can be traced back thousands of years in China. As early as the pre-Qin period, hot springs were already mentioned in *Mountain and Sea Classics*: "The Dan spring appears like boiling." Zhang Hong, an eminent astronomer in the Eastern Han Dynasty, recorded in *Ode to Hot Spring* that hot springs had effect to expel sickness. In his medical classic *Compendium of Materia Medica*, Li Shizhen, a prestigious doctor of the Ming Dynasty, divided mineral springs into hot springs, cool springs, sweet springs, sour springs, and bitter springs.

Currently, Puti Island has two hot springs. Through scientific research and thorough discussion, hot spring specialists from Japan and Taiwan reached the following conclusions:

1. Slightly Alkaline Natrium Bicarbonate Springs

This kind of hot springs lie in the tertiary aquifer of Minghuazhen Formation that is 800-1,000 meters underground. The water penetrates through the basic rock belt in northern mountainous area and cracks, joints, and lavas formed by surface water on the plain area. The temperature of the outburst water ranges between 48℃ and 52℃, which is suitable for the development of hot springs.

The water circulates deep underground, carrying fracture zones to move and forming underground hot water sources. However, it cannot be replenished immediately, but accumulates gradually for a long time.

Natrium bicarbonate hot springs have effect to moisten the skin and whiten and soften stratum corneum. Meanwhile, it can diminish inflammation and remove scars for burnt or scalded people.

Typically, natrium bicarbonate hot springs are colorless and flavorless, with slight alkaline contents. Nicknamed "beauty

第九章　菩提岛上的温泉

菩提岛地处茫茫沧海之中，植被茂盛，树荫遮蔽，是造化天地之灵秀，非人力所可为。经地质专家考察和钻探发掘，在菩提岛地下发现有丰富的地热温泉资源。

温泉疗养是现代人休闲养生、缓解压力甚至治疗疾病的途径和方法。温泉疗养，已有数千年的悠久历史。早在先秦时期的《山海经》里就有了"温泉"的记载。比如《西次三经·崖山》写道："丹水出焉……是有玉膏，其原沸沸汤汤。"东汉著名天文学家张衡在《温泉赋》一文中写道："览中域之珍轻，无斯水之神灵。……于是殊方跋涉，骏奔来臻，天地之德，莫若生兮。帝育臣民，资厥成分。六气淫错，有疾疗兮。温泉泊焉，以流岁兮，除苛，服中正兮。熙哉帝哉，保性命哉。"明代医学家李时珍在《本草纲目》中也提到矿泉，并分为热泉、冷泉、甘泉、酸泉和苦泉等。

菩提岛现有两眼温泉井，根据科学化验以及经日本和我国台湾的温泉专家共同分析，得出如下结论：

一　微碱性碳酸氢钠泉

该地热温泉位于第三纪明化镇组含水层，埋深800—1000米。由北部山区基岩裸露带和平原地表水延构造破碎带、节理、裂隙、熔岩等通道渗入，出水水温在48℃—52℃，适宜温泉开发。

由于渗水经深循环沿着地下活动，破碎断裂带不断移动，形成热地下水源，补给交替微弱延缓，需要长期微量积累，不能瞬时补给。

碳酸氢钠温泉对皮肤有滋润、漂白及软化皮肤角质层的功效，对那种烧伤或者烫伤的人，泡这种温泉也有消炎、去疤痕的作用。

碳酸氢钠温泉是无色无味的高碳酸含量的温泉，温泉为弱碱性，有"美人汤"之称。碳酸氢钠温泉泉温较一般温泉低，浸泡时在皮肤表面呈现气泡，还有天然的轻微按摩作用。

soup," they are lower in temperature than other kinds of hot springs. It can generate bubbles on the skin and thus have natural effect like slight massage.

The hot springs are rich in carbon dioxide, which can generate bubbles on the skin and has effect to reduce blood pressure without increasing heart's burden. Therefore, this kind of hot springs are also known as "heart soup." Despite their comparatively low temperature, they are effective in preserving body temperature and relieving hypertension, heart disease, rheumatics, arthritis, and cold hands and feet.

2. Chlorinous Natrium Bicarbonate Springs

This kind of hot springs lie in the tertiary aquifer of Guantao Formation that is 1,400-1,800 meters underground. So far, how water is supplied for these hot springs remains unknown. The temperature of outburst water ranges between 65℃ and 79℃, which is suitable for the development of hot springs.

These hot springs contain a little amount of chlorine, which will vaporize as soon as the water comes out of the ground. Although toxic, the chlorine can produce hypochlorous acid in water, which has effect to sterilize, sanitize, and bleach.

Moreover, these hot springs feature a high content of sulfides, which are effective in enhancing cellular metabolism, improving blood circulation and nutrition metabolism, and strengthening immunity and incretion. Meanwhile, they can stimulate nerve endings and sensors in blood vessels to produce histamines, so as to distend skin veins, improve sulfur metabolism, and soften and dissolve stratum corneum, which is good for skin disease patients.

3. Sustainable Development

In view of the decline of water supply for the tertiary aquifer of Minghuazhen Formation and its adjacency to surface seawater, the development of local hot springs must be implemented in line with strict plans, so as to prevent seawater encroachment. In the course of developing hot springs in the tertiary aquifer of Guantao Formation, water supply shall be given priority consideration, so as to ensure sustainable development.

4. Ecological Hot Springs

The development of hot springs on Puti Island shall conform to the protection of local ecosystem, so as to build ecological hot springs while maintaining its distinctive ecosystem.

How to prevent mosquitoes and other insects shall be given top priority in the construction of ecological hot springs.

Bathing in hot springs, especially in chilly winter, is not only something good for health, but also an enjoyable relaxation.

由于泉水中含有大量二氧化碳，而二氧化碳气泡附着在皮肤上具有在不增加心脏负担的前提下降血压的功效，因此，碳酸泉又被称为"心脏汤"（有益于心脏的温泉）。碳酸氢钠温泉尽管水温较低，但保温效果很好，因而具有保持体温的作用，对高血压、心脏病、风湿症、关节炎及手脚冰凉等有改善的作用。

二　含氯碳酸氢钠泉

该地热温泉位于第三纪馆陶组含水层，埋深在1400—1800米。由于该区间地热水埋藏深，补给水方式不明。出水水温在65℃—79℃。比较适宜温泉开发。

该地热温泉含有微量氯气，但出水后可以瞬间蒸发。氯气本身是有害气体，但是氯气和水反应产生的次氯酸有杀菌消毒和漂白的作用。

该温泉硫化物含量较多，可使细胞代谢增强，改善血液循环及营养代谢，加强免疫及内分泌功能。还能刺激神经末梢与血管内感受器以及产生组胺，使皮肤血管扩张，改善皮肤内的硫代谢，从而软化和溶解角质，对治疗皮肤病有辅助疗效。

三　确保可持续发展

鉴于菩提岛第三纪明化镇组含水层补给源微弱延缓，又因与表层海水接近，所以在温泉开发中，一定要专业地、有计划地控制使用量，并须严格防止海水倒灌。在开发第三系馆陶组温泉过程中，应注意补给合理搭配，确保可持续发展。

四　建设生态温泉

菩提岛的温泉开发，应该结合其原生态的优势，因地制宜，注意突出原生态的特点与个性，建设生态温泉。

在原生态温泉建设中，尤其应注意防止蚊虫叮咬。

寒冷的冬季，在大自然中洗泡温泉，既疗养保健，更是一种难得的享受。

Chapter X: Historical Celebrities of Laoting County

I. Politicians and Officials

Jin Dynasty

Han Chang, county magistrate during the Mingchang reign of the Jin Dynasty

Yuan Dynasty

Meng Guoyong, county magistrate during the Zhongtong reign of the Yuan Dynasty

Yue Zhi, a warrior stationed in Honggou and then county magistrate and education supervisor during the Zhiyuan reign

An Yi, county magistrate and military commander during the Dade reign

Chai Liben, magistrate assistant and then magistrate of Zouping County during the Zhiyuan reign

Ming Dynasty

Lu Gongmao, who acted as county magistrate of Laoting in 1369

Wang Wengui, who acted as county magistrate of Laoting in 1370

Zhang Silan, a native of Pingyuan, Shandong Province, who acted as county magistrate of Laoting in 1376

Liu Sheng, a native of Xinhua, Zhejiang Province, who acted as county magistrate of Laoting in 1386

Zhou Binfu, a native of Guiyang, Huguang Province, who acted as county magistrate of Laoting in 1403

Wei Zhun, a native of Wucheng, Shandong Province, who acted as county magistrate of Laoting in 1412

Yu Jixian, a native of Dexing, Jiangxi Province, who acted as county magistrate of Laoting in 1425

Lü Yuan, a *juren* from Fengxiang, Shaanxi Province, who acted as county magistrate of Laoting in 1435

Dong Hao, a native of Wurong, who acted as county magistrate of Laoting during the Tianshun reign

Yuan Hong, a *juren* from Anyang, Henan Province, who acted as county magistrate of Laoting during the Tianshun reign

Wang Bi, a *juren* from Qixia, Shandong Province, who acted as county magistrate of Laoting during the Chenghua reign

Li Han, a *jinshi* from Xinshui, Shanxi Province, who acted as county magistrate of Laoting in the 8th year during the Chenghua reign

Jiang Tinggui, a *jinshi* from Haiyang, Guangdong Province, who acted as county magistrate of Laoting during the Hongzhi reign

Zhang Qian, a native of Yexian, Henan Province, who acted as county magistrate of Laoting during the Hongzhi reign

Hao Ben, a *jinshi* from Yangqu, Shanxi Province, who acted as county magistrate of Laoting in 1494

Tian Deng, a *jinshi* from Wucheng, Shandong Province, who acted as county magistrate of Laoting in 1497

Yuan Xuan, a native of Yangcheng, Shanxi Province, who acted as county magistrate of Laoting in 1501

Wang Yuanxue, a *suigongsheng* from Dongping, Shandong Province, who acted as county magistrate of Laoting in 1505

第十章 乐亭历代名人录

第一节 历代政要

金 代

韩 昶 金明昌年间以奉直大夫任县令赐绯鱼袋

元 代

孟国用 元中统年间任县尹

岳 志 洪沟军人，至元年间任县尹兼监督诸君提举学校事

安 逸 大德年间任县尹兼督诸军奥鲁事

柴立本 至元年间以邹平县丞升任县尹

明 代

卢公茂 洪武二年（1369年）任知县

王文贵 洪武三年（1370年）任知县

章似兰 山东平原人，洪武九年（1376年）任知县

刘 晟 浙江新化人，洪武十九年（1386年）任知县

周彬甫 湖广贵阳人，永乐元年（1403年）任知县

魏 准 山东武城人，永乐十年（1412年）任知县

于继贤 江西德兴人，永乐十三年（1415年）任知县

吕 渊 陕西凤翔人，举人，宣德十年（1435年）任知县

董 昱 武荣人，天顺年间任知县

元 宏 河南安阳人，举人，天顺年间任知县

王 弼 山东栖霞人，举人，成化年间任知县

李 瀚 山西沁水人，进士，成化八年（1472年）任知县

蒋廷桂 广东海阳人，进士，弘治年间任知县

张 谦 河南叶县人，弘治年间任知县

郝 本 山西阳曲人，进士，弘治七年（1494年）任知县

田 登 山东武城人，进士，弘治十年（1497年）任知县

原 轩 山西阳城人，弘治十四年（1501年）任知县

王渊学 山东东平人，岁贡生，弘治十八年（1505年）任知县

Wang Bo, a *juren* from Haifeng, Shandong Province, who acted as county magistrate of Laoting in 1507

Zhao Kuan, a *juren* from Yuanqu, Shanxi Province, who acted as county magistrate of Laoting in 1509

Wang En, a *juren* from Yixing, Nanzhi, who acted as county magistrate of Laoting in 1518

Su Wen, a native of Nanyang, Henan Province, who acted as county magistrate of Laoting in 1523

Chai Ke, a *juren* from Shandong Province, who acted as county magistrate of Laoting in 1527

Ma Hui, a *jiansheng* (student in the imperial college) from Wuding, Shandong Province, who acted as county magistrate of Laoting in 1532

Wang Shu, a *jiansheng* from Jizhou, Jiangxi Province, who acted as county magistrate of Laoting during the Jiajing reign

Cai Dong, a *juren* from Suqian, Nanzhi, who acted as county magistrate of Laoting in 1535

Lu Chen, a *jiansheng* from Junzhou, Hubei Province, who acted as county magistrate of Laoting in 1538

Peng Qin, a *jiansheng* from Dingyuan, Nanzhi, who acted as county magistrate of Laoting in 1540

Chen De'an, a *juren* from Zhangqiu, Shandong Province, who acted as county magistrate of Laoting in 1541

Yang Fengyang, a **gongsheng** (tribute student by virtue of excellence) from Suzhou, Nanzhi, who acted as county magistrate of Laoting in 1543

Liang Gongshi, a *juren* from Gaotang, Shandong Province, who acted as county magistrate of Laoting in 1548

Mou Jun, a *juren* from Jiangyin, Nanzhi, who acted as county magistrate of Laoting in 1550

Lü Hong, a native of Yangqu, Shanxi Province, who acted as county magistrate of Laoting in 1554

Xiang Wenxiang, a juren from Qiantang, Zhejiang Province, who acted as county magistrate of Laoting in 1556

Hou Shu, a *juren* from Zezhou, Shanxi Province, who acted as county magistrate of Laoting in 1559

Feng Shizhong, a *juren* from Fanxian, Shandong Province, who acted as county magistrate of Laoting in 1564

Song Guozuo, a *juren* from Junzhou, Hubei Province, who acted as county magistrate of Laoting in 1565

Wang Xian, a *suigongsheng* (annual tribute student) from Feixian, who acted as county magistrate of Laoting in 1567

Li Bangzuo, a *jinshi* from Chenliu, Henan Province, who acted as county magistrate of Laoting in 1567

Yao Yunhe, a *juren* from Huaiqing, Henan Province, who acted as county magistrate of Laoting in 1570

Li Xizhen, a **gongsheng** from Jining, Shandong Province, who acted as county magistrate of Laoting in 1572

Feng Lu, a *jinsh*i from Chenliu, Henan Province, who acted as county magistrate of Laoting in 1574

Ma Su, a *juren* from Caozhou, Shandong Province, who acted as county magistrate of Laoting in 1575

Lin Jinggui, a *juren* from Dongning, Heilongjiang Province, who acted as county magistrate of Laoting in 1580

Du Hechun, a *jinsh*i from Longxi, Shaanxi Province, who acted as county magistrate of Laoting in 1582

Zhao Ziren, a *juren* from Liaoyang, Liaodong, who acted as county magistrate of Laoting in 1583

Yu Yongqing, a *jinshi* from Qingcheng, Shandong Province, who acted as county magistrate of Laoting in 1584

王　溥　山东海丰人，举人，正德二年（1507年）任知县

赵　宽　山西垣曲人，举人，正德四年（1509年）任知县

王　恩　南直宜兴人，正德十三年（1518年）任知县

苏　文　河南南阳人，嘉靖二年（1523年）任知县

柴　柯　山东人，举人，嘉靖六年（1527年）任知县

马　浍　山东武定人，监生，嘉靖十一年（1532年）任知县

王　述　江西吉州人，监生，嘉靖年间任知县

蔡　洞　南直宿迁人，举人，嘉靖十四年（1535年）任知县

卢　臣　湖北钧州人，监生，嘉靖十七年（1538年）任知县

彭　钦　南直定远人，监生，嘉靖十九年（1540年）任知县

陈德安　山东章丘人，举人，嘉靖二十年（1541年）任知县

杨凤阳　南直宿州人，贡生，嘉靖二十二年（1543年）任知县

梁公奭　山东高唐人，举人，嘉靖二十七年（1548年）任知县

缪　俊　南直江阴人，举人，嘉靖二十九年（1550年）任知县

吕　鸿　山西阳曲人，嘉靖三十三年（1554年）任知县

相文祥　浙江钱塘人，举人，嘉靖三十五年（1556年）任知县

侯　庶　山西泽州人，举人，嘉靖三十八年（1559年）任知县

冯时中　山东范县人，举人，嘉靖四十三年（1564年）任知县

宋国祚　湖北钧州人，举人，嘉靖四十四年（1565年）任知县

王　暹　肥县人，岁贡生，隆庆元年（1567年）任知县

李邦佐　河南陈留人，进士，隆庆元年（1567年）任知县

尧允和　河南怀庆人，举人，隆庆四年（1570年）任知县

李席珍　山东济宁人，贡生，隆庆六年（1572年）任知县

冯　露　河南陈留人，进士，万历二年（1574年）任知县

马　速　山东曹州人，举人，万历三年（1575年）任知县

林景桂　黑龙江东宁人，举人，万历八年（1580年）任知县

杜和春　陕西陇西人，进士，万历十年（1582年）任知县

赵子仁　辽东辽阳人，举人，万历十一年（1583年）任知县

于永清　山东青城人，进士，万历十二年（1584年）任知县

Pan Dunfu, a *jinshi* from Xiajin, Shandong Province, who acted as county magistrate of Laoting in 1590

Ye Jingyuan, a *jinshi* from Dezhou, Shandong Province, who acted as county magistrate of Laoting in 1592

Liu Fangjiu, a *juren* from Anyang, Henan Province, who acted as county magistrate of Laoting in 1593

Hu Ji, a *juren* from Fengcheng, Jiangxi Province, who acted as county magistrate of Laoting in 1597

Wang Guozhen, a *jinshi* from Anyi, Shanxi Province, who acted as county magistrate of Laoting in 1600

Li Jizu, a *juren* from Yanjin, Henan Province, who acted as county magistrate of Laoting in 1601

Zhang Jian, a *gongsheng* from Lingshi, Shanxi Province, who acted as county magistrate of Laoting in 1606

Lei Chunqi, a *juren* from Tongzhou, Shaanxi Province, who acted as county magistrate of Laoting in 1610

Sang Gao, a juren from Taiyuan, Shanxi Province, who acted as county magistrate of Laoting in 1613

Zhao Yanqing, a *jinshi* from Mengxian, Shanxi Province, who acted as county magistrate of Laoting in 1617

Li Song, a *juren* from Weihui, Henan Province, who acted as county magistrate of Laoting in 1619

Cao Yangqi, a native of Fuping, Shaanxi Province, who acted as county magistrate of Laoting in 1622

Liu Xi, a *gongsheng* from Licheng, Shandong Province, who acted as county magistrate of Laoting in 1624

Li Fengzhu, a *juren* from Le'an, Jiangxi Province, who acted as county magistrate of Laoting in 1628

Wang Zhijin, a *jinshi* from Baofeng, Henan Province, who acted as county magistrate of Laoting in 1631

Chen Changyan, a *jinshi* from Zezhou, Shanxi Province, who acted as county magistrate of Laoting in 1635

Liu Suochuang, a *juren* from Lintong, Shaanxi Province, who acted as county magistrate of Laoting in 1639

Wang Wenxiang, a *juren* from Ningzhou, Shaanxi Province, who acted as county magistrate of Laoting in 1641

Zhu Guangxi, a native of Shanyin, Zhejiang Province, who acted as county magistrate of Laoting in 1643

Qing Dynasty

Gong Maoxue, a native of Liaoyang, Fengtian, who acted as county magistrate of Laoting in 1644

Jin Tingxian, a native of Liaoyang, Fengtian, who acted as county magistrate of Laoting in 1645

Liang Yuyao, a native of Liaoyang, Fengtian, who acted as county magistrate of Laoting during the Shunzhi reign

Yao Shilai, a *suigongsheng* from Jingle, Shanxi Province, who acted as county magistrate of Laoting in 1650

Han Wang, a *jinshi* from Jingyang, Shaanxi Province, who acted as county magistrate of Laoting in 1652

Li Rirun, a *suigongsheng* from Hejin, Shanxi Province, who acted as county magistrate of Laoting in 1656

Ye Jiaoran, a *jinshi* from Minxian, Fujian Province, who acted as county magistrate of Laoting in 1662

Huang Zhaodan, a *juren* from Shaowu, Fujian Province, who acted as county magistrate of Laoting in 1663

潘敦复　山东夏津人，进士，万历十八年（1590年）任知县

叶敬愿　山东德州人，进士，万历二十年（1592年）任知县

刘芳久　河南安阳人，举人，万历二十一年（1593年）任知县

胡　绩　江西丰城人，举人，万历二十五年（1597年）任知县

王国祯　山西安邑人，进士，万历二十八年（1600年）任知县

李继祖　河南延津人，举人，万历二十九年（1601年）任知县

张　鉴　山西灵石人，贡生，万历三十四年（1606年）任知县

雷春起　陕西同州人，举人，万历三十八年（1610年）任知县

桑　高　山西太原人，举人，万历四十一年（1613年）任知县

赵延庆　山西孟县人，进士，万历四十五年（1617年）任知县

刘　松　河南卫辉人，举人，万历四十七年（1619年）任知县

曹养气　陕西富平人，天启二年（1622年）任知县

刘　檄　山东历城人，贡生，天启四年（1624年）任知县

李凤翥　江西乐安人，举人，崇祯元年（1628年）任知县

王之晋　河南宝丰人，进士，崇祯四年（1631年）任知县

陈昌言　山西泽州人，进士，崇祯八年（1635年）任知县

刘所创　陕西临潼人，举人，崇祯十二年（1639年）任知县

王文祥　陕西宁州人，举人，崇祯十四年（1641年）任知县

朱光熙　浙江山阴人，进士，崇祯十六年（1643年）任知县

清　代

龚懋学　奉天辽阳人，顺治元年（1644年）任知县

金廷献　奉天辽阳人，顺治二年（1645年）任知县

梁宇曜　奉天辽阳人，顺治年间任知县

姚时来　山西静乐人，岁贡生，顺治七年（1650年）任知县

韩　望　陕西泾阳人，进士，顺治九年（1652年）任知县

李日润　山西河津人，岁贡生，顺治十三年（1656年）任知县

叶矫然　福建闽县人，进士，康熙元年（1662年）任知县

黄肇丹　福建邵武人，举人，康熙二年（1663年）任知县

Liu Suoqin, a *shengyuan* (student in county school) from Lintong, Shaanxi Province, who acted as county magistrate of Laoting in 1667

Yao Shunmin, a *shengyuan* from Renhe, Zhejiang Province, who acted as county magistrate of Laoting in 1667

Yu Chenglong, a *yinsheng* (student by imperial beneficence) from Red-Bordered Banner of the Han Army, who acted as county magistrate of Laoting in 1668

Zhang Chengzan, a native of Liaoning, Fengtian, who acted as county magistrate of Laoting in 1670

Tang Maochun, a *juren* from Gaochun, Jiangnan, who acted as county magistrate of Laoting in 1680

Jin Xingrui, a *jiansheng* from Renhe, Zhejiang Province, who acted as county magistrate of Laoting in 1682

Chen Mengxiong, a *bagongsheng* (tribute student with distinction) from Weixian, Shandong Province, who acted as county magistrate of Laoting in 1684

Huang Ciying, a *juren* from Jinjiang, Fujian Province, who acted as county magistrate of Laoting in 1691

Zhou Cai, a *guanjiansheng* (student of noble birth in the imperial college) from Sanhan, who acted as county magistrate of Laoting in 1694

Dong Longzuo, a *guanjiansheng* from Liaoyang, Fengtian, who acted as county magistrate of Laoting in 1696

Tang Yi, a *jiansheng* from Renhe, Zhejiang Province, who acted as county magistrate of Laoting in 1699

Wang Jing, a *fubang* (tribute student by virtue of an honorable mention), who acted as county magistrateof Laoting in 1704

Zhang Deqi, a *juren* from Zezhou, Shanxi Province, who acted as county magistrate of Laoting in 1706

Zhang Min, a *juren* from Xinxing, Guangdong Province, who acted as county magistrate of Laoting in 1716

Zhang Jingsong, a *jinshi* from Wuxian, Jiangnan, who acted as county magistrate of Laoting in 1720

Zhang Junsheng, a *juren* from Shaoyang, Shaanxi Province, who acted as county magistrate of Laoting in 1721

Xiong Zhen, a *juren* from Xujiang, who acted as county magistrate of Laoting in 1722

Shen Jicun, a *jinshi* from Haining, Zhejiang Province, who acted as county magistrate of Laoting in 1723

Lai Ting, a *juren* from Fuping, Shaanxi Province, who acted as county magistrate of Laoting in 1727

Huang Qibi, a *juren* from Huaxian, Guangdong Province, who acted as county magistrate of Laoting in 1728

Yang Zhengchuan, a *jinshi* from Nanchong, Sichuan Province, who acted as county magistrate of Laoting in 1731

Feng Hongmo, a *jinshi* from Cixi, Zhejiang Province, who acted as county magistrate of Laoting in 1734

Shi Shihong, a native of Xiushui, Zhejiang Province, who acted as county magistrate of Laoting in 1735

Li Zhifan, a *juren* from Wengyuan, Guangdong Province, who acted as county magistrate of Laoting in 1739

Li Youjue, a *juren* from Quanzhou, Guangxi, who acted as county magistrate of Laoting in 1740

Dong Zhan, a native of Ganyu, Jiangnan, who acted as county magistrate of Laoting in 1743

Qin Yi, a *juren* from Rizhao, Shandong Province, who acted as county magistrate of Laoting in 1743

Ju Bingqian, a *juren* from Nanyang, Henan Province, who acted as county magistrate of Laoting in 1744

An Tai, a *jinshi* from Daizhou, Shanxi Province, who acted as county magistrate of Laoting in 1747

刘所勤　陕西临潼人，生员，康熙六年（1667年）任知县

姚舜民　浙江仁和人，生员，康熙六年（1667年）任知县

于成龙　汉军镶红旗人，荫生，康熙七年（1668年）任知县

张承瓒　奉天辽阳人，康熙九年（1670年）任知县

唐懋淓　江南高淳人，举人，康熙十九年（1680年）任知县

金星瑞　浙江仁和人，监生，康熙二十一年（1682年）任知县

陈梦熊　山东潍县人，拔贡生，康熙二十三年（1684年）任知县

黄赐英　福建晋江人，举人，康熙三十年（1691年）任知县

周　采　三韩人，官监生，康熙三十三年（1694年）任知县

董隆祚　奉天辽阳人，官监生，康熙三十五年（1696年）任知县

汤　彝　浙江仁和人，监生，康熙三十八年（1699年）任知县

王　经　陕西朝邑人，副榜，康熙四十三年（1704年）任知县

张德祈　山西泽州人，举人，康熙四十五年（1706年）任知县

张　敏　广东新兴人，举人，康熙五十五年（1716年）任知县

张景崧　江南吴县人，进士，康熙五十九年（1720年）任知县

张俊生　陕西邵阳人，举人，康熙六十年（1721年）任知县

熊　震　旴江人，举人，康熙六十一年（1722年）任知县

沈继存　浙江海宁人，进士，雍正元年（1723年）任知县

来　琜　陕西富平人，举人，雍正五年（1727年）任知县

黄其壁　广东花县人，举人，雍正六年（1728年）任知县

杨正传　四川南充人，进士，雍正九年（1731年）任知县

冯鸿模　浙江慈溪人，进士，雍正十二年（1734年）任知县

施士洪　浙江秀水人，雍正十三年（1735年）任知县

李之蕃　广东翁源人，举人，乾隆四年（1739年）任知县

李有爵　广西全州人，举人，乾隆五年（1740年）任知县

董　沾　江南赣榆人，乾隆八年（1743年）任知县

秦　翼　山东日照人，举人，乾隆八年（1743年）任知县

巨秉乾　河南南阳人，举人，乾隆九年（1744年）任知县

安　泰　山西代州人，进士，乾隆十二年（1747年）任知县

Chen Jinjun, a *juren* from Jinjiang, Fujian Province, who acted as county magistrate of Laoting in 1749

Zhang Fuhan, a **bagongsheng** from Fushi, Shaanxi Province, who acted as county magistrate of Laoting in 1757

Ning Cheng, a *juren* from Jimo, Shandong Province, who acted as county magistrate of Laoting in 1764

Cao Liang, a *juren* from Anqiu, Shandong Province, who acted as county magistrate of Laoting in 1769

Zhao Dajing, a *juren* from Dezhou, Shandong Province, who acted as county magistrate of Laoting in 1772

Tan Jianlong, a *juren* from Zhaowen, Jiangsu Province, who acted as county magistrate of Laoting in 1775

Li Yu, a *juren* from Yingshan, Sichuan Province, who acted as county magistrate of Laoting in 1778

Guo Zhaolin, a *juren* from Yangcheng, Shanxi Province, who acted as county magistrate of Laoting in 1780

Xia Weidao, who acted as county magistrate of Laoting in 1785

Yu Changzu, a *juren* from Linxiang, Hunan Province, who acted as county magistrate of Laoting in 1785

Bai Wancheng, who acted as county magistrate of Laoting in 1789

Zhou Guangyu, a **bagongsheng** from Yinxian, Zhejiang Province, who acted as county magistrate of Laoting in 1789

Xu Shao, a juren from Jiashan, Zhejiang Province, who acted as county magistrate of Laoting in 1789

Shao Zhijun, who acted as county magistrate of Laoting in 1789

Hu Danian, a *juren* from Yongding, Fujian Province, who acted as county magistrate of Laoting in 1792

Zhang (whose given name unknown), a *juren* from Guoxian, Shanxi Province, who acted as county magistrate of Laoting in 1796

Dai Shupei, who acted as county magistrate of Laoting in 1796

Zhou Yu, a *juren* from Guiding, Guizhou Province, who acted as county magistrate of Laoting in 1796

Zha Diyuan, a *jiansheng* from Louxian, Jiangsu Province, who acted as county magistrate of Laoting in 1803

Zhao Can, a *juren* from Liaocheng, Shandong Province, who acted as county magistrate of Laoting in 1803

Lü Siguan, a *juren* from Xin'an, Henan Province, who acted as county magistrate of Laoting in 1806

He Anlan, a *juren* from Dongguan, Guangdong Province, who acted as county magistrate of Laoting in 1806

Cheng Xiang, a *juren* from Nanhai, Guangdong Province, who acted as county magistrate of Laoting in 1806

Huang Heguang, a *juren* from Yongchun, Fujian Province, who acted as county magistrate of Laoting in 1809

Liu Jinjie, a *jiansheng* from Shanghang, Fujian Province, who acted as county magistrate of Laoting in 1809

Chen Nianzu, a *juren* from Changle, Hubei Province, who acted as county magistrate of Laoting in 1809

Song Qingshang, a *juren* from Wendeng, Shandong Province, who acted as county magistrate of Laoting in 1813

Lü Pengnan, a *lingongsheng* (paid tribute student) from Xin'an, Henan Province, who acted as county magistrate of Laoting in 1814

Zhu Qinggu, a *jiansheng* from Gushi, Henan Province, who acted as county magistrate of Laoting in 1817

陈金俊　福建晋江人，举人，乾隆十四年（1749年）任知县

张辅汉　陕西肤施人，拔贡生，乾隆二十二年（1757年）任知县

宁　城　山东即墨人，举人，乾隆二十九年（1764年）任知县

曹　良　山东安丘人，举人，乾隆三十四年（1769年）任知县

赵大经　山东德州人，举人，乾隆三十七年（1772年）任知县

谭见龙　江苏昭文人，举人，乾隆四十年（1775年）任知县

李　械　四川营山人，举人，乾隆四十三年（1778年）任知县

郭兆麟　山西阳城人，举人，乾隆四十五年（1780年）任知县

夏维翱　乾隆五十年（1785年）任知县

余昌祖　湖南临乡人，举人，乾隆五十年（1785年）任知县

白万程　乾隆五十四年（1789年）任知县

周光裕　浙江鄞县人，拔贡生，乾隆五十四年（1789年）任知县

徐　韶　浙江嘉善人，举人，乾隆五十四年（1789年）任知县

邵之俊　乾隆五十四年（1789年）任知县

胡大年　福建永定人，举人，乾隆五十七年（1792年）任知县

张××　山西崞县人，举人，嘉庆元年（1796年）任知县

戴书培　嘉庆元年（1796年）任知县

周　鱼　贵州贵定人，举人，嘉庆元年（1796年）任知县

查涤源　江苏娄县人，监生，嘉庆八年（1803年）任知县

赵　灿　山东聊城人，举人，嘉庆八年（1803年）任知县

吕嗣关　河南新安人，举人，嘉庆十一年（1806年）任知县

何安澜　广东东莞人，举人，嘉庆十一年（1806年）任知县

程　翔　广东南海人，举人，嘉庆十一年（1806年）任知县

黄河光　福建永春人，举人，嘉庆十四年（1809年）任知县

刘晋阶　福建上杭人，监生，嘉庆十四年（1809年）任知县

陈念祖　湖北长乐人，举人，嘉庆十四年（1809年）任知县

宋庆赏　山东文登人，举人，嘉庆十八年（1813年）任知县

吕鹏南　河南新安人，廪贡生，嘉庆十九年（1814年）任知县

祝庆谷　河南固始人，监生，嘉庆二十二年（1817年）任知县

Gu Rushou, a *jiansheng* from Shangyuan, Jiangsu Province, who acted as county

magistrate of Laoting in 1817

Bao Fuzheng, a *juren* from Nanfeng, Jiangxi Province, who acted as county magistrate of Laoting in 1817

Guo Xingfen, a *jiansheng* from Taigu, Shanxi Province, who acted as county magistrate of Laoting in 1821

Zhang Yuqian, a *juren* from Tongcheng, Anhui Province, who acted as county magistrate of Laoting in 1821

Chen Kai, a *jiansheng* from Shizai, Jiangsu Province, who acted as county magistrate of Laoting in 1822

Fusheng'e, a *jinshi* from the White Banner, who acted as county magistrate of Laoting in 1822

Yu Chongben, a *juren* from Yingshan, Sichuan Province, who acted as county

magistrate of Laoting in 1824

Xu Bo, a **bagongsheng** from Dingtao, Shandong Province, who acted as county

magistrate of Laoting in 1825

Wei Yanyi, a native of Yanghu, Jiangsu Province, who acted as county magistrate of Laoting in 1825

Zhu Xingtang, a *jinshi* from Shangyuan, Jiangnan, who acted as deputy county magistrate of Laoting in 1825

Pan Yuantao, a native of Shexian, Anhui Province, who acted as deputy county magistrate of Laoting in 1826

Zhang Lin, a **bagongsheng** from Jiaxing, Zhejiang Province, who acted as county magistrate of Laoting in 1826

Liu Yanxi, a *juren* from Dading, Guizhou Province, who acted as county magistrate of Laoting in 1832

Yang Jitang, a *jiansheng* from Haining, Zhejiang Province, who acted as county magistrate of Laoting in 1832

Wu Chengzu, a *juren* from Nanfeng, Jiangxi Province, who acted as county magistrate of Laoting in 1834

Chen Bingchang, a *juren* from Gui'an, Zhejiang Province, who acted as county magistrate of Laoting in 1835

Guo Jingyi, a *juren* from Yangqu, Shanxi Province, who acted as county magistrate of Laoting in 1839

Liu Peisheng, a **bagongsheng** from Haicheng, Fengtian, who acted as county magistrate of Laoting in 1839

Lu Weidi, a *jiansheng* from Yuanhe, Jiangsu Province, who acted as county magistrate of Laoting in 1839

Kong Zhaoran, a *jinshi* from Yangqu, Shandong Province, who acted as county magistrate of Laoting in 1841

Zhang You'an, a *juren* from Renhe, Zhejiang Province, who acted as county magistrate of Laoting in 1843

Ma Jimei, a *juren* from Yiliang, Yunnan Province, who acted as county magistrate of Laoting in 1849

Dan Chunhui, a *juren* from Dali, Shaanxi Province, who acted as county magistrate of Laoting in 1851

Yuan Shouzhi, a *jiansheng* from Jiangxia, Hubei Province, who acted as county magistrate of Laoting in

 1853 upon his working experience in Yongping Prefecture

Qian Qu, a *jinshi* from Renhe, Zhejiang Province, who acted as county magistrate of Laoting in 1853

Qi Zhirong, a *juren* from Gaoping, Shanxi Province, who acted as county magistrate of Laoting in 1854

Bo Wen, a *jiansheng* from the White Banner, who acted as county magistrate of Laoting in 1855

You Qisheng, a **gongsheng** from Tieling, Fengtian, who acted as county magistrate of Laoting in 1855

Zhang Xuequan, a *juren* from Liaoning, Jiangnan, who acted as county magistrate of Laoting in 1857

顾汝寿　江苏上元人，监生，嘉庆二十二年（1817年）任知县

包敷政　江西南丰人，举人，嘉庆二十二年（1817年）任知县

郭兴汾　山西太谷人，监生，道光元年（1821年）任知县

张裕乾　安徽桐城人，举人，道光元年（1821年）任知县

陈　楷　江苏石埭人，监生，道光二年（1822年）任知县

富升额　正白旗，进士，道光二年（1822年）任知县

于崇本　四川营山人，举人，道光四年（1824年）任知县

许　博　山东定陶人，拔贡生，道光五年（1825年）任知县

魏彦仪　江苏阳湖人，道光五年（1825年）任知县

朱性堂　江南上元人，进士，道光五年（1825年）署知县

潘元焘　安徽歙县人，道光六年（1826年）以州同署知县

张　霖　浙江嘉兴人，拔贡生，道光六年（1826年）任知县

刘延熙　贵州大定人，举人，道光十二年（1832年）任知县

杨纪堂　浙江海宁人，监生，道光十二年（1832年）任知县

吴承祖　江西南丰人，举人，道光十四年（1834年）署知县

陈炳常　浙江归安人，举人，道光十五年（1835年）任知县

郭景仪　山西阳曲人，举人，道光十九年（1839年）任知县

柳培盛　奉天海城人，拔贡生，道光十九年（1839年）署知县

陆为棣　江苏元和人，监生，道光十九年（1839年）任知县

孔炤然　山西阳曲人，进士，道光二十一年（1841年）署知县

张佑安　浙江仁和人，举人，道光二十三年（1843年）任知县

马继眉　云南宜良人，举人，道光二十九年（1849年）署知县

淡春晖　陕西大荔人，举人，咸丰元年（1851年）任知县

袁守直　湖北江夏人，监生，咸丰三年（1853年）以永平府经历署知县

钱　璟　浙江仁和人，进士，咸丰三年（1853年）署知县

祁之荣　山西高平人，举人，咸丰四年（1854年）署知县

博　文　正白旗，监生，咸丰五年（1855年）署知县

尤其胜　奉天铁岭人，贡生，咸丰五年（1855年）署知县

张学权　江南江宁人，举人，咸丰七年（1857年）署知县

Shi Xiang, a *gongsheng* from the Yellow-Bordered Banner, who acted as county magistrate of Laoting in 1858

De Cheng, who acted as county magistrate of Laoting in 1859

Ren Xincheng, a *jiansheng* from Shanyin, Zhejiang Province, who acted as county magistrate
 of Laoting in 1860

Liu Kai, a *jinshi* from Wuwei, Gansu Province, who acted as county magistrate of Laoting in 1862

Chang Zhong, a *jiansheng* from the Yellow Banner, who acted as county magistrate of Laoting in 1863

Yang Peize, a *juren* from Tianzhu, Guizhou Province, who acted as county magistrate of Laoting in 1865

Lu Tianze, a *jinshi* from Zunyi, Guizhou Province, who acted as county magistrate of Laoting in 1865

Hui Lin, a native of the White Banner, who acted as county magistrate of Laoting in 1865

Cai Zhixiu, a *jiansheng* from Songyang, Zhedong, who acted as county magistrate of Laoting in 1865

Zhang Enxu, a *jinshi* from Fushan, Shandong Province, who acted as county magistrate of Laoting in 1869

Wu Qin, a *jiansheng* from Yanghu, Jiangsu Province, who acted as county magistrate of Laoting in 1869

Er Den, a *juren* from Manchuria, who acted as county magistrate of Laoting in 1869

Zhang Guilin, a *jiansheng* from Jiaozhou, Shandong Province, who acted as deputy county
 magistrate of Laoting in 1870

Jiang Gongchen, a *jiansheng* from Huoqiu, Anhui Province, who acted as county magistrate of Laoting in 1870

Zhang Guang'e, a *jiansheng* from Yanghu, Jiangsu Province, who acted as county magistrate of Laoting in 1870

Wang Lin, a *jinshi* from Heyang, Shaanxi Province, who acted as county magistrate of Laoting in 1871

Jiang Jiabin, a *jiansheng* from Changzhou, Jiangsu Province, who acted as county magistrate of Laoting in 1874

Chen Yipei, a *jiansheng* from Hefei, Anhui Province, who acted as county magistrate of Laoting in 1874

Gu Zhaoyong, a *jiansheng* from Renhe, Zhejiang Province, who acted as county magistrate of Laoting in 1876

Wang Songhan, a *juren* from Shandong Province, who acted as county magistrate of Laoting in 1879

Dai Zuoyi, a native of Wuyuan, Anhui Province, who acted as county magistrate of Laoting in 1881

Tao Yunjin, who acted as county magistrate of Laoting in 1884

Sun Zhenhe, who acted as county magistrate of Laoting in 1886

Qian Zhengyuan, a member of Hanlin Academy from Jianshui, Yunnan Province, who acted as county
magistrate of Laoting in 1888

Luo Xiaoxian, a *gongsheng* from Jining, Shandong Province, who acted as county magistrate of Laoting in 1890

Zhang Heling, a *gongsheng* from Jinzhou, Liaoning Province, who acted as county magistrate of Laoting in 1894

Chen Ben, an honorable governor from Shengxian, Zhejiang Province, who acted as county magistrate
 of Laoting in 1894

Han Keyan, a *gongsheng* from Jimo, Shandong Province, who acted as county magistrate of Laoting in 1895

Wan Heyin, a *lingongsheng* from Dehua, Jiangxi Province, who acted as county magistrate of Laoting in

世　祥　镶黄旗，贡生，咸丰八年（1858年）署知县

德　成　正白旗，笔帖式，咸丰九年（1859年）署知县

任信成　浙江山阴人，监生，咸丰十年（1860年）署知县

刘　铠　甘肃武威人，进士，同治元年（1862年）任知县

常　忠　正黄旗，监生，同治二年（1863年）署知县

杨沛泽　贵州天柱人，举人，同治四年（1865年）署知县

卢天泽　贵州遵义人，进士，同治四年（1865年）任知县

惠　霖　正白旗，笔帖式，同治四年（1865年）署知县

蔡志修　浙东松阳人，监生，同治四年（1865年）任知县

张恩煦　山东福山人，进士，同治八年（1869年）署知县

吴　钦　江苏阳湖人，监生，同治八年（1869年）九月署知县

额尔德恩　满洲人，举人，同治八年（1869年）十月署知县

张桂林　山东胶州人，监生，同治九年（1870年）以府经代理知县

江贡琛　安徽霍邱人，监生，同治九年（1870年）署知县

张光锷　江苏阳湖人，监生，同治九年（1870年）署知县

王　霖　陕西部阳人，进士，同治十年（1871年）任知县

蒋嘉霹　江苏长洲人，监生，同治十三年（1874年）署知县

陈以培　安徽合肥人，监生，同治十三年（1874年）任知县

顾肇墉　浙江仁和人，监生，光绪二年（1876年）任知县

王崧翰　山东举人，光绪五年（1879年）任知县

戴作楫　安徽婺源人，光绪七年（1881年）任知县

陶云锦　光绪十年（1884年）任知县

孙振翮　光绪十二年（1886年）任知县

钱止园　云南建水人，翰林，光绪十四年（1888年）任知县

骆孝先　山东济宁人，附贡生，光绪十六年（1890年）任知县

张鹤龄　辽宁锦州人，优贡生，光绪二十年（1894年）任知县

陈　本　浙江嵊县人，花翎知府衔，光绪二十年（1894年）任知县

韩克岩　山东即墨人，贡生，光绪二十一年（1895年）任知县

万和寅　江西德化人，廪贡生，光绪二十六年（1900年）任知县，二十七年（1901年）调抚宁

 1900 and then governor of Funing in 1901

Tang Guozhen, who acted as county magistrate of Laoting in 1901

Shi Lifang, a native of Tieling, who acted as county magistrate of Laoting in 1901

Xie Maochun, a *bagongsheng* from Haicheng, Fengtian, who acted as county magistrate of Laoting in 1901

Chen Huaizhong, a *jinshi* from Taicang, Jiangsu Province, who acted as county magistrate of Laoting in 1901

Zhang Zezhou, a *jinshi* from Jinxian (today's Linghe City, Liaoning Province), who acted as county
 magistrate of Laoting in 1904

Wu Yong, a *jinshi* from Pucheng, Shaanxi Province, who acted as county magistrate of Laoting in 1906

Cai Jixun, a native of Zhejiang Province, who acted as county magistrate of Laoting in 1907

Han Tinghuan, a native of Shanyang, Jiangsu Province, who acted as county magistrate of Laoting in 1907

Zhao Xunnian, a *juren* from Jiangsu Province, who acted as county magistrate of Laoting in 1909

Zheng Fukang, a *lingongsheng* from Hunan Province, who acted as county magistrate of Laoting in 1910

Ming En, a native of Beijing, who acted as county magistrate of Laoting in 1911

Republic of China Period

Wang Furen, a native of Yixian, Zhili, who acted as county magistrate of Laoting in 1912

Sun Huanlun, a *bagongsheng* from Yutian, Hebei Province, who acted as county magistrate of Laoting in 1913

Li Chuanxu, a native of Feicheng, Shandong Province, who acted as county magistrate of Laoting in 1915

Chen Yurui, a *gongsheng* from Huaiyin, Jiangsu Province, who acted as county magistrate of Laoting in 1917

Chen Weixin, a native of Wenxi, Shanxi Province, who acted as county magistrate of Laoting in 1918

Zhang Yuran, a native of Fengtian, who acted as county magistrate of Laoting in 1922

Liu Qianyi, a *juren* from Yuanjiang, Yunnan Province, who acted as county magistrate of Laoting in 1923

Zhao Tingrang, a native of Fengtian, who acted as county magistrate of Laoting in 1925

Zhang Xueshu, a native of Fengtian, who acted as county magistrate of Laoting in 1925

Xie Yihe, a *gongsheng* from Dacheng, Hebei Province, who acted as county magistrate of Laoting in 1926

Sheng Jianxun, a native of Jiangsu Province, who acted as county magistrate of Laoting in 1926

Liu Yehan, a native of Fengtian, who acted as county magistrate of Laoting in 1927

Wang Jiexia, a native of Fengtian, who acted as county magistrate of Laoting in 1927

Jin Xijun, a native of Jinxi, who acted as county magistrate of Laoting in 1928

Shi Biaoqing, a native of Shanxi Province, who acted as county magistrate of Laoting in 1928

Yang Liming, a native of Hebei Province, who acted as county magistrate of Laoting in 1929

唐国珍　光绪二十七年（1901年）复任知县

石笠舫　铁岭人，光绪二十七年（1901年）任知县

解茂春　奉天海城人，拔贡生，光绪二十七年（1901年）署知县

陈怀忠　江苏太仓人，进士，光绪二十七年（1901年）署知县

张则周　锦县（今辽宁省锦州市凌河区）人，进士，光绪三十年（1904年）任知县

仵　墉　陕西蒲城人，进士，光绪三十二年（1906年）任知县

蔡济勋　浙江人，光绪三十三年（1907年）任知县

韩廷焕　江苏山阳人，军功，光绪三十三年（1907年）任知县

赵巽年　江苏人，举人，宣统元年（1909年）任知县

郑阜康　湖南人，廪贡生，宣统二年（1910年）任知县

明　恩　旗籍北京人，宣统三年（1911年）任知县

民国时期

王辅仁　直隶易县人，1912年任县知事

孙焕仑　河北玉田人，拔贡生，1913年任县知事

李传煦　山东肥城人，1915年任县知事

陈玉瑞　江苏淮阴人，优贡生，1917年任县知事

赵维新　山西闻喜人，1918年任县知事

张裕然　奉天人，1922年任县知事

刘乾义　云南沅江人，举人，1923年任县知事

赵廷勷　奉天人，1925年任县知事

张学书　奉天人，1925年任县知事

谢一鹤　河北大城人，贡生，1926年任县知事

盛建勋　江苏人，1926年任县知事

刘业汉　奉天人，1927年任县知事

王捷侠　奉天人，1927年任县知事

金希均　锦西人，1928年任县长

史标青　山西人，1928年任县长

杨励明　河北人，1929年任县长

Chen Bin, a native of Yixing, Zhejiang Province, who acted as county magistrate of Laoting in 1930

Yuan Fenggang, a native of Fengtian, who acted as county magistrate of Laoting in 1932

Xia Shutang, a native of Fengtian, who acted as county magistrate of Laoting in 1933

Guan Guangyu, a native of Haicheng, Fengtian, who acted as county magistrate of Laoting in 1934

Zhu Yi, a juren from Henan Province, who acted as county magistrate of Laoting in 1935

Li Rongqian, a native of Henan Province, who acted as county magistrate of Laoting in 1935

Zhang Peide, a native of Henan Province, who acted as county magistrate of Laoting in 1936

The Period of Japanese Puppet Government

Zhang Shusen, a native of Beijing, who acted as county magistrate of Laoting in 1939

Shen Quan, a native of Licheng, Shandong Province, who acted as county magistrate of Laoting in 1943

Zhu Yinfu, a native of Jinghai, Tianjin, who acted as county magistrate of Laoting in 1943

Li Dachang, a native of Manchuria, who acted as county magistrate of Laoting in 1944

Zhuang Minghuan, a native of Fengtian, Manchuria, who acted as county magistrate of Laoting in 1945

The Period of Kuomintang Government

Xue Muren, a native of Tianjin, who acted as county magistrate of Laoting in 1946

Hu Zhaogong, who acted as county magistrate of Laoting in 1947

Wu Tieqiao who acted as county magistrate of Laoting in 1948

陈　斌　浙江宜兴人，1930年任县长

袁凤冈　奉天人，1932年任县长

夏树棠　奉天人，1933年任县长

关广誉　奉天海城人，1934年任县长

朱　颐　河南人，举人，1935年任县长

李荣谦　河南人，1935年任县长

张培德　河南人，1936年任县长

日伪时期

张树森　北京人，1939年任县知事

沈　洤　山东历城人，1943年7月任县知事

朱荫福　天津静海人，1943年7月任县知事

李大昌　伪满洲人，1944年8月任县知事

庄明寰　伪满洲奉天人，1945年4月任县知事

国民党时期

薛沐人　天津人，1946年任县长

胡昭功　1947年任县长

吴铁桥　1948年任县长

1. The List of Party Committee Secretaries and Leaders of Laoting County

Name	Native Place	Tenure	Remarks
Wang Dezhou	Laoting County, Hebei Province	Winter 1924-Summer 1927	Secretary of Party committees of Laoting Middle School and Laoting County
Jia Kunpu	Luannan County, Hebei Province	Summer 1927-Spring 1928	
Li Yunchang	Laoting County, Hebei Province	Spring 1928-Feb. 1929	
Song Kuangwo	Laoting County, Hebei Province	Feb. 1929-Jun. 1929	Acting secretary
Xu Yinhui	Laoting County, Hebei Province	Autumn 1929-1932	
Xu Yunlong	Laoting County, Hebei Province	Autumn 1932-Early 1933	
Dai Lingzhen	Luannan County, Hebei Province	Early 1933-May 1934	
Jiang Mingyi	Laoting County, Hebei Province	May 1934-Summer 1935	
Li Huichang	Laoting County, Hebei Province	Summer 1935-Dec. 1936	Acting secretary
Li Ruiwen	Laoting County, Hebei Province	Jun. 1936-Spring 1937	
Wang Mingde	Laoting County, Hebei Province	Spring 1937-Winter 1937	
Li Haitao	Laoting County, Hebei Province	Winter 1937-Aug. 1938	
Li Ruiwen	Laoting County, Hebei Province	Aug. 1939-May 1941	Secretary of Party Committee of Laoting County
Li Haitao	Laoting County, Hebei Province	Aug. 1943-Oct. 1944	Secretary of Working Committee of Changle County
Wang Mingde	Laoting County, Hebei Province	Jan. 1945-Oct. 1947	
Wang Min'an	Luannan County, Hebei Province	Oct. 1947-Aug. 1951	
He Muzhang	Shanxi Province	Aug. 1951-May 1952	Acting secretary
Lu Da	Baoding, Hebei Province	May 1952-Sep. 1952	Acting secretary
Li Jian	Luannan County, Hebei Province	Sep. 1952-Jun. 1953	
Yi Shu san	Luanxian County, Hebei Province	Jun. 1952-May 1954	Acting secretary
Li Jian	Luannan County, Hebei Province	May 1954-Jul. 1957	
Zhang Ziming	Luannan County, Hebei Province	Mar. 1957-Oct. 1964	
Zhang Yisheng	Luannan County, Hebei Province	Oct. 1964-Oct. 1966	Acting secretary
Shen Taichang	Funing County, Hebei Province	Dec. 1968-Oct. 1969	Head of the Core Team of Revolutionary Committee
Wang Shihui	Laoting County, Hebei Province	Jan. 1971-Apr. 1978	
Sun Shanguang	Luannan County, Hebei Province	Jun. 1978-Feb. 1979	First acting secretary

一　中共乐亭县委历任书记及负责人名录

姓　名	籍　贯	任职时间（年／月）	备注
王德周	河北乐亭县	1924冬—1927 夏	乐亭中学支部、乐亭地委书记
贾坤普	河北滦南县	1927 夏—1928 春	
李运昌	河北乐亭县	1928 春—1929.2	
宋匡我	河北乐亭县	1929.2—1929.6	代理书记
徐荫会	河北乐亭县	1929 秋—1932	
徐运隆	河北乐亭县	1932 秋—1933 初	
戴凌振	河北滦南县	1933 初—1934.5	
姜明义	河北乐亭县	1934.5—1935 夏	
李惠昌	河北乐亭县	1935 夏—1936.12	代理书记
李瑞文	河北乐亭县	1936.6—1937 春	
王明德	河北乐亭县	1937 春—1937 冬	
李海涛	河北乐亭县	1937 冬—1938.8	
李瑞文	河北乐亭县	1939.8—1941.5	乐亭党支部书记
李海涛	河北乐亭县	1943.8—1944.10	昌乐县工委书记
王明德	河北乐亭县	1945.1—1947.10	
王民安	河北滦南县	1947.10—1951.8	
贺穆章	山西省	1951.8—1952.5	代理书记
陆　达	河北保定	1952.5—1952.9	代理书记
李　健	河北滦南县	1952.9—1953.6	
怡树三	河北滦县	1953.6—1954.5	代理书记
李健河	河北滦南县	1954.5—1957.7	
张子明	河北滦南县	1957.3—1964.10	
张逸生	河北滦南县	1964.10—1966.10	代理书记
申太昌	河北抚宁县	1968.12—1969.10	革委会核心小组组长
王世惠	河北乐亭县	1971.1—1978.4	
孙善广	河北滦南县	1978.6—1979.2	代理第一书记

Sun Shanguang	Luannan County, Hebei Province	Feb. 1979-Dec. 1985	
Zhao Jie	Laoting County, Hebei Province	Dec. 1985-Dec. 1986	
Dong Zhaoping	Fengnan County, Hebei Province	Nov. 1986-Jun. 1989	
Wang Shuhe	Heishan County, Liaoning Province	Jun. 1989-Sep. 1991	
Li Baozhuo	Luannan County, Hebei Province	Sep. 1991-Dec. 1995	
Liu Yinlou	Fengnan County, Hebei Province	Dec. 1995-Dec. 1997	
Fan Shaohui	Luannan County, Hebei Province	Jan. 1998-Mar. 2007	
Mao Decheng	Guye District, Hebei Province	May 2007-	

2. The List of County Magistrates of Laoting People's Government

Name	Native Place	Tenure	Remarks
Wu Shaoxian	Laoting County, Hebei Province	Sep. 1938-Oct. 1938	
Li Haitao	Laoting County, Hebei Province	Aug. 1943-Jun. 1944	
Zhang Zhao	Heilongjiang Province	Jun. 1944-Aug. 1945	Changle Cooperative County Government
Zhong Kedong	Qian'an County, Hebei Province	Aug. 1945-Nov. 1945	
Liu Zhiyi	Qian'an County, Hebei Province	Nov. 1945-Jun. 1946	Taking office in April 1946
Gao Chunyi	Luanxian County, Hebei Province	Jun. 1947-Jan. 1949	
Li Bin	Laoting County, Hebei Province	Sep. 1949-Jan. 23, 1953	
Li Jian	Luannan County, Hebei Province	Sep. 9, 1952-Feb. 13, 1953	Acting county magistrate
Zhao Yanhua	Funing County, Hebei Province	Feb. 13, 1953-Aug. 1954	
Zhao Huizhang	Laoting County, Hebei Province	Aug. 1954-Dec. 9, 1958	
Wei Zichen	Fengrun County, Hebei Province	Dec. 9, 1958-Jan. 17, 1968	
Shen Taichang	Funing County, Hebei Province	Jan. 17, 1968-Oc. 6, 1969	Director of the Revolutionary Committee
Wang Shihui	Laoting County, Hebei Province	Nov. 1969-Apr. 4, 1978	Director of the Revolutionary Committee
Sun Shanguang	Luannan County, Hebei Province	Jun. 1978-Feb. 1979	Acting director of the Revolutionary Committee
Li Yunfang	Fengnan County, Hebei Province	Jul. 24, 1979-Dec. 31, 1980	Director of the Revolutionary Committee
He Shaoxian	Laoting County, Hebei Province	Dec. 31, 1980-Dec. 31, 1980	Director of the Revolutionary Committee

孙善广　河北滦南县　1979.2—1985.12

赵　杰　河北乐亭县　1985.12—1986.12

冬兆平　河北丰南县　1986.11—1989.6

王树和　辽宁黑山县　1989.6—1991.9

黎宝琢　河北滦南县　1991.9—1995.12

刘印楼　河北丰南县　1995.12—1997.12

范绍慧　河北滦南县　1998.1—2007.3

苗德成　河北古冶区　2007.5—

二　乐亭县人民政府历任县长名录

姓　名	籍　贯	任职时间（年／月）	备注
吴绍贤	河北乐亭县	1938.9—1938.10	
李海涛	河北乐亭县	1943.8—1944.6	昌乐联合县政府
张　昭	黑龙江省	1944.6—1945.8	
钟克东	河北迁安县	1945.8—1945.11	
刘志一	河北迁安县	1945.11—1947.6	1946年4月实任
高纯一	河北滦县	1947.6—1949.1	
李　斌	河北乐亭县	1949.9—1953.1.23	
李　健	河北滦南县	1952.9.9—1953.2.13	代理县长
赵延华	河北抚宁县	1953.2.13—1954.8	
赵惠章	河北乐亭县	1954.8—1958.12.9	
魏紫臣	河北丰润县	1958.12.9—1968.1.17	
申太昌	河北抚宁县	1968.1.17—1969.10.6	革委会主任
王世惠	河北乐亭县	1969.11—1978.4.4	革委会主任
孙善广	河北滦南县	1978.6—1979.2	代理革委会主任
李运芳	河北丰南县	1979.7.24—1980.12.31	革委会主任
何绍先	河北乐亭县	1980.12.31—1981.12.31	革委会主任
何绍先	河北乐亭县	1981.12.31—1984.1	
赵　杰	河北乐亭县	1984.1—1984.6.10	代县长

He Shaoxian	Laoting County, Hebei Province	Dec. 31, 1981-Jan. 1984	
Zhao Jie	Laoting County, Hebei Province	Jan. 1984-Jun. 10, 1984	Acting county magistrate
Zhao Jie	Laoting County, Hebei Province	Jun. 10, 1984-Dec. 23, 1985	
Liu Heran	Laoting County, Hebei Province	Dec. 23, 1985-Feb. 27, 1987	
Tian Xiuqi	Luannan County, Hebei Province	Apr. 17, 1987-Sep. 1991	
Liu Yinlou	Fengnan County, Hebei Province	Sep. 1991-Mar. 1992	Acting county magistrate
Liu Yinlou	Fengnan County, Hebei Province	Mar. 1992-Feb. 1996	
Fan Shaohui	Luannan County, Hebei Province	Feb. 1996-Jan. 1998	
Wang Jingling	Fengrun County, Hebei Province	Jan. 1998-Mar. 2000	
Li Demin	Fengnan County, Hebei Province	Mar. 2000-Jun. 2001	
Huang Jingdong	Dandong, Liaoning Province	Jun. 2001-Feb. 2002	Acting county magistrate
Huang Jingdong	Dandong, Liaoning Province	Feb. 2002-Oct. 24, 2006	
Yuan Zhigang	Guyuan County, Hebei Province	Oct. 24, 2006-May 2008	
Li Zhong	Tanghai County, Hebei Province	May 2008-Mar. 2009	Acting county magistrate
Li Zhong	Tanghai County, Hebei Province	Mar. 2009-Apr. 2010	County magistrate
Wang Dongqun	Luanxian County, Hebei Province	Jan. 2011-	County magistrate

II. Jinshi of Past Dynasties

Li Hang, a *jinshi* during the Tianhui reign of the Jin Dynasty, who once acted as a prefectural governor

Li Yuandao, a *jinshi* during the Huangtong reign of the Jin Dynasty, who once acted as a prefectural judge

Li Yuanzhang, a *jinshi* during the Zhenglong reign of the Jin Dynasty, who was appointed Kaiguo Marquis of Longxi Prefecture

Zhang Tianzuo, a *jinshi* during the Zhenglong reign of the Jin Dynasty, who once acted as a vice minister

Zhang Tianyou, a *jinshi* during the Zhenglong reign of the Jin Dynasty, who once acted as Zhongfeng Dafu

Xianyu Zhongquan, a *jinshi* during the Mingchang reign of the Jin Dynasty

Yang Shaoxian, a *jinshi* granted in 1262 during the Yuan Dynasty, who once acted as Sizhi Scholar of Jixian Academy

Song Hongdao, a *jinshi* granted in 1385 during the Ming Dynasty, who once acted as Right Qiandu Imperial Inspector

Liu Gong, a *jinshi* granted in 1460 during the Ming Dynasty, who once acted as associate governor of Henan Province

Li Zongshang, a *jinshi* granted in 1490 during the Ming Dynasty, who once acted as chief secretary of the Ministry of Civil Affairs and vice minister of Taipusi (Ministry of Etiquettes)

Lu Gengqi, a *jinshi* granted in 1532 during the Ming Dynasty

Wang Haowen, a *jinshi* granted in 1550 during the Ming Dynasty, who once acted as Minister of Civil Affairs

Zhang Guorui, a *jinshi* granted in 1607 during the Ming Dynasty, who once acted as Left Governor of Shaanxi Province

Liu Tingxuan, a *jinshi* granted in 1613, who once acted as minister of Dalisi (Supreme Court)

赵　杰　河北乐亭县　1984.6.10—1985.12.23

刘鹤然　河北乐亭县　1985.12.23—1987.2.27

田秀岐　河北滦南县　1987.4.17—1991.9

刘印楼　河北丰南县　1991.9—1992.3　　　　　　　　　　代县长

刘印楼　河北丰南县　1992.3—1996.2

范绍慧　河北滦南县　1996.2—1998.1

王景龄　河北丰润县　1998.1—2000.3

李德敏　河北丰南县　2000.3—2001.6

黄敬东　辽宁丹东　2001.6—2002.2　　　　　　　　　　代县长

黄敬东　辽宁丹东　2002.2—2006.10.24

袁志刚　河北沽源县　2006.10.24—2008.5

李　忠　河北唐海县　2008.5—2009.3　　　　　　　　　　代县长

李　忠　河北唐海县　2009.3—2010.4　　　　　　　　　　县长

王东群　河北滦县　　2011.1—　　　　　　　　　　　　　县长

第二节　历代进士

李　杭：（金）天会初登进士。仕至州刺史。

李元道：（金）皇统间进士。仕至节度判官。

李元璋：（金）正隆初进士。仕陇西郡开国侯。

张天佐：（金）正隆间进士。仕至侍郎。

张天佑：（金）正隆间进士。中奉大夫。

鲜于仲权：（金）明昌间进士。

杨绍先：（元）中统三年（1260年）进士，授集贤院司直学士。

宋宏道：（明）洪武十八年（1385年）进士。任右佥都御史。

刘　恭：（明）天顺四年（1460年）进士。仕至河南参政。

李宗商：（明）弘治三年（1490年）进士。授户部主事，仕至太仆寺少卿。

卢耿麒：（明）嘉靖二年（1523年）进士。

王好问：（明）嘉靖庚戌（1550年）科进士。仕至户部尚书。

张国瑞：（明）万历三十五年（1607年）进士。仕至陕西左布政使。

刘廷宣：（明）万历四十一年（1613年）进士。仕至大理寺少卿。

Yao Xieyu, a *jinshi* granted in 1706 during the Qing Dynasty, who once acted as magistrate of Huiji County

Li Lan, a *jinshi* granted in 1718 during the Qing Dynasty, who once acted as governor of Anhui Province

Yang Kaiji, a *jinshi* granted in 1795 during the Qing Dynasty, who once acted as Fengtian Professor

Li Zhongshu, a *jinshi* granted in 1802 during the Qing Dynasty, who once acted as Professor of Daming Prefecture

Li Guangzi, a *jinshi* granted in 1809 during the Qing Dynasty, who once acted as Imperial Inspector of Fujian Province

Zhang Penglai, a *jinshi* granted in 1811 during the Qing Dynasty, who once acted as Professor of Jinzhou Prefecture

An Shutong, a *jinshi* granted in 1817 during the Qing Dynasty, who once acted as Professor of Guangping Prefecture

Zhou Lianzhong, a *jinshi* granted in 1840 during the Qing Dynasty, who once acted as chief secretary of the Ministry of Etiquettes

Ning Zenglun, a *jinshi* granted in 1840 during the Qing Dynasty, who once acted as Inspector of Zhejiang Province

Liu Zhen, a *jinshi* granted in 1850 during the Qing Dynasty, who once acted as governor of Shandong Province

Qian Dechang, a *jinshi* granted in 1859 during the Qing Dynasty, who once acted as magistrate of Tangxian County, Henan Province

Cui Guoqing, a *jinshi* granted in 1860 during the Qing Dynasty, who once acted as chief secretary of the Ministry of Civil Affairs

Yu Zonghan, a *jinshi* granted in 1865 during the Qing Dynasty, who once acted as Professor of Fengtian Prefecture

Song Guangyin, a *jinshi* granted in 1871 during the Qing Dynasty, who once acted as county magistrate of Henan

Han Zhao, a *jinshi* granted in 1874 during the Qing Dynasty, who once acted as magistrate of Huimin County, Shandong Province

Liu Chengsong, a *jinshi* granted in 1876 during the Qing Dynasty, who once acted as chief secretary of the Ministry of Justice

Wang Jinrong, a *jinshi* granted in 1883 during the Qing Dynasty, who once acted as secretary of the Ministry of Justice

Sun Guozhen, a *jinshi* granted in 1883 during the Qing Dynasty, who once acted as magistrate of Qufu County, Shandong Province

Liu Pei, a *jinshi* granted in 1886 during the Qing Dynasty, who once acted as associate secretary of the Prime Minister's Office

Xu Yuanrui, a *jinshi* granted in 1886 during the Qing Dynasty, who once acted as magistrate of Songxian County, Henan Province

Li Tan, a jinshi granted in 1886 during the Qing Dynasty, who once acted as Seal Keeper of the Ministry of Personnel

Li Xigeng, a jinshi granted in 1889 during the Qing Dynasty, who once acted as magistrate of Hui'an County, Guangdong Province

Shi Lüjin, a *jinshi* granted in 1890 during the Qing Dynasty, who once acted as director of Zhili Industry Department

Cao Zi'ang, a *jinshi* granted in 1894 during the Qing Dynasty, who once acted as magistrate of Huidong County, Guangdong Province

Zhou Pei, a *jinshi* granted in 1894 during the Qing Dynasty, who once acted as secretary of the Cabinet

Ge Liuzhi, a *jinshi* granted in 1895 during the Qing Dynasty, who once acted as chief secretary of the Ministry of Justice

Xiao Kaijia, a *jinshi* granted in 1898 during the Qing Dynasty, who once acted as chief secretary of the Ministry of Personnel

Lü Xingzhou, a *jinshi* granted in 1903 during the Qing Dynasty, who once acted as chief prosecutor of Jinlin Supreme Procuratorate

Li Fengshi, a martial *jinshi* granted in 1571 during the Ming Dynasty

姚协于：（清）康熙四十五年（1706年）进士。任会稽令。

李　兰：（清）康熙五十七年（1718年）进士。仕至安徽布政使。

杨开基：（清）乾隆六十年（1795年）进士。选奉天教授。

李中淑：（清）嘉庆七年（1802年）进士。选大名府教授。

李广滋：（清）嘉庆十四年（1809年）进士。仕至福建道监察御史。

张朋来：（清）嘉庆十六年（1811年）进士。任锦州府教授。

安树桐：（清）嘉庆二十二年（1817年）进士。任广平府教授。

周连仲：（清）道光二十年（1840年）进士。任礼部主事。

宁曾纶：（清）道光二十年（1840年）进士。仕至浙江按察使。

呼　震：（清）道光庚戌（1850年）科进士。仕至山东布政使。

钱德昌：（清）咸丰己未（1859年）科进士。曾任河南唐县知县。

崔国庆：（清）咸丰庚申（1860年）科进士。仕至户部主事。

于宗翰：（清）同治乙丑（1865年）科进士。任奉天府教授。

宋广荫：（清）同治十年（1871年）进士。任河南知县。

韩　钊：（清）同治十三年（1874年）进士。任山东惠民知县。

刘成诵：（清）光绪二年（1876年）进士。任刑部主事。

王金镕：（清）光绪九年（1883年）进士。任刑科给事中。

孙国桢：（清）光绪九年（1883年）进士。任山东曲阜知县。

刘　培：（清）光绪十二年（1886年）进士。仕至总理衙门协修官。

徐元瑞：（清）光绪十二年（1886年）进士。任河南嵩县知县。

李　坦：（清）光绪十二年（1886年）进士。任吏部掌印郎中。

李锡庚：（清）光绪十五年（1889年）进士。任广东惠安知县。

史履晋：（清）光绪十六年（1890年）进士。任直隶实业司司长。

曹子昂：（清）光绪二十年（1894年）进士。任广东惠东知县。

周　培：（清）光绪二十年（1894年）进士。任内阁中书。

葛毓芝：（清）光绪二十一年（1895年）进士。任刑部主事。

肖开甲：（清）光绪二十四年（1898年）进士。任吏部主事。

Song Zhi'an, a martial *jinshi* granted in 1737 during the Qing Dynasty

Pei Jiayou, a martial *jinshi* granted in 1742 during the Qing Dynasty, who once acted as Dousi General of Shilou Garrison in Shanxi Province

Yang Derun, a martial *huiyuan* (No.1 winner of provincial examinations) granted in 1748 during the Qing Dynasty, who once acted as Youji General of Liya Garrison in Sichuan Province

An Tingzhao, a martial *tanhua* (No.3 winner of national examinations) granted in 1751 during the Qing Dynasty, who once acted as Associate General of Taizhou, Zhejiang Province

Li Xuan, a martial *jinshi* granted in 1751 during the Qing Dynasty

Pei Jiale, a martial *jinshi* granted in 1754 during the Qing Dynasty, who once acted as an imperial guard

Li Guoliang, a martial *zhuangyuan* (No.1 winner of national examinations) granted in 1757 during the Qing Dynasty, who once acted as Army Commander of Fujian Province

An Tingzan, a martial *jinshi* granted in 1757 during the Qing Dynasty, who once acted as Associate General of Xiangshan, Guangdong Province

Yang Dajing, a martial *jinshi* granted in 1759 during the Qing Dynasty

Yin Lu, a martial *jinshi* granted in 1760 during the Qing Dynasty

Cui Guan, a martial *jinshi* granted in 1823 during the Qing Dynasty

Wu Dianyuan, a marital *jinshi* granted in 1841 during the Qing Dynasty, who once acted as a battalion commander

Xu Shouchun, a martial *bangyan* (No.2 winner of national examinations) granted in 1862 during the Qing Dynasty, who once acted as an associate general

III. Local Celebrities

Zhang Sheng, an editor of the Imperial History House of the Yuan Dynasty and the author of *Historical Records of Emperor Shizu*

Wang Haoxue, a *juren* during the reign of Emperor Jiajing of the Ming Dynasty and the author of *Collection of Migrant Arts*

Wang Hunran, a scholar during the reign of Emperor Wanli of the Ming Dynasty and the author of *Shuyoucao*

Li Zhu, a *juren* during the reign of Emperor Qianlong of the Qing Dynasty and the author of *Scripts of Jingshu Hall*

Ni Shangshu, a *juren* during the reign of Emperor Qianlong of the Qing Dynasty and the author of *Doubts on Shangshu Book* and *Doubts on Poetry Book*

Ni Qifan, a *gongsheng* during the reign of Emperor Xianfeng of the Qing Dynasty and the author of *Poetry Collection of Xuanxuan Thatched Studio*

Ge Yongning, a scholar of the Qing Dynasty and the author of *Legends of Filial Deity and Righteousness* and *Records of the Eastern Relocation of Luanhe*

Li Shuqing, a *juren* of the Qing Dynasty and the author of *Poetry of Weiwuwei Studio*

Yang Zaiwen, a *juren* during the reign of Emperor Daoguang of the Qing Dynasty and the author of *Poetry of Chujing Hall*

Zhang Jiuding, a *gongsheng* of the Qing Dynasty and the author of *Poetry of Deweicengyou Studio*

吕兴周：（清）光绪二十九年（1903年）进士。任吉林高等检察厅检察长。

李逢时：（明）隆庆五年（1571年）武进士。

宋治安：（清）乾隆二年（1737年）武进士。

裴嘉猷：（清）乾隆七年（1742年）武进士。仕至山西石楼营都司。

杨德润：（清）乾隆十三年（1748年）武会元。仕至四川黎雅营游击。

安廷召：（清）乾隆十六年（1751年）武探花。仕至浙江台州协副将。

李　萱：（清）乾隆十六年（1751年）武进士。

裴嘉乐：（清）乾隆十九年（1754年）武进士。任朝廷侍卫。

李国梁：（清）乾隆二十二年（1757年）武状元。仕至福建省陆路提督。

安廷赞：（清）乾隆二十二年（1757年）武进士。仕至广东香山协副将。

杨大经：（清）乾隆二十四年（1759年）武进士。

阴　璐：（清）乾隆二十五年（1760年）武进士。

崔　琯：（清）道光三年（1823年）武进士。

吴殿元：（清）道光二十一年（1841年）武进士。以营守备用。

徐寿春：（清）同治元年（1862年）武榜眼。以参将用。

第三节　历代名人

张　升：（元）国史馆编修。著有《世祖实录》一册刊行。

王好学：（明）嘉靖年间举人，著有《游艺集》一书刊行。

王浑然：（明）万历年间人，著有《蜀游草》一书刊行。

李　柱：（清）乾隆丙辰举人，著有《敬恕堂稿》一书刊行。

倪上述：（清）乾隆甲戌举人，著有《尚书存疑》、《诗说存疑》等书刊行。

倪启藩：（清）清咸丰年间贡生，诗画俱佳，著有《轩轩草轩诗集》刊行。

Zhang Shan, a *gongsheng* of the Qing Dynasty and the author of *Poetry and Essay Collection of Tuixue Studio*

Zhang Fengxiang, a *juren* of the Qing Dynasty and the author of *Poetry of Liyuan Garden*

Wang Peixing, a *juren* during the reign of Emperor Tongzhi of the Qing Dynasty and the author of *Calligraphy and Painting Collection of the Qing Dynasty* and *Poetry Collection of Xianhuapei*

Zhao Jianbang, a *gongsheng* of the Qing Dynasty and the author of *Hengzhang Travel Notes* and *Biansong Travel Notes*

Chang Shoufang, a *juren* during the reign of Emperor Daoguang of the Qing Dynasty and the author of *Banchanchu Notes* and *Linming Travel Notes*

Shi Menglan, a *juren* during the reign of Emperor Daoguang of the Qing Dynasty, who was cited as "No.1 Scholar in Eastern Beijing" by Empress Dowager Cixi and published more than 100 books including *Palace Poetry of All Times*

Wu Chunfang, a *gongsheng* of the Qing Dynasty and the author of *In Search of the Sources of the Book of Changes*

Yang Yingqi, a *gongsheng* during the reign of Emperor Guangxu of the Qing Dynasty and the author of *Collection of Shequ Garden*

Cui Youwen, a folk artist of the Qing Dynasty who made great contribution to the development of such folk art forms as Laoting Shadow Play, Laoting Drum, and Lianhualao Opera

Wen Rong, a famous Laoting Drum performer of the Qing Dynasty who reformed the musical instrument used in the folk art from wooden patters to iron patters, hence his nickname "Iron Patter Wen"

Lei Pengsan, a scholar of the Republic of China period and the author of *Research of Mountain Mausoleums of Ancient Emperors* and Chengleisuo Collection

Song Shixiong, born in November 1939, a native of Jingtuo Village, Leguanting Town, who is a professor of Beijing Broadcasting College, honorable chairman of China Sports Press Association and vice president of China Society of Radio and TV Anchormen. He has been reputed as "tongue of the nation."

Li Xinggang, born in April 1969, a native of Xincun Village, Maozhuang Township, Laoting County, who now acts as vice chief architect of China Architecture Design & Research Group, manager of Li Xinggang Architecture Design Studio, and chief architect of Specialized Architecture Design Academy. He once served as the Chinese representative for the design of National Stadium (Bird's Nest), the main venue of the 2008 Beijing Olympics.

Shi Shuqing, born in August 1922, a native of Shizhuang Village, Tangjiahe Town, Laoting County, is a connoisseur of cultural relics. Formerly, he acted as vice director of the Storage Department of the Museum of Chinese History and was reputed as "national treasure."

Ge Cuilin (female), born on February 25, 1930, in Qiangezhuang Village, Laoting County, is a famous children's book writer, a member of Children's Literature Commission of Chinese Writers Association, and vice chairperson of Bing Xin Award Jury

Wang Jinyuan, born in March 1939, a native of Wujialantuo Village, Xinzhai Town, Laoting County, is a national first-grade artist, chairman of Yunnan Artists Association, and president of Yunnan Painting Academy

Song Fei (female), born in January 1969 in Daxianggezhuang, Laoting County, is an erhu (a two-stringed instrument) artist and a national first-grade actress, who now acts as vice general secretary of China Nationalities Orchestra Society and chairperson of China Erhu Society. She is reputed as Erhu Queen of China.

葛永凝：（清）布衣。著有《孝义节烈传》、《滦河东迁志》等书刊行。

李淑清：（清）举人，著有《味无味斋诗草》刊行。

杨在汶：（清）道光甲午举人，著有《锄经堂诗草》刊行。

张九鼎：（清）贡生，著有《得未曾有斋诗草》刊行。

张　山：（清）贡生，著有《退学斋诗文集》刊行。

张凤翔：（清）己未举人，著有《礼园诗钞》刊行。

王佩行：（清）同治甲子举人，著有《清朝书画录》、《衔华佩诗录集》刊行。

赵建邦：（清）贡生，著有《衡漳游草》、《汴宋游草》等刊行。

常守方：（清）道光甲辰举人，著有《半禅初草》、《临滇游草》等刊行。

史梦兰：（清）道光举人，被慈禧太后誉为"京东第一人"，著有《全史宫词》等上百部刊行。

武春芳：（清）贡生，著有《易说求源》六卷刊行。

严应麒：（清）光绪甲午贡生，著《清娱阁集》六卷刊行。

赵福铭：（清）贡生，著《涉趣园集》八卷刊行。

崔佑文：（清）同治、光绪年间人，绰号"崔八厮"，对乐亭皮影、乐亭大鼓、莲花落等民间艺术的发展，有很大贡献。

温　荣：（清）著名乐亭大鼓艺人，在演唱中首改木板为铁板击节伴奏，故人称"温铁板"。

雷朋三：（民国时期）著《古帝山陵考》、《称类琐编》等刊行。

新中国成立后

宋世雄：1939年11月生，乐亭县乐观亭镇井坨村人。北京广播学院教授，中国体育记者协会名誉会长，中国广播电视节目主持人研究会副会长。被誉为"国嘴"。

李兴刚：1969年4月生，乐亭县毛庄乡新村人。现任中国建筑设计研究院副总建筑师、李兴刚建筑设计工作室主持人、建筑专业设计研究院总建筑师。2008年北京奥运会主体育场"鸟巢"方案设计者中方代表。

史树青：文物鉴定家。1922年8月生，乐亭县汤家河镇史庄人。中国历史博物馆保管部原副主任，被誉为"国宝"。

葛翠林（女）：1930年2月25日生于乐亭县前葛庄村。中国著名儿童文学家。中国作家协会儿童文学委员，冰心奖评委会副主席。

王晋元：1939年3月生，乐亭县新寨镇吴家兰坨村人，国家一级美术师，云南省美协主席，云南画院院长。

宋　飞（女）：1969年1月生于乐亭县大相各庄李家寺。二胡演奏家。国家一级演员。中国民族管弦乐学会副秘书长，中国二胡学会理事长。被誉为"二胡皇后"。

IV. Famous Businessmen

Liu Xinting, born in the time of Emperor Daoguang of the Qing Dynasty, achieved a great success in commerce as the early exploiters of Northeast China. His descendants inherited his He Company and made it a giant business kingdom.

Zhang Xikong, born in the time of Emperor Daoguang of the Qing Dynasty, earned his first bucket of gold through timber business in Northeast China. Later, the Wan Company he established became a business success in Northeast China.

Wu Baixiang, born in 1879, founded Harbin Tongji Market and Daluo New Global Department Store during the Republic of China period, winning himself the reputation "Commercial Spirit of North China."

Yang Huanting was general manager of Rishengzhan Store in Changchun, and established subsidiaries across Northeast China within 12 years.

Liu Linge, born in 1877, established Yuchangyuan Grain Store and Flour Factory in Changchun and Dalian and became a wealthy businessman.

Yang Fuqing, born in 1891, established Xinzhong Canned Food Company in Changli, and its products not only sold well not only in Northeast China, but also were exported to former Soviet Union.

Zhao Hanchen, born in 1890, established more than 30 stores in Northeast China, and his Yiheshun grain shops were found everywhere in Siping, hence his nickname "Grain King of Northeast China."

Li Yunting, born in 1905, established Tianfengyong Grocery in Harbin, with annual profits totaling 5,000 taels of silver.

Sun Xiusan, born in 1882, was the second general manager of Yifahe Store and the first general manager of Heyifa Private Bank in Changchun, which earned more than eight million silver dollars each year.

Mu Haiyue was general manager of Tianhesheng Company that specialized in banking and grain businesses. His company set up 13 branches in Northeast China. In 1926, his company was confiscated by Zhang Zuolin, a local warlord, for the Biefeng Banknotes incident.

Miao Zhuxian, born in 1916, went to Northeast China together with his father. Later, he became manger of Huitongda Grocery in Changchun. After the founding of the People's Republic of China, he was appointed principal committee member of Jilin Industrial and Commercial Federation.

Wang Yutang purchased Changchun Jidequan Liquor Plant in 1931, and became board chairman of the plant. He once acted as chairman of the Changchun Chamber of Commerce.

Li Hansan ever acted as president of Bianye Bank in Yingkou.

Lei Jingkun was manger of Fushenghou Grain and Oil Plant in Shuangcheng County, which was the county's largest grain and oil manufacturing company at the time.

Fu Zuoxin established grain stores, banks, mechanical mills, and electric light factories in Harbin, Suihua, Wangkui, and Baiquan, from which he earned considerable profits. He was ranked one of the most successful businessmen in North Manchuria.

第四节　商界名人

刘新亭：生于清朝道光年间，早期闯关东的成功商人，其后人不断在东北长春发展"合"字号买卖，成为巨商。

张希孔：生于清朝道光年间，靠木材生意在东北发迹，其"万"字头商号成了东北知名富商。

武百祥：生于1879年，民国时期创立哈尔滨同记商场、大罗新环球货店，被后人喻为"北国商魂"。

杨焕亭：长春"日升栈"总经理，12年间其分号遍布东北各地。

刘临阁：生于1877年，在长春、大连开设"裕昌源"粮米铺和面粉厂，成为富商。

杨扶青：生于1891年，在昌黎开设"新中罐头公司"，其罐头不仅占领了东北市场，还远销苏联。

赵汉臣：生于1890年，在东北开设商号30多处，其"义和顺"粮栈遍布四平，被时人喻为"关东粮王"。

李云亭：生于1905年，在哈尔滨开设"天丰涌"杂货店，年获利5000两白银。

孙秀三：生于1882年，长春"益发合"第二任总经理，和益发钱庄首任经理，生意兴隆时年获利达800万银圆。

母海岳：沈阳经营钱粮业的"天合盛"总经理，在东北的分号达13处之多，1926年因"别奉票"事件被张作霖查抄。

苗竹贤：生于1916年，1934年跟父亲到东北闯荡，后任长春"会通达"杂货庄经理，新中国成立后任吉林省工商联主委。

王玉堂：1931年收购长春"积德泉"烧锅酒厂，任董事长，曾任长春商会会长。

李翰三：曾任营口市边业银行行长。

雷景堃：双城县"福升厚粮油栈"经理，为当时该县最大的粮油加工企业。

付作新：在哈尔滨、绥化、望奎、拜泉等处创立钱粮业及火磨、电灯厂等多种商号，获利雄厚，堪称北满商界之魁。

V. Provincial and Ministerial Officials after the Founding of the People's Republic of China

Wang Sihua, born in 1904, a native of Shijiazi Village, Wangtang Town, Laoting County, who was former director and Party sectary of the National Bureau of Statistics of China

Shi Qingsheng, born in May 1927, a native of Nanzhai Village, Hujiatuo Town, Laoting County, who was former vice chairman of the People's Government of the Guangxi Zhuang Autonomous Region

Bai Shi, born in April 1927, a native of Zhoujiaying Village, Jianggezhuang Town, Laoting County, who was former vice director of the Standing Committee of the Hebei People's Congress

Liu Kan, born in May 1926, a native of Baizhuang Village, Wangtan Town, Laoting County, who was former vice director of the Rural Policies Research Office of the Secretariat of CPC Central Committee

Zhang Shiru, born in December 1941, a native of Zhangjiapu Village, Guhe Township, Laoting County, who was former director of the Information Department of the Provincial Party Committee of Hebei

Zhang Qingwei, born in November 1961, a native of Laoting County, who now acts as general manager of China Aerospace Science and Technology Corporation and vice chief commander of China Aerospace Project

Li Qing, born in June 1943, a native of Daheituo Village, Hujiatuo Town, Laoting County, who was former vice chairman of the People's Political Consultative Conference of Zhejiang Province

Li Leguang, born in November 1903, a native of Muguakou Village, Laoting County, who was former director of the United Front Work Department of the Municipal Party Committee of Beijing

Li Shenxue, born in August 1950, a native of Shizhuang Village, Tangjiahe Town, Laoting County, who now acts as general secretary of the Provincial Party Committee of Jilin and secretary of the Working Committee of Organs Directly under the Provincial Party Committee

Li Yunchang, born in September 1908, a native of Muguakou Village, Hujiatuo Town, Laoting County, who was former first vice minister of the Chinese Ministry of Justice

Li Haifeng (female), born in February 1949, a native of Liying Village, Jianggezhuang Town, Laoting County, who was former vice governor of the People's Government of Hebei Province

Li Huiren, born in November 1933, a native of Muguakou Village, Hujiatuo Town, Laoting County, who was head of the Discipline Inspection Team of the Central Discipline Committee in the Ministry of Civil Affairs

Li Baohua, born in October 1909, a native of Daheituo Village, Hujiatuo Town, Laoting County, who was former president of the People's Bank of China

Du Jingyi, born in February 1832, a native of Duxiaokou Village, Hujiatuo Town, Laoting County, who was former vice chairman of the People's Congress of the Guangxi Zhuang Autonomous Region

Yang Fuqing, born in May 1891, a native of Yuanzhuang Village, Laoting Town, Laoting County, who was former minister of the Ministry of Fishery

Chen Yu, born in March 1939, a native of Linjiazhuang Village, Hujiatuo Town, Laoting County, who was former president of the

第五节　新中国成立后省部级干部

王思华：1904年生，乐亭县王滩镇十家子村人。原国家统计局局长、党组书记。

史清盛：1927年5月生，乐亭县胡家坨南寨村人。原广西壮族自治区人民政府副主席。

白　石：1927年4月生，乐亭县姜各庄镇周家营一村人。原河北省人大常委会副主任。

刘　堪：1926年5月生，乐亭县王滩镇白庄村人。原中央书记处农村政策研究室副主任。

张士儒：1941年12月生，乐亭县古河乡张家铺村人。原河北省委宣传部部长。

张庆伟：1961年11月生，乐亭县人。中国航天科技集团总经理。中国航天工程副总指挥。

李　青：1943年6月生，乐亭县胡家坨大黑坨村人。原中共浙江省政协副主席。

李乐光：1903年11月生，乐亭县木瓜口村人。原北京市委统战部部长。

李申学：1950年8月生，乐亭县汤家河镇戈耳崖史庄村人。中共吉林省委秘书长兼省直机关工委书记。

李运昌：1908年9月生，乐亭县胡家坨镇木瓜口村人。原司法部第一副部长。

李海峰（女）：1949年2月生，乐亭县姜各庄镇李营村人。原河北省人民政府副省长。

李惠仁：1933年11月生，乐亭县胡家坨镇木瓜口村人。原中纪委驻民政部纪检组组长。

李葆华：1909年10月生，乐亭县胡家坨镇大黑坨村人。原中国人民银行行长。

杜晶一：1932年2月生，乐亭县胡家坨镇杜小口村人。原广西壮族自治区人大副主任。

杨扶青：1891年5月生，乐亭县乐亭镇苑庄村人。原水产部副部长。

陈　瑜：1939年3月生，乐亭县胡家坨镇东嵩林贾庄人。原世界新经济研究院副院长。

World New Economy Institute

Chen Yifan, born in September 1910, a native of Daluozhuang Village, Yangezhuang Town, Laoting County, who was former vice president of Sichuan Mining College

Luo Zhiling, born in February 1942, a native to Qianlantuo Village, Xinzhai Town, Laoting County, who was former director of the National Bureau of Grain Reserve

Zhao Jinfu, born in January 1943, a native of Kongzhaoxue Village, Tingliuhe Town, Laoting County, who was former vice chairman of the Standing Committee of the People's Congress of Shanxi Province

Xu Ruixin, born in 1941, a native of Xujiadian Village, Wangzhuang Township, Laoting County, who was former vice minister of the Chinese Ministry of Civil Affairs

Huan Yushan, born in June 1937, a native of Dayangzhuang Village, Tingliuhe Town, Laoting County, who was former vice minister of the Chinese Ministry of Materials

Cao Wenju, born in March 1927, a native of Dalizhuang Village, Hujiatuo Town, Laoting County, who was former vice chairman of the People's Congress of Hunan Province

Zhang Ming, born in December 1922, a native of Donggao Village, Wangtan Town, Laoting County, who was former minister of the Chinese Ministry of Civil Affairs

E Jingping, born in January 1956, a native of Sanjiazi Village, Xinzhai Town, Laoting County, who was former minister of the Chinese Ministry of Water Resources

Yan Dakai, born in May 1913, a native of Fantuo Village, Yangezhuang Town, Laoting County, who was former chairman of the Standing Committee of the People's Congress of Tianjin

Pei Ximin, born in August 1932, a native of Luhe Village, Yangezhuang Town, Laoting County, who was former chairman of the People's Political Consultative Conference of Changchun City

Wei Minxue, born in March 1942, a native of Xigeloutuo Village, Guhe Township, Laoting County, who was former vice executive chairman of the People's Political Consultative Conference of Jilin Province

Ding Guo, born in August 1928, a native of Liushige Village, Tingliu Town, Laoting County, who was former chief justice of the Supreme People's Court of Hainan Province

Wang Mingde, born in January 1914, a native of Mukousan Village, Hujiatuo Town, Laoting County, who was former chairman of the General Federation of Trade Unions of Jilin Province

Wang Shuntong, born in September 1918, a native of Xiaoshengmiao Village, Tingliuhe Town, Laoting County, who was former vice chairman of China Association for Science and Technology

Liu Runpu, born in May 1951, a native of Niuyangzi Village, Wangtan Town, Laoting County, who is vice chairman of the People's Congress of Jilin Province

Li Haitao, born in September 1912, a native of Daheituo Village, Hujiatuo Town, Laoting County, who was former vice president of the People's Procuratorate of Tianjin

陈一凡：1910年9月生，乐亭县阁各庄镇大罗庄村人。原四川矿业学院副院长。

罗植龄：1942年2月生，乐亭县新寨镇前兰坨村人。原国家粮食储备局局长。

赵劲夫：1943年1月生，乐亭县汀流河镇孔赵薛村人。原山西省人大常委会副主任。

徐瑞新：1941年生，乐亭县中堡王庄乡徐家店村人。原国家民政部副部长。

桓玉珊：1937年6月生，乐亭县汀流河镇大杨庄村人。原国家物资部副部长。

曹文举：1927年3月生，乐亭胡家坨镇大李庄村人。原湖南省人大副主任。

章　明：1922年12月生，乐亭县王滩镇东高村人。原民政部副部长。

鄂竟平：1956年1月生，乐亭县新寨镇三家子村人。原水利部副部长。

阎达开：1913年5月生，乐亭县阁各庄镇樊坨村人。原天津市人大常委会主任。

裴希敏：1932年8月生，乐亭县阁各庄镇芦河村人。原长春市政协主席。

魏敏学：1942年3月生，乐亭县古河乡西阁楼坨村人。原吉林省政协常务副主席。

丁　果：1928年8月生，乐亭县汀流镇刘石各庄人。原海南省高级人民法院院长。

王明德：1914年1月生，乐亭县胡家坨镇木口三村人。原吉林省总工会主席。

王顺桐：1918年9月生，乐亭县汀流河镇小圣庙村人。原中国科协第二届副主席。

刘润璞：1951年5月生，乐亭县王滩镇牛庄村人。吉林省人大副主任。

李海涛：1912年9月生，乐亭县胡家坨镇大黑坨村人。原天津市人民检察院副院长。

VI. Generals after the Founding of the People Republic of China

General

Cao Pengsheng, political commissar of Lanzhou Military Command

Lieutenant Generals

Tong Baocun, deputy commander of Shenyang Military Command

Hao Yan, vice director of the Science and Technology Commission of the Committee of Science, Technology and Industry for National Defense

Cao Huichen, vice political commissar of Shenyang Military Command

Major Generals

Wang Xinggang, vice director of the General Office of the Ministry of National Defense

Hao Wanming, standing member of the Naval Discipline Inspection Commission

Zhao Xijiang, political commissar of the Dalian Naval Academy of the PLA

Zhao Rongbi, political commissar of the Naval College of Politics

Wang Guansan, political commissar of the Administrative Bureau of General Staff Department of the PLA

Lei Li, vice secretary-general of the General Political Department of the PLA

Yang Molin, vice political commissar of the Lüshun and Dalian Security Area

Wang Li, political commissar of the Naval Logistics Department

Shi Shoumin, vice director of the Administrative Bureau of General Staff Department of the PLA

Li Jun, political commissar of the Armed Police College

Liu Jiasheng, vice political commissar of the North Sea Fleet of the Chinese Navy

Chao Fuhuan (female), vice president of the Academy of Military Medicine

Liu Shuchen, vice editor-in-chief of PLA Daily

Wang Enhui, deputy commander of Liaoning Military Command

Wang Yunhua, vice director of the Naval Logistics Department

Gu Lianwen, commander of the No.6370 Field Army

Niu Zhizhong, chief commander of Guangdong Armed Police Forces

Cui Zhenghua, vice president of the Commanding College of the Second Artillery Corps

Chen Wengui, director of the Fire Bureau of the Military of Public Security

Zhang Shutian, deputy commander of Guangzhou Military Command

Zhou Jinxin, president of the PLA Institute of Physical Education

第六节　新中国成立后将军

上　将

曹芃生：兰州军区政治委员。

中　将

佟宝存：沈阳军区副司令员。

郝岩：国防科工委科技委副主任。

曹惠臣：沈阳军区副政治委员。

少　将

王兴刚：国防部办公室副主任。

郝万明：海军纪律检查委员会常委。

赵锡江：海军大连舰艇学院政治委员。

赵荣璧：海军政治学院政委。

王冠三：总参管理局政治委员。

雷　厉：总政治部副秘书长。

杨墨林：旅大警备区副政治委员。

王　力：海军后勤部政治委员。

石守敏：总参管理局副局长。

李　俊：武警专科学校政治委员。

刘家声：海军北海舰队副政治委员。

晁福寰（女）：军事医学科学院副院长。

刘书忱：《解放军报》副总编。

王恩惠：辽宁省军区副司令员。

王运华：海军后勤部副部长。

谷连文：6370 部队司令员。

牛志忠：武警广东省总队总队长。

崔正华：二炮指挥学院副院长。

陈文贵：公安部消防局局长。

张书田：广州军区副司令员。

周今新：解放军体育学院院长。

VII. CAS and CAE Members

Meng Zhaoying, an electronics expert and physical scientist, who was appointed member of the Chinese Academy of Sciences (CAS) in 1955

Shi Zhiren, a railway machinery expert, who was appointed member of the Chinese Academy of Sciences (CAS) in 1955

Ma Xingyuan, a structural geologist and seismic geologist and a member of the Chinese Academy of Sciences (CAS)

Li Jilun, a famous microbiologist and a member of the Chinese Academy of Sciences (CAS)

Liu Ruiyu, an expert in marine biology and crustaceology, who was appointed member of the Chinese Academy of Sciences (CAS) in 1977

Wu Dexin (female), a microelectronics expert, who was appointed member of the Chinese Academy of Sciences (CAS)

Ge Molin, a theoretical physicist, who was appointed member of Mathematics and Physics Department of the Chinese Academy of Sciences (CAS)

Ge Baofeng, an orthopedics expert and director of the Orthopedics Institute of Lanzhou Military Command Head Hospital, who was appointed member of the Chinese Academy of Engineering (CAE) in 1999

Sun Yan, vice council chairman of China Cancer Research Fund and a member of the Chinese Academy of Engineering (CAE)

第七节　中国科学院、中国工程院院士

孟昭英：电子学、物理学家，1955年选聘为中国科学院院士（学部委员）。

石志仁：铁路机械专家。1955年选聘为中国科学院院士（学部委员）。

马杏垣：构造地质学家，地震地质学家。中国科学院学部委员（院士）。

李季伦：著名微生物学家。中国科学院院士。

刘瑞玉：海洋生物学和甲壳动物学家。1977年当选为中科院院士。

吴德馨（女）：微电子技术学家。1991年当选为中国科学院学部委员（院士）。

葛墨林：理论物理学家。2003年当选为中科院（数学物理部）院士。

葛宝丰：骨科专家。现任兰州军区总医院骨科研究所所长，1999年当选为中国工程院院士。

孙　燕：现任中国癌症研究基金会副理事长，中国工程院院士。

Postscript

Puti Island, initially named Mortar Isle or Nineteen Isle, is a famous offshore island on Bohai Bay in Laoting County, Hebei Province's Tangshan City. As the largest sandy island in North China, it boasts a primitive natural environment featuring mist-shrouded forests and spectacular sea views. Since ancient times, it has served as a holy land of Buddhism. Master Xianguang from the Linji Sect and his student Zhiyuan of the Ming Dynasty constructed a magnificent temple on the island. Then, Monk Faben from the Caodong Sect built another temple. Previously, people venerated the island as a Buddhist sacred land and a hideaway for immortals. Historically, many prestigious monarchs, chancellors, and generals left their footprints on the island, and numerous scholars visited the island and left behind countless poetic masterpieces. Due to its long history, brilliant culture and picturesque landscapes, Puti Island is reputed as a shining pearl and a bright lighthouse in eastern Hebei Province and has always blessed Laoting County.

A native of Laoting, I have deeply admired the island's beautiful natural scenery and profound history and culture, as well as local folklores with respect to famous monks like Faben from the Chaoyin Temple, since I was young. Moreover, the marvelous legends about the island are something imprinted in my mind. So, I thought I was obligated to write this book about Puti Island.

In the early 1960s, Li Xinghua, Liu Xicheng and Dong Sen, researchers from China Society for the Study of Folk Literature and Art, came to Laoting to survey local folklores, which offered me an opportunity to participate in the creation of folk literature. Besides interviewing locals in inland Laoting, the research crew also gathered information at coastal fishing villages and harbors. They realized fruitful achievements during the survey, which inspired Laoting County to further develop local folk literature. After Li Xinghua died in the 1970s, Dong Sen donated all interview scripts that they gathered to Laoting County. Encouraged by their respectable contribution, I then spared no effort to gather folklores prevailing on Puti, Xiangyun and Yuetuo Islands. To research the history of Puti Island, I visited the island more than 100 times to gather information or interview local residents. In my memories, local people that I interviewed include Wang Wu, a captain of Monk Faben's fleet, Guo Changzhi, a grandson of Faben's brother, Di Lianyi, An Jiahai, An Jiayu, Zhang Shengyun, Zhang Xiangyun, and Qi Chunhua, as well as hundreds of local fishermen and residents. So far, most of them already died, and the information they provided thus seem even more precious. The three volumes of folklores that I published in the 1980s and such brochures as *Folklores and Stories of Laoting* and *A Contemporary Romance* that I compiled, as well as many scripts in this book, are all based on the stories those forefathers told me.

In May 2008, Mr. Xu Jianyi, then owner of Puti Island, invited me to the island, where we decided to write a monograph focusing on Puti Island's history and culture, as well as local culture of Laoting County. After that, we immediately recruited a dozen writers who were acquainted to the history and culture of Puti Island to constitute the editorial crew. Then, a field survey was organized.

Before the writing began, all members of our editorial committee conducted a prudent discussion and reached a consensus that all scripts included in this book should be traceable and identical to

后 记

　　菩提岛，原名叫石臼坨，或十九坨，是渤海湾中河北省唐山市乐亭县境著名的近海岛屿，也是华北地区最大的一处沙质岛。天工造就，丽日高晶，水天一碧，丘陵草木"若云流雾骞，森奇孕秀"的原生态自然环境，向来被佛教僧侣视为佛家圣地。明临济宗僧显光上人与其传人智元，继之曹洞宗住僧法本等佛教徒，卓锡海岛，起造功德丛林，世人呼之梵宫鼎峙，仙人避居。此岛更为世俗所景仰，这里留下了帝王名臣的身影，勋僚宿将的足迹。文人墨客，慕名而至，临岛吟咏，写下的名篇佳作，经世传诵，脍炙人口。菩提岛历史之悠久，文化底蕴之渊深厚重，自然环境之清纯优美，似孤悬溟海的一颗璀璨的明珠、一座熠熠生辉的灯塔，辉映着冀东大地，荫庇着唐山乐亭。

　　笔者为乐亭土著，自幼对菩提岛美丽的自然景观、深厚的历史文化内涵以及潮音寺法本大师等名僧的奇闻逸事无限敬仰。而对那些来自菩提岛的美丽传说故事，更是魂牵梦萦，心驰神往。及至能捉笔拙耕，撰写一部菩提岛的介绍，义不容辞。

　　20世纪60年代初，中国民间文艺研究会研究员李星华、刘锡诚、董森一行来乐亭采风收集民间故事，为我参与民间文学写作带来了契机。星华一行除在内陆大黑坨等地进行采访外，还把乐亭沿海北港等渔村码头作为重点进行了广泛收集。这次采访，收获之丰厚，令人艳羡。同时也为乐亭的民间文学工作的进一步开展给予了启示。20世纪70年代星华病逝后，董森同志把当年在乐亭收集到的采访文稿全部奉献给了乐亭。受星华、董森等同志的启发，我在事后的岁月里，对于收集菩提岛、祥云岛、月坨岛等地散布在民间的传说故事，从未有过半点倦怠。忆及当年，为收集菩提岛的历史资料，或是专题上岛，或是乘机采访，何止百次。尚有记忆的，曾先后采访过法本的"大木鱼"船长王武，法本的族孙郭长智，捞渔尖邸连义，安家海安世玉及贾滩上村张生云、张祥云，三家子邰春华等数以百计的渔民与熟悉岛上情况的民众。时至今日，这些受访者多数已经作古，当年他们所提供的资料就显得弥足珍贵了。乐亭20世纪80年代的三套集成民间故事卷和今天我们记写菩提岛的许多稿件，乃至我所编《乐亭民间传说故事集》、《近世风流》等几部小册子，多得益于那时这些先辈们的耳提面命之资料积蓄。

　　2008年5月，菩提岛"岛主"徐建义先生特意邀我上岛，议定编写一部以反映菩提岛人文历史为主兼及乐亭地域文化的专著。事后，立即遴选写作人员，从文化圈朋友中请出了十几名谙熟菩提岛人文情况的写作高手组成了专门的写作班子，并先行组织到外地考察。

　　写作前，全体编委首先进行了审慎的研究论证。一致认为要秉持唯物观，凡进入书稿的文章，必须是历史有据、事出有因、有稽可考的历史题材，不让那些荒诞不经的篇什进卷。

　　写作开始后，徐建义先生亲力亲为，一丝不苟，严格甄选史料，认真校勘典籍，谋篇布局，

previous historical records, so as to avoid absurd and inauthentic contents.

In the course of the book's compilation, Mr. Xu Jianyi spared no effort to ensure all historical records are carefully selected and all documents are strictly examined. His responsible spirit, earnest attribute and strict work style impressed everyone who participated in the compilation work.

Most writers have full jobs elsewhere, and some even hold important posts. So, they had to complete their writing assignments in spare time. To ensure the quality of their writings, they dedicated painstaking efforts and their holidays. Some even worked late to midnight. The texts were revised again and again until they satisfied the editor-in-chief.

Upon Mr. Xu Jianyi's suggestion and the discussion of all editors, the book only focuses on the culture, history, and landscapes of Puti Island, rather than include local culture of Laoting County. Even so, it took us two years to complete the publication.

Everything has two sides. The prolonged period of publication enabled us to have enough time to choose materials and examine texts more carefully and further enrich its contents. For instance, we consulted eminent historians like Tang Xiangrong and Lü Xueheng on stele inscriptions such as *A Brief Record of Chaoyang Nunnery* and *Stele Inscriptions of Chaoyang Nunnery*. We also consulted Mr. Jing Wei, secretary of former president of Chinese Buddhist Association Zhao Puchu, Master Jingyuan from the Kwan-yin Temple, and other Buddhism specialists like Wang Zhenyu. Particularly, although in his 80s, Hu Jingshan, former vice magistrate of Laoting County, dedicated himself to writing, which tremendously encouraged all other writers and editors. Despite his age and bad physical conditions, Dong Zongren, a retired professor from Liaoning University, committed all energy to the annotation and proofreading of poems included in this book. Liu Jiangtao from the Information Department, Zhang Zhigang from the Tourism Bureau, and Xu Yaping from the Memorial Hall to Li Dazhao, provided a large amount of images to the book. Chen Yajie, a teacher from Laoting Vocational School, contributed many illustrations. Hereby, we express our sincere gratitude to those who ever helped the publication of the book.

For some reason, the articles of some writers aren't included in the final book. Even so, their selfish contributions also deserve our thankfulness.

This is the first time for us to compile such a reference book. Due to the lack of relevant specialized materials and knowledge, we encountered many difficulties in the course of compilation, especially the chapters concerning plants and animals on the island. Therefore, this book must have some regretful errors and omissions. Any criticism or advice from all experts and readers are greatly welcomed and appreciated.

He Zongyu

August 28, 2010

操觚染翰，这种对历史负责的精神、认真做事的态度、严谨务实的工作作风，深深地激励着每一位参与写作的同志。

写作班子中，多数是身任现职的工作人员，有的且是居于重要领导职位的同志，因此写作时间只能多是利用勤务中的业余时间。为了稿件的精当，他们不辞辛苦，宁可牺牲自己宝贵的节假日时间，有的人甚至是挑灯撰稿，通宵达旦，成篇后一改再改，直到主编人员认可。

在写作过程中，遵照徐建义先生的意见，经编者研究，书稿从原来囊括乐亭地域文化诸多方面，锁定到进卷书稿必须贴近菩提岛的人文历史和海岛风貌，为此时逾两年直到日前书稿总纂成卷。

世间事物无一不具两分法，某种意义上时日拖延却给编写此书带来了时空的宽容，从而使编者选材更为精细，内容更为丰富翔实，文字更加精确。比如，我们注释的《朝阳庵记略》、《朝阳庵碑记》等多篇碑刻文稿，不耻旁问，曾向县外唐向荣、县内吕学恒等资深文史学家求教；多篇有关佛教的文章，曾向中国佛教学会原会长赵朴初的秘书景伟先生、观音堂释净缘师父、王振宇居士等佛学专家请教。特别应提及的是，年近八旬的乐亭县原副县长呼景山同志不计名利尊卑，参与写作，这就对全体编写人员从精神上给予了巨大鼓励与支持。写作过程中，辽宁大学退休教师董宗仁先生，不畏高龄体弱，对书稿诗词部分认真作了诠注校正。县委宣传部刘江涛同志、旅游局张志刚同志、李大钊纪念馆徐亚平同志为此书提供了大量图片。乐亭职校陈亚杰老师，热心为此书绘制多幅插图。在此，我们对上述诸位，及对此书编写给予过帮助的专家、同志们表示衷心的感谢。

此书编写过程中，因情况的变化，内容的取舍，有的同志因故最终未能参与编辑，有些撰稿人的文章未能入卷，对于他们付出的心血和辛劳，表示衷心的感谢。

编写这样一种版本的资料工具书，对于我们尚属首次。加之有些资料的匮乏和对有关专业的生疏，尤其是对于岛上动植物的考证，给编写带来了困难。毋庸讳言，此书一定存有这样那样的缺点、疏漏与遗憾，为此我们敬请各位专家、读者、社会贤达阅后不吝赐教，提出宝贵的修改意见。

何宗禹

2010年8月28日

责任编辑：吕大千

图书在版编目（ＣＩＰ）数据

人间仙境菩提岛 ： 汉英对照 / 徐建义主编. -- 北
京 ： 中国旅游出版社，2011.7
　　ISBN 978-7-5032-4196-3

　Ⅰ. ①人… Ⅱ. ①徐… Ⅲ. ①岛－旅游指南－乐亭县
－汉、英 Ⅳ. ①K928.44

中国版本图书馆CIP数据核字(2011)第131624号

人间仙境菩提岛

出版发行：中国旅游出版社
　　　　　（北京建国门内大街甲9号　邮政编码：100005）
　　　　　http://www.cttp.net.cn
　　　　　E-mail：cttp@cnta.gov.cn
版　　次：2011年7月第1版　2011年7月第1次印刷
印　　刷：北京今日新雅彩印制版技术有限公司
开　　本：889毫米×1194毫米　1/16
印　　张：18.5
定　　价：192元
ISBN 978-7-5032-4196-3